THE COPYWRITER'S
TOOLKIT

MARGO BERMAN
THE COPYWRITER'S
TOOLKIT
THE COMPLETE GUIDE TO
STRATEGIC ADVERTISING COPY

WILEY-BLACKWELL

A John Wiley & Sons, Ltd., Publication

Blackwell Publishing was acquired by John Wiley & Sons in February 2007. Blackwell's publishing program has been merged with Wiley's global Scientific, Technical, and Medical business to form Wiley-Blackwell.

Registered Office

John Wiley & Sons Ltd, The Atrium, Southern Gate, Chichester, West Sussex, PO19 8SQ, UK

Editorial Offices

350 Main Street, Malden, MA 02148-5020, USA
9600 Garsington Road, Oxford, OX4 2DQ, UK
The Atrium, Southern Gate, Chichester, West Sussex, PO19 8SQ, UK

For details of our global editorial offices, for customer services, and for information about how to apply for permission to reuse the copyright material in this book please see our website at www.wiley.com/wiley-blackwell.

Library of Congress Cataloging-in-Publication Data

Berman, Margo, 1947-
  The copywriter's toolkit : the complete guide to strategic advertising copy / Margo Berman.
     p. cm.
  Includes bibliographical references and index.
  ISBN 978-1-4051-9952-0 — ISBN 978-1-4051-9953-7 (pbk.)
1. Advertising copy—Handbooks, manuals, etc.   I. Title.
  HF5825.B47 2012
  659.13'2—dc23

                                      2011042973

A catalogue record for this book is available from the British Library.

Set in 10/12.5 Minion Pro by Thomson Digital, Noida, India
Printed and bound in Singapore by Markono Print Media Pte Ltd

1   2012

I would like to dedicate this book to my parents who gave me the discipline and creative freedom to solve complex problems.

BRIEF CONTENTS

CONTENTS

CHAPTER FOUR
THE STICKY WORD: HEADLINE AND SLOGAN TECHNIQUES 44

CHAPTER FIVE
THE WRITTEN WORD: PRINT 59

CHAPTER SIX
THE SPOKEN WORD: RADIO 85

PREFACE

It doesn't matter whether you're a student, novice, or seasoned professional, this book will hone your copywriting skills. Beginning with strategy and technique, each following chapter focuses on writing for a specific medium: from print, broadcast, and out-of-home through social, interactive, and digital media. Writing examples are shown using a gamut of industry standard formats, which are useful reference points when writing. You'll quickly see how radio scripts differ from TV scripts, how television storyboards are presented, and how print copy is typed up to facilitate typesetting.

You'll discover why thinking from the production end first helps writers create better broadcast copy. Starting with the end result in mind helps you consider which talent to cast and what sound effects or music cuts to include. These conscious choices force you to write for a specific voice and with a completely produced spot in mind.

Other writing areas of discussion will help you avoid other production errors like inaccurate script length, legal issues created by the absence of talent releases, and screen safety problems in television post production. Special callout boxes will make major principles easy to remember and simple to apply.

You may already realize that it's not enough for you to know how to create headlines and slogans or to write strong copy. You must also know how to create gripping messages in every medium, from traditional to emerging. Besides having an understanding of current trends, you should also be creative enough to bend or invent new media vehicles. You should avoid creative stagnation and innovative inertia. With all your mental muscle, you should push your imagination past the status quo. And create new avenues of expression.

In order to this, you must have a solid writing foundation. You need to understand various script formats, creative brief templates, media restrictions, and compositional structures. Then, you need to build on that knowledge and cement it with strategic thinking, analytical insights, audience-relevant messages, and sound writing techniques.

This book will give you an entire toolkit of tips to write in all size spaces, all venues, and all touchpoints. Whether you're creating messages for small print or mobile coupons, packaging, or "gianormous" billboards, interactive or any other media, you'll be able to apply the principles set forth in this volume and succeed in writing compelling copy.

Great advertising writing isn't just clever; it's convincing. It's persuasive. It's interruptive. It's intrusive. Most of all, it's unforgettable. The ad campaigns that create "talk value" (are talked about over office water coolers) also generate free press and propel the campaign into everyday events and mainstream consciousness.

How do you begin to create these kinds of messages? You start by understanding that every assignment has an objective. An audience it's targeting. An array of media where it encounters that consumer. And a specific strategy to deliver that message.

To help you get started, each chapter is devoted to one aspect of writing. I would recommend you read the first four chapters first, so you have a solid foundation of the basics: targeting your audience, presenting key benefits, creating a brief (chapter 1), selecting a strategy (chapter 2), applying writing techniques (chapter 3), and developing a main message (chapter 4). After that, you can read any chapter in any order (from chapters 5 through 14). That's because the book is modular.

Therefore, each chapter stands on its own. So, if you'd like to read about writing for television, you could read that chapter. Or if you're interested in blogging, you could go to that chapter. Or if you're curious about multilingual or international campaigns, you start with the last chapter. People learn best when they satisfy their curiosity. With that said, you can begin wherever you want. Then, go to whatever interests you most. Here's the order of each medium that's explored.

- Chapter 5: Print (ads, brochures, catalogues)
- Chapter 6: Radio
- Chapter 7: TV
- Chapter 8: Direct mail, mobile and small-space writing
- Chapter 9: Out-of-home and transit
- Chapter 10: Digital dialogue, virtual community, blogging
- Chapter 11: Websites
- Chapter 12: Interactive engagement, social media and viral marketing
- Chapter 13: Integrated campaigns
- Chapter 14: International campaigns

I also recommend familiarizing yourself with the content set in callout boxes. They're designed so you can find what you're looking for. If you want to review the checklists, you can find them listed in the table of contents or the index. If you want to read tips for writing, simply look those up. Or, if you want to check out the info boxes, rules, and so on, go right ahead. You can also scan the book and read the callout quotes. They're little bites of wisdom that are easily digestible.

To best absorb the information in each chapter, allow yourself the necessary time to do the following:

1 Read the copy in all the examples.
2 See how it relates to the image.

3   Look carefully at typography for hierarchy of message. (See what's emphasized by the size, position, and style of the type.)

4   Review the terminology lists.

5   Visit the listed websites.

6   Complete, or at least examine, the exercises.

7   Become an active observer. Notice new media everywhere.

8   Practice your analytical skills every day, whenever you see advertising messages.

9   Be a gracious recipient of criticism. You'll grow faster.

10 Read more. Be receptive to all kinds of writing. In all media and formats, from plays to promotions.

What I have intended to set forth is a "Writer's Depot" where you can browse all the tools on the virtual shelf and select the ones you need to add to your creative tool shed. Take what you want, review what you'd like, and cart off as many as you can. That way, you'll be prepared for any upcoming project.

If you're committed to your own creative growth, you'll become a stronger writer, even if you jump around from medium to medium. You'll soon discover, after reading this complete guide, you'll be prepared to create compelling copy in any medium. Mostly, because you'll be equipped with a handy, all-in-one toolkit.

But, don't stop there. You'll also find an online toolkit that's packed with ancillary materials. These will serve as additional tools to reinforce the skill sets you'll be building.

Just visit www.wiley.com/go/copywriterstoolkit and you'll be privy to a plethora of informative supplements, including:

1   145-page Test Bank

2   84-page Instructor's Guide

3   14 PowerPoint presentations (one for each chapter)

4   Interactive terminology

5   5-page Syllabus

Feel free to refer to them for creative exercises, quiz questions, chapter reviews, key point summaries, or critical analyses. The online toolkit is an invitation to start a creative scavenger hunt where advertising solutions start with strategic thinking.

ACKNOWLEDGMENTS

The completion of this book would not be possible without the help of many people who generously offered their time and graciously devoted their attention throughout the creative process. I am eager to thank each of them individually to show them how deeply grateful I am. I can hear them saying, "That's not necessary." But, I assure you, it is. If by any chance, I inadvertently omitted someone, please accept my deepest apology.

The first person I would like to thank is my husband, Jack. I've been sequestered away researching and writing for so much of the time, he probably wouldn't recognize me if I wandered out of my office. Next, I would like to thank Jennifer and Paul Minnich, co-creative directors of M2Design, for keeping me focused and centered. They enthusiastically join my celebratory moments when another image or quote was acquired. Third, I wish to thank Monica Hudson, my rainbow of creative solutions. Fourth, I want to thank Selacia, for her support as I navigated through complex challenges. Fifth, I would like to give a big thank you to my niece, Ronni Alexander, who provides a loving life compass.

Next, I must thank some people at Wiley-Blackwell. First, Elizabeth P. Swayze, senior editor, Communication and Media Studies, who not only wholeheartedly supported my vision, but also allowed me to digress and "grow the manuscript" into what it has become. Second, I would like to acknowledge Deirdre Ilkson, development editor, who patiently worked "side-by-side" with me throughout the revision and organizational process. Third, I wish to acknowledge Margot A. Morse who first established a comfortable editorial relationship in her earlier position as senior editorial assistant, followed by Allison Kostka, editorial assistant, who moved the process along. I also wish to thank Julia Kirk, books editorial project editor, who carefully carried this work through production into print, Simon Eckley, production manager, who supervised the beautiful design; Matthew Brown, project manager, whose attention to detail was unrivalled; Eldo Barkhuizen, copy editor, who helped find the tiniest of errors; and Joanna Pyke, project manager, for combing through the final page proofs for last-minute corrections. Finally, I would like to thank members of the marketing team who have shown enthusiastic support: Amanda Banner, associate product manager, and Virginia Graham, list marketing manager.

Now, I wish to thank all of the creative talents and various executives at ad agencies (in alphabetical order), who never complained about my seemingly endless requests and interruptions to handle the mundane tasks of interview scheduling, image acquisitions, text content corrections, caption and credit approvals, while sharing relevant campaign insights.

At 22squared, Curt Mueller, creative director and writer, for sharing the strategic thinking behind the Red Brick Beer packaging copy; and Julianna Bowman, director of corporate communications, for carefully shepherding through permissions, quotes, acquisitions, and images.

At 60 Second Marketer, Mr. Jamie Turner, Chief Content Officer, for allowing me to use information from his website: http://60secondmarketer.com/blog/2010/04/09/top-52-social-media-platforms/(accessed June 7, 2011).

At Altimeter Group, Brian Solis, principal and author of *Engage!* and JESS3, for graciously granting permission to include his comments and feature his inventive infographic, "The Conversation Prism."

At Bel Brands USA, Colleen Nash, Brand Manager for her tireless work on my behalf to secure permission from Fromageries Bel to include The Laughing Cow radio scripts.

Drayton Bird, writer, speaker, marketer, and author, for sharing his writing tips for various media.

At Chick-fil-A, Sherry Kangas, corporate legal supervisor, for managing to move the permission process through completion; and Michael E. Ruberti, senior manager, corporate legal attorney, for granting final permission to include the Chick-fil-A image.

At Crispin Porter + Bogusky: Steve Sapka, vice-president/director agency communications, for judiciously and quickly answering every correspondence, from information compilation and interview scheduling to quote and image approvals; Rob Reilly, partner/co-executive/creative director, for granting an interview and sharing his creative insights on innovative campaign development.

At DDB: Pat Sloan, media relations DDB Corporate, for orchestrating information gathering and image acquisition in various parts of the world; Jeff Swystun, chief communications officer, DDB Worldwide, for permission to quote from the DDB website; Bonnie O'Hara, PR manager in London for tracking down permission to include the "Monopoly Live" information and visual; Sara Cosgrove, European communications director in London, for her assistance in facilitating the permission process for the "Monopoly Live" and VW "Das Auto" campaigns; Sylvia Phipps, international database manager in Berlin, for coordinating the final content, obtaining images, clarifying the campaign strategies, and granting approval/permission for VW "Das Auto" campaign discussed herein; Jason Lusty, global business lead VW, for his assistance with the approval process on VW "Das Auto" campaign; Erik Chmil, photographer of the German Eos images (Figures 14.22–14.25), for magnanimously granting permission to showcase his photographs; Michael Bugaj, social media director for his guidance in gaining information and approval for the VW "The Fun Theory" campaign; Fabiana Antacli, DDB Latina's director of communications, Rodrigo Figueroa Reyes, founder & CEO, FiRe Advertiament, and Victoria Cossentino, assistant, for their help with background information and approval of the Kosiuko campaign.

At DeVito/Verdi: Paul McCormick, director of new business, for liberally sharing comments and allowing inclusion of the Legal Sea Foods campaign; Kelly Durcan, director of public relations for conscientiously coordinating all correspondence and final image releases; and Chris Arrighi, video specialist, who eagerly provided images in the required format.

At Digital Surgeons: Peter Sena II, founder and chief technology officer, for freely discussing the digital development of creative work including the Arm & Hammer "Jill's Secret Solution" interactive campaign.

At Draftfcb: Jonathan Harries, chairman and worldwide chief creative officer, for quickly responding to my request for information; Teddy Brown, senior vice president, executive creative director of the Orange County office, for freely sharing background information about and indispensable insight into Taco Bell campaigns; Josh Dysart, manager, corporate communications, who miraculously managed to finalize all approvals; and Soraya Eltomey, former associate corporate communications, who initiated and monitored the permission process.

At Emory University: Reshma Shah, assistant professor of marketing in the Goizueta Business School, for generously allowing me to quote from http://60secondmarketer.com/blog/2010/04/09/top-52-social-media-platforms/.

At Euro RSCG: Alison Lazzaro, account director, for overseeing the communication and approval process; Cherie Malone, account supervisor, for arranging interviews, acquiring images, and double-checking all the tedious details; creative directors Drummond Berman and Simon Nickson, the writing and art direction team who created the celebrated "Talk to Chuck" campaign discussed in this work, for their openness about the development and conceptualization process, detailed comments and exciting images; and Nicole Portet, brand marketing director at Charles Schwab, for her ongoing patience and assistance.

At Fantasy Interactive (Fi): David Martin, founder and CEO, for considerately granting permission to quote from his agency's website: http://www.f-i.com/.

At Goodby, Silverstein and Partners: Christine O'Donnell, PR Director, for her assistance in interview scheduling and script acquisition; Judy Ybarra, business affairs manager, for granting permission to include the HP story script; and Sara Rose, former senior copywriter, for her interview and thoughtful comments.

At Hasbro: For everyone's diligent assistance in obtaining permission to use Mr. and Mrs. Potato head images.

At Hubspot: Kipp Bodnar, inbound marketing manager, for permission to include his invaluable list he's posted of "24 Awesome SEO blogs everyone should read."

At Joy Radio: Joy Golden, founder/creative director, for her frank comments, tips, for providing The Laughing Cow radio scripts, and for her consent for inclusion.

At Kaplan Thaler Group: Robin Koval, president, for initializing and supporting the research process; Tom Amico, creative director/copywriter and co-creator of the Aflac Duck, for carefully answering questions, providing a visual for inclusion, and imparting his creative wisdom; Tricia Kenney, director of corporate communications, for her direction and facilitation of correspondence; and Erin Creagh, account coordinator, corporate communications, for following up with all correspondence.

At Kellogg Company: Brian O'Donnell, Counsel, Intellectual Property, for leading the decision process and granting final permission for images and comments relating to the **Kellogg's Frosted Flakes®** campaigns; Deb Ball, assistant to Gary Pilnick, for ushering the paperwork through for final consent.

At McCann Erickson: Alessandra Lariu, senior vice president, digital group creative director, for her enthusiastic participation and invaluable discussion of digital marketing.

At McDonald Marketing: Kelly McDonald, president, for clearly explaining her Latino Acculturation Stratification Model and sharing her expertise.

At Leo Burnett: Abby Lovett, director, global PR, for activating the internal information research process; Cindy Maguire, account director, for fastidiously checking all copyright references and gaining image, caption, credit line, and excerpt approvals; Jeff Cowie, talent manager, for helping to clear final permissions; Kevin Moriarty, vice president and creative director, for eagerly offering his creative insights on the **Kellogg's Frosted Flakes®** campaigns.

At the Marketing Pilgrim: Andy Beal, founder, for his kind permission to quote from his blog, www.marketingpilgrim.com.

At Miami Ad School: Pippa Seichrist, president, for her eager participation and permission to include the Miami Ad School bottled water copy and image (Figure 8.3).

At RinkTime.com: John Kirker, founder, for the authorization to include his compilation of websites posted at http://topcopywritingsites.com/.

At SapientNitro: Matt Ziselman, creative director, for imparting his astute perceptions on digital marketing, and for granting the go-ahead to quote from the agency website.

At Sweetspot Agency: Robert Borges, creative director, for assisting in gathering information on interactive campaigns.

At Tablet Computer Geeks: Shane Ketterman, founder/blogger, for permission to feature his article "Five Tips for Better Results with Mobile e-Mail Marketing."

At The Escape Pod: Vinny Warren, creative director, for offering insight into strategic planning, providing images, scripts, writing tips, and permission for innovative campaigns including Feckin Irish Whiskey.

At The Happy Marketing Guy: David Leonardt, founder, for his kind permission to use his blog post "The Golden Rules of Guest Blogging."

At The Richards Group: Stephanie Mullins, brand management, for her diligence in arranging interviews, images, scripts, and approvals for the Bridgestone Tires campaigns; Jack Westerholt, copywriter, for providing lucid insights into concept and copy development for various campaigns, including the Mr. and Mrs. Potato Head commercial ("Taters") for Bridgestone Tires; Stephanie Johanson, brand management, for her dedicated supervision of Motel 6 interviews, comments, images, caption and credit lines, and permission approvals; Christopher Smith and Lance Miceli, creative directors, for sharing their creative strategies behind the ever popular "Tom Bodett" Motel 6 campaign; Lorraine Holland and Adalys Castellanos, brand management for their valiant efforts to secure image, caption, and credit line approvals for Chick-fil-A. Rebecca Babin, brand management, whose attention to detail ushered permission approvals through for the Orkin images; Adam Fish, photographer, for kindly granting permission to use his Orkin postcards (Figures 8.1 and 8.2) with his photographs.

At The San Jose Group: George L. San Jose, president and COO, for offering his expertise on multicultural marketing, image permission, and thoughtful quotes, Julie Sestan, account executive for her tireless help compiling images, supervising image credits, and overseeing excerpt revisions; Erika Cano-Albor, account supervisor, for her help in gathering images and scripts, coordinating correspondence, and ushering through the necessary permissions.

At Thunder Bay Media: Derek Cromwell, founder, CEO, copywriter and/or content marketer, for permitting me to quote freely from his blog posts: http://www.thunderbaymedia.net/blog.

At Vitro: John Vitro, principal and chief creative officer, for enabling the information gathering process on various campaigns, including ASICS; Tom Sullivan, CEO and principal, for the initial impetus to obtain answers to research questions; KT Thayer, creative director, for his important copy tips; Elena Rodriguez, assistant to John Vitro, for persistence in ushering the critical comments, creative content, and campaign images.

At Wieden+Kennedy in the US: Danielle Black, PR director, Joani Wardwell, press relations global, for their combined efforts in arranging for interviews and permission; Sheena Brady, creative director/copywriter, for her explanation of the creative concepting process and application of universal truths.

At Wieden+Kennedy in London: Lauren Glazer, director of PR, and Bella Laine, PR director, for their concerted assistance in coordinating and supervising the interview and permission process; Neil Christie, managing director, for guiding the permission process and granting approval; and Ben Walker, creative director/copywriter, for his helpful tips to other copywriters.

At www.copyblogger.com: Brian Clark, founder, for generously allowing inclusion of his posted article "Warning: Use These 5 Headline Formulas at Your Own Risk."

At www.famousbloggers.net: Hesham Zebida, founder, for his gracious permission to showcase his blog post "How to Cook an Irresistible Blog."

At Young & Laramore: Paul J. Knapp, CEO, for his continued support of my research through his supervision of information accumulation, image compilation, and permission finalization; Tom Denari, president, for his consent to the inclusion of agency work; Carolyn Hadlock, executive creative director, for providing images, explaining the Peerless Faucet campaign's creative process; and Charlie Hopper, creative director, for sharing the strategic thinking behind various campaigns, including Ugly Mug Coffee.

At xynoMedia: Lena L. West, president, for her tips on blog writing and for allowing quotations from her articles and blogs.

At Zubi Advertising: Joe Zubizarreta, chief operating officer, for his permission to include copywriting information and for granting access to former and current creative talents; Carlos Menendez, copywriter, for offering interesting comments and helpful writing tips; and Juan Santiago Lagos, former associate creative director, for providing tips on writing for the Hispanic market.

I would also like to thank the following people for their encouragement and generosity.

At Florida International University: Lillian Kopenhaver, dean, School of Journalism and Mass Communication, for her faithful commitment to my ongoing research efforts.

Fernando Figueredo, department chair, Advertising and Public Relations, for his loyal and palpable support.

In addition, I would also like to thank my colleagues, university students, and seminar audiences who inspire me and drive my inquisitive nature to seek out new avenues of research.

Lastly, I would like to thank everyone who believed in this project from the very first moment when it was just an idea.

1

THE PERSUASIVE WORD

Strategy ABCs: audience, benefits, and creative briefs

> *Having a clear vision of what it is that you are heading for, and know it when you see it and dismiss it when you don't see it, is really, really important. Just think from the outset about what it is that you're writing because writing is not an accident.*

DRUMMOND BERMAN, CREATIVE DIRECTOR/ COPYWRITER, EURO RSCG [1]

Thinking about strategy first

Examining the brief: an up-close look

Gaining deeper audience insight through VALS and observational research

Understanding secondary audience versus primary audience

Delving into consumer insights

Realizing the importance of a benefit

Creative strategy exercises

In this first chapter, you'll examine a campaign's creative starting point: the strategy. You'll take an up-close look at the creative brief, which acts as the campaign's directional guide. You'll analyze the structure and function of the creative brief, see how it drives the strategy, and find out how it's based on several key aspects including market research, consumer insights, specific objectives, and product positioning.

You'll also learn how to create effective media intersections, or the best places for your message to collide with the consumer. In no time, you'll grasp how to use these "collision venues" or touchpoints to change or reinforce consumers' impression of the brand. You'll see selecting the right tactics (specific distribution vehicles, like online ads or mobile messages) helps propel your message to the targeted audience.

In addition, you'll realize that creating a two-way conversation with consumers can result in an unexpected backlash. That happens when consumers share their feelings (good and bad) about the brand. You'll quickly recognize that being able to analyze your audience through various means like VALS will help you create authentic and credible messages.

You'll soon comprehend the difference between primary and secondary audiences, be able to identify them, and know why you need to consider both. You'll gain insight into why some agencies copy test (ask consumers their opinion of ad messages) and some still conduct focus groups, surveys, mall interceptions, and other means of consumer research discussed later in the chapter. Finally, you'll be reminded of the importance of focusing on the benefit in your main idea. So, let's start looking at strategy right now.

Thinking about strategy first

Every advertising campaign needs a specific objective, a clear message, a target audience, and a "strategy." The strategy is the overall creative direction of a campaign, which is determined by the account and creative teams. They work together to develop an underlying solution that addresses a specific consumer benefit or need, clarifies the product or service, or solves a brand's marketing challenge. The strategy acts like a compass and allows the agency to double check that the campaign direction is on-course. For example, if the agreed-upon strategy was to show the whitening power of a detergent and the ad talked about a special two-for-one offer, then the message was off-strategy. It should be highlighting the whitening ability, not the price.

How does each agency decide the strategy? First it conducts research to gain consumer insights. What does the audience want or need? How can this product deliver a solution? What is the benefit, the reward for the consumer to make this purchase? The agency team looks to answer these and other questions and gain a deeper understanding of consumers and how they think. What they value. What's important to them? What solution the product offers. Why should they choose this product and not another.

The agency team uses the creative brief to answer these and other specific questions in order to develop a creative strategy statement to steer the campaign. The account team always thinks about the big picture, concentrates on the overall strategic direction, and looks for long-term creative solutions in its messaging. To gain greater insight into the creative-problem-solving process, we'll start by examining the elements of a creative *brief*. Then, we'll see how it serves as an outline for the campaign *strategy*, or basic creative destination.

But, before we get to the brief, we should take a look at how much of this strategic thinking has been changed over the years by technology and consumer behavior. Starting in 1900, when N.W. Ayer first introduced campaigns to fulfill the advertisers' marketing objectives,[2] agencies used to work in this way:

1 Brief
2 Creative strategy
3 Concept
4 Execution

First the brief was created based on client input, market research, consumer insight, advertising objectives, product positioning (in the mind of the consumer), competitors, product's uniqueness, tactics, main message, and so on. Then, the strategy was created based on the brief, a main concept was developed from the strategy, and the concept was executed.

Today, marketers are thinking about the execution as they're creating the brief. Why? Because the advertising isn't just about the concept; it's also about where the message and consumer intersect. These *media intersections* are "touchpoints," places where the campaign messages are seen by the target. Another key point is that consumers now participate in delivering the brand's message. They do this through consumer-created content and user-generated content. The difference between these two is that user-generated content are messages developed by people who use the product, not just the general public. With so many people involved in social media like Facebook, LinkedIn, Twitter, and Flickr, consumers can continue a dialogue between themselves and the brand. Or they can initiate an open conversation among members of their online community.

Consumers can share their opinions, photos, videos, and even their own impression of the brand through self-created commercials. This puts the power of selling a brand's message in the hands of the consumer, without anyone's permission. Marketers have to be careful because once a negative impression is circulated on the Internet, it's difficult to change it. Advertisers have to protect their brands' images. There are several ways they attempt to do this. Notice the word "attempt," because it's not that simple to achieve. First, they need to constantly monitor their social media sites. Second, they need to immediately address consumer complaints. Third, they need to be willing to face harsh criticism in a graceful and responsive way.

Now, unhappy consumers can create damaging user-generated content. One unforgettable 2008 United Airlines incident was globally publicized online. While the band Sons of Maxwell was on tour they witnessed the careless handling of its $3,500 guitar by the United Airlines' baggage crew. After several unsuccessful attempts to have the airline resolve the problem, the band created a video detailing the event. It posted it on YouTube where it instantly went viral. Unlike years ago, companies today that are nonresponsive to customer complaints have to face irate, public backlash. Consumers are no longer going to sit idly by when they can broadcast their poor customer service complaints. Smart marketers are wise to address problems immediately. Most likely, that would be any brand's best corporate strategy.

Taking that one step forward, Crispin Porter + Bogusky, named agency of the decade by *Advertising Age* (December 14, 2009 issue), flies over this process entirely and starts with the end in mind: press coverage. Creative talents must write a jaw-dropping press release before they begin any creative conceptualization. They must present what the press will write about.

Then, they have to find a way to make that happen. The campaign's "big idea" must transcend medium and format. It must be so powerful it cannot be ignored. In thinking about the reaction to their work, their strategic thinking teams include cognitive anthropologists (account managers), creatives, digital technologists (developers), and anyone else who would like to work on the campaign. It's a collaborative effort in which everyone shares ownership, with credit lists of possibly 75 people.

Now, let's get back to the function and format of the brief, which is more commonly used at agencies, and how that guides the strategic direction.

Examining the brief: an up-close look

Although agencies differ in their briefs, most include the same key information. Here's a template to use for your briefs. It forces you to determine the audience, product competitors, consumer opinions, product uniqueness, and other critical areas.

We will look at the basic or shorter brief (text box 1.1) and the more expanded, detailed brief (text box 1.2).

You can see there are only eight parts to this basic brief. This will give you a good start in your overall thinking. However, before you can begin outlining your creative direction, you should go through and complete the longer brief (text box 1.2). Be sure to answer every one of the questions and fill in each answer specifically.

The brief is a series of questions that need to be carefully answered before developing a solid campaign strategy. First you need to fully understand all of the terminology. First, we'll examine some of the words used in box 1.2.

The brand is advertising to say something to _____ (VERB – persuade, convince, inform, educate) the audience (SPECIFIC CONSUMERS) that this _____ (PRODUCT, SERVICE OR BRAND) will _____ (STATE THE BENEFIT) because _____ (FEATURES THAT EXPLAIN WHY AUDIENCE SHOULD BELIEVE IT. THIS ACTS AS A SUPPORT STATEMENT).

TEMPLATES 1.1 The shorter creative brief

1   What is the *brand's character* or personality?

2   Why does the brand *want to advertise*?

3   Who is the *audience*?

4   What do they (audience members) *currently think*?

5   What do you *want them to think*?

6   *Why should they buy* this product/service?

7   What is the *big message* you want them to know?

8   What *kind of tactics* (specific ad/promotional techniques) do you want to use? For example, do you want to use viral marketing, interactive online components, out-of-home messages, print ads, transit (buses, subways, taxis, etc.), new media, direct mail, or other vehicles?

TEMPLATES 1.2 The creative brief

1 Why does the brand *want to advertise*? What does it want to accomplish?
(Use this template.)

Creative strategy statement template

To _____ _____ that _____ will _____ because _____.
    (verb)   (audience)   (brand)   (benefit)   (support statement /
                                                 reason why)

Example

To convince fastidious moms that Tide will get out the toughest stains because of its enzyme-fighting formula.

2 Who is the *audience*?

  a *Demographics*– Provides insight into audience by their age, income, education, gender, occupation (employment status), etc.

  b *Psychographics*– Examines how audience lives. Think lifestyle, attitude, personality, behavior (like brand loyalty), and value (what's important to them). (VALS and OBSERVATIONAL RESEARCH. Explained after box. See below.)

  c *Geographics*– Explores where (location and kind of setting: urban, suburban, rural) audience lives.

3 Who are the brand's competitors?

4 What do they (audience members) *currently think* (about the brand)?

5 What do you *want them to think* (about the brand)? (THINK CONSUMER BENEFIT. What the product does for the end-user.)

6 *Why should they buy* this brand (product or service)? Clearly answer: "WHY BUY?"

7 What is the *big message* you want them to know? (THINK SLOGAN.)

8 Determine what the brand's positioning is. Do you want consumers to say it's safe, cool, fun, reliable, etc.? (WHAT IS THE BRAND KNOWN FOR?)

9 What is the brand's *USP*? (UNIQUE SELLING POINT OR PROPOSITION?) What separates this brand from its competitors?

10 What is the *brand's character* or personality?

  a What kind of personality does the brand have?

  b Who would the brand be as a famous person?

  c Who would that famous person be in relation to the consumer? (A coach, friend, uncle, sister, neighbor, dad?)

  d How would that person (friend, brother, boss) speak to the consumer? How would a coach speak to team members? THINK ADJECTIVE. A coach would be authoritative, encouraging, concerned, etc. This is the brand's *TONE OF VOICE*. (Use it in #11 below.)

11 What is the *tone of voice*? (HOW YOU SPEAK TO YOUR AUDIENCE: Think adjective. Refer to #10d, above.)

12 What *kinds of tactics* (specific ad/promotional techniques) do you want to use? For example, do you want to use viral marketing, interactive online components, ambient messages, print ads, transit (buses, subways, taxis, etc.), new media, direct mail, or other vehicles?

13 Think about what kind of campaign will generate press and create buzz.

The creative strategy, as shown in the brief (# 1) is a deceptively simple formula that explains the broad direction of the campaign. Although it looks like an easy-to-develop sentence, the challenge is to write it in the most descriptive and accurate language, specifically relating to the brand. Just fill in the blanks. Use the capped words in parentheses as explanatory guides.

The point here is to explain in detail why the brand is advertising; however you don't want to just say "to increase sales" or "to build awareness" because that could apply to any brand. Those statements are too general. This is where you want to differentiate your brand from any other. You must answer this general question in a very specific way: What do you want this campaign to do for the brand? Don't just rush in with the first obvious answer. Look deeper into the audience profile you'll outline before proceeding. Who are they? Why are you targeting them? What benefit will they derive from this product or service? What features explain why they should pick this brand and not one of its competitors?

The trick to writing a great brief is in drilling down the information. Think of it as if you're a chef and you're reducing the ingredients in a pan to create a sauce. You must reduce the information down to its core essence. This one sentence must act like a one-line review in a newspaper if this were a restaurant. Then, the campaign or "menu" is what will attract diners to taste the food or brand.

Gaining deeper audience insight through VALS and observational research

Two other important terms appeared in the brief under "Who is the Audience" in section 2b above, "Psychographics." These were *VALS* and *observational research*. VALS connects consumer personality traits to future purchasing behaviors. VALS stands for Values, Attitudes, and Lifestyles and was created in the 1970s by SRI International, a research company, in Menlo, California. VALS market segmentation places audiences into easy-to-refer-to, shopping-prediction categories. Observational research is a method

> The brief has a tiny hole. You must make an elephant go through it without tearing the paper. **JUAN SANTIAGO LAGOS, ASSOCIATE CREATIVE DIRECTOR, ZUBI ADVERTISING, NOW AT ALMA/DDB**[3]

of collecting consumer information by seeing them firsthand in a natural, everyday setting like at home rather than learning about them through their answers in a focus group. So, instead of asking them what magazines they read, they can see them usually lying around their homes. This sidesteps a common consumer desire to impress others in the focus group or tell researchers what they think they want to hear.

These are just two of many ways to analyze audiences. There are target groups by age-group titles. Some of the dates vary depending on the source, but you can get a quick idea of the various target groups here. These labels include the Baby Boomers (born between 1946 and 1964); the Generation X or "Gen X" (born between 1965 and 1976); the Gen Y or "Millennials," "Gen M," "Generation Next," or "Generation Y" (born between 1977 and 1994); the Gen Z or "Net Generation," "Internet Generation," "Digital Natives," or the "Verge Generation" (born between 1994 and 2004). These groups have attitudinal likeness or similar perspective. Even though it's unfair to categorize any individual, researchers will create a one-word nickname, or short expression to act as a short cut to identify a group. For example, the Baby Boomers are the "never get old" group. Gen X are "independent." Gen Y are team players. Gen Z are "digital savvy."

There are ethnic groups, which you reach through their cultural similarities. There are interest target groups, which you speak to through their common interests, like technology buffs, wine lovers, conscientious environmentalists, and so on.

VALS, on the other hand, allows marketers to predict consumers' future shopping behavior by considering different buying motivational categories based on consumer attitudes and values. The first VALS, or VALS 1, which explored consumers' lifestyles and buying motivations, was later refined to reflect consumers' ability to pay for products they desired. The revised VALS, or VALS 2, blended demographics into the mix and considered income, education, and health. VALS 2 answered the question of the strength of consumers' buying power. Today all of the categories are used, to reflect different audience's lifestyles, buying motivations and purchasing power. Let's compare the two different VALS one after the other as they are so clearly explained in *Ads, Fads and Consumer Culture*.[4] After this, we'll compare these to VALS 3 (text box 1.3).

VALS 1: from lowest to highest income

Group I: Needs-driven consumers – Financially challenged.

1   *Survivors* – Poor and elderly, who are just scraping by.
2   *Sustainers* – Young and clever with a desire to succeed.

Group II: Outer-directed consumers – Representative in attitude, geography, and financial status as "Middle America"; concerned about other people's opinions of them; want to leave a positive impression.

3   *Belongers* – Conservative traditionalists, who long for yesterday, and stick to what's tried and true, rather than experimenting with something new.
4   *Emulators* – Eager, status-driven and competitive, these are up-and-comers on the path to financial success.
5   *Achievers* – Have reached their financial and material goals, community leaders.

Group III: Inner-directed consumers – Make purchases from their own desires, not to impress others.

6 *I-Am-Me's* – Young, self-focused freethinkers who do their own thing.

7 *Experientials*– More mature individualistic naturalists who seek self-improvement and personal growth.

8 *Societally Conscious* – Environmentalists interested in global conservation and consumer product protection.

9 *Integrateds* – Self-assured and confident, less responsive to advertising messages, may be unintentional trendspotters because of their good taste.

VALS 2

Starting at the lowest income group, moving to highest, we start with the Strugglers (Survivors in VALS 1) and end up with the Actualizers (Integrateds in VALS 1). Now there are only eight categories as follows:

1 *Strugglers* – Lowest income, those barely surviving financially.

2 *Makers* – High energy, lower income group who enjoy constructing things.

3 *Strivers* – Emulating Achievers without the income or skill set.

4 *Believers* – Like Fulfilleds with a lower income, conservatives who prefer name brands.

5 *Experiencers* – Avid shoppers, risk takers who relish unusual, novel, even wacky, items.

6 *Achievers* – Accomplished and structured, goal-oriented consumers whose purchases reflect their status.

7 *Fulfilled* – Mature, financially stable, who value durable, functional products, and are receptive to new ideas.

8 *Actualizers* – Wealthy individuals who reached their personal goals, their purchases reflect their sophisticated taste.

VALS 3

A third VALS segmentation also breaks consumers into eight categories (with some different labels) and three groups. At the bottom of the financial ladder are the Survivors with limited resources and little creative innovation. In the top group are the opposite. These are Innovators with deep resources who are highly innovative. In the middle are these six groups that represent the primary buying motivations based on their (1) ideals, (2) achievements, and need for (3) self-expression. In each of the middle groups (numbers 2–7) are low- and high-income subsets. For example, the "Ideals" group has Thinkers (higher income) and Believers (lower income).[5]

Group I: Survivors – Lowest income and lowest ability to innovate.

1 *Survivors* – Reluctant, brand-loyal shoppers, focus on needs not wants.

Group II: Ideals – Idealistic, inspired by moral principles and beliefs.

2 *Thinkers* – Informed and analytical, educated consumers who seek new knowledge, value structure, and appreciate durability (higher income)

3 *Believers* – Deep moral values, brand loyal, predictable conservative shoppers with a preference for anything familiar, strong community and religious alliances (lower income).

Group III: Achievement – Goal-oriented, motivated by accomplishments.

4 *Achievers* – Committed to success and family values, driven by career and family goals, seek prestigious products that reflect social status, conservative and risk averse (higher income).

5 *Strivers* – Status purchases demonstrate their need for approval, lack job skills to advance in the marketplace, have jobs not career positions (lower income).

Group IV: Self-expression – Stimulated by expressing themselves.

6 *Experiencers* – Young impulsive shoppers looking for the cool factor, attracted by novel and quirky items (higher income).

7 *Makers* – Enjoy being self-sufficient and making or building things themselves, more impressed with getting their money's worth than status purchases or luxury products (lower income).

Group V: Innovators – Highest income and ability to innovate.

8 *Innovators* – Strong self-image, upscale leaders, sophisticated shoppers.

The point of considering VALS categories before you begin writing is to try to actually picture your audience. To see them as people with specific lifestyles, attitudes, and different values so you can speak to them in a way that singles them out. You want the readers or viewers to feel as if you're talking directly to them. Even if you don't have the category titles perfectly in your mind, you can at least have a strong sense of the audience's way of life. Always remember to remind yourself of your audience when looking at a brief and beginning every assignment.

In thinking about the audience, Teddy Brown, senior vice president, executive creative director of the Orange County office at Draftfcb, explained that Taco Bell talks to a psychographic, not a demographic. He said:

> *So, it's really more about what this audience believes more than necessarily who they are. It's quite a broad target in general, so we spend more time talking about how this target audience acts and how they live their lives, than we do if they're male or female.*[6]

Review all the observational research and internalize the consumer insights provided to you by the account team. Ask questions to the account and research teams if you need audience clarification. The more clearly you understand your audience, the more effective your message will be. Writing just to explain product features won't drive anyone to make a purchase, but writing to show what those features mean and how they can solve a problem or improve someone's life will. Ask yourself when you're about to create an ad in any product category what has or would compel you to buy it. Pay attention, whenever you buy anything, to your decision process. If you were skeptical at first, what did you see, hear, or read that swayed you?

It's this kind of thinking that is the backbone of the brief. It forces you to examine various aspects of marketing and fully understand the product's overall advertising goals, competitors, consumer beliefs, tactics, as well as its character, *tone of voice*, uniqueness,

USEFUL INFO 1.3 VALS comparison starting with highest incomes on top

The categories in all caps do not line up with VALS 1 groups. Subgroups are in italics. Notice that VALS 2 has no subgroups.

VALS 1	VALS 2	VALS 3	CAMPAIGNS
Integrateds		*High Resources and High Innovation*	
9. Integrateds	8. Actualizers	8. Innovators	*Charitable causes,new approaches*
	7. FULFILLEDS		*New, durable products*
Inner-directed			
8. Societally Conscious			*Eco-friendly campaigns*
7. Experientials		*Self-expression*	*Sky diving, hiking,*
6. I-Am-Me's	6. Experiencers	7. Experiencers	*biking, exploring, etc.*
	5. MAKERS	6. MAKERS	*Home Depot, Lowe's*
Outer-directed		*Achievement*	
5. Achievers	4. Achievers	5. Achievers	*Luxury items: Gucci, Dior*
4. Emulators	3. Strivers	4. Strivers	*Designers for less, T.J.Maxx, Marshalls*
3. Belongers		3. Thinkers	*Tried-and-true, reliable brands*
Need-driven		*Ideals-driven(higher income)*	
2. Sustainers	2. Believers	2. Believers (lower income)	*Designers at deeper discounts: outlet malls*
1. Survivors	1. Strugglers		*Walmart, Costco*
		Low Resources and Low Innovation	
		1. Survivors	*Goodwill, thrift shops*

and main message. You need to consider everything when you're developing the campaign's direction and creative strategy.

Sheena Brady, creative director/copywriter at Wieden+Kennedy, explained how important the brief is in reaching client objectives this way:

> I think what the brief is, is what the client is trying to do. So that's going to have a direct impact on the work. Then we, as creative people, find the best way of creatively solving that problem. Without a brief, there's no way of knowing whether we're doing our job for the client.[7]

Understanding secondary audience versus primary audience

In addition to the primary target who eventually buys the product, another audience should also be considered. This secondary audience is made up of the people who influence the primary audience: those are the people who make the purchase and use the product. The secondary audience could be a friend, relative, business associate, mentor, or anyone who affects the buyers' purchasing decisions. According to Larry Percy, there are five different groups of people who influence purchasing decisions. They fall into the following "purchasing role" categories:

1   *Initiator:* person who first suggests buying the product or trying the service.

2   *Influencer:* someone who encourages or dissuades the buyer.

3   *Decider:* the actual person who makes the final decision purchasing selections.

4   *Purchaser:* the shopper who buys the item.

5   *User:* the person who ultimately uses the item or service.[8]

When creating a campaign, it's helpful to think about how the *tone of voice* could also speak to these groups, so they're impacted by the message. Also when you're working on new product introductions, think about whether your audience members are early or late adapters. If they're the type of people who would wait online for hours to be one of the first consumers to buy the latest Nike or high-tech gadget, then you might entice them with a be-the-first-to-own kind of message. If they're late adapters, the people who wait until all the bugs are out of a new computer, smartphone, software, and so on, you might talk humorously about how this model has been "bug-proofed" with a digital exterminator.

Delving into consumer insights

There's more to understanding the consumer than psychographic VALS categories, primary and secondary audiences, and purchasing roles. There are also insights gleaned from observational and other types of consumer research. Here's a short list of some types of advertising-based research.

Focus groups provide information gathered from small groups of people placed together to review products and evaluate campaigns. Sometimes one person dominates and drives the discussion, thereby "tainting" or influencing the opinion of others in the group.

Pre-testing or *Copy testing* allows copy to be tested before it's released in an ad campaign. Subjects are asked to comment on myriad ad messages. Some questions might include:

1   Whether they'd seen comparable ads and/or would consider buying the product (overall ad appeal).

2   What the audience's overall impressions were (general impressions).

3   What they like or disliked about the ad, whether it seemed to be cohesive or confusing (ad consistency).

4   Whether they responded to the ad in an emotional way (ad emotional effect).

5   How they might use the product (usage effect).

6   Whether they'd talk to others about the ad.

Their responses are used to predict ad performance in these and other areas: (1) audience attention, (2) brand awareness, (3) purchase motivation, (4) emotional response, (5) ad recall, and (6) clarity of message.

Post-testing or *Ad-tracking* evaluates the brand's performance by monitoring these and other results from the advertising campaign: (1) product/brand sales, (2) brand name recognition, (3) top-of-mind awareness, (4) unaided advertising awareness, (5) aided advertising message recall, (6) aided and unaided brand awareness, (7) brand preference (loyalty), (8) product adoption (usage), and (9) consumer opinion.

Mall interception reveals consumer opinions as they're going about their normal mall shopping. People are stopped randomly and asked to answer some questions.

Surveys indicate how consumers feel about the questions asked. Survey questions are designed to glean specific consumer insights. Often very lengthy surveys offer free products to the participants.

Digital Anthropology shows consumers' online behavior, including which sites they visit, how long they stay; what items are purchased; which articles, podcasts, vodcasts are viewed and shared; and so on. Marketers are looking to understand how to communicate with online communities through "tribalization" studies.

Multi-platform research tracks which media consumers prefer to consume: television, radio, print, online, and so on and helps advertisers evaluate which platforms are the most effective communication vehicles.

Observational research (or *Ethnography*) is conducted at consumers' natural settings, as they go about their everyday routines. The idea is to watch them in their own environment. It's easy to see the books or magazines they read. The kind of décor they prefer. The types of electronic gadgets they use. The brands they prefer, and so on. Understanding consumers' lifestyle is more than statistics. It's having a visual reference, an actual image of these people, so they're three-dimensionally real to the writer.

You also want to know how they feel about the brand and its competitors. Not only if they use it, but also if they do, why? And if not, why not? What do they really think about the product? If they don't like it, why not? What exactly don't they like about it? Having more insight into how consumers make buying decisions gives you more firing power so you'll hit your target with relevant messages. Think of your client's product as "your product." It will make your creative approach more personal. Ask yourself if you can answer these questions:

1   What do they like about "your product" (the one you're advertising)?
2   What do they like better about its competition?
3   What can you say to persuade them to choose "your product" the next time?
4   What haven't you mentioned before that could sway their decision?
5   How can you show them their personal benefits?
6   What need does it fulfill?
7   How does it enhance their lifestyle?
8   How can you differentiate "your product" in their eyes?

Most importantly, think like the consumer. Write that in big letters next to your computer. Before you create any promotional message, answer this: What would you need to hear to take action?

Realizing the importance of a benefit

There's no point in creating a vague campaign. The target audience wants to know why they should make a purchase. They need to find out how this brand will improve their lives, solve a problem, address a specific need, and so on. They don't have time to decipher a complicated message. Put a spotlight on your benefit or W-I-I-F-M (what's in it for me) and place it center stage.

The reason Apple sold so many iPods, iPhones, and iPads is that the advertising shows how easy they are to use and how they can simplify owners' lives. All of the messages answer consumers' objections to learning new technology by demonstrating them in use. The ads don't just say, "Here's a cool new gadget." They make consumers feel confident that the devices are user-friendly and promise a quick-to-integrate learning curve. They remove any hesitancy consumers might have about using a new device.

Try to understand what problem your product or service solves or how it fits into your target audience's lifestyle. If you don't know why they should buy it or order it, your message will be meaningless and ineffective. You must give them an indisputable reason to buy. At the same time, your creative solution must also realize the brand's objectives for advertising. Remember, you want to avoid common reasons such as generating traffic or increasing name recognition. These two goals are not definitive enough. You should be able to encapsulate the campaign message in a short phrase. Think about famous slogans and how they zero in on one sticky idea. It's important to showcase product features; just don't forget to explain how they ultimately help the audience.

For example, Taco Bell's campaigns are usually product-focused and sometimes use exaggeration to drive home a product feature. In the "Volcano Nachos" spot, an actor's face was flaming and smoke was coming out of him to show the product was hotter than other menu items. The "Grand Quesadilla" spot showed a young, pregnant woman boarding a bus. Climbing on board right after her is a young guy with an equally big belly who makes a remark suggesting that she must have enjoyed her Taco Bell lunch as much as he did. The product promises to satisfy your hunger. Brown explained Taco Bell strategies like this:

> The thing with our product is "that new news drives the whole category." So, it must be newsworthy. It's always solving some sort of consumer need or problem. The point of difference is that our product stands out and is celebrated.
>
> The difference between brand marketing and product marketing is that our work is always food-centric. It's the product that inspires the brief, but the story is always centered around the food. In that bus stop spot it's all about the main message. I'm looking at a brief here that states: "the quesadilla that actually fills you up."[9]

Whenever you create a message, you must consider the target audience. See them as three-dimensional people, not just a general group with certain characteristics or identified by a VALS, demographic, psychographic, or cultural category. How would you speak to them one on one? What do they value? What would be your *tone of voice*? Your *point of view*? What would be the main benefit most important to them? If you begin by focusing on who's receiving your message, you'll be able to tell them what you want to in the most relevant way. In the next chapter we'll talk about the strategies behind message development.

Creative strategy exercises

Exercise 1: deconstructing the thinking behind the message

Part 1 Examine one long-running, multimedia campaign like Monster.com "Monkeys," Absolut, Coke "Polar Bears," e-Trade "Talking Babies," and so on.

a   Identify the main idea in the campaign.

b   Decide the primary audience.

    c   Determine the key benefit.

    d   Analyze the main message.

    e   Identify the *tone of voice*.

Part 2 Now create another ad in the campaign, targeting the same audience, using the same *tone of voice*, and main campaign message. What other medium could you introduce? Could you create a new place to place a message to reach the audience? Could you use an ambient ad?

Part 3 Create a message for a different audience by using the same basic strategy. Where else would you run this message to reach this audience? How would you change the *tone of voice*?

Exercise 2: where have you seen new messages?

Can you think of a new place to advertise besides luggage carousels, manhole covers, telephone wires, escalator steps, elevators, store floors, sidewalks, taxi tops, shopping bags, subway hand straps, and online? Think beyond traditional media. Consider an interactive vehicle.

Notes

1   Drummond Berman, personal communication, April 8, 2009.

2   http://adage.com/century/timeline/index.html (accessed November 14, 2010).

3   Juan Santiago Lagos, personal communication, January 12, 2010.

4   Arthur Asa Berger, *Ads, Fads, and Consumer Culture: Advertising's Impact on American Character and Society* (Lanham, MD: Rowman & Littlefield, 2000), 84–89.

5   Strategic Business Insights, http://www.strategicbusinessinsights.com/vals/ustypes.shtml (accessed July 5, 2010).

6   Teddy Brown, personal communication, October 26, 2009.

7   Sheena Brady, personal communication, May 8, 2009.

8   Larry Percy, *Strategies for Implementing Integrated Marketing Communications* (Oxford, UK: Butterworth-Heinemann, 2008), 252.

9   Teddy Brown, personal communication, October 26, 2009.

THE STRATEGIC WORD
Strategy categories

> *To me, the first thing to being a good writer is to listen to and read a lot of good writing.*

CHRISTOPHER SMITH, CREATIVE DIRECTOR AT THE RICHARDS GROUP [1]

Using strategic thinking strengthens each touchpoint

Analyzing types of strategies

Keeping a handy reference list of strategies

Evaluating strategies and needs

Applying different types of positioning

Inventing the USP: selling uniqueness

Creating the main message: campaign slogans

Deciding the *tone of voice*

Considering competitors

Designing tactics

Final creative direction checklist

Creative strategy exercises

The Copywriter's Toolkit: The Complete Guide to Strategic Advertising Copy, First Edition. Margo Berman.
© 2012 Margo Berman. Published 2012 by Blackwell Publishing Ltd.

When you start working on creative solutions, you want them to be on-strategy and on-target. To do that, you'll need to constantly reexamine your concepts and double check that you haven't veered off course. In this chapter, you'll learn how strategic thinking maximizes the impact of each message. This is especially true when the selected touchpoint is particularly relevant to that audience. That means if your target is online, you as a writer should have a clear understanding of what's important to your audience (what they value), how they access the Web, and what they need to hear to respond to your ad.

In the following pages, you'll start to think about developing a strategy that specifically targets your audience. You'll first consider the six basic strategy categories. Then, you'll explore the fifty different strategies you can add to your creative toolkit. These include strategies (strategic-based concepts) that highlight the consumer, product, and savings, plus messages that deliver emotions, stories (storytelling), and interactivity (or audience engagement).

You'll also discover or possibly review common needs that are divided into easy-to-refer-to categories and charts by Jib Fowles, Abraham Maslow, and others. In addition, you'll investigate different types of product positioning. You'll beg into consider how to more clearly position your brand "in the mind of the consumer." So consumers perceive the brand as you want them to.

You'll be reminded to (1) feature the *unique selling point* (USP), so your target knows what makes your brand different from its competitors, (2) create a sticky main message (slogan), (3) develop a distinctive and appropriate *tone of voice,* (4) consider competitors' messages, and (5) be selective about your *tactics.* Now, we'll begin by examining the relationship between strategic thinking and relevant *touchpoints.*

Using strategic thinking strengthens each touchpoint

Be sure you think through all the questions in the brief for even a one-time promotion. Remember every consumer touchpoint can be a breakthrough to that consumer. Touchpoints are every place your audience sees your ad. These include out-of-home messages, online banner and interactive ads, TVs spots, floor and shelf talkers, print ads, social networking sites, and so on.

So, where do you begin with your strategic thinking after you've examined the brief, reviewed or created the media vehicles, considered audience touchpoints, studied consumer insights and current audience trends? You must consider where and how you'll be speaking to your audience. Knowing where your message will intersect the consumer's life is critically important. This is how VALS can help because it focuses on the psychographic profile of the audience: how they live their lives. Also, think about the audience's demographics. Then, think about the most effective campaign touchpoints. For example, for an interactive text messaging campaign, you'd consider a younger, more connected audience who might be I-Am-Me's or Experentials. For a do-it-yourself, home improvement campaign, you'd consider Makers and maybe also Innovators who had sufficient income to purchase the exact materials they want to create what they imagine.

In thinking about your strategy, today you must evaluate your audience's possible participation. An online, interactive dialogue on a blog or social media site would not be approached the same way as a traditional, one-way TV message. For example, an out-of-home advertising communication could include an audience directive. It could tell viewers to dial a number and text a message or even download a free, mp3 song to their cell phones. That's what Absolut did in 2006 on a Times Square billboard when it offered a 4-minute mp3 Lenny Kravitz track. Naturally, the audience needed to have a Web-enabled phone to participate.

It has become more and more clear that interactivity and engagement strengthen consumers' bond with a brand. The more vested the target market is, the more loyalty they feel toward that brand. However, here's one note of caution. You don't want to create interactivity for its own sake. You want it to reward the participant. After people are engaged, they must discover a benefit, be entertained, or at least have fun in the process.

When we discuss interactivity later in chapter 12, we will look at some of the most successful uses of audience engagement. For now, realize that every message must be relevant and resonate with authenticity. Gimmicks insult the audience. People don't have time for useless information and resent having their energy wasted. Your creative strategy, regardless of where it is executed, should zoom into the needs of that particular audience and make those people feel as if they're having a personal, one-on-one conversation with the brand.

Now we will examine different types of strategies that you can consider using when you're developing your next campaign.

Analyzing types of strategies

There are many different ways to portray the product and address the audience. What you want to do is create a message with legs, one that can keep going and *spin out* or work in all media. Think back on some campaigns you've seen that have become ingrained in your memory. Then, examine the strategies below and see which one they fit into. Some brands use several strategies at the same time. This is because each strategy targets a different market or drives the audience to take a different action. Let's look at a few of these.

First there's PEDIGREE® the brand that used three separate strategies:

1 *Charity or cause-related strategy* with its "Adoption Drive: Dogs Rule" campaign and its "Help Us Help Dogs" line.

2 *Quality strategy* with its healthy ingredients message and humorous, anthropomorphic campaign.

3 *Benefit strategy* with its reminder of how dogs enhance our lives campaign and its "We Love Dogs" slogan. Each strategy had its own goal. In the first, the cause-related strategy, PEDIGREE® wanted people to go to their local pet shelter and adopt, as well as to buy PEDIGREE® dog food because a portion of the proceeds went to aiding shelter dogs find homes. For the second quality strategy, it told dog owners to feed their pets PEDIGREE® because of the healthy ingredients. In the third benefit strategy, it reminded dog lovers how their pets were an integral part of their lives and reminded them about the joy of "pet parenting."

Taco Bell also used two strategies concurrently. These were messages that addressed (1) *abundance* and products that featured (2) *value*. With the *abundance strategy*, Taco Bell presented larger, more filling menu items like the Grande Quesadilla. For the *value strategy*, it featured items at a special savings. Most of these are shown on TV and then posted on-site in the windows of the restaurant on large, colorful posters. Each strategy targets a different group. The abundance strategy is talking to those with a larger appetite. The value strategy is singling out the consumer looking for savings, like the coupon shopper. Taco Bell directly asks consumers, "Why pay more?" in its campaign slogan. (See more in chapter 7.)

According to Teddy Brown, who leads the creative for the Taco Bell account, value advertising is critically important in a down economy:

> *The advertising is becoming more scrutinized and we could see where this year (2009) was taking us. So, we took a look at all of our work that was going to run in the back half of the year. We wanted to make sure that it was strong enough and retail-focused enough. It's very difficult in this climate when there's this sort of notion that America's on sale.*

He went on to say that commercials that tested extremely well with consumers before the economic downturn didn't perform quite as well during the year (the quick-service restaurant sales, that is, the fast-food industry, were down by one billion visits in 2009). He added that copywriters on the Taco Bell account write 1,000 TV commercials each year. Yes, 1,000. Two hundred are tested. That means they're shown to consumers for their opinion of and reaction to the spots. Finally, 40 are actually aired. Most brands don't require the development of so many in ordinately high number of scripts; however, Taco Bell wants to find the most effective spots and testing is one way to do so.[2]

Most brands focus on one strategy for each campaign. As a copywriter, you would benefit from identifying the strategy behind every campaign you encounter. This will strengthen your analytical skills and heighten your creative awareness. Make it a habit to actively evaluate all messages, so you can identify the (1) target audience, (2) campaign strategy, and (3) *universal truth*. In chapter 5, we discuss universal truths in detail. However, let us clarify the term here. A universal truth is an instantly understood statement that is accepted as fact regardless of gender, age or nationality. Here are a few examples: (1) Hard work pays off. (2) Never underestimate your opponent. (3) He who owns the gold rules the world. (4) You can't concentrate when you're hungry. Each time you hear or see an advertising message, look for the universal truth. Because it helps to quickly deliver the underlying meaning, making the ad more relevant to the audience.

Now, let's take a look at the strategy list. It will give you a library of strategic directions before you begin any creative assignment.

Keeping a handy reference list of strategies

As you review the list, realize that new strategies can be added at any time. If you find another category, add it to this list. Remember, the strategy you choose should be so easy to understand that it can be reduced down to a few words as shown below. It should be so simple that the moment you see the definition, you understand the strategy. Take a few moments to log onto YouTube and view as many of the spots as possible. That will give you an instantly applicable frame of reference.

Notice that the 50 strategies fit into six basic categories: (1) *Consumer-Focused*, which are campaigns that show the W-I-I-F-Ms or how the consumer benefits from using the product; (2) *Product-Focused*, which are campaigns that showcase the product's features; (3) *Savings as the Star*, which are campaigns that emphasize price; (4) *Emotional Approach*, which are campaigns that involve consumers' emotions; (5) *Storytelling*, which are campaigns that tell the audience about the product in a story; and (6) *Audience Engagement*, which are campaigns that encourage consumer participation.

Consumer-focused

1   *Benefit strategy* – This explains how the product will help you. It highlights your W-I-I-F-M and answers your question "What's in it for me?" like the iPhone, iPod, and iPad campaigns. They all show how the devices make consumers' lives easier whatever they're doing: phoning, texting, or surfing the Web; storing images, music and files; or reading books, researching online, or evaluating information; sharing images, and so on. The benefit could even be social status, a sense of individuality, or even a whatever-makes-you-feel-good or cool benefit.

2   *Before and after strategy* – This illustrates the difference the product makes, like Jenny Craig or Weight Watchers campaigns.

3   *Picture yourself strategy* – This shows you what result you can expect from the product – like cosmetic surgery or Bowflex campaigns.

Product-focused

4   *Feature strategy* – This shows an important product feature and then should relate it to your needs. So if the feature is durability that means you won't have to replace it soon.

5   *Abundance (quantity) strategy* – This demonstrates that consumers will have a big selection of items or receive a large portion of something, like a super-sized meal.

6   *Quality strategy* – This illustrates the excellence, claiming superiority to other brands. A few examples would be Neiman-Marcus, W Hotels, Rolls Royce, and De Beers, even Ford's line "Quality is job 1."

7   *Product demonstration strategy* – This exemplifies the product's results, like detergents, deodorants, stain removers, or Breathe Right nasal strips. Take a look at the UPS "Whiteboard" campaign for some excellent examples.

8   *Product comparison strategy* – This places two competitors in a head-to-head competition, like the "Mac versus PC" campaign's "Crash" commercial. (Be sure to see several spots on YouTube.)

9   *Testimonial strategy* – This allows people to explain what they like about the product, like the "Beautiful" Stanley Steemer spot or the earlier "Jared Fogle" Subway campaign. If a celebrity is delivering the testimonial, it's called a *celebrity endorsement*, like Jessica Simpson for Proactiv; Michael Phelps for Speedo, Subway, and PowerBar; or Victoria Secret models, Gisele Bündchen, Adriana Lima, Selita Ebanks, and Izabel Goulart, talking about the brand. If celebrities only talk about the brand, they are part of a *celebrity spokesperson* campaign.

10   *Icon strategy* – This uses an iconic character in the campaign, like Nabisco's Keebler Elves, the Weight Watchers "Show Hungry Who's Boss" orange Hungry Monster, or the Brawny Man.

11   *Information strategy* – This explains product in detail like pharmaceutical ads or Colgate Total toothpaste's announcement that bacteria are building up in your mouth right now.

12 *Uniqueness strategy* – This shows what's different about this product than its competitors, like 7-Up's classic "Uncola" ads with Geoffrey Holder.

13 *Product as hero strategy* – This places the product center stage, like the "Absolut Perfection" campaign, with the bottle artistically portrayed, or Coke's "Open Happiness" campaign.

14 *Come from behind strategy* – This asks for the audience's empathy, like Avis's classic "We're Number 2" campaign.

15 *Brand-centric strategy* – This focuses on the brand, its features, and how it works in consumers' lives, like Google's "Parisian Love" spot.

16 *Product-centric strategy* – This focuses on a specific product, like Taco Bell menu item spots. (See more in chapter 7.)

17 *Company history strategy* – This reminds the audience of a firm's long-standing tradition, like "With a Name Like Smucker's, It's Got to Be Good."

18 *Company's founder or corporate leader strategy* – This presents the company message from the voice of one of its owners or business leaders, like Perdue Chicken's Frank Perdue, Orville Redenbacher's popcorn with his namesake, or Chrysler's Lee Iacocca and his famous campaign line "If you Can Find A Better Car Buy It." This also integrates a *challenge strategy*.

19 *Performance strategy* – This epitomizes the product's commitment to top-level performance like Nike's dedication to enhancing every athlete's performance or Ford's "Built Ford Tough" (since 1979).

20 *Positioning in the marketplace strategy* – This depicts the brand's placement in the industry. It could relate to one aspect such as sales, safety, or customer service.

21 *Stamp of approval strategy* – This states that experts have approved the product, like "Crest's The Dentist's Choice" or "Four out of five dentists agree" that this product whitens teeth.

22 *One-word strategy* – This identifies the brand with one memorable word, like Disney's "Magic" or Nike's "Boom."

Savings as the star

23 *Value strategy* – This promises the audience they got a great deal, leading them to believe they received more than they paid for, like two-for-one dining.

24 *Makes sense strategy* – This explains why the product is a logical choice, like a fuel-efficient car model rather than a gas-guzzler.

Emotional approach

25 *Humor strategy* – This approaches the audience in a comedic manner, like Tide To Go's "Talking Stain" campaign. (Be sure to watch it on YouTube, if you haven't seen it.)

26 *Honesty strategy* – This tells consumers the real, unfiltered information, like the anti-smoking Truth® campaign's "Body Bag" spot that depicted 1,200 body bags

on a sidewalk to visually depict the number of people who die daily from smoking. This spot is also an example of the *shock strategy* below.

27 *Anthropomorphism strategy* – This shows animals with human emotions, like the many Budweiser Super Bowl spots. One example is "Hank," the so-named Clydesdale that wanted to make the hitch team and was "trained" by a Dalmatian for a year with *Rocky* music in the background.

28 *Role reversal strategy* – This places a character in an unexpected role, like Doritos "Keep Your Hands Off My Mama," the e-Trade "Babies" as the financial experts, or the Mrs. Paul's "Whole Fillet" commercial with the little girl demanding an answer to these "grown-up" questions about another brand's fish sticks: "You feed me minced? You ever catch a minced fish?"

29 *Exaggeration strategy* – This obviously inflates the real benefits of the product, like the For Eyes campaign with inflated promises like claiming the eyeglasses can speak French ("French"), or they can shoot laser beams ("Laser"), or they can make an elderly lady see her senior-citizen husband as a young man ("Husband"), or the Doritos 2010 Super Bowl spot with Betty White playing football and representing a young guy who's "playing like a girl."

30 *Challenge strategy* – This invites the audience into a product test, like the "Activia 14-Day Challenge"; "You Can Do It, Nicorette Can Help" campaign, inviting people to quit smoking; or the Dove Beauty Bar "Discover the Truth about Soap" promotion, enticing women to see for themselves the residue other soaps leave behind.

31 *Emotional blackmail strategy* – This makes consumers feel insecure as if they'd be in trouble if they didn't use the product, like Michelin's "There's a Lot Riding on Your Tires."

32 *Temptation strategy* – This promises irresistibility for consumers, like the Axe "Chocolate Man, Dark Temptation" TV spot.

33 *Shock strategy* – This plays on surprising the audience in some way. It can be positive (www.pizzaholdout.com), negative (Sierra Club "Saving the World One Tree At a Time"), or controversial (the Audi "Suicide Commercial").

34 *Playful strategy* – This is a lighthearted way to present the product, like the Coke animated "Beautiful" commercial.

35 *Deprivation strategy* – This exemplifies what life would be like without the product, like the earliest "Got Milk" campaign. (See the Got Milk commercials "Aaron Burr," "Body Cast," and "Heaven or Hell" on YouTube.)

36 *Sexy strategy* – This portrays the brand or the consumer in a sexually enticing manner, like the GoDaddy.com Super Bowl spots with buxom girls in different commercials or the Victoria Secret campaigns.

37 *Parody strategy* – This pokes fun at a trend, culture, or creative direction, like the Volkswagen "Um-pimp Your Ride" I, II, and III spots, Smirnoff "Tea Partay," and the Sienna Minivan "Swagger Wagon." (Don't miss these great parodies on YouTube.)

38 *Letting off steam strategy* – This allows actors to vent in a fun way, like punching someone in the arm and calling out the color of a passing-by car with "Yellow one," or "Blue one," as in the Volkswagen "VW Punch Dub" campaign. There's humor

mixed into the spot when Grammy Award-Winning singer Stevie Wonder calls out "Red one." His friend asks how he did that? The joke is the singer is blind, as he answers with a confident, "Hah!" as if he's saying "Gotcha!"

Storytelling

39 *Mini movie or "vignette" strategy* – This presents a little story, like the De Beers "25th Anniversary" story-of-our-lives spot.

40 *Continuing story strategy* –This is a campaign with an ongoing storyline, like the Budweiser "Lizards," which followed up after the "Frogs" campaign.

41 *Continuing characters strategy* – This establishes one character and continues using him or her, like the Progressive Insurance's quirky character Flo, played by Stephanie Courtney, or Geico's Caveman.

42 *Breaking news strategy* – This exploits news that relates to the product, like the 2010 spot celebrating Canada's first Olympic gold medal.

43 *Green strategy* – This spotlights the ecological consciousness of the brand, like the Audi lighthearted 2010 Super Bowl spot "Green Police." Although this is a *cause-related strategy* (#49), environmental issues have become so important, they merit a separate category. Starbuck's took a more serious approach than Audi. It suggested on its interactive website how everyone could be more environmentally responsible: www.planetgreengame.com. This site also falls into the next category. (This currently inactive site is discussed at http://www.treemedia.com/treemedia .com/Starbucks_Planet_Green.html.)

44 *Futuristic strategy* – This places the product benefits in the future, like the Hewlett-Packard "Touch the Future Now Light Show" and the HP TouchSmart PC commercials "Experience," "Ad 2," and "Maestro." (See them all on YouTube. Pay attention to the use of exciting visual special effects.)

45 *Reposition the brand strategy* – This is used when the product has been modernized, upgraded, reengineered to appeal to a different or reappeal to the same audience.

Audience engagement

46 *Interactive strategy* – This engages the audience, like the Pepsi "Refresh" campaign, the Toyota "Tell Us Your Story and Win a Free Toyota" with "Erica's Surprise," "Elan's Big Day," as well as the "Brawny Academy" campaign. (See them all on YouTube.)

47 *Social networking strategy* – This uses social media sites, like the www.facebook.com/ Toyota or creating a Facebook fan page, to connect to the audience.

48 *Fill in the blank strategy* – This invites the audience to figure out some part of the message like the Budweiser "Frogs" who were reading the Bud-wei-ser sign reflected in their pond.

49 *Charity or cause-related strategy* – This heightens consumers' charitable consciousness, like the "RED" fight AIDS in Africa multibrand campaign with HBO, Hallmark, Starbucks, and other sponsors; the American Express annual Christmas drive "Charge Against Hunger" (since 1994); the Unicef "Tap Project" to provide pure water in a hundred countries; and the Susan G. Komen "Cure Breast Cancer," commonly called "Pink," campaign. The Anti-Advertising agency wanted to point out how excessive out-of-home advertising had become, so they created several *anti-advertising campaigns*. Ambient communication, placed over existing posters, and other out-of-home ads, reminded consumers that they didn't need the items being advertised. (See "You Don't Need It Stickers" at http://antiadvertisingagency.com/you-dont-need-it-stickers-2/.) This group even *blacked-out* existing ads, fully covering them, and replacing them with a new statement: the word "Graffiti" stenciled. This new message labeled the original ads as graffiti. For example, "Graffiti" was placed over flat screens in the "Light Criticism" campaign (http://www.youtube.com/watch?v=rboHOj1FgYk).

50 *Pop culture strategy* – This lets the brand reflect a cultural behavior or create a popular phrase that becomes integrated into everyday language, like Budweiser's "Whassup!" or Wendy's "Where's the Beef?"

Before you keep reading, can you imagine other campaigns and decide which strategies they used? Think back to a spot or promotion you really enjoyed. Now, ask yourself what you liked about it and what *strategy* and *universal truth* it depicted. Do you think you were the primary targeted audience? If the campaign resonated as authentic for you, and you instantly connected to it, you probably were. Have you noticed that some commercials use several strategies in one campaign? For example, the e-Trade "Talking Baby" spots use a continuing character, exaggeration, humor, and little vignettes (mini movies).

Can you sum up the message in a phrase or a word? If so, you just clarified product positioning in the mind of the consumer. Here are two examples: "Blue Light Special" for Kmart or "expensive" for Rolls Royce. This positioning, as opposed to other kinds of positioning, relies on the consumer's opinion of the brand. If your opinion is not what the advertiser wants you to think, new messages will be developed to create a different positioning statement. There are more than two types of *positioning*.

Evaluating strategies and needs

The most sophisticated marketers know that the more detailed the audience information, the more accurate the creative direction. Understanding the three audience components – demographics, psychographics, and geographics– is one part of the puzzle. Looking at the different strategies is another. Considering consumers' basic needs is yet another. You're probably already familiar with Maslow's commonly known Hierarchy of Needs (Figure 2.1). Perhaps you may know about Jib Fowles's list of Advertising 15 Basic Appeals,[4] based on more than 25 Social Motives as listed in *Explorations in Personality by* Henry A. Murray in 1938.[5] The 70th edition was published in 2007.

Advertisers use consumer needs in many ways. Products demonstrate how they satisfy different needs. Here are a few examples using Abraham Maslow's Hierarchy of Needs:

1 *Physiological* needs with food and beverages.
2 *Safety* needs with insurance or alarm systems.
3 *Belongingness* needs with Facebook fan pages.
4 *Status* or "esteem" needs with luxury products and designer brands like Gucci.
5 *Cognitive* needs with advice like Butterball's Thanksgiving Day turkey cooking tips.

> Positioning is an organized system for finding windows in the mind. **AL RIES AND JACK TROUT**[3]

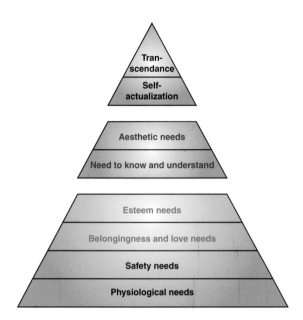

FIGURE 2.1 Maslow's hierarchy of needs. Source: http://honolulu.hawaii.edu/intranet /committees/FacDevCom/guidebk/teachtip/maslow.html (accessed July 14, 2010).

6 *Aesthetic* needs with art and home decorating classes.

7 *Self-actualization* needs with self-growth courses.

8 *Self-transcendence* needs with mentoring programs like Big Brothers and Big Sisters.

It's crucial that you absorb the various strategies, motivations, and needs lists and then apply them in your strategic thinking. Look at the list (Figure 2.2) and see how the strategies align with the list of motivational appeals and needs. Now consider what products, services, or brands could use the strategies to answer specific consumer needs. For example, when could you use a product demonstration strategy? What need(s) could that fulfill? Okay, let's consider a color-safe detergent. You could demonstrate how it gets stains out without fading (safety need) the garment's color. The campaign shows both the cleaning power and the color protection qualities of the detergent. People want clean and not faded clothes.

There are other categories of needs, as well. You could consider The Institute for Management Excellence (2001), which suggests there are nine basic human needs:

1 Security

2 Adventure

3 Freedom

4 Exchange

5 Power

6 Expansion

7 Acceptance

8 Community

9 Expression

BERMAN Strategies that Relate to Fowles's Appeals & Maslow's Needs (Brand examples)	JIB FOWLES Advertising's 15 Basic Appeals (Buying Motivations)*	MASLOW Hierarchy of Needs
1. *Sexy strategy* (#36) (Victoria's Secret)	1. *Need for sex* – according to Fowles this may be too overt and may distract the audience's attention from focusing on the product. Back in the early 1980s, only 2% of the ads used this approach.	**HELPING INFORMATION** **(#1 Physiological & #2 Safety)** *1) Physiological needs*: basic drive for survival, hunger, thirst, bodily comforts, etc. – ALSO ALIGNS WITH APPEALS #15 - FOWLES
2. *Interactive strategy* (#46) 3. *Social networking strategy* (#47) 4. *Pop culture strategy* (#50) **(www.GetTheGlass.com - Milk)** **(www.facebook.com/Toyota)** **(Bahamasair Interactive Campaign)**	2. *Need for affiliation* – wanting to socialize Can be used in a positive or negative way. Showing you how to gain friends or reminding you that you could lose them without this product.	**ENLIGHTENING INFORMATION** **(#3 Belongingness)** *3) Belongingness and love needs*: desire to join, connect with, and be accepted by others
5. *Charity, cause-related strategy* (#49) **(www.RedCampaign.org - fighting AIDS in Africa)**	3. *Need to nurture* – people's natural parental and protective urge	
6. *Information strategy* (#11) **(www.Butterball.com - recipes/info, Google)**	4. *Need for guidance* – looking to be advised and cared for	**(#4 Esteem, #5 Cognitive, & #6 Aesthetic)** *5) Cognitive needs*: aspire to gain information for clarification (Part of Empowering information)
7. *Letting off steam strategy* (#38) **(www.ComcastMustDie.com – customer service complaints)**	5. *Need to aggress* – seeking vengeance when you feel wronged	
8. *Celebrity spokesperson strategy* (#39) **(Valerie Bertinelli for Jenny Craig or Jennifer Hudson for Weight Watchers)**	6. *Need to achieve* – striving to accomplish something very difficult	*4) Esteem needs*: hope for accomplishment, recognition, competence, and appreciation
9. *Positioning in the marketplace strategy* (#20 **("Avis. We're Number 2")**	7. *Need to dominate* – wanting to control your environment	
10. *Company history strategy* (#17) **(Barbie's 50th Anniversary)**	8. *Need for prominence* – wanting recognition and social status	*7) Self-actualization needs*: wish to gain self-fulfillment, reach your potential and do what you're born to do
11. *Quality strategy* (#5) **(Tiffany – little blue box)**	9. *Need for attention* – hoping people will notice us	
12. *Before and after strategy* (#2) **(cosmetic surgery - www.StraxRejuvenation.com)**		
13. *Picture yourself strategy* (#3) **(anti-wrinkle creams like Retinol Night Cream)**	10. *Need for autonomy* – wanting to be unique 11. *Need to escape* – desiring adventure	
14. *Uniqueness strategy* (#12) **(Benihana)**		
15. *Feature strategy* (#4) **(iPhone apps - Apple)**	12. *Need to feel safe* – wanting to feel safe and unthreatened	*2) Safety/security needs*: long to stay out of harm's way and avoid danger
16. *Emotional blackmail strategy* (#31) **("There's a Lot Riding on Your Tires." Michelin)**	13. *Need for aesthetic sensations* – desiring to experience art, music and other kinds of beauty	*6) Aesthetic needs*: want to have order, organization, beauty and experience joy in arts and nature
17. *Performance strategy* (#19) **("Just Do It." Nike)**	14. *Need to satisfy curiosity* – wanting to know accurate and detailed information supported by data	
18. *Product demonstration strategy* (#7) **(Proactiv)**	15. Psychological needs - Fowles includes sex in this category (item #1) biological needs like sleeping, eating, drinking, and reproducing	*1) Physiological needs*: basic drive for survival, hunger, thirst, bodily comforts, etc.
19. *Testimonial strategy* (#9) **(Carol's Daughter)**		
20. *Benefit strategy* (#1) **(Colgate Total Plus Whitening Toothpaste)**		

FIGURE 2.2 This "Strategies-Motivations-Needs" chart, created by Margo Berman, shows how various Berman's Advertising Strategy Categories line up with Fowles' 15 Basic Appeals and Maslow's Hierarchy of Needs. It presents a quick cross-reference for consumer insight and acts as a tool for strategic thinking. Source for Jib Fowles: Jib Fowles, "Advertising 15 Basic Appeals," *Et Cetera*, Vol. 39.3 (1982): pp. 273-290.

You can see how most of these fit into Fowles's list. For example the institute's #2 "adventure" would be Fowles's #11 "need for escape" and #3 "freedom" could correlate to #10 "need for autonomy." You don't have to know every single category ever created, you just have to know the needs your audience have that your product/service/brand satisfies. Think of the strategies, movitations, and needs chart (Figure 2.1) as a guide to creative thinking and an easy-to-refer-to-problem-solving method. Notice that not all of the strategies are listed, just the ones that correlated to specific needs.

If all of these needs confuse you, you can think about the four basic or buying motivations, which group several of Fowles's and Maslow's into just these four categories. This might simplify your creative process. These four groups are as follows.

1   *Biogenic needs* – basic requirements for survival: food, water, rest, procreation, and so on.

2   *Psychogenic needs* – needs based on cultural pressures like status, power, affiliation, and so on.

3   *Utilitarian needs* – desire for useful and functional solutions in products or services.

4   *Hedonic needs* – yearning for pleasure, experiences, and excitement.

This shortened version enables you to think of creating campaigns that appeal to consumers' physical, psychological, functional, and pleasure needs. You can easily see how a beer, spa, or exotic resort commercial would go under hedonic needs. Home gyms would fit under utilitarian needs. Cosmetics, social networking sites, and designer clothes would fit under psychogenic needs. Restaurants would fit under biogenic needs.

Consumer needs are what drive their spending. They're the motivations behind the actual purchase. Here it is interesting to note that some of the motivations actually create a psychological conflict in consumers. For example, if they're torn between two good choices, like two equally wonderful vacations, this is called *Approach-Approach Conflict.* If the conflict drives people to resolve existing conflicts between their beliefs or their behaviors, like they're against the death penalty but feel conflicted about the severity of the punishment when a child was murdered, it's called *Cognitive Dissonance Reduction.* If they have a conflict between reaching a goal and the behavior modification required to reach it, like dieting, it's called *Approach-Avoidance Conflict.* If consumers have to decide between two unpleasant choices, like buying a new car or repairing an old one, it's called *Avoidance-Avoidance Conflict.*

One campaign that deftly handled the Approach-Avoidance Conflict was the Weight Watchers "Show Hungry Who's Boss" campaign with the lovable and comical, yet all-too-true, orange Hunger Monster.

Once you realize all advertisements want to change or reinforce behavior, it will help you think about how you want the audience to respond and what you want them to do. For example, if they hardly use the product (inertia involvement), you want to increase their purchase, so they move toward more purchases (flow state or high involvement). If they're already fans, you want them to become fanatics (cult-like involvement). You don't just want people to know about your product; you want them to begin to get involved and actually "sell" your product to their friends. This is the highest form of product involvement, because it embraces engagement and interactivity, increasing the consumers' relationship with the brand.

Then, after you consider strategies and needs, you should look at the different kinds of product positioning. For copywriting, the one you want to focus on is the first one: positioning in the mind of the consumer, discussed below.

Applying different types of positioning

Most advertisers want to create an impression in the consumer's mind. This kind of positioning is called *positioning in the mind of the consumer*. Earlier, we also discussed *sales-related positioning*. But those are not the only ones. By knowing the brand's different positioning, you could choose to feature one in a campaign. For example, Cadillac used to be your grandfather's car. However, it was *repositioned* to be a cooler car both for the individual and the family. Likewise, you could emphasize the brand's number rating in customer service or safety, as Volvo did years ago. Review the list below and think about how any of these could be integrated into your campaign message.

Here is a list of the various types of positioning.

1   *Positioning in the mind of the consumer* – What the consumer currently thinks about the product/brand. This is critical when developing your message. If consumers have the right impression, you want to reinforce that, if not, you want to change their opinion.

2   *Positioning in sales* – What place this product/brand holds in relation to sales: First place, second place like Avis, and so on.

3   *Positioning in real estate* – Where the product sits in stores: eye-level shelves, at the front of the store (in bookstores), end caps (facing out at the end of the isle), freestanding displays (separated island with product), and so on. The placement of products is directly linked to the selling power of the brand.

4   *Positioning in the media* – What media vehicles are used for the ad message: TV, radio, Internet, out-of-home, transit, and so on.

5   *Positioning in the medium* – Where the ads are placed in a specific medium, like surrounding the news on TV, morning or afternoon drive time for radio, banner ads on sites targeting a specific audience, key billboards for out-of-home, inside subways for transit, and so on.

6   *Positioning in the marketplace* – Where is the product sold: globally, nationally, or regionally?

7   *Positioning in performance* – Where consumers rate the brand through customer service and safety awards.

8   *Positioning in the Internet* – What is the size of the brand's digital footprint? This is especially important for small businesses, entrepreneurs, and solo-preneurs.

9   *Repositioning of the brand* – What is the new way you want to present the brand's image? Just because it used to be old-fashioned doesn't mean it can't get an image facelift. Brands can reengineer the styling, performance, or technology of one product or the entire line of products to regain a previous market or target a new audience, as in Cadillac. This is can also be used as a strategy (#50).

You must consider the brand's current position in each of these categories and decide if you want to showcase that in your message. You've seen car commercials that boast about their customer service awards or safety ratings. If the car's been recognized as the safest in the automotive industry, you may want to share that information with the consumer. If you realize your audience listens to the radio in different dayparts (specific blocks of times in a 24-hour cycle, as discussed in chapter 6), you would schedule your commercials during those segments. Positioning awareness and emphasis is key for all marketing.

Besides positioning, you should be 100 percent clear on what differentiates your product or brand from the competitors. Let's focus now on the USP, or *unique selling proposition* (or position).

Inventing the USP: selling uniqueness

The target audience needs to know why they should pick your brand, product, or service. You must be able to answer the following: How is your beer different? What makes your exercise equipment more efficient? Why is your pizza better? Strong brands do that. Think about Papa John's slogan "Better ingredients. Better pizza," which simply states what distinguishes its pizza compared to everyone else's.

Think about Bayer aspirin's slogan "Take it for pain. Take it for life." As soon as research proved that an aspirin could actually save a heart-attack victim's life if taken immediately when the symptoms appear, Bayer claimed that benefit. By being the first to state Bayer can save your life, it made people believe only Bayer aspirin had this power. Some people today don't realize that any aspirin, not ibuprofen, can offer the same benefit.

Just as mp3 players existed before iPods, Apple showed people how easily they could carry their favorite songs with them. By being the first to clarify why consumers needed the product, Apple became the first successful mp3 player brand by popularizing the technology.

Not being first isn't as important as being the first to clearly state the unique selling proposition. Clarity is key. That's how the main message sums up the point in an easy-to-remember or "sticky" slogan.

Creating the main message: campaign slogans

What's one of the stickiest slogans you know? "Just do it." Right? That's because it doesn't tell you what sport to do. Just to be sure you go out and exercise. The brand's promise is to help improve your performance in any sport because it has shoes specially designed for different activities: walking, hiking, running, and so on.

When you're thinking of a slogan, think about all the ones that are stuck in your head. Those are sticky. Think of messages that are short. To the point. And instantly understood. They're the battle cry of the brand. They're unique, original, and fresh. Be sure you check in chapter 4 for slogan techniques as you develop your ideas.

You want consumers to not only remember your slogan, but also to remember the brand. Slogans that could apply to any other brand need to be reexamined. Of course you could say "Just do it" could work for another brand. Just realize Nike's ability to drive home the message in multiple formats, multiple media, and without interruption. That doesn't take away from the power of the message. It was strong to begin with and a big-budget campaign only enhanced its impact.

Deciding the *tone of voice*

Although we'll discuss *tone of voice* in greater detail in chapter 3, in order to better understand how it fits into the brief, we need to look at it for a moment. The *tone of voice* is the way you speak to your audience. Is the message going to be delivered in a serious or other *tone of voice*? Think about an adjective. What would be the best way for the brand or product to talk to the audience? Should it be playful? Authoritative? Informative? Intimidating? Friendly? It's not what the message is saying; it's the way it's presented. It's not the media vehicles. Those are tactics, which we'll discuss last. Now, we'll look at the product's competitors in the marketplace.

Considering competitors

Why do you need to know your competitors? For several reasons. First, you can understand what they're doing to reach your audience. What is their message and where are they reaching them? Next, you can think about how you can differentiate your brand so your audience picks yours.

Designing tactics

When you think about advertising vehicles, don't just make a list of media outlets. Evaluate which media are the most likely places your message will intersect with your audience. Are your audience members involved in social media? Do they like to play online games? Do they watch sports live or on TV? By understanding how your audience gets information, engages in discussions, and uses technology, you'll be better equipped to select target-relevant avenues where you can capture your audience's attention. You want to implement the creative direction in a relevant and effective way. Your main goal is to develop an on-target and on-strategy message. Here's what Charlie Hopper, creative director/copywriter at Young & Laramore, suggested when you're thinking through writing for various media vehicles.

 ADVICE FROM THE PROS 2.1   **Charlie Hopper's writing for specific media tips**

We feel pretty strongly that we start with where people are going to encounter it. Then, you can absolutely surprise and delight them that you know where they are. That gives you the chance to really craft the piece to be appropriate to its medium.

There's a little green light that goes on in a person that knows it's a manhole cover or it's sitting on a gas pump. It isn't just the slogan. It somehow acknowledges where you come across it. That's why your first question, as a writer, ought to be: Where will people be seeing this?

"Oh, it's an outdoor board, so it should be seven words." Now we have all the different ways to getting at people. In the old days, there were outdoor things that were innovative. But, now you've got online as a whole, new world, and you've got cell phones ringing in people's pockets, and you've got all the different technologies for outdoor that you didn't used to have, or things that stick on to stuff.[6]

Notice how writers today are thinking about the medium first to be sure the message will work wherever the audience will see it. You can't just write a TV spot and hope you can turn it into a billboard or an online banner or an interactive website. You need to plan the message as you're creating the campaign. You need to be thinking backwards: from the *touchpoint* to the message.

Final creative direction checklist

Enough cannot be said about strategy. Every piece of copy has to be aligned with a predetermined creative direction and must clearly support it. The overall message has to reflect that objective. For example, if the campaign is for Jif peanut butter where the slogan (tagline or main theme line) is "Choosy moms choose Jif," but the copy talks about price, the message would be off strategy. All copywriters must recheck the final copy against the initial strategy to be sure the message delivered is the one originally intended. Double-check your creative solution against this list:

1 Did you *create an on-strategy campaign* that reflected the Creative Strategy Statement objectives?
2 Did you clearly *identify the psychographic profile of the audience?*
3 Did you develop an *on-target message,* one that speaks directly to that particular target audience in a relevant and authentic way?
4 Did your message properly *reflect the brand's image?*
5 Did your concept allow for multiple executions, so it *can "spin out"?*
6 Did your solution clearly *highlight the main consumer benefit?*
7 Did your audience walk away with a message that *reinforced or changed their beliefs* about the brand, product, or service?
8 Did you *correctly position or reposition the product* in the mind of the consumer?
9 Did you *answer the consumer's question "Why buy?"*
10 Did you clearly *project the brand's USP?*
11 Did you succinctly *state the big idea* that will drive the slogan?
12 Did your concept *illustrate the brand's personality?*
13 Did you *use the appropriate tone of voice* for the brand and the audience?
14 Did your tactics *reach the appropriate touchpoints* for the right audience?
15 Did you create a campaign that *would create buzz?*

Creative strategy exercises

Exercise 1: how can you use traditional media in a new, unexpected way?

For example, placing a gigantic comb in power lines to demonstrate how a detangling product unsnarls unruly hair. Go to http://www.gushmagazine.com/category/Edgy-and-Innovative-Ads and look at some exciting examples of new media. What can you come up with that's unique and surprisingly effective?

Exercise 2: write two briefs and think about your creative direction

1 Select a product (client) and a short creative brief. (See chapter 1, text box 1.1 or example below.) Short creative brief example:

- What is the *brand's character* or personality?
- Why does the brand *want to advertise*?
- Who is the *audience*?
- What do they (audience members) *currently think*?
- What do you *want them to think*?
- *Why should they buy* this product/service?
- What is the *big message* you want them to know?
- What *kind of tactics* (specific ad/promotional techniques) do you want to use? For example, do you want to use viral marketing, interactive online components, out-of-home messages, print ads, transit (buses, subways, taxis, etc.), new media, direct mail, or other vehicles?

2 Using the same product (client), expand the brief into a longer one. Remember to describe your audience using the appropriate VALS, such as Belongers, Emulators, Achievers, and so on. (See chapter 1.)

3 List the *touchpoints* where you'd reach your audience.

4 Consider competitors' campaigns. How could yours stand out?

5 Review the six categories of 50 strategies.

6 Select the one that would work best for this "client."

7 Decide how that strategy could become a campaign that would *spin out* to different *touchpoints* (media).

8 Be sure you considered *consumer benefits*.

9 Think about a campaign direction.

10 Double check that your campaign is *on strategy* based on your Creative Strategy Statement (#1) from your brief.

Notes

1 Christopher Smith, personal communication, August 19, 2009.

2 Teddy Brown, personal communication, October 26, 2009.

3 Al Ries and Jack Trout, *Positioning: The Battle for Your Mind* (New York: McGraw-Hill, 2000), 21.

4 Jib Fowles, "Advertising 15 Basic Appeals," *Et Cetera* 39.3 (1982): 273–290.

5 Henry A. Murray, *Explorations in Personality*, 70th ed. (New York: Oxford University Press, 2007).

6 Charlie Hopper, personal communication, November 26, 2008.

3

THE CHOSEN WORD
Writing Techniques

> " The overall point is that you can't think of the writing without thinking of how and where and when people will encounter it.

CREATIVE DIRECTOR/COPYWRITER, YOUNG & LARAMORE
CHARLIE HOPPER[1]

The Copywriter's Toolkit: The Complete Guide to Strategic Advertising Copy, First Edition. Margo Berman.
© 2012 Margo Berman. Published 2012 by Blackwell Publishing Ltd.

As you read through this chapter, you'll accumulate your personal arsenal of writing tools. You'll soon discover the appropriate use of vernacular, and realize when it's acceptable to digress from stringent grammatical rules to deliver a more conversational style. The goal is to create copy that sounds as if you're talking to your best friend. You want readers to feel as if you're having a personal conversation with them. Great copy mirrors the spoken word. It's a skill you can learn through easy-to-apply techniques and by reading aloud. Be sure you review the list of writing tips in this chapter to use as a guide. Remember that copy that talks about serious topics like healthcare, medical procedures, insurance and others normally veers away from a casual *tone of voice*. Normally, but not always. Think about the Aflac Duck and how he speaks like an everyday person and not an insurance salesperson. If your campaign creates a whimsical character in a usually solemn, complex, or informative product category or service, you may use a lighthearted creative direction.

As you examine the following library of writing techniques, you'll see how idea development, execution, and production in multiple media, specifically apply to the verbal message. Let the brief guide you as you think about your audience and advertising objective (Creative Strategy Statement). Before you create advertising copy, be sure to think about conceptual messaging, *tone of voice* (how you speak to the audience), and *point of view* (who's speaking). While you're writing, you'll know when to implement *ABA* (referring back to the headline [that's the first "A"] in the closing line [that's the second "A"] after the body copy [that's the "B"]), parallel construction (repeating a phrase, word or part of speech, like "no salt, no sugar, no calories"), and weave (connecting one main idea from the headline throughout the copy). These are discussed again later in the chapter. Let's start with the development of a strong message.

Developing a strong message with legs

After you review the brief and have a strong sense of your audience, competition, tactics, and overall direction from your creative strategy statement, you want to establish a message that can stand up in multiple media. It's equally important for it to work in a predetermined medium, as it is to be media neutral and work in new, unexpected, or unforeseen media. The campaign concept needs to be so big it transcends the media. That's when you know you have a powerful idea.

Think about when the M&M'S campaign launched new colors. People could vote for their favorites. Create M&M'S characters in their likeness. And order customized M&M'S with their own messages on the outside. The idea of engaging the audience in different ways worked equally well everywhere: from print to TV and online.

So, as you're thinking through your messaging, be sure to look at the intended media. Will your message *spin out*, that is, will it translate easily into any promotional vehicle? Does it have "legs," meaning will it have longevity like the character-based slogan "*Snap! Crackle! Pop!*" of **Kellogg's® Rice Krispies®**?

What you're looking for is the big idea that doesn't have constraints. Like a chameleon, it can take on any backdrop and blend in perfectly. It's flexible, malleable, and translatable. It's a message that can be transcreated (recreated in other languages) and still retain its core idea. Did you realize that McDonald's slogan "I'm lovin' it" was originally created in Germany? Yet it's relevant to the American market. The message is conversational and uses vernacular or everyday speech like "lovin'" instead of "loving." The way, verbal manner, the message is delivered is called the *tone of voice*.

Determining the tone of voice

This is how you speak to your audience. Think about adjectives. Should the message sound whimsical, authoritative, informative, concerned, lighthearted, mysterious, friendly, cool, trendy, sophisticated, or something else? If you were discussing open-heart surgery, you wouldn't want to sound too casual. You're talking about a potentially life-threatening surgical procedure to repair a serious condition. No one wants to hear a funny message when you're discussing this kind of topic. They want to be reassured, not joked with. Choosing the right *tone of voice* for the product and audience is crucial to a successful campaign.

Take your time when you're thinking through the *tone of voice*. One good idea is to think of the brand as a famous celebrity. It has to be someone your audience would immediately know. Then, consider who that celebrity would be if he or she were in the consumer's life. Would that person be a friend, sister, mentor, neighbor, teacher, coach, or someone else? The more you see this celebrity as someone who could be part of the consumers' life, the more accurate the message will be. Just look at the difference between the PC geek and the Mac guy who's cool. You instantly see the cool guy as your friend, your buddy. So how would that buddy speak to you? He'd be casual, cool, and friendly. Precisely the way the Mac guy is portrayed.

Now, select an adjective that depicts how our brand would speak to the consumer, the same way the Mac guy sounds "cool." For example, if you had an ultra expensive, luxury brand, you might think of adjectives like sophisticated, polished, refined. These would create an elegant *tone of voice*. However, regardless of how chic the product is, "chic," although it's an adjective can't be a *tone of voice*. Here's the rule of thumb: Ask yourself to speak in a "chic" *tone of voice*. If you can't, then it's an ill-fitting adjective for tone. However, you could speak in a sophisticated, polished, or refined manner or *tone of voice*. These would be appropriate adjectives for the "voice" of the campaign.

This is an extremely useful mental exercise that you should include in your message development. After you've decided your *tone of voice*, now you determine your *point of view*, namely who's delivering the campaign message?

Finding the point of view

There are several points of view. Choose the one that best supports your strategy. Ask yourself who will speak on the brand's behalf? Whose voice will be heard? Will it be the company that talks about its consumer service, performance, or safety ratings? Will it be a consumer who states a testimonial, singing praises? Will it be the consumer's conscience that warns consumers what could happen if they don't use the product? Or will it be the brand speaking for itself? Here's a short list explaining these four *points of view*:

1   *Self-serving* – The brand/product/company boasts about its achievements and awards. The consumer is not delivering the message. For example, "You can't drive a safer car," or "We're number one in customer service." It's all about the brand. Yes, the benefit is mentioned, but it's told to, not stated by, the consumer. It's a promise

of quality and a guarantee of performance that the brand makes to its audience. One recognized example, created in 1965, is the slogan for Hebrew National (all-beef cold cuts and hotdogs): "We answer to a higher authority."

2   *Testimonial* – Product users rave about the product. They eagerly share what they love about it and enthusiastically talk about how it improved their lives. Comments like "I tried every diet and none of them worked. Look at me now! I lost fifty pounds and kept it off. And, so can you." Because she's a real person and not a superstar with a fitness trainer and personal chef, she's more relatable. If a celebrity is speaking, not a consumer, that campaign is called a celebrity endorsement. Here are a few examples: (1) Ashton Kutcher for Nikon, (2) Queen Latifah for the Cover Girl "Easy, Breezy, Beautiful" and her own "Queen Collection" campaigns, and (3) Jennifer Hudson for Weight Watchers. If a celebrity talks only about the product but doesn't claim usage, that star is a celebrity spokesperson, like Carly Foulkes or Catherine Zeta-Jones for the T-Mobile campaign.

3   *Emotional Blackmail* – The consumers' conscience is warning them of a potential problem they could avoid by using the product. One example would be the "Hertz? Not Exactly" campaign, which warned if you rented from another company you'd be missing all that Hertz promises as the number one car company rental. A great example of emotional blackmail was the Tide To Go "Talking Stain" campaign. It's worth a moment to see it on YouTube. The stain on the young interviewer's shirt is talking and drowning him out so the potential employer is distracted and can only hear the stain's voice. If only the applicant had used Tide To Go, the problem would have been averted!

4   *Brand Stand* – The brand takes a stand in its own voice with a distinct personality convincing consumers to buy. For example, go to www.elfyourself.com and discover how much fun OfficeMax created in its Elf Yourself campaign. People could upload their image or their pet's image and create animated elves. The interactive campaign has returned for another playful year.

Writing the way you speak

Writing copy for ads is not like writing a scientific article or term paper. You're not delivering a dry lecture or making a formal speech. Instead, you're having a conversation. You're chatting with the consumer. So just how friendly should you be? This is where knowing your audience and your brand's *tone of voice* is crucial. Your language needs to both speak to the audience and properly represent the brand and its message. If either one is wrong, there's a disconnect between the brand and the consumer. If your message is *off target* it's incorrect for the audience. If it's *off strategy* it's going in the wrong creative direction.

1   *Use vernacular when it fits* – So when do you use vernacular, or everyday, informal speech? When it's appropriate. That casual *tone of voice* works perfectly for its audience of young, carefree college-aged guys, as depicted in Budweiser's "Whassup?" campaign or its "Beer House" 2010 Super Bowl spot. Remember there are degrees of casual. You would have to decide whether to use texting with its abbreviated spelling, or a relaxed tone with "gonna" or "woulda,"or a cultural or

regional "dialect." For instance, would writing using idiomatic expressions like "ma'am," "ya'll," or "fuggetaboutit" from Texas, the deep South, or New York enhance the message and target a specific audience? Ultimately, the *tone of voice* you choose and the delivery mechanism, such as vernacular or regional expressions, are crucial in establishing a credible link with your consumer.

2   *Choose simple, easy-to-grasp language* – Whatever you write, use simple, easy-to-grasp language. Avoid complex words, insiders' jargon, and "techie" terminology. Unless you're writing to a specific market that naturally uses those types or terms, leave them out. Don't you hate reading something that's supposed to explain how to use a product and you can't understand it? Many product manuals have been simplified so consumers can quickly understand the directions.

3   *Write in phrases, not lengthy sentences* – Shorter is usually better. See how easy it is? Just keep it short. The way you speak. Next time you're at a café, in the park, at a train station, listen. Pay attention to how people often don't even finish their thoughts or use one-word sentences. Get it? Great.

4   *Write in a conversational style* – Actually picture your consumers. What do they look like? How would they dress? How would you talk to them? Then, just say what you want to say aloud. That's how you'll hear your own voice and natural delivery. Use it. But, this time write it.

5   *Read your copy out loud* – After you've written it. Read it again out loud. Are you stumbling anywhere? Does it sound stiff or awkward or unnatural? If so, restate it and rewrite it the way you said it.

6   *Use punctuation to guide the reader's pace and focus* – Stop and start the reader with short sentences and periods. Like this. See?

7   *Choose active, not passive voice* – Keep the action alive by using straightforward writing, such as the active subject-followed-by-the-verb sentence construction. So, you'd say, "That guy SNAPPED a photo," not "The photo WAS SNAPPED by that guy."

8   *Weave* – Use the main idea throughout the copy. So if your headline talks about "Creating Buzz," you would weave "buzz" in interesting ways in the copy.

9   *Consider parallel construction* – This is a specific kind of phrasing or wording that you've heard or read many times: "To be or not to be." "It's not just coffee. It's Starbucks." "No salt. No sugar. No calories." "Get it? Got it. Good." It could just be the same word or part of speech used *over* and *over* and *over* or like this: here, there, and everywhere.

10 *Apply ABA format* – Often used in many of the arts, this structure repeats the headline's main idea in the closing line of the copy. The first "A" refers to the headline. "B" refers to the body copy. The last "A" refers to the last line of copy. So, if the headline used Maxwell House's slogan "Good to the last drop," the closing line could read, "One sip and you'll know why it's good to the last drop." The closing line doesn't have to repeat the headline word-for-word, just embody the concept.

11 *Use connectors*–These are words that tie each sentence or paragraph to the next, like "and," "so," "the truth is," "naturally," etc. Think of them as little stepping-stones that create a path that leads the reader through the woods.

12 *Start writing in the middle* – This means don't have a long intro. Jump right into your message or you might lose your reader.

13 *Think about alliteration* – This is another technique you're familiar with: "Sally sells sea shells by the sea shore." Monday Madness," "Fabulous Fun Fridays," "Ho, Ho, Ho!" for the holidays.

14 *Use a button* – This is a clever closing line that does *not* refer back to the headline. It can be a pun or a witty line that makes the reader smile.

15 *Rewrite until it's right* – Don't be satisfied with your first effort. Look the copy over. Is it wordy? Vague? Hard to read? Too complex? Take out superfluous words and unnecessary phrases. Then, reread it. Does it need more editing? Be honest!

16 *Know when to break grammatical rules* – In advertising copy, it's okay to start a sentence with because. Why? Because it works. You can end a sentence with a preposition because that's the way we naturally speak: "Who'd you sent the letter TO?" sounds better to the ear than "To whom did you send the letter?" even though the second one is proper English. You want to connect to the audience, not sound stuffy and affected. Some slogans use incorrect spelling or improper English. That's fine in this kind of writing. When Apple used this tagline, "Think Different," grammarians were upset, saying it should have used an adverb "Think differently." What Apple claimed was that "different" was a noun, not modifying the verb "think." Likewise, Toyota deliberately used the wrong spelling in the slogan "Toyota Everyday." Cordiant's Saatchi & Saatchi Advertising developed the slogan. It should have read "Toyota Every Day," because everyday, as one word, is an adjective modifying a noun like everyday routine. But you'd say, he goes to that restaurant every day. The reason the agency creatives wrote "every day" as one word was for two reasons. First, they wanted the audience to read the slogan like a verbal logo. Second, people would absorb the slogan faster if there were only two words to digest. Hence, "Toyota Everyday."[2] Even Leo Burnett, the advertising legend, agreed that "ain't" could be used if it precisely expressed the point. Here's a much-quoted Burnett comment using "ain't":

> *A good basic selling idea, involvement and relevancy, of course, are as important as ever, but in the advertising din of today, unless you make yourself noticed and believed, you ain't got nothin'.*[3]

Writing to your audience

In the first chapter we spent a lot of time talking about the different types of audience categories (VALS). The reason for this was to prepare you to think about your audience as a living, breathing human being, not a statistic. You want to get inside the mind of your consumers and know how they think. What's important to them. What they value. And, how they live their lives. Numbers are one thing. But, seeing your product from their *point of view* is everything. Probably the most important tip is to "Think like the consumer." Write down that phrase in big letters and post it on your computer. You won't go wrong – off strategy or off target – if you remember this point.

Always ask yourself what you would want to hear to take action. What would motivate you to make that purchase? To order that service? To hire that company? Then, select a *tone*

CHECKLIST 3.1 A quick "Grammar" copywriting checklist

1   *Use slang (vernacular):* gonna, gotta, hey, lemme, 'em, wanna, shoulda, lovin', etc. work for many types of products, like the line Red M&M'S says, "Gimme a break." But, if your client's tone is formal, covers a serious problem, or deals with health, medical, or insurance issues, you need to reconsider.

2   *Put prepositions at the end of the sentence* if that's where they naturally fall. For example: Who's the audience you're talking to? The dangling preposition is fine for ad copy.

3   *Write in fragments.* Not sentences. Like this.

4   *Create short paragraphs.* Even with just one sentence.

5   *Use short sentences.* They read faster.

6   *Use contractions* like we'd, you'd, she'll, not we had, you would, or she will. M&M'S used this headline: "Hey, How'd that get in there?" The image is of an X-ray of an M&M'S with the pretzel inside. Notice the use of "how'd" instead of "how did"?

7   *Sound conversational.* Like you're talking to a friend. (Notice the fragment, starting with "like.")

8   *Make up a new word* so the message is catchier, like "Comcastic" for Comcast, or "Peanutopolis," "Nougetaboutit," and "Hungerectomy" for a Snickers billboard campaign in 2009.

of voice that sounds natural for the brand and right for the audience. Write a message that will be ready to interrupt your target wherever they are.

1   *Catch their attention with a compelling headline.* What could you say that would be intrusive? Actually make them stop what they're doing at that precise moment in time and hear what you're saying. Keep working until you find an interruptive or disruptive message. For example, this message was on the top of a double-decker bus in London: "For people in high places." The advertiser was *The Economist,* a financial publication. Only those people, who worked in tall buildings, usually where financial institutions had offices, could see the ad.

2   *Show the benefits up front.* No one wants to wade through miles of copy to find out what's in it for them? (Notice "them" should have been "him" or "her." But, "them" is more conversational.) People want to know the answer to "Why buy?" immediately. Place the benefits in the headline or subhead so they'll read on.

3   *Select a familiar tone of voice.* Be sure your tone is correct for both the brand and the consumer. How conversational or casual is appropriate? You will know this if you have insight into your brand's personality and your consumer's core (or key) values.

4   *Include relevant copy points.* Tell consumers how the product will fit into their lives, solve a specific problem, or fill a need. This is where the copy has a chance to further explain the *consumer benefits* and the product features. Is the product lighter, faster, safer? What features prove these points?

5   *Determine VALS language.* If you're speaking to "Makers," you should be talking about how simple it is to build this bookcase or to customize this deck. They enjoy the process of construction and like to celebrate their creativity.

6 *Consider regional dialects.* Should you use them? Do they reflect the tone of a regional brand or a specific audience? Do they catch the target's attention? Do they present the brand in an acceptably humorous way without being offensive?

7 *Connect directly using NLP.* NLP, *neuro-linguistic programming*, also called NLC, *neuro-linguistic conditioning*, shows the connection between the people's state of mind (mood) and their physical reaction (health). A quick example is the way you cannot smile when you're in the middle of a fight. That expression would be incongruous with your feelings. However, if you wanted to change from angry to calm, something that makes you smile, like a baby's laugh, can help you change your mood. This neuro-linguistic link shows the connection between how you feel and how you look. If I told you that you just won a million dollars, you'd smile, sit up straighter and feel great, instantly. That's how quickly your mood can change.

When people want to change their behavior, they model the habits and gestures of successful people. They change their carriage and gait when they walk. They stick their chests out with pride. Just changing your physiology can change how you see yourself. This can lead you to opening yourself up for greater success.

When used in advertising messages, NLP singles out audience members by modeling their patterns of language. There are three ways we process information. Most of us are stronger in two of these. They are (1) *kinesthetic* (by touch), (2) *auditory* (by hearing), and (3) *visual* (by sight). People will tell you which one they are by the language they use.

The *kinesthetic* person will make comments like "Feels good to me," "I have a handle on it," and "I need to wrap my brain around it." These are the people who kick the tires and have to feel the interior of a car they're buying.

The *auditory* person will say sentences like, "I like the sound of that," "Sounds good to me," and "Listen up."

The *visual* person will say statements like, "Can you picture it?" "Take a look at this," and "See what I mean?"

Whenever you see a message that uses language like "Listen up," "We see how you feel," or "Sounds too good to be true? Well, it is true," it's talking to the audience in a way that will generate a response from a particular way those people best absorb information, that is in an auditory, visual, or kinesthetic manner.

When you're writing to an audience and don't have a sense of how they process, it's good to use words to target these three senses: touch, hearing, and sight.

Writing for the medium and the senses

We just discussed writing for three of the senses. With advertising, each medium addresses one or more of these. When writing for a specific medium, think about engaging the senses, how your choice of words can awaken one or more of them.

1 *For print: eye, ear, nose, and hand (touch)* – Print ads can incorporate more senses than sight. Now there are sound chips and scent advertising that can be added. Think about the Hallmark cards where you can record your own message. That's done with a sound chip. Remember scent strips in perfume ads in magazines? That's scent advertising. Even though most print ads involve only sight, consider adding sound and scent to the medium when appropriate. With print, you're physically holding the message.

2 *For online: eye, ear, and hand* – Online messages can include hearing when there's animation or a video with a sound track. If you're creating an online message, you may be working with a strip or narrow ad. For a banner ad, it would be a horizontal strip, and for a skyscraper ad, it would be a vertical strip format. Should you involve a multipanel ad (with same-size boxes) that includes animation and sound effects as the action moves from one scene to another? Or does the ad work well enough by itself without movement and sound? Will it click through to another site?

3 *For radio: ear* – This is the one pure medium. The only sense is hearing. This is why you need to think visually. When writing for this medium, carefully decide the music and sound effects. They will put the listener in the exact setting.

4 *For TV: eye and ear* – The next time you watch TV, notice how much of it is enhanced with sound. To prove this, shut the sound off. You immediately feel as if you're missing half the story. Because you are. When writing for this medium, carefully decide the location and visual effects. Then, consider what additional sounds and music can be added to further tell the story.

5 *For ambient: eye, ear, nose, and hand* – Actually, this medium can connect all the senses. As with print advertising, you can use visuals, sounds, and scent. For example, for a fair, you could have a carousel horse going up and down, kids' screams and giggles, and spray the scent of French fries, cinnamon buns, or hot fudge. This could be a 3-D billboard, at a bus shelter (within the safety glass), at kiosks in a mall. You could use two or three senses. For example, the back of escalator steps could show people in seats going up the Ferris wheel with the sound of people laughing. The point is to think about your audience's reaction to multiple sensations. Or you could show people in rollercoaster seats with the sound of a wooden track clicking with each elevating step. Or you could place the message on subway turnstile handles.

6 *For mobile* – Think eye, ear, and hand. Portable devices allow you to create messages while consumers are on the go. They could be shopping or surfing. Using their apps or texting. What kind of message would you want to receive on your device? Coupons? Invitations to events? Special offers? Think about an older market. Perhaps they'd like to have medication renewal reminders and senior savings. Don't be judgmental and think they don't use a smart phone, Kindle, or iPad. Look around. You may be surprised to see your grandparents are sending you photos from their phones.

7 *For other touchpoints* – Ask yourself where else your consumers are seeing this message. In supermarkets? On shopping carts? On shelves in stores? How can you activate the audience's senses in unexpected ways?

"

There's already so much writing in the world, nobody is actively interested in reading what YOU have to write, especially if it's on behalf of somebody who's trying to sell them something. **CHARLIE HOPPER, CREATIVE DIRECTOR/COPYWRITER, YOUNG & LARAMORE**[4]

Writing for celebrities

This is a skill you will want to develop. Start right this minute and listen carefully to a few famous celebrities. Watch them on TV, YouTube, Hulu, or wherever you can. Do they speak quickly or slowly? Do they have a slight accent, like Kyra Sedgwick, or a slight lisp, like Holly Hunter, or rich vocal tone like Demi Moore? Do they have a distinctive voice like James Earl Jones or Denzel Washington or Al Pacino? Try to find their cadence, their rhythm, their inflection, and their pace. Then, write for it.

For print–If you're writing a quote as if the celebrity actually said it, you need to write in that star's individual *tone of voice*, using natural phrasing and expressions. Most stars have a manager who needs to approve the copy before allowing it to be used in an ad.

For broadcast– In this case if the celebrities are delivering the lines you wrote as voice-over talents for radio or on- or off-screen as actors, each phrase must sound authentic, as if that was something they would say. This is where copy length is crucial. If you have a star with a slow delivery, you might only write 15 seconds of copy for a 30-second spot. In this way, you're using the celebrity's normal inflection and pace, for a natural sounding delivery. When talents appear to be rushing through the script, especially in a testimonial, the commercial loses its credibility.

For the Web– If stars appear in an online video, they have to sound as if they're speaking to the audience one-on-one. The same rules apply for online copy, even if the audience, and not the talent, is reading the message. Everything has to sound true to the star's style of speech.

The best thing you can do is immerse yourself in watching the star in as many movies, films, TV shows, and so on to capture the celebrity's vocal mannerisms, idioms, phrasing, and idiosyncrasies. Some stars might pepper their speech with colloquial expressions, like "y'all" or "sugar" if they're from a Southern state. Or you might use a phrase or word that would reflect the celebrity's attitude like "winning" for a famous athlete. If that's how they naturally speak, there's no reason not to use those phrases. It makes the star and copy sound genuine.

Finding your own voice: some tips

Write and rewrite your copy until it sounds natural. Listen to how you speak. Record a few of your conversations, so you can hear your natural delivery. Would your way of speaking work for your client? Do you use too many qualifiers, such as "like," "sort of," "kinda," and so on? If so, edit those out. What other habits do you have that might not work?

Now write a paragraph of copy for the "client." Read it aloud. Does it sound stiff or contrived? Or does it sound like you? Reading aloud helps you find your rhythm and capture it on paper.

You may want to mimic other copywriters to hear how your voice differs. Write another commercial, tweet, post a blog, or use another form of communication following the rhythm of another writer. It's not that easy to pinch and step into someone else's voice, is it? However, you may need to do that if a copywriter can't get to a recording session and the copy has to be edited. This is a great exercise to help you learn another way to express ideas. Then, when you get back into your own voice, it will be like sliding into a comfy pair of slippers. A perfect fit.

Quick chapter overview

Take a look at the checklist below before you begin writing. It's a quick reminder to write in an easy-to-grasp manner so your target audience can "get" your message. Remember, less is more. Try to write as succinctly as possible. Create interest and curiosity, and get the point

CHECKLIST 3.2 Writing technique tips checklist

1   Review the Brief.

2   Read the Creative Strategy Statement.

3   Consider using *ABA* format, *parallel construction*, *weave*, *alliteration*, *connectors*, or a *button*.

4   See your audience as three-dimensional people, not as a statistic.

5   Create a strong message that can *spin out*.

6   Select the appropriate *tone of voice*.

7   Decide the campaign's *point of view*: who's speaking.

   a   The brand (self-serving)?

   b   The consumer (testimonial)?

   c   The conscience (emotional blackmail)?

   d   The brand's unique personality (brand stand)?

8   Write naturally. Sound conversational.

9   *Weave* the main idea of the headline through the copy.

10   Read your copy aloud for flow.

11   Use familiar *slang* (gotta, getta, etc.), simple language, short phrases, and contractions.

across. Think of copywriting as a conversation with the reader. If you read your copy out loud, you may discover sections where you're stumbling. Don't worry about what's wrong with the copy. If you can't read it effortlessly, just rewrite it.

Creative writing exercises

Exercise 1: creating a consistent message

Part 1 Look at multimedia ads for your local zoo. How did the campaign work for print compared to TV? Look for consistency in language and graphics. Does the website reflect the campaign images and *tone of voice*?

Part 2 Develop another, related message to spin out the campaign. Would you use a different medium like mobile? Could you create an interactive game on the website?

Exercise 2: using vernacular

Part 1 What kind of "client" could use vernacular in the campaign?

Part 2 Write three headlines in a campaign for different media: out-of-home, bus sides, magazine, or online. Make sure you use the same writing technique for each.

Part 3 Could this campaign be used for an ambient message? What type and where? For example, could you create lawn signs for parks?

Exercise 3: write two to three paragraphs of body copy, using one or more of the techniques below

1   *Parallel construction* – For example: "He loves me. He loves me not."

2   *Alliteration* – For example: "Betty Botter bought some butter."

3   *Weave* – Make the copy refer to the headline concept throughout the ad.

4   *Connectors* – Insert words to connect some lines or paragraphs, such as "but," "the best part is," "additionally," and so on.

5   *Button* – Introduce a witty, unexpected closing line.

6   *ABA* – Wrap up the last line of copy by relating back to and reinforcing the headline.

Notes

1   Charlie Hopper, personal communication, November 26, 2008.

2   Margo Berman, "Teaching Grammar Through Lyrics, Film and literary Quotes. The Grammar Controversy." *American Society of Business and Behavioral Sciences*, 10 (1998): 67–a73.

3   Brainy Quote, www.brainyquote.com/quotes/authors/l/leo_burnett.html (accessed August 12, 2010).

4   Charlie Hopper, personal communication, November 26, 2008.

THE STICKY WORD

Headline and slogan techniques

If a client says to use something we never thought of and it makes that a better ad, we more than welcome it.

WILLIAM BERNBACH, ONE OF THE FOUNDERS OF DOYLE DANE BERNBACH (DDB) [1]

Devising ad structure: headlines, subheads, body copy, and slogans

Remembering the call to action

Thinking up catchy headlines and subheads

Reviewing different kinds of headlines

Making up sticky slogans: the backbone of campaigns

Adding power to your writing

Copywriting insights and tips

Making your copy sticky

Creative writing exercises

In the following pages, you'll walk through various techniques to create unforgettable headlines and slogans. You'll learn the structure of ad copy, with between eyebrows, headlines, subheads, body copy, call to action wording, closing lines, and slogans. You'll discover specific types of headlines that you can easily refer to when you're concepting, like the celebrity endorsement, the metaphor, or the story.

You'll find out what makes slogans sticky and how to create them using 16 different techniques. Most importantly, you'll recognize the importance of writing in a conversational way and creating a message that's relevant to your audience. In short, you'll begin to think like the consumer. You'll look at how they shop, where they shop, what's important to them. And so on. You'll become a more active listener, a mental-note keeper of natural speech, a collector of great ad references, and a more powerful writer.

Best of all, you'll read some invaluable copy tips from master copywriters. Now, let's take a good look at the construction of copy messages up close.

Devising ad structure: headlines, subheads, body copy, and slogans

After creating a heart-stopping *headline* make sure it will work as part of a campaign, and not just as a stand-alone message. This headline needs to be able to work as one in a series of ads, each one related to the next. Remember, you're always looking for a big idea that spins out in various formats and different media.

Some headlines have a supporting line or *subhead*. Think of this as a supporting actor in a movie who plays the lead's best friend. The role of this character is to support the main idea and help explain it further.

Some ads have paragraphs of copy, as in magazine articles, brochures, and web copy. Mini headlines or subheads are used to separate the copy into digestible sections. They're easy to find because they're usually bold or in a contrasting color to highlight them. These separations are considered *blocks of copy*. Blocks range from one to several paragraphs.

Here's a quick overview of the structure of advertising copy. Each part has a specific function.

1 *Eyebrows* – These are a line of text that targets a particular audience, like "Arthritis Sufferers" and appears before the headline.

2 *Headlines* – These deliver the main message of the ad. They must be strong enough to stop readers and get them to notice the ad. Headlines in a series of ads should continue stating one big idea with multiple executions. Well-integrated campaigns send a singular impression by presenting variations on one concept. Together they present one cohesive theme. They also need to have the same format. So, if one headline states a command, they all will. If one headline uses vernacular, they all will. If one headline uses parallel construction (as in the preceding sentences), they all will.

3 *Subheads* – These strengthen the headline and reinforce the stated benefit. The purpose of subheads in lengthy copy is to guide the reader from one key idea to the next. Think of them like directional signs on the highway. Readers can skip ahead to the sections they want to read next.

4   *Body copy* – This is the area where writers can explain specific benefits and features. They help readers understand why they should buy the product. Effective body copy is fluid. It flows from one point to the next, carrying the reader along. It usually incorporates other writing techniques discussed above, like *weave* (connecting the headline throughout the copy), *ABA* (restating the headline in the closing line), and *alliteration* (using the same first sound in sequential words).

5   *Call to action* – This tells the target what you want them to do: dial a phone number, hop on a website, visit a store, and so on.

6   *Closing line of copy* – This last line gives readers closure. Do you want to use a *button* (short, catchy phrase) or reinforce the headline through *ABA* format? Remember, you're thanking the reader for getting to the end of your copy. Make it rewarding.

7   *Slogan* – This is a verbal logo. It's the one line that remains constant and doesn't change with each ad or touchpoint. *Slogans*, also called *taglines*, *theme lines*, or *catch phrases*, encapsulate the brand's message in a sticky phrase. Nike's "Just do it," created in 1988, is still one of the most powerful slogans. It was voted as the number two slogan of the century by *AdAge*.[2] Number one was the De Beers "A diamond is forever." If a slogan is read aloud in a radio or TV spot, the actor's voice should be consistent with the brand's voice. You wouldn't want a comedian to deliver the slogan in jest for a heart surgeon. When appropriate, you may have the slogan incorporated into a jingle, making it a musical slogan.

8   *Sig (signature)* – This is required copy (or "mandatories") that include contact information like the company address, phone, fax, website, and so on.

Remembering the call to action

The final thing your audience needs to know is what you want them to do. Go online. Call an 800 number. Ask their doctor. Go to the store. Redeem a coupon. Post a comment on a blog. Create your own product-centric video. Vote for your favorite competitor. Become a Facebook fan. And so on. Although many ads don't include a call to action, they are for brands so well known that consumers don't need any direction. Like Nike, Apple, Wii from Nintendo, or Coke.

If you don't tell consumers what to do, chances are they'll do just that: nothing. They need to be encouraged to respond to your message by taking action. Your message has to motivate them to get off the couch or away from the computer. Then, they need to know what they should do.

Now we will discuss several creative areas that explain how to strengthen your writing skills.

Thinking up catchy headlines and subheads

There are many approaches to writing great headlines. Using an unexpected, well-targeted message is always refreshing. Surprising the audience with a shocking, little-known fact is another. You want to get readers' attention so they stop and actually spend three seconds reading your ad. Yes, three seconds. If you think that's a short time, they only spend one second deciding to read it once they look at the *headline*. Amazing, right? Well, now you know how critically important the headline is. It's the main message of the ad and it has to stop readers cold. No matter what they're doing and get them to read on.

To grasp the different ways to create print campaigns, take a look at some other books on copywriting for a quick reference. Here's a handy list of some of them. This list includes the latest editions of these works in alphabetical order by author:

1 Edd Applegate's *Strategic Copywriting* (chapters 6 and 7).

2 Tom B. Altstiel and Jean M. Grow's *Advertising Creative Strategy, Copy + Design* (chapter 9).

3 Bruce Bendinger's *The Copy Workshop Workbook* (chapter 13).

4 Margo Berman's *Street-Smart Advertising* (chapter 5).

5 Margo Berman and Robyn Blakeman's *The Brains Behind Great Ad Campaigns* (chapter 5).

6 Robert W. Bly's *The Copywriter's Handbook* (chapter 6).

7 Philip Ward Burton's *Advertising Copywriting* (chapters 6 and 7).

8 George Felton's *Advertising Concept and Copy* (chapter 7).

9 Randall Hines and Robert Lauterborn's *Print Matters* (chapter 5).

10 Bonnie L. Drewniany and A. Jerome Jewler's *Creative Strategy in Advertising* (chapter 6).

11 Luke Sullivan's *Hey Whipple, Squeeze This* (chapter 4).

Realize that the list of strategies in chapter 1 can help guide you to a powerful headline. Also, the slogan techniques that follow can be used to generate headlines.

Reviewing different kinds of headlines

Although there are many, here are some of the most common headline approaches.

1 *The results* – This headline highlights the product's benefit. Any time you want to demonstrate products that remove stains, whiten teeth, reduce wrinkles, stimulate weight loss, build muscles, make plants grow, eliminate weeds, and so on, this is a tried-and-true headline. Dramatic changes are often depicted through before-and-after images. The image paired with a candid message can create an "Oh, wow!" moment. Consider the Bowflex campaign that promises to give you that longed-for six-pack.

2 *The comparison* – This allows one brand to challenge another's effectiveness. Instead of just showing the results of your brand, you compare those side by side to a competitor. The point is to show off your brand's advantage in lifting stains, whitening clothes, straightening hair, adding shine to shoes, and so on. Think of it as advertising bragging rights: "My brand can beat up your brand." Think about the Bounty "Quicker-Picker Upper" promise to outlast against its competitors. One line on its website challenges the consumer with "Bring It," ensuring it can clean up the toughest spills (http://www.bountytowels.com/en_US/index.shtml).

3   *The celebrity endorsement* – This approach gives the 'microphone" to a celebrity to talk about the product. Celebrities from all industries, from entertainment to sports, instantly raise brand awareness, especially for little-known products. There are also the likeability and watchability factors. Ashton Kutcher has wide appeal as the Nikon spokesperson because he seems like someone who feels like a friend. Whoopi Goldberg in Weight Watchers and other campaigns makes you want to watch her. You're curious about what she's going to say. The main downside to using celebrities is the crash-and-burn syndrome. If the star or athlete has a run in with the law, is caught in the center of a controversial issue, or is involved in a personal scandal, that incident can quickly tarnish the brand's image and negatively affect sales.

4   *How to* – This enables you to show consumers how to solve a problem or get a desired result. People can learn "how to have shinier hair," "how to instantly look 10 pounds thinner," or "how to prime and paint in one coat." Brands like Pantene hair care products, Spanx body-slimming shapewear, and Behr all-in-one paint have used this approach.

5   *The product as the star* – This main message spotlights the product, like the "I'm a PC" campaign. The earlier Absolut campaign that used two-word headlines like "Absolut L.A." is another example. One more is the 3M Post-it Notes "Organize Your Head."

6   *The teaser* – This headline tempts the reader with a bit of information. Usually used in a campaign, teasers reveal the advertiser in the last ad in the series only. An example is the campaign that introduced the Florida Lottery with all-type ads that used only one word: "Ha." Each ad added another "Ha." In the end, the vertical strip ad (narrow, vertical panel ad) had many "Ha's" stacked one over the other. The closing line stated that if you play the Florida Lottery you could laugh all the way to the bank. Finally, it revealed the advertiser.

7   *The blind headline* – Here the headline is deliberately vague, sometimes with a surprising "reveal." Once readers find the logo, they get it and are able to grasp the message. *The Economist*, a financial publication, has used blind headlines. One example is this print headline: "Dissection. Good if you're a story. Bad if you're a frog." You don't know who the advertiser is until you see the logo. Then, you, as the reader, put the message together, surmising that you'll read a carefully researched article in *The Economist*.

8   *The stacked headline* – This headline allows writers to use words that are stacked one over the other. Although this is a layout-based headline, it gives writers a way to present related and unrelated words in a numbered or unnumbered list to lead readers to reach the end. For example, the headline could stack this way to draw you into reading the copy.[3]:

> Keep
> Reading.
> You're
> Almost there.

There are also visually driven figures of speech headlines like those listed below in numbers 9 through 14 below. Be sure to check out the ihaveanidea website (www.ihaveanidea.org) for more figures of speech examples, great writing tips, interviews with creative giants, and more. Be sure you read the two-part article with exciting visual examples and great tips for writers: "An Inconvenient Truth for Copywriters: How to Write Headlines and Why Your Career Depends On It."[4]

9   *The metaphor* – Unlike using a simile, the headline shows a comparison without using "like" or "is." One example is the series of one-word ambient ad headlines on three-dimensional objects to advertise The Miami Rescue Mission: (1) "Kitchen" for a dumpster, (2) "Closet" for a shopping cart, and (3) "Bed" for a bus bench. Or the door hanger message created by Knock Knock: "Out to Lunch But that's a Metaphor."

10 *Personification* – This headline gives human characteristics to an inanimate object, like "time flies." One example is for Gay Lea spreadable butter: "Margarine Is Like So Freaked Out Right Now." Or for Maynards candies, which showed a police lineup of various sweets, from gummy bears to character-shaped sours under the headline "Maynards' Most Wanted," as if they were criminals with funny names like "Jerry Bomb" and "The Swede." Or for Workers Injury Law & Advocacy Group with an image of a weasel in a business suit and the headline "Winning a War Against Weasels."

11 *Hyperbole* – This is an obvious, can't-be-true exaggeration, like "the bag weighed a ton," or this headline for the restaurant 321 East: "How Good Is Our Steak? Last Week a Man Who Was Choking on a Piece of Meat Refused the Heimlich Maneuver." Or this headline for a window cleaner: "Every Window Becomes Invisible to You." This wouldn't an exaggeration until you saw the visual of a bird with his wing set in a sling and his head wrapped in gauze. The reader had to connect that the bird just crashed into a super clean, or invisible, window.

12 *Irony* – This headline says one thing but means another, like the phrase "laundering money." For example, a lost dog poster read, "Lost: Search & Rescue Dog." Or this headline for the HBO hit TV series, *True Blood*: "All Flavor. No Bite." The visual looked like an alcohol bottle of blood with the label reading "100% Pure True Blood." (The closing line was equally humorous: "HBO reminds vampires to drink responsibly.") Another example is the sign that stated, "Please Vote Against Campaign Signs on City Utility Poles." Or the "ThinkB4USpeak" campaign that tried to teach tolerance and sensitivity to phrases like "That's So Gay" with headlines like these: (1) "That's 'So Jock Who Can Complete a Pass But Not a Sentence," and (2) "That's So 'Cheerleader Who Can't Like Say Smart Stuff." At first, readers might be amused by the headlines, but then realized these were stereotypical and offensive messages.

13 *Paradox* – This headline is an absurd, contradictory, or seemingly untrue statement like "Eat More. Weigh Less." Or, as exemplified in the book title, *The Paradox of Choice: Why More Is Less* by Barry Schwartz, which suggested having more product options may adversely affect consumer-buying behavior. Or this headline: "It's Cheaper to Print on Some Money than Paper," which was superimposed over African bank notes to show how much they have been devalued. Another headline in the same campaign was "Thanks to Mugabe This Money is Wallpaper." The bank notes were spread across a bulletin board and refer to the negative effect of the Mugabe regime.

14 *The pun* – This headline uses a play on words, like this headline for Starbucks, "Beware of a Cheaper Cup of Coffee. It Comes with a Price." Or the headline for Mercy (hospital): "All Arteries Connect to Mercy." Or this headline for the film *The Boys in Company C:* "To Keep Their Sanity in an Insane War They Had to Be Crazy." Or the headline, "Renew Now It's Werth It," in support of keeping baseball pitcher Jayson Werth on the Nats (Washington Nationals) team.

Here are a few more headline categories presented by Bruce Bendinger in his book *The Copy Workshop Workbook.*

15 *The one-liner* – This catchy, attention-grabbing headline is like the one-line joke. It's fast and immediate, with a little twist. For example, a TV spot for Zazoo condoms with a screaming kid having a temper tantrum in a store was accompanied with two words superimposed: "Use condoms." That line could work as a headline if the campaign went to print.

16 *News* – This technique presents information like a news story. "Wrinkle breakthrough! Fewer lines without surgery." Then, the copy would explain how this new pharmacological product is better than the others at reducing wrinkles.

17 *The spiral* – This headline keeps on going, seemingly without end to entice the reader to continue. One line weaves into the next like the song *One Little, Two Little, Three Little Indians.* For instance, a headline for a jewelry store for Christmas could say, "On the First Day of Christmas, Her Boyfriend Gave to Her, a Diamond in a Pear Shape. On the Second Day of Christmas, Her Boyfriend Gave to Her, Two Ruby Earrings, and a Diamond in a Pear Shape."

18 *The story* – This presents a story featuring a consumer, corporate executive, or the brand. If told by the consumer, the stories usually have an emotional appeal and are based on real-life experiences like Jared Fogle's weight loss by eating healthy sandwiches at Subway. For a cosmetic surgery center, a headline could read: "Once Upon a Time There Was a Little Girl Who Loved Herself, but Hated Her Nose." You'd read on to see what she did about it.

19 *The sermon* – The headline preaches. One example was imprinted on the inside of Vazir Breweries beer bottle caps. Once the bottle was opened the cap was dented in. The message inside simply said: "Don't Drink and Drive."

20 *The outline* – The headline continues down the page using subheads or numbers to continue the message. This allows writers to chunk lengthy copy down to small pieces of easy-to-grasp information. "Ten Reasons to Safeguard Your Credit." Then, the reasons would be numbered one through ten in ten blocks of copy.[5]

Making up sticky slogans: the backbone of campaigns

One thing that I find invaluable, and I don't really know how a writer can be a writer unless they do this, is to read a lot.

MATT ZISELMAN, CREATIVE DIRECTOR, SAPIENTNITRO[6]

Slogans have an important job. They wrap up the product's message in a tidy package. They remind the audience why they should use that item (or service). They can make a promise to consumers and also establish a relationship with them. Easy-to-remember slogans hang like sticky notes in the consumer's mind. You can probably finish each of these slogans without prompting:

1 "Melts in your mouth, not in your _____."
2 "Better Ingredients. Better _____."
3 "The _____ of Macy's."
4 "The incredible, edible _____."
5 "Home of the _____."
6 "Once you pop, you can't _____"
7 "America runs on _____."
8 "What would you do for a _____ bar?"
9 "Like a good _____, State Farm is there."
10 "Sometimes you feel like a _____ sometimes you don't."

You get the idea. Whether the slogan is new or old, you can see how these have the unforgettable factor. Did you get them all right? Did you know all the company names? Here are the answers so you can double-check:

● "Melts in your mouth, not in your *hands*." (M&M'S, 1954)
● "Better Ingredients. Better *Pizza*." (Papa John's, 1998)
● "The *magic* of Macy's." (2008)
● "The incredible, edible *egg*." (American Egg Board, 1977)
● "Home of the *Whopper*." (Burger King, 1957)
● "Once you pop, you can't *stop*." (Pringles, 1968)
● "America runs on *Dunkin'*." (Dunkin' Donuts, 2006)
● "What would you do for a *Klondike* bar?" (1984)
● "Like a good *neighbor*, State Farm is there." (1971)
● "Sometimes you feel like a *nut* sometimes you don't." (Peter Paul Almond Joy and Peter Paul Mounds, 1953)

So what makes these particular slogans so sticky? They're catchy and easy to remember. They might be humorous, witty, surprising, or blatantly direct, like "Kotex. Fits. Period." Or "Get to a better State. State Farm Insurance." They can be a line used in a TV spot that suddenly becomes a popular catch phrase like the Budweiser line "Whassup!" or Wendy's "Where's the beef?" They're lines that may repeat a word or phrase like the Meow Mix jingle "Meow. Meow. Meow." Or the Energizer Bunny that "Keeps going and going and going." As simple as they seem, they're both clever and have structure. You'll find they're often based on one of the 16 following techniques. Once you learn these, see if you can identify which techniques were used.

1 *Name* – When you include the company's name in the slogan, you've instantly reinforced name awareness. This is especially true if the slogan is only a few words long. Or, if it's a name that's easy to make fun of or difficult to remember. Let's start with the short slogans like "Toyota. Moving forward." "Take Aim against cavities." Or "Pepsi refresh project." Pepsi uses a secondary or *subslogan*,

which some call a *tagline*, for this specific campaign For longer ones, notice how this one supports a challenging name: "With a name like Smucker's, it's got to be good." Aflac simply had an endearing Duck quack for the name and that became the slogan. The slogan and the logo become one: a sLOGOn, coined by Michael Newman.[7]

2 *Rhyme* – The reason these slogans are so sticky is that we learned nursery rhymes even before we could read. "Jack and Jill went up the hill." "Hickory dickory dock. The mouse ran up the clock." "Old King Cole was a merry old soul." You don't need any more prompting. You know the rest of the rhyme. It's the same with these kinds of slogans. They're easy to recall. "Swiffer gives cleaning a whole new meaning." "Twizzlers. The Twist You Can't Resist." "Must see TV" (NBC). "Feel the heal" (Cortizone-10 for Eczema). "Crave the wave" (Ocean Spray). "Flick my Bic" (lighter). "The best part of waking up is Folgers in your cup." "Takes a licking and keeps on ticking" (Timex) was created back in the 1950s by W.B. Doner & Co. and agency predecessors. This type of slogan increases name awareness.

3 *Alliteration* – Repeating the first letter or sound of a word creates alliteration. You've said alliterative phrases many times. Peter Piper picked a peck of pickled peppers. Alliteration slogans are sonorous: "Be certain with Certs," "Intel inside." "Ruffles have ridges." "Whiskas. What cats want." "Fluent in finance" (Barclays Bank). Others have longevity. The famous Campbell's Soup slogan "Mmm mm good!" was created back in 1935 by BBDO. "I'm cuckoo for Cocoa Puffs!" first said by Sonny the Cuckoo bird in 1962, created by Gene Cleaves and illustrated by Bill Tollis, creative head and art director at Dancer/Fitzgerald/Sample.

4 *Play on words* – This is a witty line that has a second meaning: "Chase what matters." Notice, it's only three words long and the first word is the name. This is also an example of a combination slogan (technique #16) because it uses the name, a play on words and a command (imperative, technique #11). Other great examples are "All the news that's fit to print" from the *New York Times*. "Don't treat your puppy like a dog" from Ralston Purina dog food. "Discover what One can do" (Purina One dog food). "Works like a dream" (Ambien sleeping aid). "Kraft your snack" (Kraft salad dressing). "Zero's Subs. We're Hot and on a Roll." "Takes the 'fur' out of furniture" (Scotch Fur Fighter pet hair remover). "The best tires in the world have Goodyear written all over them." "Aflac. We've got you under our wing." "The best seat in the house" (Jockey Underwear). "What moves you" (Scion). "Think outside the bun" (Taco Bell). Morton Salt's slogan, "When it rains, it pours," created in 1912.

5 *Parallel construction* – This was described earlier as a writing technique and it works just as well as a slogan. It's memorable because it's repetitive. A word, phrase, or part of speech is repeated like these examples. "American by birth. Rebel by choice" (Harley-Davidson). "Kid tested. Mother approved" (Kix cereal). "Share moments . . . Share life" (Kodak). "The few. The proud. The Marines" (U.S. Marine Corps). "Bring out the Hellmann's. Bring out the best." "Sometimes you feel like a nut, sometimes you don't" (Peter Paul Almond Joy & Mounds). "Be clear. Be confident. Be Proactiv."

6   *Statement of use or purpose* – The company gives a promise to the audience. It answers what people can expect when they make a purchase. It's a commitment to the consumer. For example, "Imagination at work" (GE). "We know money" (AIG). "You're in good hands with Allstate." "It's not just for breakfast anymore" (Florida Orange Juice Growers). "100% juice for 100% kids" (Juicy Juice). "When banks compete. You win" (Lending Tree). "We do chicken right" (Kentucky Fried Chicken). "The greatest show on earth" (Barnum & Bailey Circus). "We know drama" (TNT). "There's Fast Food, Then There's KFC." "Expect more. Pay less" (Target). "Save money. Live better" (Walmart). The problem with the last two slogans is that they can be confused. Both Target and Walmart target the same audience with a similar message. You want to create a message that's indisputably your client, not its competitor.

7   *Testimonial* – This type of phrase gives the "microphone" to consumers and lets them praise the product or service. "I'm a Toys R Us Kid." "That was easy" (Staples). "I am stuck on Band-Aid, and Band-Aid's stuck on me." "My wife, I think I'll keep her" (Geritol). Notice in this one, "Kibbles and Bits! Kibbles and Bits! I'm gonna get me some Kibbles and Bits!" From Kibbles & Bits dog food, the "consumer's voice" is the dog speaking. Another one in the dog's voice is Purina Beggin' Strips tagline, "It's bacon!" A famous celebrity can act like the end-user and comment about the brand. People today, however, know that the celebrity is being paid and may make the message less credible.

8   *Simile* – This approach uses "like" or "as" to connect similarities between two items. A metaphor compares without using like or as. "He is a tiger in war." He is not "like" a tiger. He is a ferocious tiger. These are slogans that use similes. "Easy as Dell." "There's nothing like Australia." "Cats like Felix like Felix" (Felix cat food). "Like a good neighbor, State Farm is there." "Chevy. Like a rock."

9   *Onomatopoeia* – The beauty of this technique is that it engages two senses: sight and hearing. Onomatopoeic words imitate an object or action. Hear the words "Ding-dong" and you're picturing a doorbell. "Click" sounds like the snap of a pen, a computer mouse, or a door closing. "Click" sounds like the action itself. Listen to the Mazda slogan "Zoom-Zoom" and you think of a car. Alka-Seltzer sounds just like the product in use: "Plop, plop. Fizz, fizz," when dropped into water. Of course, you know how much *"Snap! Crackle! Pop!"* sounds just like **Kellogg's® Rice Krispies®** when milk is poured over it.

10 *Emotional blackmail* – These slogans conjure up a sense of guilt or fear. It makes consumers wonder what would happen if they chose another product. They make people second-guess themselves and doubt their purchasing choices. How sure are you about your deodorant? Probably fine until you were asked to "Raise your hand if you're Sure." It makes you wonder. Doesn't it?

       If "Choosy moms choose Jif" how good a mom are you if you use another brand of peanut butter? Consider: "There's a lot riding on your tires." If you bought another brand, how safe do you feel?

11 *Imperative statement* – One iconic phrase is the Nike slogan, "Just do it." Without preaching, it invites people to continue enjoying whatever sport they choose. Do what you want, but do it. Some other slogans that use a command or imperative statement are these: "Subway. Eat fresh." "Play. Laugh. Grow" (Fisher-Price).

"Invent" (Hewlett-Packard). "Never let 'em see you sweat" (Gillette Dry Idea). "Eat fresh" (Subway). "Say it with Flowers" (FTD). "Eat up!" (Quiznos).

12 *Interrogative statement* – A catchy phrase that poses a question is an interrogative slogan. One of the most recognized is "Got milk?" (California Milk Processor Board). Here are a few more: "Doesn't your dog deserve Alpo?" "Gatorade. Is it in you?" "Have you laughed today?" (The Laughing Cow cheese).

13 *Vernacular* – This type of slogan sounds natural because it imitates consumers' everyday speech or slang. Using common phrases, casual language, and contractions like "gonna," "'em," "woulda," "goin'," "yeah," make people feel comfortable. Some slogans catch on and become part of the American culture. Here are a few pop phrases: McDonald's "I'm lovin' it," "Whassup!" from Budweiser, and even Jim Cramer's "Booyah" from his CNBC show *Mad Money*.

14 *Reason why* – This kind of tagline tells consumers why they should choose this product over another. Reason why slogans encapsulate "because." You purchase this because it's "So easy a caveman can do it" (Geico). Or, because you want "The world on time" (FedEx). Or, because you want to "Stop dieting. Start living" (Weight Watchers). Maybe you like "Hot eats. Cool treats" (Dairy Queen). Or you want to "Drink better water" (VitaminWater). Maybe you need more energy, so you drink Red Bull because it "gives you wings." When you reach for a chocolate, you expect that "There's a smile in every Hershey Bar." You know "There's always room for J-E-L-L-O." You ship with FedEx because it promises you, "Relax. It's FedEx." The underlying message with Federal Express is that you don't need to stress because your package will arrive. Since 1959 when Ogilvy, Benson & Mather created its slogan, Maxwell House has answered "Why buy?" with this promise: because it's "Good to the last drop."

15 *Challenge* – This type of catch phrase dares the audience. It sets up the challenge in the slogan. Everyone on a diet knows you can't eat just one potato chip. That's why the Lay's Baked Potato Chips line is perfect: "Betcha can't eat just one." Here's another line that dares you to say no: "Nobody can say no to the honey nut O's in Honey Nut Cheerios." Slim Fast has challenged dieters with this line "Give us a week, we'll take off the weight." Lowe's invites its audience to take on a home project with "Let's build something together." Underneath the slogan is the idea that people want to improve their homes. They just need a little help.

16 *Combination* – These theme lines blend several types of slogans together. Notice how "Real people. Real results" from Bowflex uses *parallel construction*, *statement of purpose*, and *reason why* you would use this fitness equipment. Gerber baby food says, "Start healthy. Stay healthy." It also uses the same techniques as Bowflex: *parallel construction*, *statement of purpose*, and *reason why*. Playstation 2 offered this question: "Fun anyone?" It *rhymes* and it's a question (*interrogative*). This line, "Don't live a little, live a lotto," incorporates *imperative*, *parallel construction*, and *reason why*.[8]

> "
>
> The majority of our advertising [for Taco Bell] is all centered around one particular product, one benefit, one main idea that we want to communicate.
>
> **TEDDY BROWN, SENIOR VICE PRESIDENT, EXECUTIVE CREATIVE DIRECTOR OF THE ORANGE COUNTY OFFICE AT DRAFTFCB**[9]

Adding power to your writing

Start today to make the following suggestions a habit. They will help you strengthen your writing immediately. Your copy will sound more conversational. More relatable. And more relevant to your audience. By becoming an active listener, you're fine-tuning your writing. By becoming the consumer, you're focusing on consumer insights. By becoming an interactive consumer, you understand the draw of engagement. By becoming an online shopper, you're experiencing what your audience is when they make a purchase. By becoming an avid observer, you're collecting reference material for inspiration.

1   *Become an active listener* – To help your copy sound natural, listen to conversations wherever you are: in restaurants, coffee shops, parks, train stations, gyms, at parties, at meetings, or even in lines at store. Just listen to how people speak to each other. Notice the short phrases ("Okay, great"), idiomatic expressions ("See what I mean?"), vernacular phrases ("Gotta go"), contractions ("I'm runnin' late"), and connectors ("Yeah, but").

2   *Become the consumer* – Ask yourself what would make you buy that product? Remember to consider how you would feel and think if you were the targeted audience's age. Now, is that message you're writing appropriate for that age group? Is the *tone of voice* the best one to use?

3   *Become an interactive consumer* – What engages you? What piques your attention? What makes you participate with the brand? Is what you're developing exciting enough to capture your imagination?

4   *Become an online shopper* – Okay, you're at the website. Now what? Would a special offer prompt you to take action? Would being able to customize the product excite you? If you're working on a product website that could allow customization for, say, shoes or belts, can you help make that happen?

5   *Become an avid observer* – Pay attention to TV commercials you love. Why do you love them? What visual or verbal techniques could you borrow? Focus on radio commercials. Do the scripts sound contrived or convoluted? If so, why? What make them sound unnatural? Keep a mental note of these observations, so you'll refer to them when you're writing for any medium.

6   *Become a collector* – Save great examples of promotional messages wherever you find them. Use your cell phone to snap a photo. Print out creative work from agency websites. Keep great brochures you may find or direct mail pieces you receive. Yes, there are some great direct mail examples.

Copywriting insights and tips

1   Craig Miller, creative director at Crispin, Porter + Bogusky:
   - We used to know what it was going to be: TV, radio, and so on, now I have no idea what it's going to be. It's back to the core idea. For all media we think in press releases. We write press releases for the big idea. What's the press going to write about?
   - Let the idea drive the media, not the media drive the idea. It's purifying. What are you trying to say? What can this campaign do to get attention?

Rather than what kind of ad can I do for Domino's? What can I do to make this press worthy?

- I do more idea generation in four years than in the 10 years before that.[10]

2 Teddy Brown, senior vice president, executive creative director of the Orange County office at Draftfcb, discussing the "Why Pay More" campaign:

- When you're dealing with humor, it definitely needs to be smart humor. You don't want it to be whacky or goofy or really radical or different just for the sake of being different.

- Our briefs from our *point of view*, from any creative's *point of view*, are all trying to drive towards that single most important thing: that main message.

- For the most part, there is a habit, or perception, or a belief that we're trying to change or reinforce. Then, we have our main message. And then, we have our consumer take away: 'What is it that we want the consumer to like?'

- The way we break our briefs down is to get to quite simply: (1) What the consumer currently thinks, (2) what our message is going in, and (3) what will the consumer think as a result of this advertising.[11]

3 Drummond Berman, copywriter/creative director at Euro RSCG.

a Be absolutely ruthless because no one other than you can be as ruthless as you could be on your own stuff.

b Too many people sit there and write a bunch of lines and the best of those is the one that they'll put forward. It's not about quantity; it's about quality.

c Having a clear vision of what it is that you are heading for, and know it when you see it and dismiss it when you don't see it, is really, really important. Just think from the outset about what it is that you're writing because writing is not an accident.

d The best headlines are based on an idea rather than just moving words around until they sound cool.

e Absolutely avoid borrowed interest at all costs. And what I mean by that is bringing in other things that have got nothing to do with what you're talking about because you can't think of interesting ways to talk about it. (Ex: If you're talking about a breakfast cereal, stay in the world of breakfast cereal. Don't start comparing it to another world. Because you end up just blurring the whole thing.)

f Make what you've got interesting. Make what you've got make sense. Make what you've got appealing. As a writer, it's important that you really understand that when you have an ability to spin something in a way that makes what you actually have in front of you sound interesting to other people, it's probably one of your best lines.[12]

Making your copy sticky

By creating messages that target the audience with headlines that have stopping power, copy that's relevant to the reader, super sticky slogans, and media-specific language, you'll develop unforgettable campaigns.

Review the writing tips in each chapter and apply them when you write. Analyze every advertising message you read. Dissect each one to see why they work and why they don't. Be sure to collect all kinds of print materials with great copy, so you always have examples you can refer to. The best way to improve your writing is to read great writing. Lastly, and most importantly, become an avid reader who's always looking for inspiration.

Creative writing exercises

Exercise 1: continuing an existing campaign message

Part 1 Choose a campaign that you relate to. Look for a print campaign with strong headlines.

Part 2 Create two more headlines using the same creative approach. For example, if all the existing ads ask a question, your next two headlines must do the same. If the headlines use parallel construction, yours must too. If the campaign uses humor, your ads must also be funny.

Part 3 What other out-of-home or print media could work to spin out this campaign? Would a billboard work? A poster? A direct-mail piece?

Part 4 Write an advertising message that fits into the campaign and blends with the new ads you just created.

Exercise 2: write a headline using the techniques below

1 *A blind headline* – The audience shouldn't have a clue what the ad is for until they see the logo.

2 *A news headline* – Develop a message that reflects something in the news or sounds like a news story.

3 *A stacked headline* – Create a headline that would work better if it were set one word above another.

Exercise 3: creating sticky slogans

Part 1 Using the same brand or product in Exercise 1, now look through the list of slogan techniques in the section "Reviewing different kinds of headlines."

Part 2 Select two techniques and write a slogan using each one. For example, create one using *parallel construction*, another using *testimonial*, and a third using *reason why*. Try to include the name in at least one of the slogans.

Part 3 Decide which slogan is stronger. Answer why that one works better.

Notes

1   Denis Higgins, *The Art of Writing Advertising: Conversations with Masters of the Craft* (Chicago: NTC Business Books, 1965), 24.

2   *AdAge Advertising Century*, "Top 10 Slogans of the Century," 2005, www.adage.com/century/slogans (accessed August 27, 2010).

3   Margo Berman, *Street-Smart Advertising: How to Win the Battle of the Buzz* (Lanham, MD: Rowman & Littlefield, 2010), 92–93.

4   http://ihaveanidea.org/articles/2007/09/23/an-inconvenient-truth-for-copywriters-how-to-write-headlines-and-why-your-career-depends-on-it/ (accessed June 17, 2011).

5   Bruce Bendinger, *The Copy Workshop Workbook* (Chicago, IL: The Copy Workshop, 2009), 324–365.

6   Matt Ziselman, personal communication, January 30, 2009.

7   Michael Newman, *Creative Leaps: 10 Lessons in Effective Advertising Inspired at Saatchi & Saatchi* (Singapore: John Wiley & Sons, 2003), 232.

8   Berman, *Street-Smart Advertising*, 84–87.

9   Teddy Brown, personal communication, October 26, 2009.

10 Craig Miller, presentation, August 4, 2010.

11 Teddy Brown, personal communication, October 26, 2009.

12 Drummond Berman, personal communication, April 8, 2009.

THE WRITTEN WORD
Print

The Copywriter's Toolkit: The Complete Guide to Strategic Advertising Copy, First Edition. Margo Berman.
© 2012 Margo Berman. Published 2012 by Blackwell Publishing Ltd.

Writing for print can be more exciting than you realize. Especially with the addition of scent and sound, 3-D and holograms, pop-ups and more. In this section, you'll be shown why your message must be just as dynamic today as the special effects. You'll be reminded to always remember the reader. You'll think of your audience not as a statistic, but as real people. You'll realize that great copy appeals to their needs and desires. You'll review the writing techniques in chapters 3 and 4, apply the strategies in chapter 2, and learn about *mandatories*, *eyebrows*, basic copy format, and categories of effective messages.

You'll find out how to construct your copy by a careful consideration of *strategy*, an analysis of *audience*, a clarification of *benefits*, a determination of *tone of voice*, an assessment of *relevance*, a reflection of *concept*, and a presentation of *message*.

You'll also examine examples of exciting print ads, like Ugly Mug Coffee, Charles Schwab, and ASICS campaigns, among others, and hear from creative talents who developed them. What's more, you'll delve into the successful use of wit and humor in print ads. Finally, you'll find some helpful writing tips from award-winning copywriters. You'll have a print checklist at the end of the chapter that will help you before you begin the exercises. Now, let's read more about the world of print advertising.

Writing for the printed page

Print advertising, contrary to popular belief, isn't dead. There are still opportunities to develop exciting messages for a wide range of magazines as well as newspapers, financial and business-to-business publications. In fact, with scent and sound chips, pop-up designs, 3-D and holographic images, plus other special effects, print ads can practically come to life. Even without any additional creative, executional techniques, print ads on their own can still deliver powerful messages.

Writing for the printed page is different from writing for broadcast, out-of-home, or the Internet. First, it's not a short-lived message because the actual page can be saved and read again, in hard copy. Some ads have longer shelf life because they are in consumer magazines and business journals that subscribers often save around the house or office to refer to later.

In addition, the printed word delivers a message to the audience in a wide range of vehicles or formats: from ads, brochures, postcards, table tents, posters and flyers. Furthermore, the copy length varies from abridged copy in catalogue writing and coupons to longer, multiple-page collateral materials like annual reports and newsletters. Each vehicle demands a special, uniquely suitable approach. Persuasive body copy, regardless of length, will drive a home a point as long as the main message, or headline, stopped consumers and made them take a moment to read it.

As with all media, you need to understand the consumers' frame of mind. Sheena Brady, creative director/copywriter at Wieden+Kennedy, said you must "put yourself in your audience's place." What are they looking for? Do they want to be entertained as in interactive media and TV? Do they want to be surprised as in ambient messages? Do they want to be educated as in newspapers and financial publications? She went on to say:

> *If I'm reading a business journal, I'm probably looking at that medium for information.*
> *So you're probably not going to do an ad that's just sheer entertainment value. So I think*
> *it really helps to know your medium and tailor that messaging to it.*

It's critical to understand your audience's expectations in different media. That will help you create a medium and target an appropriate message. She added that although you need to tailor the brand attributes, that is, those particular qualities that make a car a car or a shoe a shoe, "the idea of a one-on-one communication with someone, that doesn't change."[2]

Formulating one focused message

Whatever your print vehicle, it's important to focus on one main message. Don't confuse readers with endless benefits and product features. Zoom in on the one take-away you want them to get and stay with it. Kevin Moriarty, vice president and creative director at Leo Burnett, offered a physical example of this point he learned at a presentation. The presenter had three circular objects in his hand, maybe baseballs or apples. What the objects were isn't important. What they represented was. He explained:

> He tossed one to this student and he caught it. And he tossed all three at the same time and he dropped all three of them. And his point was if you put one message in there, chances are people will remember it. If you put three in, they may not remember any one of the three.[3]

The idea is to simplify your message to the audience, so they can absorb it. Stay focused on one singular idea. Even ads without text, or "no copy ads," not even a headline, can make a clear statement. They can still showcase a writer's critical thinking, because, as Moriarty explained:

> An ad can have no words in it and still be a reflection on a great writer because he or she was interested in the ad communicating. So it didn't necessarily require words, it required communication.[4]

Writing takes thinking. It's not just about throwing ideas out in a brainstorming session. It's about throwing relevant concepts around. The critical point here when looking for a strong concept with legs is relevance, not just bold creativity. Drummond Berman, copywriter/creative director at Euro RSCG, clarified that thought this way:

> There are too many writers, I think, who sit down and think, "If I write 100 headlines, three of them must be great." That is just not the way to write. You have to have a clear vision before you even put pen to paper, or finger to keyboard, or whatever you want to call it. Having a clear vision of what it is that you are heading for, and know it when you see it and dismiss it when you don't see it, is really, really important. Just think from the outset about what it is that you're writing because writing is not an accident.[5]

New writers often get impatient: They want to have a great idea immediately. But, they eventually learn that some headlines take hours of tweaking. Several seasoned copywriters suggested that all writers should be very hard on themselves. They should be demanding and self-critical. Rather than being in love with every idea they have, copywriters should try to become more objective. Let concepts sit for a few days. Then, if they're still excited about them, the ideas are worthy of consideration. Berman said, "Be absolutely ruthless because no one other than you can be as ruthless as you could be on your own stuff."[6]

Remembering the reader

Writers still need to be self-critical even if the number of people reading ad copy may be smaller than anyone cares to admit. However, the quality of anyone's writing is not contingent upon the size of the audience. Vinny Warren, founder and creative director of

The Escape Pod, confessed that he hardly reads all the print copy and he's in the industry. He acknowledged the decline of the newspaper audience and the low number of print ad readers, explaining how readership can impact the copywriter's process. A key point was "presuming interest is a big mistake."[7] Charlie Hopper, creative director and copywriter at Young & Laramore, concurred:

> *There's already so much writing in the world, nobody is actively interested in reading what YOU have to write, especially if it's on behalf of somebody who's trying to sell them something.*[8]

Hopper continued to say, "Everything is [read] in context. That's the key to the writing anyway. I hate long copy. Nobody wants to read."[9]

Warren considered himself one of a small number of people still reading newspapers today. Of those few people how many actually spend time reading copy at all? If they are reading, what will they absorb and how far into the ad will they read? Warren posed and answered the following question, which gives writers another way to think about how to entice an audience:

> *How do you get people to read what they need to read to get your message? That's the way I always look at it. That means keeping it down to a minimum and making the writing the necessary part of the ad. In other words, the ad isn't complete until you read the copy.*[10]

Keep in mind the audience who bothers to read the copy should be rewarded with clear, concise, persuasive, and engaging copy. You have a living, breathing person who will take the time to read your work. Write with the readers in mind, remembering that even though you may never meet them, you are still appreciative of their time. Think about that every time you write. Reward readers for reading by bringing copy to closure with techniques discussed in chapter 3, like:

- *ABA* – reinforcing the headline in the last line of copy.
- *Weave* – continuing the headline idea throughout the body copy.
- *Buttons* – creating an imaginative closing line, unrelated to the headline.

In addition to writing techniques, you must think about the best way to deliver the message. What's important to your audience? What specific needs do they have? What problem(s) are they trying to solve? How does your product/service/brand help them? Here is a copy checklist to review as you're weaving the copy.

CHECKLIST 5.1 Copy checklist

1   Reinforce the *benefits*. Answer, "Why buy?" Show the consumer the reason to make the purchase. Clearly state what the consumer's going to get from the product/brand. For example: Tide To Go gets stains out when you're out and about.

2   Showcase the *product features*. Explain how the product works, like Apple's product (iPod, iPhone, iPad, etc.) *product-demonstration* messages.

3   Speak in an appropriate *tone of voice*. If you're reaching out to families looking for a fun vacation look at how Disney vacations always sound like exciting adventures.

4   Choose the most effective *point of view*. Should the *brand* be bragging about its features, design awards, or customer service rewards? Should consumers offer raving *testimonials* about their product/brand experiences? Should people's *conscience* warn them of avoidable problems the brand can prevent?

5   Look at the audience. How do they live their lives (psychographics)? Does it enhance their lifestyle? What do they *value*? Does the brand share any *core values* with the audience? Which *decision maker* ("decider") are you targeting? (See chapter 1.) You'd speak differently to the end-user than you would to the *initiator*. To refresh your memory, let's review this list once more.

   a   *Initiator*: suggests buying or trying the product or service.

   b   *Influencer*: encourages or dissuades the final shopper.

   c   *Decider*: makes the final purchasing decisions.

   d   *Purchaser*: buys the item.

   e   *User*: uses the item or service.[11]

6   Consider audience *needs*. What are they looking for? Status? Comfort? Clear skin? Weight loss? Are they *Inner-Directed* (make purchases to please themselves, not to dazzle others)? Are they *Outer-Directed* (seek to establish status and gain acceptance)? Or are they *Needs-Driven* (purchase only necessities at this time)?

7   Portray the *brand's personality.* Is it lively like T.G.I. Friday's restaurant chain? Convenient like an urgent-care center? Sophisticated like a champagne bar?

8   Integrate the *brand's heritage* or *history*. Is there a Colonel as in the KFC story, a Jack Perdue in Perdue Chickens, or an Orville Redenbacher as in Orville Redenbacher Popcorn? Has it been around for more than 150 years like Macy's, boasting the largest store in the world?

9   Drive home the message. Make sure it's *relevant* to your audience. Keep it clear, simple, and instantly digestible. If anyone can't read it and "get it," change it.

10 Show what makes the brand *unique*. What separates it from its competitors? Faster service? Newer technology? Better integration between mobile and nonmobile devices?

11 Decide which one of *50 strategies* you want to use. Start by selecting from the six main categories (see chapter 2):

   a   *Consumer-Focused* – show benefits.

   b   *Product-Focused* – emphasize product features.

   c   *Savings as the Star* – focus on price.

   d   *Emotional Approach* – appeal to consumers' emotions.

   e   *Storytelling* – present product in a story.

   f   *Audience Engagement* – encourage consumer participation.

12 Think about the *specific publication(s)* or *location* where the ad or poster will appear. Does anything need to be tweaked for a better fit? For example, the sexy Axe deodorant ads can be even spicier in a magazine like *Maxim*. Would you want to change it for a train station wall or a store window?

13 Check that your overall direction follows the *creative brief* so your concept, strategy, message, and tone are all *on-strategy* and in line with the key marketing objective.

There are times when you'll have an attentive, eager reader, for example when you create annual reports, trade show flyers, newsletters, and manufacturers' literature. You may think these are more informative or promotional rather than advertising materials. Remember, each printed piece is still communicating a message, whether it's from the company to the consumer or from one business to another (called *B-2-B* or business-to-business marketing). With annual reports, you need to think about what investors are looking to learn. In this case, writers should do the following:

- Highlight company's success and growth.
- Showcase new products.
- Feature awards and recognitions.
- Consider what you would want to hear as an investor.

If you're writing a newsletter, know if it's an internal (to employees) or external (to consumer and/or other businesses).

Discovering basic copy format

All copy needs structure, meaning a format and a *template* or *shell* to follow. This helps you to organize your thinking and prioritize the copy points and *mandatories* (must-have information). The shell is simple. It allows space for the *headline, subhead,* and *body copy* separated by *additional subheads, logo,* and *slogan.* If your ad uses an *eyebrow,* it would be listed before the headline. The *eyebrow* is a line of copy that targets a specific audience like this: "Eyeglass wearers," "Headache Sufferers," or "Cookie Lovers." It singles out that particular individual. Then it delivers the headline. The signature or "*sig*" normally appears outside the body copy, near the logo. It includes the product, company, service, or store's mandatory information: phone, e-mail, website, location, hours, and so on.

Here are the basic print templates. They can be used for flyers, annual reports, manufacturers' literature, and even web copy.

 TEMPLATES 5.2   Basic print ad copy format

Eyebrow: (if needed)

Headline:

Subhead:

Body copy:

Logo:

Slogan:

Sig:

TEMPLATES 5.3 Basic brochure copy format

Headline:

Subhead: (Identify location, for ex: Inside Left Panel)

Body copy:

Subhead: (Identify location, for ex: Inside Right Panel or Inside Spread if it fits across two pages)

Body copy:

Subhead: (Identify location, e.g., Back Cover)

Body copy:

Logo:

Slogan:

Sig: (Address, phone, hours, website address, etc.)

If you're working at an ad agency, adopt the firm's format immediately. Then, use it for every assignment. Using a consistent copy format has several benefits. It helps do the following:

- Organize your copy.
- Prioritize copy points by sections.
- Facilitate typesetting.
- Focus your writing and readers' attention.

Whether you're writing a small amount of copy for a table tent, sign, small flyer, or print ad, get right to the point. Think in bites of text: tiny messages or packets of information. Edit out all unessential copy. Usually, in advertising messages less is more. However, there are some products or services that require lengthy copy. Even then, just include the most crucial information. Highlight the *main benefit* and *key message*. The point is, get to the point. But first, get their attention with a *powerful headline*.

Focusing on strategy, audience, benefits, tone of voice, message, and relevance

Before you start brainstorming for a message, implement the strategic thinking in chapters 1 and 2. This will fine-tune your critical thinking. Next, review the 50 strategies, such as abundance, continuing story, testimonial,

If it doesn't speak volumes without you having to explain it to anyone, then it isn't good enough. **DRUMMOND BERMAN, COPYWRITER/ CREATIVE DIRECTOR, EURO RSCG**[12]

and shock. Consider the various audience categories (VALS), such as *Achievers*, *Makers*, *Experiencers*, and *Innovators*. Picture your audience as real people, not a list of statistics. Think about how to make your message relevant to this particular *primary*, and possibly *secondary*, *audience*. Analyze consumer insights. Determine the appropriate *tone of voice*. Should it be emotional: casual, authoritative, flirty, or concerned? Or should it be rational: informative, educational, authoritative, or instructional? Decide which benefit(s) will be featured. Focus on the unique traits that differentiate the product (USP). Choose how you want the audience to think about the brand (positioning in the mind of the consumer). Imagine your message at different *touchpoints*. Be sure you're writing to the correct senses (sight, hearing, scent, touch) for that medium. If you have a *creative brief*, refer to it and let it guide you.

Ask yourself what kind of *headline* you could use: results, comparison, how-to, teaser, and so on. If you need to create a *slogan*, what type would be *sticky* and *relevant*: *name*, *challenge*, *reason why*, *vernacular*, and so on? Question whether you should create a unique word like Comcastic for Comcast or "Hungerectomy" for a Snickers campaign or "Imagineering" for The Walt Disney Company research and development department. This is an example of a word created, or a *portmanteau*, by joining two words: imagination and engineering.

Whenever you can create something that's unique and easy-to-remember, you've added stickiness to your message. The whole point of any advertising campaign is to first get the consumers' attention so the message can persuade them to take action.

Recognizing categories of effective messages

What makes a headline practically jump off the page and strike up a conversation? How do some of them single you out when you're the consumer? Why do some seem like a personalized, individual message? How do they reach out and tap you on the arm like a good friend about to confide a secret?

Headlines work for different reasons. Their message and *tone of voice* sound credible. They also sound authentic. The humor is unforced. The language reflects the culture. The message is relevant. When creating headlines, check to see if your message resonates with believability. Here's a short list of reasons why headlines work. They've been grouped into different categories for easier reference.

1 *Credible*
   a Believable
   b Truthful
   c Honest
   d Sincere
   e Trustworthy
2 *Authentic*
   a Genuine
   b True-to-life (Realistic)
3 *Relevant*
   a Informative
   b Comparative
   c Demonstrative

4   *Natural*
   a   Unforced humor
   b   Vernacular speech
   c   Casual
5   *Emotional*
   a   Concerned
   b   Urgent
   c   Serious
   d   Sympathetic
   e   Empathetic
   f   Compassionate
   g   Inspiring
   h   Motivating
6   *Personal*
   a   Friendly
   b   Intimate
   c   Seductive
   d   Secretive

Exploring playful, humorous, empathetic print ads

One campaign that speaks to the audience in a humorous, "we-know-how-you-feel" way is for Ugly Mug Coffee. Created by Young & Laramore, both the ads and the package copy (in chapter 11) talk to the consumer in a light-hearted, humorous *tone of voice*.

The headline reads, "The snooze button is a pusher" (Figure 5.1). Instantly you're drawn into the fun of the ad. The play on words is irresistible and forces you to read on.

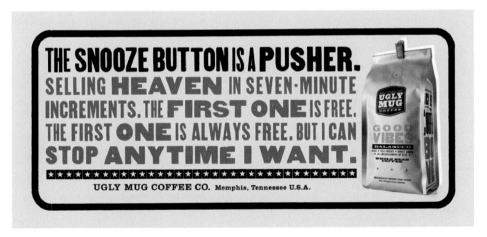

FIGURE 5.1 This print ad was created by Young & Laramore for Ugly Mug Coffee. Image courtesy of Young & Laramore.

FIGURE 5.2 This print ad was created by Young & Laramore for Ugly Mug Coffee. Image courtesy of Young & Laramore.

The copy addresses a universal truth: We all hate to wake up when the alarm sounds. The copy describes the craving we all have for the last few blissful moments of sleep and the subsequent addiction to the sleep button. The last line reiterates all addicts' dubious claims that they can quit whenever they choose. What makes it funny is that with our sleep-button addiction, we really can.

> *Selling heaven in seven-minute increments. The first one is free. The first one is always free. But I can stop any time I want.*

The second states, "You can't get a restraining order for the sun" (Figure 5.2). Again it refers to our longing for more precious sleep. We'd like the night to continue holding back the dawn so we can get more rest. But, we just can't stop the light from bursting through in its unruly, intrusive, lawless manner. The copy, using personification by humanizing the sun, explains:

> *It comes and goes as it pleases. A gaseous, unwelcome peeping Tom peeking in between the blinds. The sun is above the law.*

As mentioned earlier, you want to keep the reader reading. Hopper showed how the writer's thought process worked with an interesting comparison:

> *So, the strategy is how you're going to keep them on the line. It's like dating. It's like wherever it is that you would meet someone – the bar is a cliché – keeping them interested long enough for them to understand that there's something there. You're doing the same thing with the ads. You're trying to keep them from moving on before they get what's good about you.*[13]

What kind of creative thinkers developed the Ugly Mug Coffee campaign? Hopper described how this actual creative team worked. The writer was naturally funny and comfortable expressing his humor.

> *In this particular campaign, the writer is one of the funniest guys you've ever met. He's funny in the way that he isn't always trying to be funny. He's so confident; he's not one of these joke-a-minute types of guys. He actually has a lot of comedy credentials as it were. But, he is absolutely in love with design and all its forms and is one of the leaders of our*

digital design units. The other leader works on this campaign so the art director is also involved in what it says. So when you get into an agency, you get this blurring of the lines.[14]

He went on and explained that the campaign was a true representation of teamwork, blurring and possibly eliminating the lines between writing and designing. They both worked together on Ugly Mug Coffee, adding, "The designer having very strong opinions about the writing and the writer having very strong opinions about the design."[15]

Most strong creative teams work as one collaborative idea factory. The titles of copywriter and art director become insignificant. Each one contributes to the strategic thinking and conceptual solutions. When the partnership works, unforgettable and brilliant campaigns are the result.

Studying more ads that empathize with the target

One strikingly effective example of creative work is the Charles Schwab "Talk to Chuck" campaign. The original idea is attributed to Israel Garber, the person who led the pitch at Euro RSCG. Since then, the creative director team of Drummond Berman and Simon Nickson has imaginatively spun out the concept. What makes this campaign so memorable is its believability. The *tone of voice* is casual and relaxed, like a friend chatting, and the message is honest. It's the way investors feel about how they're often underappreciated by the brokerage houses. It spoke to the everyday investor. According to Berman, the copywriter on the account, the client was "looking for something that could differentiate them from the rest of the investment category."[17] The team delved into the background of the company. They discovered that Chuck's name kept coming up. Berman explained everyone they spoke to at Charles Schwab was saying, "Chuck did this and Chuck did that." Everyone called the head of this major investment firm by his first name, as if they all knew him personally. Berman traced the campaign back to this:

> *It just felt like a really good way to lower the barriers and make people feel that there was an approachable company, or an approachable person, or a name in this business, and that was the beginning of it. "Talk to Chuck."*[18]

The word "approachable" epitomizes the tone of the entire campaign. People who see the campaign think of the firm as "Chuck," a real person they can relate to, unlike the other stuffy investment houses. The team developed the campaign by deciding what they *didn't* want to do. They didn't want to sound like every other financial institution. They wanted to sound friendly and easy to talk to. They didn't want to show the typical visual clichés of the wealthy: built-in, wood-paneled libraries, oversized Adirondack chairs, Martinis and cocktail parties. Simon Nickson, the art director on the campaign, expounded how they developed it:

*The way that we've always talked about how we came up with the idea of the "Talk to Chuck" campaign itself was that we explained that it was as much about what we **didn't** want to do as it was about what we **did** want to do.*

We didn't want to produce another financial advertising campaign. We didn't

> People are going to critique your work and they're not going to care how much time you spent working on it, or how much sleep you lost worrying about it. **MATT ZISELMAN, CREATIVE DIRECTOR, SAPIENTNITRO**[16]

want to put out a bunch of fake images of people enjoying their retirement, being able to afford a house on the beach, and a yacht, a jet ski, and all that kind of stuff. We didn't want to produce a campaign that used financial jargon. We didn't want to produce a campaign that went over people's heads.[19]

What this campaign did was break through the financial clutter and speak to real people in a real way. The messages were presented in matter-of-fact language for down-to-earth people. The result was advertising that was *relevant* and *resonated* with authenticity, which made it easy to *remember*. It encapsulates "The Three Rs" set in italics and discussed again, along with this campaign, in chapter 7.

Let's look at a few print ads now to understand how powerful these to-the-point headlines are. The first ad (Figure 5.3) asks "Nickeled and Dimed?" as the headline, quickly answered by the subhead "I feel like I'm being quartered." The play on words is unmistakable. Many people feel their financial institutions from banks to investment firms charge them for every little service. The retort responds in a witty way, referring both to coin change (the quarter) and being practically tortured (quartered) financially. Put them together and you've wrapped up how people were treated: inconsequentially like small change and financially exploited with excessive fees. The body copy reinforces the message, continuing in the same honest *tone of voice*. Notice the use of the word "transparent" to emphasize the point.

> *Copy:* "We prefer to focus our energy on making your portfolio bigger, not smaller. At Schwab, there were no account service fees, no hidden fees, and you can make online equity trade for as little as $9.95.
>
> In fact, our pricing is completely simple, transparent and clearly laid out – so you can always know how much, when, and why."

The second ad (Figure 5.4) again underlines how insignificant many day-to-day investors felt with their current brokers. Their dry cleaners treated them better. Look at how the headline and subhead made this point:

> *Headline:* "At My Dry Cleaners, I'm 'Sir.'"
>
> *Subhead:* "At my brokerage, I'm 'Who?'"

The body copy explains the difference in individualized attention they'll receive at Charles Schwab.

> *Copy:* "Schwab clients don't have to 'meet certain criteria' to be treated with respect. You also don't have to 'qualify' to get our best research; you just get it. At Schwab, all our clients get access to our industry-recognized Schwab Equity Ratings,® our analysis-rich quarterly reports, third-party research, and our meticulously screened list of no-load, no-transaction-fee mutual funds. The way we see it, you're an investor. And at Schwab, that's all that matters."

The last two lines say everything. Every Schwab client is an investor, regardless of the portfolio size. Just having a Schwab account ensures equal attention and information access.

Most importantly the entire "Talk to Chuck" campaign has a relaxed tone and easy-to-understand language. No financial lingo or investment babble, just plain, yet often witty, speech.

The slogan "Talk to Chuck" is as much an invitation to start a conversation with Chuck, as it is a *call to action*. Thus, there's no reason to ask the audience to take action. The slogan takes care of that.

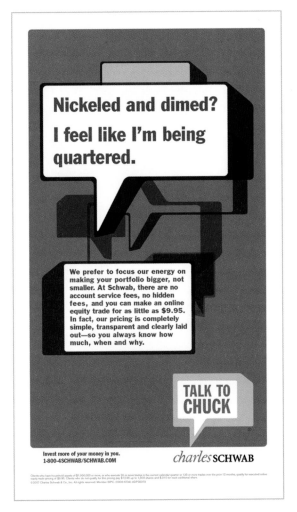

FIGURE 5.3 This "Talk to Chuck" print ad was created by Euro RSCG for Charles Schwab. Image courtesy of Euro RSCG.

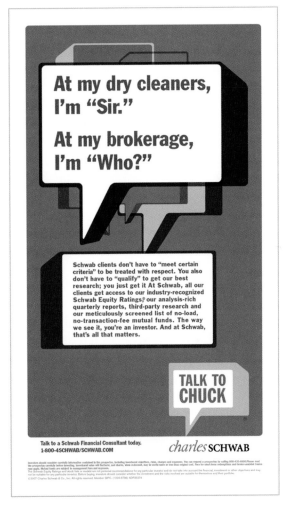

FIGURE 5.4 This "Talk to Chuck" print ad was created by Euro RSCG for Charles Schwab. Image courtesy of Euro RSCG.

Identifying ads with an insider's understanding

One campaign that talks directly to the audience as an athletically driven insider is ASICS. It uses clever play on words that shows it understands how consumers who take their sports endeavors seriously demand more from themselves to reach their athletic goals. Just look at the headlines in these three no-copy ads. The messages are so strong no explanatory copy is needed. The first two ads were for running. The third one was for team sports.

1   "Happiness Is Pushing Your Limits and Then Watching Them Back Down" (Figure 5.5).

2   "Intensity Can Be the Quickest Path to Tranquility" (Figure 5.6).

3   "Funny How Defying Gravity Can Ground You" (Figure 5.7).

FIGURE 5.5 This "Happiness" print ad was created by Vitro for ASICS America Corporation. Image courtesy of Vitro.

FIGURE 5.6 This "Intensity" print ad was created by Vitro for ASICS America Corporation. Image courtesy of Vitro.

FIGURE 5.7 This "Defying Gravity" print ad was created by Vitro for ASICS America Corporation. Image courtesy of Vitro.

The everyday athletes who want to increase their strength and improve their personal performance push themselves in their workouts. They can easily relate to the targeted headlines because each one is speaking their language in a relevant way.

The type is set in a three-dimensional perspective toward a vanishing point. That paired with bold colors energizes the message. When asked whether the visual image preceded the verbal message, KT Thayer, creative director at Vitro, answered:

> It's hard to say which drove the other, the lines may have come first, but the bold colors and typography definitely influenced the tonality. Once we got the layout to a place we were happy with, we rewrote some of the lines to be shorter, bolder and punchier.[20]

While developing the strategy for the campaign, Thayer explained, "As a challenger brand, the top priority for ASICS is to build awareness."[21] The objective was to differentiate it from its two name brands, Nike and Adidas, giving the consumer a personal choice. He went on to discuss the slogan.

> "Sound Mind, Sound Body" is more than ASICS' tagline. It is the founding philosophy and the root of the name. Anima Sana In Corpore Sano is a Latin phrase that translates to, "a sound mind, in a sound body." This position drives every decision, innovation, and communication that comes from ASICS.[22]

The 2009 campaign demonstrated that the way to a sound body and sound mind is to be physically fit. The campaign started out showing how running helps consumers achieve mental and physical health. Later other sports were added, highlighting the same universal benefits. The campaign is based on the *Benefit* and *Honesty* strategies (#1 and #26 in chapter 2) and spoke candidly. Thayer shared these thoughts:

> *The 2009 campaign was internally called, "Running Truths" as the message had to come from a genuine, honest place that any level of runner could understand and believe. By educating or reminding runners of the full benefits of running, mental and physical, ASICS stood out and carved out an ownable space in running, with plenty of room to grow.*[23]

All of that communication was delivered through gripping headlines that reached out to the specific audience and demanded to be heard. The brand's voice demonstrated an unmistakable appreciation for its audience.

Shaping witty headlines that say it all

Sometimes, as we've already seen, the headline carries the entire message. No subhead copy is required. In the Geek Squad "Wireless Awareness" campaign, created by Crispin Porter + Bogusky, the headlines show a dry wit that engages the audience's imagination. The image is an orange Ethernet cable playfully twisted into the shape of a cause ribbon to add a little more humor. Take a moment to digest each of the headlines.

1 "It's True You Can Get Wireless Just From Talking to a Geek."
2 "If You Have Wireless, You Could Be Giving Wireless to Everyone."
3 "To You It's a Wire. To Us It's a Mission."

Using a play-on-words technique, the first two headlines talk about wireless as if it were a virus that's contagious. They make readers do a double take and then "get" the message. The first one states a simple fact in a clever way. The second one ingeniously warns Wi-Fi users that they inadvertently could be sharing their signal. The third talks about the passion geeks have for their work. Consumers having computer problems want someone passionate, not apathetic. "To You It's a Wire. To Us It's a Mission" Separates the computer aficionado from the simple end-user. That's who you want working on your system: Someone who thrives on solving challenging computer problems.

Notice how these ads address the *audience's objections* and *needs*. Why don't people call for help? Most likely, because they've been disappointed with substandard computer repairs. What do they need? The problem solved right the first time.

The Motel 6 campaign discussed later in chapter 6 had a print component as well. The no-nonsense layout with only a few lines of white type on an all-black background projected an *on-strategy* message visually and verbally (Figure 5.8). The *universal truth* here is: Why pay for amenities you don't need? The headline reads, "When You're Sleeping, We Look Just Like Those Big Fancy Hotels. Motel 6."

It makes a point relevant to many business travelers. They just need somewhere to sleep because the rest of their day is busy with meetings, conferences, exhibits, and so on. The message hits home even harder because there is nothing on the page to detract from it or distract the reader's attention. Its simplicity reflects the brand's no-frills personality.

> " Just figure out, in advance, what is the one thing you want people to walk away and remember from your ad and stick to it. **KEVIN MORIARTY, VICE PRESIDENT AND CREATIVE DIRECTOR, LEO BURNETT**[24]

When you're sleeping, we look
just like those big fancy hotels.
Motel 6

FIGURE 5.8 This "When You're Sleeping" print ad
was created by The Richards Group for Motel 6.
Image courtesy of The Richards Group and Motel 6.

Another brand with a distinctive personality is the Aflac Duck. It's funny and lovable. The headline in this ad (Figure 5.9), which was also a poster, integrates the company name: "Get the Aflacts." The subhead follows, creating more urgency: "Why you need Aflac now more than ever." Each subhead that separates the key points spins off the main idea, highlighting the benefits.

Subheads: "Aflac is different from health insurance; it's for daily living."

"Aflac is an extra measure of financial protection."

"Aflac pays you cash benefits to use as you see fit."

"Aflac benefits help with unexpected expenses."

"Aflac belongs to you, not your company."

The slogan offers another benefit of protection: "We've got you under our wing."

Take a close look at the body copy. It's not real copy. It's *Greeked in*. Artists use *Greek* type (English letters arranged in nonwords like "lorem ipsum dolor" to fill space, or copy blocks. It's not designed to be read. It's just to be used for layout purposes.

Another series of print ads with powerful headlines is the Republic Airways campaign, created by Young & Laramore. The main message is this is no ordinary job. If you want the expected, you don't want to work at Republic Airways. The headlines single out the adventurers, those people who are part of the *Experiential*, the *I-am-Me*, and *Experiencer* audience groups. They seize opportunities and enjoy life in their own unique way.

Look at the headlines and subheads in the following ads (Figure 5.10, Figure 5.11, Figure 5.12). The subhead is the same for all three: "Choose a career less ordinary." The only copy

FIGURE 5.9 This print ad was created by the Kaplan Thaler Group for Aflac. Image courtesy of the Kaplan Thaler Group.

FIGURE 5.10 This print ad was created by Young & Laramore for Republic Airways. Image courtesy of Young & Laramore.

FIGURE 5.11 This print ad was created by Young & Laramore for Republic Airways. Image courtesy of Young & Laramore.

ruts can't form at
30,000 feet.

choose a career less ordinary.
now recruiting flight attendants at rjet.com

REPUBLIC AIRWAYS

trusted by six major airlines.

FIGURE 5.12 This print ad was created by Young & Laramore for Republic Airways. Image courtesy of Young & Laramore.

is a call-to-action line: "Now recruiting flight attendants at rjet.com." Notice how the visuals complement the headline and complete the message.

Headline #1: "Creatures of Habit Need Not Apply."

Visual: Old-fashioned green clock, wall of time cards in their green, metal holders, and three stacked, black in-baskets.

Headline #2: "100 Pages Per Minute vs. 500 Miles Per Hour."

Visual: Hands of office worker making copies at the copy machine.

Headline #3: "Ruts Can't Form at 30,000 Feet."

Visual: Bay of beige, metal file cabinets with woman retrieving or replacing files.

Each ad depicts the mundane office environment and boring, repetitive tasks workers face every day. The images reinforce office life as usual. However, if you're the kind of person who detests the ordinary, you've found a company with a corporate culture to match your lifestyle.

Noticing ads that don't look like ads

Some campaigns don't resemble advertising. Instead they can look like a publicity campaign or even press releases or a series of internal memos. In the "Indiana Fever" campaign for the Women's National Basketball Association (WNBA), Young & Laramore (Y&L) wanted to create a campaign that looked like informal communication. Charlie Hopper, Y&L creative director and copywriter, explained that the print campaign included strategic, yet humorous, bus sides. The messages were created not as an extension of or sister to the men's basketball team, but for an entirely new women's team that appealed to its own audience: women. He continued to say:

The print campaign on that was an attempt to jump right into the middle of making it seem like there was daily communications needed between the fans and the head office. So, we had this head office stationery look that had humorous statements, everything from announcements of upcoming games to season tickets. We were able to get it all within this very tongue-in-cheek sort of writing to make it seem that there was already a huge fan base. They were to look like daily communications that couldn't be too formal or pretty.

The newspaper ads, which were created like press announcements on letterheads, were supposed to look as if they were quickly created in and released from a press office. They wanted to give the impression that the team, the Indiana Fever, was having a tough time keeping up with the fans and sending out announcements. Some offered up-to-date info and others looked as if they had been torn from a typewriter or taken out of a printer. Their news-of-the-day look had two objectives according to Hopper:

1   *Some of these were general [announcements].*
2   *Some of these are trying to get ticket and sales.*
3   *And some are trying to get you to games.*

Hopper explained the way these were written like this:

You have to write it as if you were the press secretary for the Fever, typing this straight-faced announcement, but then of course, incorporating the humor that actually makes it the voice of the campaign.

If you examine the first ad, "Note to WNBA Fans" (Figure 5.13), the ad looks like a personal note to the fans. The copy continues in the same casual *tone of voice*:

FIGURE 5.13 This press release look-alike print ad was created by Young & Laramore for WNBA. Image courtesy of Young & Laramore.

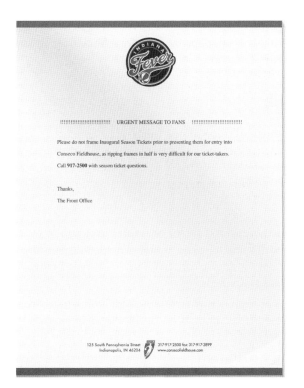

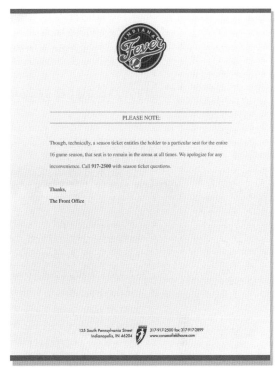

FIGURE 5.14 This press release look-alike print ad was created by Young & Laramore for WNBA. Image courtesy of Young & Laramore.

FIGURE 5.15 This press release look-alike print ad was created by Young & Laramore for WNBA. Image courtesy of Young & Laramore.

Copy: "Contrary to rumor, each Season Ticket is not encoded with a special 'flavor seal' in flavors ranging from raspberry to mango. Please do not present wet tickets to our ushers. For accurate season ticket information, call 917-2500. Thanks, The Front Office."

Notice how natural the humor is and how the closing line is like a signature from the press secretary.

Following with the same theme, the second ad, "Urgent Message to Fans" (Figure 5.14), is also written as if typed on a typewriter and the copy shows a dry, unforced wit. It has the same easy closing line of thanks.

Copy: "Please do not frame Inaugural Season Tickets prior to presenting them for entry into Conseco Fieldhouse, as ripping frames in half is very difficult for our ticket-takers. Call 917-2500 with season ticket questions. Thanks, The Front Office."

The third ad, "Please Note" (Figure 5.15), looks like a press release or even an office memo. The read-it-if-you-want-to approach piques the curiosity of any WNBA Indian Fever fan. It doesn't force the audience to read it. It simply notifies them of an "important" announcement.

Copy: "Though, technically, a season ticket entitles the holder to a particular seat for the entire 16 game season, that seat is to remain in the arena at all times. We apologize for any inconvenience. Call 917-2500 with season ticket questions. Thanks, The Front Office."

Once more, the subtle humor is heard when ticket holders who normally have an assigned seat should leave the seat in the stadium, implying that they shouldn't go home with them as a souvenir. That's very funny.

Copywriting: a closer look

In looking at all these examples, although the campaigns differ, they all have several components in common.

Print writing tips

1   "I find the people that struggle in this business are the ones that can't let go of an idea and move on and come up with something else. If they're not letting go of the idea, what's happening is they're not coming up with new ideas" – Sheena Brady, creative director/copywriter, Wieden+Kennedy.[25]

2   "If these are tips to young writers or beginner writers, with print, I think more so maybe than even TV – well, I wouldn't say more so, but again – try to be simple-minded. People are turning the pages of a magazine and – in every magazine there are ads for pharmaceuticals, and shampoos, and this and that, and whatever your product is – you want to stop them with something that even with that two seconds they glance at it, they take it away. A lot of times we give print assignments to some of the younger creative teams. Just as I did when I was their age, you're hoping to win this year's Gold Lions at Cannes with every ad you do. So, you break the bank trying to do the greatest print ad of all times. Very often, it becomes a complicated mess. There's nothing wrong if you're trying to sell a Keebler cracker, for instance, which is part of **Kellogg's®**, with just having a big picture of a cracker and a line

USEFUL INFO 5.4 Common qualities in featured campaigns

Notice how each one does the following:

1   Delivers an *on-target* and *on-strategy concept*.

2   Shows a deep understanding of the *audience's lifestyle*, *needs*, and *values*.

3   Presents a particularly *relevant* and *relatable message*.

4   Shows a *sense of humor*.

5   Surprises the reader with an *unexpected concept*.

6   Entertains the audience with a *clever turn of phrase*.

7   *Thanks the reader* for having "stopped by."

8   *Fulfills* a need, *solves* a problem, *answers* an objection, or *presents* a challenge.

that communicates why you should want them. Sometimes I think they think, 'Oh, that's too easy.' But there's a reason it's too easy. Well, because it's so simple. But, that makes for a much better ad quite often, not always.

But just to be simple visually and copy wise, too. If possible, try to tell the story with just a headline and no body copy. You may have to have body copy, but if possible, try to do it without it" – Kevin Moriarty, vice president and creative director, Leo Burnett.[26]

3   "Writing for print media should typically be more formal, since readers tend to peruse the entire article or spread more thoroughly. One benefit to this is that including sidebars of information, like the resources in these pieces, are more likely to be taken in by the reader" – Deltina Hay, author of *A Survival Guide to Social Media and Web 2.0 Optimization.*[27]

4   "As a writer you have to be able to convey ideas that are sometimes difficult. You have to be able to write about things that are visual. How do you explain that? How do you make people feel something for an idea that they've never seen? Some clients are incredibly visual and can grasp things and some clients aren't. Just like some people are and some people aren't. And so, you have to figure out how to convey your idea in a way that makes it understandable to everybody" – Sara Rose, former senior copywriter, Goodby, Silverstein & Partners.[28]

5   "Too many people sit there and write a bunch of lines and it doesn't make, you know, the best of those is the one that they'll put forward. It's not about quantity; it's about quality. Simon and I would much rather agonize for three hours on one line than write 20 lines and just pick the best one" – Drummond Berman, copywriter/creative director, Euro RSCG.[29]

6   "Obviously, with print, if they're reading at all, and that's a big if, then keep it short, keep it flowing, and just don't imagine that they're reading it for fun, because they're not" – Vinny Warren, founder and creative director, The Escape Pod.[30]

7   "Have a strategy. You even have a strategy just for getting through your day. You can't just dutifully represent your client. You have to somehow get people engaged in it. That's why we have to think about the strategy. You can't just start talking about Stanley Steemer being this great carpet cleaner. You have to think about what's a way to get people interested in this if they haven't thought about it already. 'Oh, you're walking on crap and tracking it in your house. You don't see it, so you don't really think about it being there. But, it's there.' Boom! You have a Stanley Steemer strategy. Then, everything will fall off of that. That comes from knowing you have to have a way in" – Charlie Hopper, creative director and copywriter, Young & Laramore.[31]

8   "Ride the bus, go to the supermarket, walk around the city and LEARN what people do, what people say, what they wear, what concerns them, what they buy, and what they don't" – Juan Santiago Lagos, associate creative director, Alma/DDB[32]

Creative print checklist

So, let's review what makes a terrific print message. Before signing off on your print campaign, answer the questions in checklist 5.5.

CHECKLIST 5.5 Print campaign checklist of questions

1   About the concept.

   a   Is it *relevant* to the audience?

   b   Does it speak from the *audience's point of view*?

   c   Would it *generate press attention*?

   d   Would it *create talk value* or "buzz"?

   e   Does it *entertain*, *inform* and/or *engage* the reader?

   f   Does it *promise a benefit* or *solve a problem*?

   g   Does it deliver one, instantly *understandable message*?

   h   Do all of the related materials project *one cohesive message*?

   i   Does it reflect the *brand's personality*?

2   About the body copy (review chapter 3).

   a   Does it *flow*? (Can anyone read it out loud without stumbling?)

   b   Does it *weave the main idea* from the first sentence to the last?

   c   Does it use short, *concise sentences*?

   d   Does it *offer little phrases*? If they work? Like this.

   e   Does it use *simple language*, not technical jargon?

   f   Does it incorporate *sticky writing techniques* (discussed in chapter 4) that make your message easy to retain and digest, like the following:

      i   *Alliteration* – "The Magic of Macy's" tagline.

      ii   *Parallel construction* – "Save money. Live better" (slogan for Walmart).

      iii   *Rhyme* – "Hooray for the everyday" (headline for 2011 Ikea catalogue, http://onlinecatalog.ikea-usa.com/2011/ikea_catalog/US/).

      iv   *Simple promise* – "No ordinary airline" (Virgin Atlantic Airway).

      v   *Button* – clever closing line, like "Priceless" (at the end of MasterCard ads and commercials, which doubles as the tagline).

      vi   *ABA* – last line of copy reiterates the headline, for example, if the headline were "In an Absolut World," the last line could say, "Now you can help create an Absolut world."

      vii   *Bullet points* – to emphasize important ideas.

      viii *Connectors* – to join sentences and paragraphs, like on the other hand, because, but, the best part is, etc.

3   About the layout.

   a   Can the reader *find* the most *important message*?

   b   Does the layout *guide the reader* to the most important points first (referred to as visual hierarchy)?

   c   Does the *visual support the headline*? Do they work as a single, conceptual unit?

   d   Is the *headline type broken in phrases*, for easier comprehension?

e Does the body copy have *objectionable widows* (one word sitting alone at the top of a new copy block) or *orphans* (one word dangling at the end of a paragraph)?

f Is the *font* (type style) *appropriate* for the brand and audience? (E.g., you wouldn't use a funky or novelty font for a funeral home.)

g Is the body *copy set flush left* (aligned on the left side) for a faster read? Centered type is okay for just a few lines. Flush left (last words are aligned on the right side) can work for a visual effect with short copy.

4 About the medium.

a Should this be placed in a *media-specific vehicle* (like *Maxim* magazine for a male audience)?

b Would you need to *edit down the copy* for a smaller-space ad?

c Do you need to *rewrite the headline* and *some of the copy* to target a *different audience*? (E.g., would the concept need to be tweaked for a business publication as opposed to a fitness magazine? Or is the concept strong enough to work in any publication?)

d Is there *another print vehicle* you would suggest?

Creative print ad exercises

Exercise 1: create a print campaign for cereality

Cereality is a restaurant chain that primarily serves custom-designed cereals and toppings. Check out www.cereality.com for more details. Be sure to create a campaign for university students. So, use a *tone of voice* and message that would resonate with them.

a. Write two different, but related, *headlines*.

b. Create a *tagline*.

c. Find or create a *visual*.

d. Write at least five sentences or phrases for *body copy*.

e. Remember to make Cereality a "*must-go-to destination*" for a perfect anytime snack or quick meal.

f. Think about *another medium* that would extend the campaign, like out-of-home messages on billboards or ambient ads, such as lawn signs on college campuses.

Exercise 2: now, write a print campaign for its competitor, the cereal bowl

This is a direct competitor that offers similar fare. Visit www.thecerealbowl.com for more information. Repeat all steps (a through f). Try to create a strong campaign to challenge Cereality. Remember, each campaign must be distinctive, so as not to confuse the audience. Think about how head-to-head competitors, like Coke and Pepsi or Denny's and IHOP (International House of Pancakes), face off in their campaigns.

Exercise 3: compare the two campaigns

Be honest. Which one is stronger? Why?

Notes

1   Drummond Berman, personal communication, April 8, 2009.

2   Sheena Brady, personal communication, May 8, 2009.

3   Kevin Moriarty, personal communication, August 24, 2009.

4   Kevin Moriarty, personal communication, August 24, 2009.

5   Drummond Berman, personal communication, April 8, 2009.

6   Drummond Berman, personal communication, April 8, 2009.

7   Vinny Warren, personal communication, September 4, 2009.

8   Charlie Hopper, personal communication, November 26, 2008.

9   Charlie Hopper, personal communication, November 26, 2008.

10   Vinny Warren, personal communication, September 4, 2009.

11   Larry Percy, *Strategies for Implementing Integrated Marketing Communications* (Oxford, UK: Butterworth-Heinemann, 2008), 252.

12   Drummond Berman, personal communication, April 8, 2009.

13   Charlie Hopper, personal communication, November 26, 2008.

14   Charlie Hopper, personal communication, November 26, 2008.

15   Charlie Hopper, personal communication, November 26, 2008.

16   Matt Ziselman, personal communication, January 30, 2009.

17   Drummond Berman, personal communication, April 8, 2009.

18   Drummond Berman, personal communication, April 8, 2009.

19   Simon Nickson, personal communication, April 8, 2009.

20   KT Thayer, personal communication, September 9, 2010.

21   KT Thayer, personal communication, September 9, 2010.

22   KT Thayer, personal communication, September 9, 2010.

23   KT Thayer, personal communication, September 9, 2010.

24   Kevin Moriarty, personal communication, August 24, 2009.

25   Sheena Brady, personal communication, May 8, 2009.

26   Kevin Moriarty, personal communication, August 24, 2009.

27   Deltina Hay, personal communication, July 19, 2009.

28   Sara Rose, personal communication, April 24, 2009.

29   Drummond Berman, personal communication, April 8, 2009.

30   Vinny Warren, personal communication, September 4, 2009.

31   Charlie Hopper, personal communication, November 26, 2008.

32   Juan Santiago Lagos, personal communication, January 12, 2010.

6

THE SPOKEN WORD
Radio

> " Most original thinking isn't even verbal. It requires a groping experimentation with ideas, governed by intuitive hunches and inspired by the unconscious. "
>
> DAVID OGILVY, FOUNDER OF OGILVY & MATHER
> (ORIGINALLY HEWITT, OGILVY, BENSON & MATHER) [1]

Becoming a radio aficionado

Learning some radio tips from the masters

Observing a few more radio writing "rules"

Applying basic radio copy format

Finding out more about radio format

Thinking about production from the start

Using union and nonunion talent, music, and sound effects

Working with and directing the talent

Understanding radio dayparts

Exploring examples of great radio scripts

Writing radio tips

Reviewing radio: the wrap up

Creative radio exercises

You know what a radio spot sounds like. You're familiar with the format. You may even listen to the radio every day. But, do you really listen? When you hear a spot you particularly like, have you ever thought about what makes that spot work?

In this chapter, we'll talk about the main radio script format that is double spaced, all caps, and breaks each line at the end of a phrase; other script formats; some radio "rules": like leaving two seconds for sound effects and music cuts; using ellipses to "billboard" or emphasize a word or phrase; thinking about production while you're writing, including the talent, delivery, sound effects and music you'll use; writing for the ear, not the eye as in print or TV; casting, booking, and directing talent; creating scripts for specific celebrities; targeting different radio "day parts" (times the spots air on radio); applying handy radio writing tips; and listening for great radio spots to use as references.

Becoming a radio aficionado

Starting today, you're going to do that with every great radio spot you hear. You're going to analyze what you like about it and why it works. You'll deconstruct spots the second you hear them. Identify spots that catch your attention. Group them in your mind: lousy ones, so-so ones, good ones, and great ones. What makes the difference? Is it the overall concept? The music? The talent? The sound effects? Does it sound natural to the ear or forced? Radio, like TV, is an oral medium, meaning the lines will be said aloud, not read silently by the consumer. So, scripts that include dialogues need to sound natural, the way people actually speak in their everyday conversations.

Okay, how many times have you heard a contrived dialogue like this one on the air?

ASHLEY: Oh, Jessica. I love your hair. What is the name of your hair salon?
JESSICA: I go to Great Hair at 120 Catalina Drive.
ASHLEY: Where's that?
JESSICA: That's at the northeast corner of 8th Street and 4th Avenue.

What's wrong with this script? Well, people just wouldn't talk like that. They wouldn't give the exact addresses. Okay, at this very moment, stop reading. Ask yourself: Do you know the exact address of your hair salon, or drycleaner, or bank? No. You just need to know what shopping center they're at or what intersection they're near. Just to get started, let's look at a more conversational version of this spot. This time, Ashley and Jessica would sound more like this:

ASHLEY: Oh, Jessica. Your hair looks great. Where do you go?
JESSICA: Brad at Great Hair. They're great, and right near by. You know, on Catalina Drive.
ASHLEY: Oh, across from that big shopping center?
JESSICA: Yeah, on the corner of 8th.

Of course, grammatically, you'd want to say, "Brad at Great Hair. HE'S great." But, we mix our subjects up when we speak. First, Jessica's talking about Brad at Great Hair. Then, she switches to the salon. Instead of saying, "It's great and right near by," she used "they." Of course, it's incorrect. But, that's how we speak. Most of us say "they" when we're talking about a company. Grammatically, it's wrong, but it's perfect for broadcast.

The more natural the language is, the more it sounds like a real conversation. Writing in the vernacular is crucial.

Let's take a moment and hear what some of the radio greats have to say about writing for this medium.

Learning some radio tips from the masters

Many great advertising giants knew how to create unforgettable messages in all media, including radio. Some writers think it's the most difficult medium because there's no visual component.

TIPS AND RULES 6.1
How to write for the ear

- Take listeners on a journey.
- Paint pictures so listeners can imagine the scenario.
- Place them in a setting with
  - sound effects
  - dialogue
  - ambient, random conversations
  - music
- Make dialogues sound natural and conversational.
- Close with a clear statement, wrap up, button, or call to action.
- Read aloud.
- Let other people read the script aloud. If they stumble, rewrite those lines.

Others think it's the most exciting because it taps into the listeners' imagination. David Ogilvy found that a research study identified four main factors needed in radio spots. These were:[2]

1   *Identify your brand early in the commercial.*
2   *Identify it often.*
3   *Promise the listener a benefit early in the commercial.*
4   *Repeat it often.*

Then, he promptly added that 90 percent of commercials don't do any of these things, but they still work. How many times have you heard a commercial and didn't know what it was for until the very end? Some of the most interesting spots keep you waiting the same way a blind headline works in print: you don't know who's advertising until you read the ad.

Instead of just listening to what the research said, he came up with his own checklist of eight steps when writing great radio spots. These were:[3]

1   *Get people to listen.*
2   *Surprise them.*
3   *Arouse their curiosity.*
4   *Wake them up.*
5   *Once they are awake, talk to them as one human being to another.*
6   *Involve them.*
7   *Charm them.*
8   *Make them laugh.*

The truth is, the second list is as applicable now as it was in 1983 when Ogilvy wrote it. Today marketers are looking to engage the audience to involve them with a brand, like Apple, as mentioned above (in #6): involving them creates an emotional attachment to the brand's product line, such as the series of iPods and iPads.

Kenneth Roman and Jane Mass in *How to Advertise* explain that radio can target a specific audience in a local market, making it a versatile medium. With so many types of music and so many different groups listening to their favorite formats, radio can speak to people with the same musical taste, reaching a specific niche. They offer 10 tips for radio writing that would be extremely helpful to the novice and seasoned professional alike. These are:[4]

1   *Focus on one idea.*
2   *Think about the program environment.*
3   *Don't splinter your efforts. (Use the same music for TV, for example.)*
4   *Stretch the listener's imagination.*
5   *Register your brand name.*
6   *Use the strength of music.*
7   *Advertise promotions.*
8   *Listen to the commercial in context.*
9   *Make it topical and timely. (Advertise ice cream in the summer when it's hot, for instance.)*
10   *Talk one-to-one.*

When looking at these, pay particular attention to listening to the commercial in context (#8). In other words, how does this spot sound on your car radio or in the office. When producing a spot, be sure to listen to it on several different types of speakers to check that the music is audible, yet not too loud. But, also consider how the music in the spot works with the music on the station. If your spot includes classical music, it will stand out when played on stations with contrasting music like Reggae, Jazz, or Top-40, or other formats.

Just as we discussed car products for morning and afternoon drive times, think about advertising seasonal products (#9) just before the season starts, like showcasing snow blowers in the fall, or featuring lawn seeds in late winter. Some advertisers, who are not sponsors of the Olympic Games, wrap their commercials before and after the full schedule of events is aired. The idea is to make audience members think they actually were the official sponsors.

Again, the tenth tip reminds writers to speak to listeners as if you were talking to a friend. Be personal and create an open dialogue. The warmer the message, the more comfortable the listener.

Each of these suggestions has invaluable insights into writing powerful radio scripts. Keep them handy when you're writing radio. You can never have enough tips when you're writing to the ear.

Notice how naturally this **Kellogg's Frosted Flakes®** spot moves along. You can hear the girls chanting in unison as if they're doing a training run preparing for an upcoming athletic meet. See how the one-syllable words like "go" and "know" are broken into two syllables to fit into the chant format: "go-oh" and "know-oh." Prior to girls' running 5K events, this spot aired in participating cities. Girls were directed to go to one of two websites, www.girlsontherun.com and www.frostedflakes.com, for more information on the exact time and location of the meets.

KELLOGG'S® RADIO SCRIPT

CLIENT:	**FROSTED FLAKES®**
JOB:	:60 Radio
TITLE:	"Training Run"
LEADER:	OKAY, GIRLS. TWO MILES DOWN, ONE TO GO.
	(MARCHING CHANT) EVERYWHERE WE GO-OH.
ALL GIRLS:	(MARCHING CHANT) PEOPLE WANT TO KNOW-OH.
ANNCR:	AS YOUNG GIRLS APPROACH THEIR TEENS,
	LIFE CAN GET CHALLENGING IN MANY WAYS.
GIRLS #1:	(MARCHING CHANT) WHO WE ARE-AR.
GIRLS #2:	(MARCHING CHANT) SO WE TELL THEM.
ANNCR:	GIRLS ON THE RUN IS A UNIQUE, AFTER-SCHOOL PROGRAM
	THAT EDUCATES AND PREPARES PRETEEN GIRLS
	FOR A LIFETIME OF SELF-RESPECT AND HEALTHY LIVING.
TONY:	WE ARE TIGERS!
ALL GIRLS:	(MARCHING CHANT) MIGHTY, MIGHTY TIGERS.
ANNCR:	**KELLOGG'S FROSTED FLAKES®** IS A BIG BELIEVER
	IN "GIRLS ON THE RUN."
	TONY THE TIGER® ENCOURAGES ALL KIDS TO WORK HARD.
	EAT RIGHT, AND NEVER STOP EARNING THEIR STRIPES.
TONY/GIRLS:	(MARCHING CHANT) WE ARE TIGERS! MIGHTY,
	MIGHTY TIGERS.
TONY/GIRLS:	(MARCHING CHANT) WE ARE TIGERS! MIGHTY,
	MIGHTY TIGERS.
ANNCR:	TO LEARN MORE, VISIT GIRLSONTHERUN.COM OR
	FROSTEDFLAKES.COM.
	AND HELP PUT A GIRL ON THE ROAD TO A HAPPY AND
	HEALTHY FUTURE.
ALL GIRLS:	EARN YOUR STRIPES!
TONY:	**THEY'RE GRRRRREAT!®**
SFX:	(GIRLS GIGGLING)

*(This "Training Run" :60 radio spot was created by Leo Burnett for **Kellogg's Frosted Flakes®**. Script courtesy of Leo Burnett and the Kellogg Company.)*

The campaign not only increased girls' fitness and courage; it also engaged them in athletic participation and self-awareness. An essay contest invited girls to explain how "Girls on the Run" helped them be more fearless. Ten girls could win $500 each and another $3,500 for their corresponding Councils. The more interactivity with a brand, organization, or event, the greater the audience's emotional response.

Now, let's look at a few more important points you should consider when you write for radio.

TIPS AND RULES 6.2
Basic radio writing rules

For the body of the script, just use:

- All caps.
- Double spacing.
- Two columns.
- Contractions like "we're" not "we are."
- Everyday phrases like "you're kidding," "no way," or "that's ridiculous" (not words that work better in print, like "moreover" and "therefore").
- Conversational style, especially in dialogues.
- Phrases instead of full sentences.
- As many complete phrases as possible on each line of the script.
- Dashes to spell something out like this: *P-L-A-Y.*
- Narrow, half-inch margins on right and left side to allow more script per page.
- Easy-to-remember phone numbers only (and repeat three times).
- Two full seconds for every sound effect and music cut.
- The client name at least three times.
- Short, simple phrases.
- Three dots before (and sometimes after) a word to "billboard" (emphasize) it, like this: *Remember . . . friends drive you home or call a cab.* Use these dots sparingly.
- Italics to emphasize a single word.
- Repeated letters to drag a word out like this: *GRRRRRRROW* UP, ALREADY!
- A stop watch to be sure you don't exceed, even by a second, the length of the spot. A 30-second spot is not 30.5 seconds.
- The same page for a talent. Don't break a talent's lines at the bottom of the page and continue it on a second page

Like this:
BARB: I CAN'T BELIEVE SHE SAID THAT. THAT WAS SO MEAN.
              I THOUGHT SHE WAS A FRIEND.
Not like this:
BARB: I CAN'T BELIEVE SHE SAID THAT. THAT WAS SO MEAN.
(Script continues on next page)
BARB: I THOUGHT SHE WAS A FRIEND.

Observing a few more radio writing "rules"

When writing for radio, you also need to know the correct length of time. For length, a 60-second spot can run to 60, but not a second longer. Some people write 59.5 seconds, just to be sure. If the spot runs past 60 seconds, even by a half of a second, it can get cut off at the end by the DJ, a show host, or an automated system that's preset to 60 seconds or 30 seconds for shorter spots.

As mentioned earlier, radio scripts have a specific format that is used at radio stations, recording studios, and production houses. This format is universally accepted as are these basic rules for writing radio spots.

You must also realize that it's important to write using a specific format or template that's common in the radio industry. Now, let's look at correct script format.

Applying basic radio copy format

Before we go any further, the script we just discussed should be in two columns and in all caps like this:

ASHLEY: HEY, JESSICA! YOUR HAIR LOOKS GREAT.
             WHERE DO YOU GO?
JESSICA: BRAD AT SUPER HAIR. THEY'RE GREAT, AND RIGHT NEAR BY.
             YOU KNOW, ON CATALINA.
ASHLEY: OH, ACROSS FROM THAT BIG SHOPPING CENTER?
JESSICA: YEAH, ON THE CORNER OF 8TH.

Aside from the format, notice how it's written: in phrases not sentences. Also look at the use of vernacular, or everyday speech: "*hey*" and "*yeah*." This is the way friends speak to each other, in little bites of information. Instead of "*Where do you go?*" Ashley could have also asked, "*Who does your hair?*" or "*Who does it?*" That's still conversational. Ashley could have said, "*Where's that?*" if she didn't know it was "across from that big shopping center." Or she could have asked, "*Where's it at?*" even if that's incorrect English. Why? Because people use that phrase. Remember writing for radio is not about proper grammar. It's about real communication when there's dialogue. Listeners have to imagine the relationship, the setting, and the scene.

If you're writing a one-voice spot, the copy can be just as natural sounding, enticing, and engaging. Think about the kind of talent you want for this spot. If you can, cast a voiceover talent with a unique voice that would help capture the listener's attention. One-voice spots can be dramatic, like an auditory film trailer; or compassionate, like a public service announcement trying to raise funds and awareness for a needy cause; or humorous, like someone talking herself out of eating a dessert when she's on a diet.

Now, let's take a detailed look at basic radio format.

Finding out more about radio format

The two columns make it easy to see who's speaking and what's being said. The left column identifies the actor speaking, plus it indicates where to place the music and sound effects. The top of the page includes all the file information. That's the only part of the script that's set single-spaced. Right from the very beginning, get in the habit of using clients' names, dates, job numbers, script length, and edit version number. That way you won't have any unidentified scripts sitting around without full client information.

You might ask why the script is in all caps and double-spaced. Even though caps are usually harder to read, for radio announcers and voiceover talents caps are generally the preferred format. The double spacing between the lines makes sense because it allows the talents to make notes to themselves.

Break lines in phrases means that you start a new line at the beginning of a phrase. Try to fit as many phrases on a line as possible, so the script doesn't run past two pages. Here's an example:

Like this:

BRIAN: BRAD, I CAN'T BELIEVE YOU DIDN'T TELL ME.
                WHY DIDN'T YOU SAY ANYTHING?

Not like this:

BRIAN: BRAD, I CAN'T BELIEVE YOU DIDN'T TELL ME. WHY DIDN'T
                YOU SAY ANYTHING?

Can you see the difference? It's more natural to keep "*Why didn't you say anything?*" on the same line, rather then, breaking after "*Why didn't . . .*" That chops the sentence up and leaves an unfinished phrase. You wouldn't say, "*Why didn't.*" You would say, "*Why didn't you.*" Read aloud to hear where to best break the line.

The reason to break lines in phrases is that it reflects the talent's natural rhythm, making for a smoother read. To have the talent highlight or "billboard" word or phrase, you can use three dots, but use them sparingly. Once or twice in a spot is fine. You may find the three dots at the end of the spot, just before the client's slogan or name. The three dots look like an ellipsis, but they don't indicate an omission. For a single word, use italics.

Now, let's take a look at an example of a correct radio format to use as a template.

After mastering radio format, next you should be familiar with the shorthand that's used in scripts. Below is a quick overview of some of the most common radio and broadcast terminology (Useful Info 6.4). Keep this list handy when you're writing for radio or booking the studio and talent.

 TEMPLATES 6.3 Standard radio format

DATE: 01/15/10
CLIENT: Ticket Fighters
JOB #:   TF-6502
RE: :60 Radio Spot – "No Points"

BOB: I CAN'T BELIEVE HE GAVE ME A TICKET.

LINDSEY: WELL, YOU DIDN'T HAVE TO FLOOR IT AT THE LIGHT.

BOB: I DIDN'T KNOW HE WAS A COP.

LINDSEY:	I TOLD YOU THEY WERE GIVING TICKETS ALL WEEK.
BOB:	WHAT A PAIN!
ANNCR:	DON'T GO TO COURT. GIVE YOUR TICKET TO THE TICKET FIGHTERS.
SFX:	(LOUD PUNCH)
ANNCR:	THEY GO TO COURT.
SFX:	(GAVEL)
ANNCR:	SO YOU DON'T HAVE TO. WITH A 95% SUCCESS RATE, YOU COULD AVOID POINTS ON YOUR LICENSE AND MIGHT ONLY GO TO TRAFFIC SCHOOL, DEPENDING ON YOUR DRIVING RECORD.
ANNCR:	THE TICKET FIGHTERS. 888-4-TICKET. THAT'S 888-4-TICKET.
LINDSEY:	(TEASINGLY) STUDY UP IN SCHOOL, BOB!
BOB:	(SARCASTICALLY) NICE!
ANNCR:	GOTTA TICKET? CALL 888-4-TICKET AND LET THE TICKET FIGHTERS . . .
SFX:	(LOUD PUNCH)
ANNCR:	REDUCE THE PAIN.
BOB:	I REALLY HATE TRAFFIC SCHOOL.
LINDSEY:	WHO DOESN'T?
BOB:	BUT IT BEATS POINTS ON MY LICENSE.
LINDSEY:	YA' GOTTA POINT, BOB! (LAUGHS) ONLY KIDDING!
BOB:	FUNNY, REAL FUNNY!

 USEFUL INFO 6.4 Common radio terms

Air-ready	A completed, fully produced spot that's ready to be aired on a radio station.
Air times	Specific schedule of times of the spot will run.
ASCAP	American Society of Composers, Authors and Publishers. Organization that protects the rights (intellectual property) of musical artists.
AFTRA	American Federation of Television and Radio Artists – actors' union.
ANNCR	Announcer.

Billboard	To emphasize a word or phrase. Indicate by using three dots . . . like this.
BMI	Broadcast Music Incorporated – Where businesses, agencies, studios, etc. obtain a license to play or use recorded music and avoid copyright infringement.
Book the studio	To schedule a time and day to record your spot in a recording studio.
Book the talent	To hire a voiceover talent or actor.
Button	A clever closing line that may refer back to something mentioned earlier in the script.
Buyout	To pay a one-time fee to a nonunion talent, allowing unlimited use of the recorded spot.
Call to action	A reminder to the listener to do something: go to a website, visit a store, call for an appointment, etc.
Cast the talent	To audition various talents for a spot, and then select the actor(s).
Character voice	An actor who can create a distinctive personality, speech pattern, or regional accent, like a Southern farmer, New York gangster, "mad" scientist, cowboy, diva, snob, sweet old lady, wise guy, or even a quirky, cartoon-like character.
Check or ride levels	To adjust the volume of voices, effects, and music during production.
Copyright	Music, lyrics, recorded sound effects, and other intellectual property (creative works) are protected from being copied (plagiarism and piracy) or played (copyright infringement) without consent and/or compensation.
Copyright infringement	Inappropriate use of copyrighted material without permission from the work's creator.
Dayparts	How the stations divide up specific segments of time.
Morning drive	6 A.M. to 10 A.M.
Midday	10 A.M. to 4 P.M.
Afternoon drive	4 P.M. to 7 P.M. (some stations start at 3 P.M.)
Evening	7 P.M. to midnight.
Overnight	Midnight to 6 A.M.
Demo (talent)	Online and/or digital CD or DVD recording used to showcase the talent's voice and/or image for future bookings.
Echo	Add an effect, like an echo, behind the voice.
Filter	Used as a special effect to create a muffled sound, or to replicate talking on the phone.
Flight	Pre-arranged radio schedule detailing how many spots will air at what time and on which stations.
Intellectual property	Creative work including, but limited to music, lyrics, novels, plays, books, screenplays, TV shows, etc.
Levels	The volume of the different tracks containing voices, effects, and music.
Library	CD sets with compiled selections of sound effects.
Line reading	Saying a line in the script to the talent, demonstrating how you want the line read.
Live announce	Radio host reads spot live on the air.

Mic	Microphone.
Mix	The combining of each voice, music cut, and sound effect into a final spot.
Music cuts	Short, edited selections of music.
Music fades	Music gradually fades away.
Music post	The way the music hits in a certain place to emphasize copy point or set a mood.
Negotiate rates	Media buyers work with radio stations to get lower rates and/or special packages.
Nonunion talent	An actor who does not belong to a union (AFTRA for radio or SAG for film – see above and below in list).
Phone patch	To direct the talent in another studio via a telephone connection.
Producer	Person who goes into the recording studio, supervises the production, and directs the talent and recording engineer.
PSA	Public service announcement – A commercial for a social or charitable cause, non- or not-for-profit organization, or other community service entity that is usually given free air time and may be created pro bono (without creative and/or production fees) by an agency, production house, recording studio, or radio station.
Punch in	To insert a corrected, new line to fit into a specific amount of time.
Radio buy	The agreed-upon on-air schedule for radio spots, including dayparts: morning/afternoon drive, midday, evening, and overnight "flights."
Rate card	A sheet listing the cost of radio spots during dayparts.
Recording engineer	Someone who records the voiceover talent(s), music, and sound effects, adjusts levels, and creates the fully produced, final spot so that it's air-ready.
Remote broadcast	When a radio station broadcasts live from an advertiser's site, outside the station.
ROS	Run of station – Spots air randomly between 6 A.M. and midnight.
SAG	Screen Actors Guild – A labor union for film and TV, not radio.
SFX	Sound effects.
Signatory	An authorized union representative who can handle and submit the required paperwork for booking union talents.
Scale	The going union rate for talent per market, per 13-week cycle.
Tag	A specific ending on the spot that advertises a certain location, event, or date.
Track	The individual channel that separately records each voice, music cut, and sound effect.
Union talent	Actors who are members of AFTRA or SAG (see above in list).
Up and under	Music comes in and remains playing (under the spot).
Up and out	Music comes in and cuts right out (of the spot).
VO	Voiceover.
Wild line readings	To have the talent read the same line several different ways, one "read" after another, so you have many versions as options for your final, completed spot.

Thinking about production from the start

Before you start writing, while you're developing the overall concept and main message of the spot, you need to focus on the entire production, including talent, sound effects, and music. You should remind yourself to leave at least two seconds for each sound effect. Count a slow ONE–TWO for timing when you're reading aloud. Remember to also leave time for music. At least two or three seconds per music cut, depending on how the music will "*post*" or punctuate the spot. Be sure to listen carefully to more radio spots. Pay attention to what music is used. Notice whether it's the same music throughout the spot or whether there are different cuts (short selections) of music. Listen to how and where the music comes in and/ or out.

Remember, you must paint a picture. Radio, often called "theater of the mind," must appeal to the listeners' imagination. They must be able to picture what is being stated, feel what is being portrayed, then hear and absorb what is being said. So, they can imagine the scene.

Consider where the spot is taking place. Realize that everywhere you are has ambient noise. For example, in a plane there are many sounds: the hum of the engine, the whir of the air conditioning, people sneezing, babies crying, people typing on their laptops. In a restaurant, there are plates, glasses, and silverware clinking; people talking; background music; and the popping of wine bottles and champagne being opened. On the beach, there are the sounds of waves breaking on the shore, sea gulls, volleyballs being hit, and kids squealing and splashing in the water. Listen everywhere you are. Close your eyes. Then, ask yourself what sounds put you where you are? Are these sounds distinctive and instantly identifiable, like the clicking of a pen or the sizzling of meat on a grill? If not, replace them with more easily recognizable effects.

As you're writing the spot, consider the music. What kind of music would work? Do you want several different cuts (selections) of music? Or, should the spot not have music, just voice and sound effects? Now, ask yourself where would you place sound effects? Should you start with an attention-catching sound, like kids arguing, a car engine revving, or a bee buzzing? Interrupt the spot with an unexpected noise like a helicopter's blades whirling? Close the spot with an effect like a closing door? Of course, the sound effect has to work. You don't want to just get the listener's attention with a distinct sound or even word that doesn't have anything to do with the spot.

If a spot started with a loud "Ouch!" but the topic was a dental office, it would be completely inappropriate because of the common fear of going to the dentist. Yes, it caught the audience's attention, but then it focused on everyone's trepidations. Including a sound effect just to have an effect is never the right solution. As mentioned earlier, leave at least a full two seconds for each sound effect. Always read every spot aloud and allow enough time for music and sound effects to register in the listeners' minds. Decide if you would need to add a filter to one of the voices in a dialogue to replicate a phone conversation. If one voice sounds muted, it's as if you're listening personally to someone on the other end of the phone line.

One other sound effect to consider is white noise, or natural room noise. Just listen to the sound in the room you're in right now. If you're home, you might have the TV on, a heater or air conditioner might be running, the dishwasher or washing machine might be on in the background. If you're in an office, you might hear the clicking of someone typing on a computer, or someone on the phone, or someone making copies. If you're in an elegant restaurant, you might hear silverware on a plate, corks being popped, quiet conversations, footsteps, servers announcing menu specials, or any other familiar restaurant sounds. The point is, there's almost always ambient noise wherever you are. So creating a radio spot with no background noise, could either sound unnatural, or could stand out because of its stark background, like an all-white room.

Next explore possible vocal talents. Who should voice the spot?

Using union and nonunion talent, music, and sound effects

As you're creating the spot, hear the talent's voice or voices in your mind. What kind of voice do you have in mind? Determine if you want to use local colloquialisms like "Fuggetabout it," "Who 'ya kiddin'?" or "Ya talkin' to me?" for a New York audience.

Does the actor have to portray someone with a distinctly different voice? Do you hear an accent or a regional dialect? Do you imagine a high or low voice? A character voice (see box above)? A dramatically powerful voice? A rich, resonating voice? A heavenly voice? Are you imagining a guy- or girl-next-door voice? A celebrity with an instantly recognizable and/or distinctive voice?

Every time you watch TV or see a movie, listen to the exact timbre (tone quality and depth) of the actors' voices. Can you recognize any of them with your eyes closed? Can you pick out any actors just by hearing their voices without seeing them on the screen? If so, do those actors have distinctive voices? For example, can you hear the voice of Owen Wilson or Robert Di Nero? What about Whoopi Goldberg or Keira Knightley? Or Robin Williams or Matthew McConaughey? Or how about Jennifer Lopez or Reese Witherspoon? Do you see how you can actually hear their voices because they have a unique sound?

Replay different actors in your mind whenever you're writing a script so you can determine what kind of voice to cast, especially if you're not using a celebrity. Listen to voiceover demo CDs from both union and nonunion talent. Look at demo DVDs of actors in your budget. All serious voiceover talents and actors will present each agency with their demo reels. If you've heard of some talents and don't have their demos, contact them or their agents and request one.

Be open-minded. You might find an undiscovered talent who isn't seasoned, but would be perfect. Audition voiceover talents and actors you haven't worked with before to be sure they are right for your spot. If at all possible, participate in the process of casting the talent.

If you're using union talent, be sure you've arranged for a *union signatory* to be on site at the recording session. Most recording studios have signatories on staff. Be sure you double-check that. Union talents are paid by market and in 13-week increments. This means you cannot replay any commercial after the initial 13-week run without paying the talent for the next cycle.

If you're using nonunion talent, remember to bring two copies of a talent release detailing the time, date, studio name and location, client name, job number and title of the spot, as well as the name of the talent with the amount he or she was paid. This is a legal document that verifies the nonunion talent was financially compensated in full. If your release states that you have unlimited use of his or her voice, that arrangement is called a *buyout*. This means you can replay the commercial in any market for as long as you wish without paying the nonunion talent any additional fees. If you book union and nonunion talent in the same commercial, the nonunion talent must be paid union fees, called *union scale*.

Just as you need to pay for talent, you need to remember to include music and sound effects charges in the budget. Even though as a writer, you may not be involved in budgetary discussions, you must still be cost-conscious when you're working on a small account or for a mom-and-pop establishment. In this case, you need to be cognizant of the fact that each music cut or selection is a separate fee that must be paid to cover the music rights. Just because you own a CD doesn't mean you can use the music in a commercial spot. Only if you wrote and recorded the music yourself are you free to use it. If you included other singers or musicians on your recording, they must be financially compensated and must sign a talent release to protect you in any unexpected legal disputes.

Likewise, sound effects selected from a studio library – a CD collection of recorded effects – need to be paid for to avoid copyright infringement. Recording studio owners and engineers can give you the current pricing for music and sound effects cuts so you have a frame of reference as you're conceptualizing the spot.

Always know that you must pay for and have the proper authorization if you want to use any part of any recording. Let's say you want to use a hit song. If it's on the charts listed in *Billboard Magazine*, it's expensive. Therefore, unless you're working with a client that can afford tens, or even hundreds of thousands of dollars, chances are you won't be using a chart-topping artist or song. You might consider using local artists and giving their work exposure for a more affordable fee.

If you're looking to develop custom music, the more specific you can be when working with the composer the quicker the process. You might hire a jingle writer or contemporary composer or rap producer if there's a singularly unique musical sound you want to create. Don't limit your thinking to just jingles. Any musical phrase can punctuate a spot and act like a sound logo. For example, the three notes that musically represent the General Electric Corporation are the same as those in the corporate name: G, E, and C. Your custom music needs to be completed before you enter the recording studio so it can be integrated into the spot.

If you're involved in producing radio commercials, it's critical that you know how to work with the engineer and the talent so you execute the spot exactly as you imagined it. Now let's discuss some aspects of the production process.

Working with and directing the talent

It's one thing to write the spot. It's another to produce it. The best writers/directors have an extremely clear picture of what the spot should sound like. They can hear the finished spot with the correct inflection and emphasis long before they enter the recording studio. This is why it's vitally important to know the following:

1   How to *work with talent*.
2   How to tell the recording engineer *exactly where the sound effects and music should post*.
3   How the *completed spot should sound*. He or she needs to know what you want and not be left guessing what you had in mind.

Likewise, working with voiceover talents requires that you can give them an accurate line reading, so they know the delivery or "read" you want. By acting out every spot aloud, you will hear when a line sounds awkward. You may want to record yourself reading the script on a digital tape recorder. That way you'll be able to rewrite any lines that don't work well before the studio clock starts ticking the dollars away. You should be able to hand your script to people you've just met and they should be able to read it flawlessly the first time. They don't even have to be familiar with the campaign or the product. Well-written spots just flow. There are no clumsy lines or stiff phrases. They're written the way people speak. The easier your scripts are to read, the faster they'll be read and the better they'll sound. Great writing is a time and budget saver.

Now, back to directing the talent. This is a skill worth learning. You can't walk into the studio and say, "Oh, you're a professional: read it the way you want." It's okay to allow voiceover talents to deliver several interpretations, but you must always know the end result you're seeking. You could e-mail your digitally recorded line readings to the talent preproduction to give the talent an idea of the delivery you want. This could save some studio time. Sometimes talents will offer some excellent conceptual ideas or various character portrayals you may not have considered. Be willing to listen to alternative suggestions and be ready to accept other "reads." A fresh perspective can transform a good spot into a terrific one.

It usually takes most talents a few run throughs to get the gist of how the spot should be read. Make the talent as comfortable as possible and encourage early exploration. Just remember you're the guide, so don't wander too far away from the approved creative direction.

Award-winning radio writers and producers like Joy Golden, president of Joy Radio in Manhattan, explain that getting the results you want from the talent requires that you have them imagine that they're actually in the setting, not in the studio. Here's what Joy Golden said:

> *The key to making a good radio commercial is to know how to direct the people . . . What I often do, especially with some of the new people, is set up a visual scenario for them. I'll say, "You're a husband and a wife in bed, right? And, it's early in the morning, and he's feeling lousy and she's feeling ____." I'll give them a whole physical and personality scenario, so they can perform, in their minds, in a setting that isn't so audio. Because I want a bigger thing to come out . . . In the studio, most of the time it requires ten, twelve, fifteen takes for the talent to get it right, especially if it's a monologue. We do and we redo and we redo.*[5]

Dick Orkin, a celebrated radio specialist, along with other voiceover talents including his brother, Sandy Orkin, and Christine Coyle founded The Famous Radio Ranch, an award-winning, full-facility recording studio. Visitors to the company's website (www.radio-ranch.com) can hear many of their famous and funny commercials. Some of the spots are listed as outrageous and you may question how they ever aired. Take a listen and see if you can determine what makes these spots such award winners. Be sure to notice how each one is set in a particular place that you can quickly imagine. Pay attention to the way the scripts are read and to the line readings and talents' voices. Also, be particularly observant of how conversational and engaging these spots are.

Understanding radio dayparts

If you know what the *radio buy* might be, you could write certain versions for certain times of the day, called dayparts. For instance, if your spot is for a nightclub, you might consider talking to listeners during afternoon drive time (4 P.M. to 7 P.M.) to remind them about your club as they're making their evening plans. If it's for a bank or financial institution, you may want to remind listeners about your competitive car or home loans during morning or afternoon drive time, so they can think about your rates to and from work. You might have a special offer that tells listeners to say they heard about your loans on a certain station.

If you have a popular, local radio celebrity on a particular station, you could also incorporate a few "live announcements." The fan base will pay attention when their favorite radio personality says something. If the message is offered as a relaxed, conversation-like read, as if the on-air personality were chatting with you, the audience, it will sound like a celebrity endorsement. Other live spots can be aired when you arrange radio remotes. These are shows aired on-site from advertisers' locations. People can stop by and visit the "show" as it airs because these often take place on weekends.

With radio, you can speak to the audience while they're driving, so any car-related messages are particularly relevant, like specials on tires, car repairs, tune-ups, car washes, car rentals, and so on. When writing radio consider what messages would be particularly effective if you were behind the wheel. During rush hour, while drivers are frustrated sitting in traffic, a spot that discussed the convenience of using a train, metro rail, tram, trolley, or carpool lane might make computers think about other transportation options. A spot that said this kind of message could really resonate.

ANNCR:	RIGHT NOW YOU COULD BE CATCHING UP ON E-MAIL OR TAKING A NAP INSTEAD OF . . .
SFX:	(TRAFFIC NOISES, HORNS HONKING, DRIVERS SHOUTING)
BILL:	HEY, BUDDY, WAKE UP! THE TRAFFIC'S MOVIN'!
ANNCR:	SITTING BEHIND THE WHEEL. TAKE THE TRI-RAIL TRAM AND TAKE A BREAK.
SFX:	(SNORING)
ANNCR:	YOU EARNED IT. YOU'VE BEEN WORKIN' HARD ALL DAY.
SFX:	(PHONES RINGING)
WOMAN:	(FRANTICALLY) HEY, BILL! IT'S BOB. NOW HE NEEDS THE REPORT IN AN HOUR!
ANNCR:	WORKS OVER . . . UNLESS YOU'RE STUCK IN TRAFFIC.
SFX:	(SIRENS, CARS HONKING)
ANNCR:	THEN YOU'RE WORKIN' . . . JUST TO GET AWAY FROM WORK. TRY THE TRI-RAIL TRAM.
SFX:	(TRAIN MOVES ON TRACKS. DOORS OPEN, COMMUTERS CHATTING.)
ANNCR:	TRI-RAIL. TRAM IT TOMORROW!
SFX:	(TRAIN MOVES ON TRACKS. DOORS OPEN.)
ANNCR:	TRI-RAIL TRAM. TURN RUSH HOUR INTO HUSH HOUR.
SFX:	(SNORING)

Exploring examples of great radio scripts

Young & Laramore has created many attention-grabbing scripts. Several radio campaigns for retail clients like Silver in the City, a jewelry and home décor boutique, Weaver Popcorn, and Goodwill stand out. The way the following two scripts immediately draw the listener in show how immediately personal and intimately conversational radio writing can be.

Notice, too, how the scripts are written in a nonradio format, just in a block of type and how the length is shown as ":60," not written out as "sixty seconds," or ":30" for a thirty-second spot.

As you read each script, pay attention to how the writer draws you in right away. It helps to think of radio writing as if you're writing a play, but without the first act. Just jump right into act two and you'll put the audience in the center of the action. Radio is so short, you won't have the time to set up the scene. There are no prologues, no intros, no preludes. That's why you need to get going from the start. See how each of these spots makes you keep reading, the same way they made the listener keep listening.

Also see how these scripts veer away from traditional radio format and are written in blocks of text, in upper and lower case. But, notice how they use all caps for sound effects and the actor's character name. Each agency determines its own way of writing scripts, although radio stations tend to use the same format.

In the following spot, "Seasons/Vortex," notice the descriptive language in the second line, when the writer describes the rhythm of life as seasons that continue "sweeping us along like so many dead lives, sucking us inevitably into a black vortex of oblivion, until all we are is dust in the wind." It's poetic, allowing the listener to see the words in pictures, playing to radio's often-dubbed "theater of the mind."

 SCRIPT 1: Silver in the City :60 radio, "lead lining"

SFX: MUSIC UNDER

NEHAMKIN: Nothing in life is certain, but this much is certain: there's simply, absolutely and positively no substitute for silver. Don't believe me? Why don't you believe me? "Every cloud has a lead lining." "She was born with a zinc spoon in her mouth." "You make me all squishy inside, you aluminum-tongued devil, you." See? Without silver, those clichés are hollow and sad. And quite frankly, so is your life. Ah, but aha, that's why there's Silver In The City. Silver In The City is a hip (but not tragically so) jewelry boutique, right here in Indianapolis that offers a staggering array of unique, handcrafted sterling silver jewelry, accessories and decorative items. Silver In The City is owned by Kristin Kohn, a quiet but intense young woman whose dark brown eyes seem to pierce your very soul. Kristin scours the globe for silver pieces, just so you'll be able to lord your infallible fashion sense over your so-called friends. Like silver? You'll love Silver In The City. Of course, if you want something, you'll actually have to come in. Or do you expect Kristin to hand it to you on a tungsten platter? Silver In The City. 434 Massachusetts Avenue.

(This :60 radio script, "Lead Lining," was created by Young & Laramore for Silver in the City. Script courtesy of Young & Laramore.)

SCRIPT 2: Silver in the City, :60 radio, "seasons/vortex"

SFX: MUSIC UNDER

NEHAMKIN: There is a rhythm to life. A natural cycle of ebb and flow, seasons coming and going, sweeping us along like so many dead leaves, sucking us inevitably into a black vortex of oblivion, until all we are is dust in the wind. Hey, it happens. But until then, we all need a conveniently located friendly store to supply us with unique home accessories. A store that knows that seasons change, and that décor must change with them. A store that stays ahead of trends. A store that, for the purposes of this commercial, we'll call At Home In The City. There, you'll find everything you need to keep your surroundings current: from lighting and mirrors, to glassware and mobiles, to seating and shelving, owner Kristin Kohn and her guaranteed-never-to-be-snooty At Home In The City staff will work with you tirelessly to pinpoint the exact items that reflect both your personal psychodynamics and the zeitgeist of the season. Or they might just suggest you bop in, grab a pair of salt-and-pepper shakers shaped like froggies, and call it a day. Yes, there is a rhythm to life. And if you don't want to head into the black vortex of oblivion part of it without dated décor, then you'll shop At Home In The City. At Home In The City. 434 Mass Avenue.

(This :60 radio script, "Seasons / Vortex," was created by Young & Laramore for Silver in the City. Script courtesy of Young & Laramore.)

In the following "His, Hers and Ours" Goodwill spot, the Y&L writer shows one of the problems when people marry: the combining of two homes packed with his stuff and her stuff. How do you know what to keep and what to toss? This is an often-overlooked dilemma. Yet, this dilemma is a treasure trove for Goodwill stores. As you read the script, dissect how it is written. Pay attention to the use of parallel construction with the lines that start with "or," like "Or a love of travel. Or a mutual appreciation for Ukrainian folk dancing," and "Or two sofas. Or two Wedgwood gravy boats." This helps consumers imagine the duplicity of household items when couples marry. Be sure not to miss how the closing line wraps up the spot and gives the listener a clever and clear call to action: "We understand that when you're married, what's his is hers, and what's hers is his. We'd just like you to consider making what's both his AND hers . . . ours."

SCRIPT 3: Goodwill, :60 radio, "his, hers and ours"

SFX: WEDDING-ISH MUSIC UNDER

GOODWILL GUY: When two people get married and move in together, it's safe to assume they share a lot of things in common. Like a sense of humor. Or a love of travel. Or a mutual appreciation for Ukrainian folk dancing.

Of course, two people with similar tastes might also have too much in common when they start adding their possessions together. For instance, they may have two copies of the same book. Or two sofas. Or two Wedgwood gravy boats.

So what does one couple do with twice as much stuff as they want? We'd like to suggest they give the half they don't need to Goodwill. (As to which half – we're not getting in the middle of that.)

The money we earn from donated goods – be those clothes, chairs, or even cars – helps people in our community become better prepared for life and work.

We understand that when you're married, what's his is hers, and what's hers is his. We'd just like you to consider making what's both his AND hers . . . ours.

ANNCR: Goodwill. Good cause.

(This :60 radio script, "His, Hers, Ours," was created by Young & Laramore for Goodwill. Script courtesy of Young & Laramore.)

In the Weaver Popcorn "TV Spot on the Radio" commercial, look at how Mike introduces himself to establish credibility. He's not an actor. He's a third-generation president, telling the listener that his family has a vested interest in this message. The next part of the message states that his company is interested in saving you money, something every consumer likes to hear. Then, the writer uses sound effects to "show" the audience the unpopped kernels from its competitors. How is this done? By first popping the popcorn and them pouring it, along with the unpopped kernels, into a ceramic bowl. Anyone who's ever popped popcorn knows the sound of unpopped kernels.

This is a great strategy to remind listeners about a frustrating problem and to present the Weaver Popcorn solution: more popcorn, fewer wasted, unpopped kernels. Mike also starts joking with the listener by saying that they were "going in for the close-up," which of course he can't do because he's on radio. Then, he adds he doesn't have the budget for close-ups, making it even funnier. Notice how this agency doesn't use two aligned columns in their script formats.

 SCRIPT 4: Pop Weaver Popcorn, :60 radio, "tv spot on the radio"

MIKE: I'm Mike Weaver, third generation president of Pop Weaver popcorn, where we're always looking for ways to make better popcorn – and save you money.

So, this is our TV ad. I'll just describe it. That way, we save on film developing, and you can get a big box of Pop Weaver for less money.

SFX: MICROWAVE, POPPING

MIKE: We open on a professional hand model pouring popcorn into bowls.

SFX: SOUND OF POPCORN BEING POURED INTO CERAMIC BOWLS FROM PAPER MICROWAVE BAGS, WITH THE LITTLE DINGING OF UNPOPPED KERNELS

The unpopped kernels you heard came from the competitor's bag, which you would see is a major brand even though we blurred out the name. Actually, it doesn't matter which brand it is, because they all have more unpopped kernels than Pop Weaver. We also have a better corn hybrid, too, so as we go in for the close-up you see our big fluffy pieces of popcorn. That's not a special effect – I can't afford special effects. Next, a highly paid announcer comes on but heck I'll just do it.

(IN A LOWER VOICE) Pop Weaver. Today, popcorn. Tomorrow . . . more popcorn.

(This :60 radio script, "TV Spot on the Radio," was created by Young & Laramore for Weaver Popcorn. Script courtesy of Young & Laramore.)

SCRIPT 5: Pop Weaver Popcorn, :30 radio, "arlene"

MIKE: I'm Mike Weaver, third generation president of Pop Weaver popcorn, where we're always looking for ways to make better popcorn and save you money. Today we're cutting costs on actors by talking to long-time employee, Arlene.

ARLENE: Now what?

MIKE: Talk about what we do.

ARLENE: All we do is popcorn. All I've done for the best years of my life.

MIKE: (HURRIEDLY, AS HE REALIZES IT'S NOT WORKING) Okay, thank you Arlene.
(HE ADDRESSES THE AUDIENCE) Go look for Pop Weaver!
(HE CUES HER TO DELIVER THE TAGLINE) . . . Arlene?

ARLENE: Pop Weaver. Today, popcorn. Tomorrow . . . more popcorn. Is that supposed to be cute?

MIKE: Yes it is.

(This :30 radio script, "Arlene," was created by Young & Laramore for Weaver Popcorn. Script courtesy of Young & Laramore.)

The following campaign, which started in 1986, put Motel 6 on the proverbial map and made Tom Bodett, the only spokesperson for the chain, an instant celebrity. The beloved, light-hearted, award-winning spots were created by The Richards Group based in Dallas, Texas. Here's one example from the unforgettable series. Notice this agency uses "ANN," not "ANNCR" for announcer.

SCRIPT 6: Motel 6, :60 radio, "comparison"

CLIENT: MOTEL 6
JOB: :60 Radio
TITLE: "Comparison"

ANN: *Hi. Tom Bodett for Motel 6 a comparison. You know, in some ways, a Motel 6 reminds me of those big fancy hotels. They've got beds, we've got beds. They've got sinks and showers, by golly we've got 'em too. There are differences, though. You can't get a hot facial mudpack at Motel 6 like at those fancy joints. And you won't find French-milled soap or avocado body balm. You will, however, get a clean, comfortable room, and a good night's sleep for the lowest prices of any national chain. Always a heck of a deal. Motel 6 has over 750 locations from coast to coast. And we operate every darn one of 'em, which means they're always clean and comfortable. Oh sure, it'll be rough to survive one night without avocado body balm or French-milled soap, but maybe the money you save'll help you get over it. It always works for me. I'm Tom Bodett for Motel 6, and we'll leave the light on for you.*

(This "Comparison" :60 radio spot was created by The Richards Group for Motel 6. Script courtesy of The Richards Group and Motel 6.)

Notice the script format for this spot. It uses upper and lower case, not all caps. Agencies differ on their script formats. Learn which one your agency uses and adopt it consistently, so all your script formats are uniform. Also pay attention to the use of vernacular contractions like "save'll" in the phrase "but maybe the money you *save'll* help you get over it."

It's always useful to look at classic radio commercials that reached celebrity status. One of the most celebrated radio commercials ran from 1985 to 1990 and was the campaign for Fromageries Bel's The Laughing Cow Brand Cheese. TBWA New York asked Joy Golden to create a campaign to boost sales. The spots used "heavy ethnic" talent: female actors with a New York accent and Valley Girl dialect (a regional California teenage sound at that time).

There were several spots created as a series. So radio listeners could follow the story. The first three spots, using the Valley Girl accent, feature a budding romance that blossoms into marriage. It starts with the Valley Girl being stopped by the highway patrolman, "Highway," and ends up with his asking her to marry him, "Proposal." Golden explained how she created the humor in The Laughing Cow series like this:

> *The story of The Laughing Cow cheese commercials is one of miscommunication. Is the product a cow or a piece of cheese? Two spend 60 seconds attempting to solve this important question. And their dialog is what forms the basis of the humor that ran on the radio for 5 years in many different spots. Finding the right actors to carry this off was a huge challenge. As a matter of fact all radio casting is a huge challenge. Great film or theater actors don't necessarily have the vocal genius to translate characters for a strictly audio medium. They don't have the rhythm, the timing, the quirkiness. Radio is like music. Obviously you can't see it. So what you hear is the whole show. And with comedy radio, if the script is funny, an actor better laugh before he or she does the first take. If he doesn't, it's goodbye Murray.[6]*

The series with Enid, a woman, with a New York accent, shows funny little scenes from her life. One is a conversation about her daughter's "Sweet Sixteen" party and another is about her friend's "Divorce Sit Down Dinner."

Sales increased a staggering 52% after advertising in six markets over only 13 weeks. Here's an example of one of those famously successful, award-winning spots.[7]

 SCRIPT 7: The Laughing Cow "Valley Girl" and "Enid" radio campaign

VALLEY GIRL #1: "HIGHWAY"

VALLEY GIRL:
Like I was driving down the freeway, ok
and this totally gorgoso highway patrolman stops me.
I said like wow there's wheels on your motorcycle and
wheels on my car. That's really kharmoso. He said
you were speeding. I said have to get my little round
Laughing Cow in the red net bag into the fridge, ok. He said
where's the cow? I said in the trunk, ok. He said you're not
authorized to carry livestock. I said officer that is

like really heavy. The Laughing Cow isn't a real
cow, ok. It's like cheese, ok. Mild Mini Bonbel. Nippy Mini
Babybel. And new Mini Gouda. You know like really
awesome and naturelle. Five delicious round cheeses
in little net bags.
Each one wrapped in wax with a cute little zip thing. He
said open the trunk. I said ok. He said you need a key. I
mean this guy was totally brilliant ok. I said so you want a little
Laughing Cow. So he said ok. So I said ok. So we said ok.
So then he asked me for my license. And I said when can I
see you again. He was so totally freaked like he
dropped the cheese
and bit the ticket.
And so now it's two weeks and he never called.

VALLEY GIRL #2: "COUNTING SHOES"

VALLEY GIRL:

Okay, so like I was sitting here
eating a little round Laughing Cow
in a red net bag
and counting how many pairs of shoes I owned
when the phone rang. I said like hello.
And this deep voice said like hi.
And then like I totally freaked.
I said this isn't the highway patrolman?
He said yes it is. I said no it isn't.
He said yes it is. So I said really?
Then he said like what're you doing.
I said eating a little Laughing Cow and counting my
shoes. He said got any extras?
I said they're too small for you.
He said that's ok, I eat twenty of them.
I said even the suede ones?
He said oh no. I said officer, why don't you come over
and have The Laughing Cow
instead.
Mild Mini Bonbel. Nippy Mini Babybel.
And Mini Gouda.
You know like really awesome and naturelle.
Six delicious cheeses in little net bags.
Each one wrapped in wax
with a cute little zip thing.
He said what's your address?
I mean talk about an inquisitive mind, right?

I said you want crackers, too? He said ok.
So I said ok. So ok, ok?
So *then* I said what should we do
after we eat the cheese.
He said I'll watch you count your shoes.
I mean like
I've had heavy relationships before,
but this is intense.

VALLEY GIRL #3: "PROPOSAL"

VALLEY GIRL:

So like hold on to your nail tips – ok – you're not going
to believe this –the gorgoso highway patrolman
asked me to marry him.
I mean talk about matching white shoes and bag, ok?
I am like totally freaked. Because like who would have guessed
that this hunkola who stopped me for speeding when I had the
little round Laughing Cow in the red net bag in my trunk
would be my groomoso for life, ok? Can you see this wedding
with like real Frenchola champagne and trays of Laughing Cow
cheeses in little red net bags everywhere? Mild Mini Bonbel.
Nippy Mini Babybel. And mellow Mini Gouda, too.
Like really awesome and naturelle. And me in flowing lace for days.
Anyhow it happened when we were eating Laughing Cow cheese
for lunch and talking about how many grains of sand are on the
beach because we are both like really deep. Then like all of a sudden
he said you want to get married? I said ok. So he said ok. So ok, ok.
So then he gave me a little round diamond ring in a red net bag.
And I said officer that is like so intensely sentimental. And he said
he couldn't find wrapping paper with cows on it. I mean talk
about romance. This is like movietown, USA.

ENID: "HOT TUB"

WOMAN:

Last Sunday my friend Bambi invited me to a hot tub
brunch. I said I'll bring a little something. She said,
not Stuart. I said how about a little round laughing
cow in a red net bag. She said forget it, I'm having 14,
it won't fit in the tub. I said you don't put it in the
tub. You put it on the table under the umbrella. She said
if you're worried about sunburn dump the red net bag and
put the cow in a caftan.
I said Bambi your hot tub is running tepid. The Laughing Cow

Is a real cow, it's cheese. Mild Mini Bonbel, Nippy Mini
Babybel, and new Mini Gouda. Five delicious natural bite size
Cheeses in their own little net bags. Freshly wrapped in
wax with an easy open French Zipper. She said good it's a
kinky crowd anyway.
So I went to Bambi's brunch and what do I see, a big bull,
complete with horns. She said it's for your Laughing Cow.
This is a couples party. So I put the mini cheese on the table
and I went in the hot tub. When I got out the cheese was gone.
I said Bambi, I don't believe it, the bull ate The Laughing Cow.
She said hurray for Hollywood.

ENID: "SWEET 16"

ENID:

My daughter Tiffany said she wanted to do something totally awesome
for her sweet 16.
I said I'll put a little round Laughing Cow in a red net bag
on a silver platter and surround it with orchids.
She said that's cute, ma, but it isn't awesome. Better you
should put it in mink and drive it up in a stretch limo.
I said Tiffany watch my lips. The Laughing Cow isn't an
animal act, it's cheese.
She said will the girls be impressed with Laughing Cow cheese
on a cracker?
I said Tiffany your girlfriends have so many birds on their
antennae, they wouldn't be impressed with a dancing bear on
a bagel. But they'll love The Laughing Cow. Mild Mini
Bonbel and Nippy Mini Babybel. Five little round cheeses in
their own red net bags. Delicious. Natural. Bite-size.
Freshly wrapped in wax with an easy open zip.
She said OK it sounds good to me ma.
So we served The Laughing Cow at Tiffany's sweet 16 and all
her friends were impressed except Heather Rubini who expected
a real cow and brought a bale of alfalfa. So everybody
had cheese with a roll in the hay. I want to tell you it
was awesome.

ENID: "DIVORCE SIT DOWN DINNER"

ENID:

My neighbor Blaze Blenheim after 30 years of her marriage
made in heaven to Marty, invited me to her divorce sit down
dinner. I said did she need anything. She said something
for sitting by the fire with soft lights and music. I said a

little round Laughing Cow in a red net bag would be perfect.
She said more perfect would be tall, thin and serious in an
Italian suit. I said Blaze, The Laughing Cow is an ideal
companion with crackers, with fruit, with brandy. She said I
had a companion for 30 years. He finished all the crackers,
fruit and brandy in the house. I'm looking for different. I
said The Laughing Cow is different. She said listen, Enid,
times are tough but I'm not ready for nights by the fire with
some wacked out heifer in a see through sack. I said Blaze,
open the flue, your chimney is clogged. The Laughing Cow is
cheese. Mild Mini Bonbel, Nippy Mini Babybel and Mini Gouda
too. 5 round cheeses in their own net bags, freshly wrapped in
wax with an easy open zip. She said now I get it Enid.
So bring The Laughing Cow. Marty will love it. I said I
thought you were divorcing Marty. She said he has to eat.

ENID: "CRAVING"

ENID: (FAST PACED)
Last night my husband woke me and said he had a little
Craving. I said, "I'll go to the all night super market
and get you a little round Laughing Cow in a red net bag."
He said, "I don't care if she's in lace with high heels.
It isn't what I had in mind."
I said, "So what do you want Stuart?"
He said, "Something sort of soft and a little nippy."
I said, "So, you want Mini Babybel from The Laughing Cow."
He said, "No."
I said, "So you want Mini Bonbel. It's a little more mild."
He said, "No."
I said, "So what do you want Stuart?"
He said, "Cheese."
I said, "What did you think I was talking about?
So I went to the dairy case and I bought two red net bags.
With mini cheese in each. Mini Bonbel and Mini Babybel.
Delicious. Natural. Bite size. Then I went home and I said,
"Look Stuart, I bought you a little Laughing Cow in a red
net bag freshly wrapped in wax with an easy open French zipper."
He said, "Enid don't talk naughty to me."
Then he ate all 10 mini cheeses and said it was the best treat
He ever had in bed. So I smacked him.

(These Laughing Cow Cheese :60 radio commercials were written and produced by Joy Golden for Fromageries Bel. The Laughing Cow, Bonbel and Mini Babybel are registered trademarks of Fromageries Bel Script courtesy of Joy Golden and Fromageries Bel.)

ADVICE FROM THE PROS 6.5 Joy Golden's 10 secrets for creating successful comedy radio commercials

1 You must have worked for at least 147 agencies without ever writing a radio commercial.

2 You must have worked for at least 147 agencies, none of which let you be funny.

3 You must have spent 38 years writing small space, black and white douche ads.

4 You must have a moderately unraveled family. An Aunt Yetta who can chew celery without making noise is a help.

5 You must have had 20 years of intense therapy with a shrink who slept through the last 10.

6 You must be a card-carrying hypochondriac at all times.

7 You must have been at a dentist who does Groucho Marx imitations.

8 You must have a lawyer who wants to give it all up and be a voice over.

9 You must have an Uncle Sy who says "Explain to me again what it is you do for a living."

10 You must love to write and produce radio commercials better than sex, or death-by-chocolate ice cream. Well, maybe not better than ice cream.[8]

What gave these commercials celebrity status was the use of distinctive, regional accents like the Valley Girl mentioned above and another female talent with an obvious New York accent. The combination of a female voice presented as a specific character in a vignette paired with a particularly identifiable accent gave the campaign an instantly recognizable sound, increasing brand awareness.

One award-winning radio campaign, hailed as having some of the greatest radio spots ever created, is still running today, with more than 100 variations. The first two spots in the campaign were "Mr. Footlong" and "Mr. Toupee." The Bud Light "Real Men of Genius" was developed in 1999 by Bob Winter when he was a copywriter at DDB, before joining Leo Burnett. The announcer was Peter Stacker and the singer is Dave Bickler, formerly with Survivor, who mimics the announcer. The composers, Sam Struyk and Sandy Torano, were from Scandal Music in Chicago. The spots pay tribute to many ordinary, yet annoying, characters most people have encountered, comically addressed as "Real American Heroes." One salutes "Mr. Bumper Sticker Writer" and attributes to him the ridiculous line "You can't hug with nuclear arms." The singer echoes back, "I need a hug now!" You'll find the full scripts online, as well. This one is posted at http://thefuntimesguide.com/2005/03/bumper_stickers.php.[9] Be sure you take the time to listen to these spots online at these and other websites:

1 "Mr. Cargo Pants Designer" at http://thefuntimesguide.com/audio/Bud_Light_Real_Men_of_Genius_Mr_Cargo_Pants_Designer.mp3

2 "Mr. Centerfold Picture Retoucher" at http://franklin.thefuntimesguide.com/2007/08/the_face_behind_the_blog.php

3   "Mr. Over-Zealous Foulball Catcher" at http://www.youtube.com/watch?v=K8gUojXK7sc

4   This is the link to an entire list of these spots: http://thefuntimesguide.com/2004/10/bud_light_real.php

Writing radio tips

Charlie Hopper, creative director/copywriter at Young & Laramore, offered the helpful tips below. He discussed writing backwards, that is writing with the medium, the talent, and the production in mind. He explained how writers need to understand casting talent and the production process in order to get the exact read and sound they have in mind. His comments are very helpful. Read through them and refer to them the next time you're writing for radio.

 ADVICE FROM THE PROS 6.6 Charlie Hopper's tips for writing for radio

The Process

Starting with the production and working backward, you gotta know that you're going to be changing the script in there [the studio] at some point. So you gotta know how to walk in with the script written the right way. You gotta read it out loud at your desk, and not rush it because you want it to fit. That happens to every writer, and I sit here, as the creative director, having done it and having learned my lesson the hard way, I keep telling the writers as they're writing, "You've gotta make it shorter. Make it shorter. Make it shorter." They start off and they don't want that to be true. They think you're just being mean and you want them to cut out a joke or something. You get into the recording session and it just doesn't fit. Then, you end up writing on the spot. Maybe you're good at that and maybe you're not. It's stressful and everybody's waiting and you're burning the studio time. You gotta rewrite it right there and then. It just isn't working because you didn't read it slowly enough with a stopwatch.

The Script

Certain radio ads are simply sixty seconds of a guy talking. Others have sound effects, so you end up having to make it easy for the guy to read it. That's the key. I feel like sometimes I can manipulate and save time in the studio by typing it a certain way, so the guy reads it the way I want it right off the top. He gets the spot. He knows how he fits in the spot and isn't trying to guess what you want.

You can indicate the sound effects within the block. Or you can break it up and put it into blocks, and you can decide if you want to do each block individually when you're recording him. Or whether you want to do the body of the spot and punch him back in. I'm famous in the radio circles around here for belaboring my talents because I believe in two things.

The Direction of Talent

Your first takes are your freshest. Your announcer is going to have a little twinkle in his eye and a little sparkle in his tone that you can't quite put your finger on, but it's there in the first five takes.

The second thing I "believe" in: that you learn things about your script as you go and you have to stay spontaneous and open to change. The problem is, in those first five takes, you're learning things about your script, like "Oh, it's too long. That joke isn't funny. That phrase isn't as pronounceable as I thought it was, or whatever." You're learning stuff like that. Maybe they're hitting a word wrong and calling caramel, CAR-MEL, CARA-MEL. You're not supposed to do it that way. Little things like that. Then, what happens is I get those first takes for their *esprit*, but then we've belabored everything after that. So, I get all the little nuances the way I want them if I'm working with somebody who isn't automatically getting it.

If you're working with someone great, they get all those nuances, those little twists and turns, that you want them to take that you can't necessarily direct because it's too much for them to hold in their head. A really good voice talent does that. By and large, the level that most people are working, they don't get to work with the real voice talents. They don't get to work with Dan Castellaneta [the voice of Homer Simpson]. They get to work with some random guy from a talent agency who's pretty good. He's got good pipes, but he's not that good of an artist or a performer that he gets all those little ins and outs.

The Production

That's when you have to go in and punch in all these little phrases. You need to really work with your engineer and bond with him so that he knows, "Okay, that pause after that word was right on this take and wrong on that take. But, the latter take is best overall. So, we'll take the pause from the earlier take and cut it into this other one."

You end up really having the ability to control the result. Radio is a writer's solo flight. Radio is the writer's chance to really make something. That's the funny thing about being a writer. We don't actually ever make anything. We're always an interim step. We've gotta be on it. We have to be ready to kill a widow [one word hanging alone at the end of a paragraph on top of a page] and rewrite it so it fits the space better. And, "Oh my gosh, I wrote too much. Let me go edit that." Let's make sure that when I'm on set [for TV spots] and the announcer's not reading it right, let me get that in the director's head so that he isn't burning a bunch of film with the wrong read because I know we need to do it this other way.

The Writer's in Charge

The writer has all these duties including sharing responsibility for the overall look and concept of anything you're involved with, but as far as actually physically making something, radio is your only real chance. I get a weird, sweaty feeling going in to do radio because as a writer I so seldom make a final product. Writers make an interim product, but don't finish off the layouts and send them to production like the art directors do. Writers don't finish up the final edit the way the editors do. Writers are usually just commenting the whole time. Radio is the exception where the writer has to go, "Yes, we're done," and that's the fun part. That's the hard part: deciding you're done.

You can always make something better, but you have to stop at some point. There's actually a good quote that I like from Roger Miller, the guy who wrote *King of the Road*: "Half of art is knowing when to stop." You just have to know where we have to stop. We gotta move on. That's hard to know for the writer sometimes because he doesn't usually do that. He usually relies on his editor, or his art director, or creative director or client or someone else to say, "Okay, that's good. We're going to go with that." The writer can say, "That's good. Let's go with that," but then he's not physically finishing it. Radio is your chance to do that.

Starting with the production and working backward, you gotta know that you're going to be changing the script in there [the studio] at some point. So you gotta know how to walk in with the script written the right way. You gotta read it out loud at your desk, and not rush it because you want it to fit. That happens to every writer, and I sit here, as the creative director, having done it and having learned my lesson the hard way.

Then, you've gotta know how Pro Tools works. You don't actually have to touch Pro Tools, but to some degree your engineer is going to be doing what you say. You've gotta know that you can cut in that word from the other take here. You can take that phrase out; it's not necessary. We've already released the talent, but now we want this pause to be longer over here. So, we have to take this phrase out, and you say, "Okay, you could take that out," or "Oh, you couldn't take that out because he blends those words together." "Oh, went for a half an hour about this."

But, about typing the script, we're kind of loose about that because we're going to get in there and roll up our sleeves. We just want to do whatever's going to make it work.[10]

Reviewing radio: the wrap up

Remember when writing for radio, you only have one sense: hearing. So, everything you create has to be instantly understood aurally. You can't expect anyone to know it's snowing unless a voiceover talent mentions it. You can't see clouds, but you can hear plane engines. If you're setting a scene, use sound effects and/or music to portray that setting, like island music playing, palm fronds rustling, ocean waves breaking, and seagulls "talking." Think production right from the start. Do I want one voice or more? Do I want to depict a story or deliver a message? Do I want a strong or soft delivery by the talent? Do I want several different music cuts or one uninterrupted music bed? Am I casting an actor or a character voice? What else will help sell the product or tell the brand's message? Radio has been called "theater of the mind" for years because everything that happens must be projected through sound alone.

Close your eyes and listen to every sound you hear. Can you tell where you are? Do you hear the hum of a computer-cooling fan, the typing of someone at a keyboard, the ringing of a phone, or the sound of people chatting? Each sound you hear around you helps define where you are. Think about this when you're writing radio scripts. Always ask yourself, Can I tell where this is taking place?

Then ask, Does my copy sound natural, like real people speaking? Or, does it sound "forced," like people talking about the product in an unnatural way? For example: "Maria, did you see the new gym on the corner? It has weights and treadmills, and yoga classes. It's awesome." Maria answers, "No, I haven't. Gee, that sounds great." People don't usually tell friends a list of features as an announcer would. We just don't talk like that.

Finally, be sure you read all your scripts aloud. Rewrite any place that causes you to stumble. Don't worry about what's wrong in the script. Just revise it so it flows more easily.

Radio is a challenging, yet exciting, medium. Don't let it scare you. Jump right in and speak the lines as you're writing them. This will help you find your own natural voice.

Creative radio exercises

1 Work in teams of four or five.

2 Choose one of your favorite Super Bowl spots. You can go to http://www.spike. com/superbowl, http://www.myspace.com/superbowlads, or http://www.youtube. com to view them before deciding. This YouTube page has the top 10 of the year: http://www.youtube.com/watch?v=_6Ce-SJreIA

3 How could you extend the campaign creatively?

4 Write a 30-second radio spot to continue the campaign and "marry" into the strategy of the TV spot by using the same talent, characters, creative approach, music, and sound effects. Consider what sound effects would place the listener in the same scene.

5   Now write the same commercial as a 15-second spot. Think about what you can edit out yet still get the message across.

Notes

1 David Ogilvy, *Confessions of an Advertising Man* (New York, NY: Atheneum, 1981), 20.

2 David Ogilvy, *Ogilvy on Advertising* (New York: Vintage Books, 1985), 113.

3 Ogilvy, *Ogilvy on Advertising*, 113–114.

4 Kenneth Roman and Jane Mass, *How to Advertise*, 3rd ed. (New York, NY: Thomas Duane Books, 2003), 126–130.

5 Peter B. Orlik, *Career Perspectives in Electronic Media* (Ames, IA: Blackwell Publishing, 2004), 86.

6 Joy Golden, personal communication, July 28, 2010.

7 Pete Schulberg and Bob Schulberg, *Radio Advertising: The Authoritative Handbook*, 2nd ed. (Chicago, IL: NTC Business Books, 1996), 155–156.

8 Joy Golden, personal communication, July 28, 2010.

9 http://thefuntimesguide.com/2005/03/bumper_stickers.php (accessed September 4, 2009).

10 Charlie Hopper, personal communication, November 26, 2008.

THE ANIMATED WORD
Television

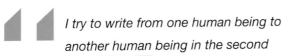 *I try to write from one human being to another human being in the second person, singular.*

**DAVID OGILVY, FOUNDER OF OGILVY & MATHER
(ORIGINALLY HEWITT, OGILVY, BENSON & MATHER)** [1]

Scrutinizing television writing: what's the secret?

Analyzing TV writing: where to begin

Reviewing universal truths

Discovering more about universal truths

Portraying common goals

Seeing how exaggeration, humor, and strong copy drive home benefits

Realizing a great tip for TV spot length

Investigating ways to present TV ideas

Learning from beloved Super Bowl spots

Identifying types of TV commercials

Writing TV scripts

Absorbing key copywriting tips

Tom Amico's tips (Kaplan Thaler Group)

Sara Rose's tips (Goodby Silverstein & Partners)

Vinny Warren's tips just on screenwriting (The Escape Pod)

Casting TV talent

Becoming familiar with TV terminology

Creative TV exercises

The Copywriter's Toolkit: The Complete Guide to Strategic Advertising Copy, First Edition. Margo Berman.
© 2012 Margo Berman. Published 2012 by Blackwell Publishing Ltd.

In this section, you'll scrutinize the art of writing for TV so you can increase your proficiency. You'll investigate the three Rs, delve deeper into universal truths to see how they're used in TV, compare different kinds of script formats, inspect storyboards by some of the most popular icons, from Mr. and Mrs. Potato Head to **Kellogg's® Tony the Tiger®**.

You'll also learn to identify different types of commercials, including the talking head, continuing characters, reason why, and more. You'll become familiar with the basic rules for TV writing, like writing for both the eye and the ear. Plus, you'll hear first hand about TV writing tips from several successful copywriters, including Tom Amico, who creates copy for the Aflac Duck and Vinny Warren, best known for the Budweiser "Whassup!" campaign.

Finally, you'll have access to a list of commonly used industry terms at the end of the chapter. Now, let's find out the secrets to great TV writing.

Scrutinizing television writing: what's the secret?

If you want to be a better TV writer, watch more terrific commercials. Become an active viewer, a clever deconstructionist, an insightful analyzer, and a discerning critic. The next time you see a great commercial, dissect it. Ask yourself why it hit you so hard. What captured your attention? What resonated with you? Most likely, you were the primary target because the spot caused a response and you unconsciously connected to the message.

Successful campaigns are those that use what I like to call "The Three Rs." If you remember these three particular "Rs," your writing will speak directly to your audience in a meaningful way and create a reaction in the viewer (or reader, if in print).

These types of powerful, targeted communications get in under consumers' radar and are referred to as BLT or "below-the-line" messages. They're so perfectly constructed they penetrate past consumers' shields that block out unwanted advertising communications. They speak directly to the audience in the consumer's language. They get delivered before the shields go up. They sneak in, invisible to the radar detectors.

How do creative teams create these kinds of campaigns? They start with gaining consumer insight and having a clear understanding of the audience. They go beyond demographics (age, income, education, etc.) and geographics (residence location), and lock in on psychographics (overall lifestyle). It's not enough to know how old the audience is and what they earn. Marketers want to get inside the mind of these consumers so they can position the brand in a way that singles them out and specifically targets them. The next time you see a spot and you react strongly to it, be sure you allow yourself time to reflect and answer what pulled you in. Was it the visual(s)? The language? The message? The humor? Always remember to analyze every ad that interrupts your day-to-day activities and gets you to stop, read, look, listen, or respond.

TIPS AND RULES 7.1
The three Rs

Messages that are RELEVANT and RESONATE with authenticity are REMEMBERED.

Analyzing TV writing: where to begin

When writing for TV, as with radio, start in the middle of the action. Don't write a prologue or introduction. Begin with act two, as if you were creating a play. This will immediately engage the audience's attention because something is already happening. They don't need to know the preceding scene. Remember, you're writing to the senses. Your dialogue needs to sound conversational. You need to write in little bites or phrases. Not lengthy sentences. Just like this. Watch your use of language. If you don't say "however" in your everyday speech, you can't include that word in TV or radio. Read out loud. If you're stumbling, you're not writing naturally. If your writing sounds like you're reading from a brochure, it's too stiff. Also, with TV, if you show it, you may not need to say it.

If the spot has someone speaking to the camera, as in the Charles Schwab spot "Broker's Kids" (Figure 7.1), viewers feel as if the actor's speaking to them, in a one-on-one conversation. It has a personal, intimate feel to it. Look at the first line: "So I was talking with my broker the other day." Then, it continues with a real-life conversational tone, "It was the usual small talk, you know . . . 'How's the kids? How's the family?' . . . all that . . ." Notice the inclusion of a commonly repeated phrase: "you know." Instead of editing that out, it's written in to sound as if someone were actually talking to a friend, not reading a script.

The actor goes on, "And then it dawned on me." He didn't say, "Then, it dawned on me." He said, "And then . . ." Why? Because that's the way we speak. We connect our thoughts with "ands," "you knows," and "umms." The middle section continues with his inner thoughts, "When you think about all the years I've been paying those big commissions on everything we've bought and sold . . ." The closing line is a button, a clever comment that wraps up the spot and rewards the viewer for listening: "Were we really discussing my kid's future or his kid's future?" What a telling statement. It reveals an underlying universal truth: "Each man

"Broker's Kids" :30 TV

Scene: *Open on guy in his mid-forties sitting on a park bench.*

Man: So I was talking with my broker the other day… It was the usual small talk, you know… "How's the kids? How's the family?" …all that… And then it dawned on me. When you think about all the years I've been paying those big commissions on everything we've bought and sold… Were we really discussing my kid's future or his kid's future?

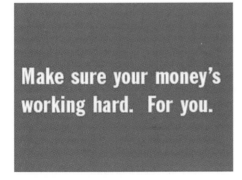

FIGURE 7.1 This "Talk to Chuck" TV commercial was created by Euro RSCG for Charles Schwab. Image courtesy of Euro RSCG.

for himself." What this means in this case is that brokers are also working for themselves and their own families. (Figure 7.1)

The creator of the famous "Talk to Chuck" line was Israel Garber, who also led the original pitch at Euro RSCG that landed the account. It was born from conversations with staff members at Charles Schwab and their clients. Everyone spoke about Chuck (Charles Schwab) as if they were working directly with him in one-on-one conversations. People called him by his nickname, Chuck, not Mr. Schwab, the way you would expect them to out of respect for one of the world's wealthiest men.

Drummond Berman, copywriter/creative director, and Simon Nickson, art director/creative director, the creative team on the account, explained it this way:

> It just felt like a really good way to lower the barriers and make people feel that there was an approachable company, or an approachable person, or a name in this business, and that was the beginning of it, "to Chuck" and it all came from there."

When asked how they continue to spin out this theme and develop witty, new ideas for the "Talk to Chuck" campaign, they said the following:

> We didn't want to produce a campaign that spoke in a language that nobody else spoke, and spoke to people as if all they thought of every single minute of every single day was their future, their investments, their money, and when they were going to retire. Because all of that stuff was false and fake and none of it rang true, when we started delving into the way that's how our target audience really did think about their money and their retirement and their future, and the way they invest.
>
> And so, we set out **not** to do a financial advertising campaign. I still think that that is the kind of guiding principle for everything we do, right? Even 4 years into it, we don't produce financial advertising. We just produce a great advertising campaign that resonates with real human beings.[2]

It's obvious that the campaign did exactly that. Look at the opening line in the Talk to Chuck "Cha-Ching" spot (Figure 7.2). The first words are "I mean," something we all say every day. Here's the rest of the line, "I mean, is there anything they don't charge you for these days?" It closes with "these days," an acknowledgment of frequently heard comments people make about how much times have changed. Just the two words "these days" speaks to another universal truth comparing today to the past, like: "Those days are gone," referring to societal behavior changes like "common" courtesy and honesty in business dealings.

These tiny social and cultural references in the copy speak volumes in a few short phrases. The spot continues with a clear consumer insight. People are tired of being charged for every little service. "Every time I make a trade? Big commissions. Buy a few mutual funds? Bam! I mean, just having an account in the first place? Cha-ching! Pretty soon you'll get a bill just for walking past their office." Wow, what a statement! Notice the use of vernacular: "bam" and "cha-ching," in addition to adding a second "I mean." Here the actor is voicing what so many people are feeling: overcharged.

In fact, as we discussed earlier in chapter 5 when we talked about print advertising (Figure 5.3), the headline "Nickel and dimed" really says it all. It's actually a universal truth: "Being nickel and dimed." It's not often that an actual common complaint is stated so clearly. But, that's the genius behind the copy in this entire campaign. It sided with the

"Cha-Ching" :30 TV

Scene: *Open on a guy in his late-forties eating at an expensive steakhouse.*

Man: I mean, is there anything they don't charge you for these days? Every time I make a trade? Big commissions. Buy a few mutual funds? Bam! I mean, just having an account in the first place? Cha-ching! Pretty soon you'll get a bill just for walking past their office.

FIGURE 7.2 This "Talk to Chuck" TV commercial was created by Euro RSCG for Charles Schwab. Image courtesy of Euro RSCG.

consumers' complaints and offered an instant solution. It spoke directly to the consumers' concerns in their own language, not stuffy investment lingo, and broke free of the typical financial ads. Instead, it talked in an honest and empathetic *tone of voice* that reflected investors' angst.

Likewise, in the "Sir/Who" spot (Figure 5.4), the investor protests about being someone important to his dry cleaner, but an unknown to his broker. It's a sad, but unfortunately true, comment. The person handling your financial security may have no idea who you are.

Berman further explained how the campaign's truthfulness strategy impacted financial advertising, "Because we've created such a different type of brand in this category, it sort of changed the rules for everyone else now. I think that everyone feels that there needs to be a measure of honesty and truth in their advertising."

Before the financial fallout in early October of 2008, investors were more comfortable about allowing "experts" to handle their investments. They were fine handing their money over and expecting a fair return, paired with some moderate losses. But, after a major downturn in the market and seeing their savings disappear, the same investors were now more focused on preserving and protecting their future investments. As Berman stated, "I just think those issues are different and the way people think about their money is different. So the campaign has adapted to that."[3]

You can see how commercials that resonate with authenticity are those that address a universal truth. Most often these are just implied rather than stated. However, they're understood on a subconscious level, even if they can't be restated perfectly. There may be several similar underlying, universal truths, as well. It doesn't matter which one you choose as long as it has the same message.

Reviewing universal truths

As soon as possible, get into the habit of dissecting every TV commercial. Look for the universal truth and then restate it in everyday speech. For example, Sheena Brady, creative director/copywriter at Wieden+Kennedy, explained the importance of integrating consumer thinking this way:

> *Most of my experience comes from trying to find a universal human insight that works across many cultures. But depending on what you're doing, you might need to tailor it. For example, soccer isn't as well known in the states and it is very established in Europe. You would speak to it differently. But for the most part, what I work on is I try to find a universal truth that is relatable to a lot of people.*
>
> *We all want love, and family, and compassion towards others. There are certain inherent qualities that are across the board whether you're Puerto Rican, or you're German. Most of my work has been focused on finding those truths that we can all relate to.[4]*

She went on to explain her writing process before she develops her message and said that the brief is the starting point rather than what she called "blue-sky thinking." She added:

> *You know what you are trying to solve and you can then have the fun and the freedom of solving for that in an interesting way.[5]*

Memorable campaigns exemplify fun, yet strategic problem-solving, solutions. For example, let's take a look at how one spot for Bridgestone Tires exemplifies presenting a universal truth, "Backseat drivers drive you nuts," in a fun and creative way. In a spot called "Taters" (Figure 7.3), Mr. and Mrs. Potato Head are riding in a convertible down a winding, mountainside road. Mrs. Potato Head is in the passenger seat complaining about her husband's driving. He's driving too fast. The wind's messing up her hair. She's the typical "back-seat driver." When they suddenly see a herd of sheep in the middle of the narrow road, Mr. Potato Head jams on the brakes, stops short and avoids hitting them. She screams, "Great! Now, look what you've done. I told you not to drive so . . ." Then, there was silence. When the car stops suddenly, her lips fly off and cascade down the side of the mountain. Realizing she has no mouth, she switches to her "angry eyes." Her expression says everything without her being able to utter a sound. It's just hilarious. And, it speaks to everyone who's ever suffered in a car next to a nagging, backseat driver. The closing line brings the viewer back to the benefits of the tires: "For those who want to get the most out of their cars, it's Bridgestone or nothing."

What's especially noteworthy is the natural dialogue and scene. Nothing is forced. It's so lifelike, the spot captures one single moment that portrays the dynamics of the relationship, and the silent stoicism of husbands everywhere.

THE TATERS
High-performance Bridgestone tires leave
Mrs. Potato Head speechless.

Open on a beautiful, winding mountain highway. A yellow, convertible sports car is going through its gears.

It's apparent that the driver is an expert by the way the car corners and moves along the road. It's a gorgeous day. Above the sweet sound of engine noise, a voice is nagging.

MRS.: *Slow down! Slow down! You're driving too fast…*

Cut inside the car to reveal a life-size Mr. and Mrs. Potato Head. He's driving intensely; she's nagging.

MRS.: *Slow down! Slow down! You're gonna fry us both—you're driving like a maniac. Are you listening? You know I can't stand it when you ignore me. What's the hurry? Can't we enjoy the scenery? How many times have I told you…blah…blah…blah… yak…yak…yak…*

Just then, they round a corner and see a herd of mountain goats crossing the road, right in front of them.

Mr. Potato Head slams on the brakes.

FIGURE 7.3 This "Taters" :30 TV spot was created by The Richards Group for Bridgestone Americas Tire Operations. Storyboard courtesy of The Richards Group and Bridgestone Americas Tire Operations. MR. POTATO HEAD and MRS. POTATO HEAD® & © 2010 Hasbro, Inc. Used with permission.

FIGURE 7.3
(Continued)

Cut to the tires, which stop perfectly, just before hitting any of the goats. Mrs. Potato Head screams.

MRS.: *Aaaaaaaarrggggggghhhhhh!*

As the car stops, there is a loud POP. Mrs. Potato Head's mouth flies off her face, bounces off the windshield, and rolls down the side of the mountain. It's still screaming and talking.

MRS.: *Aaaaahhh. Now look what you've done, you crazy spud. I told you not to drive like that. But—oh, no—you just HAD to do it, didn't you? If your mother ever knew…blah…blah…blah…*

Cut to a mountain goat eating grass on the side of the cliff. The mouth flies by, still talking and screaming. The goat turns to look at it, still chewing. The voice trails off as the mouth tumbles below.

Cut back to the car. Above the idling engine, there's an awkward silence in the crisp, mountain air. Mrs. Potato Head blinks her big eyes at Mr. Potato Head. He stares back blankly. She has no mouth—just a hole now.

She reaches into her purse and grabs something.

She looks at her husband, removes her regular eyes, and pops in her "angry eyes." They're large, with flared eyebrows and red veins. It's obvious that she's really mad.

Mr. Potato Head raises an eyebrow, ever so slightly. He's got a slight grin on his face. He's satisfied with his good fortune. It's his lucky day. He shifts into gear. The engine revs, and the car peels off again down the mountain.

VO: *For drivers who want to get the most out of their cars…*

VO: *…it's Bridgestone or nothing.*

SCRIPTS AND EXAMPLES 7.2   Bridgestone TV script: "taters"

CLIENT: BRIDGESTONE
JOB: :30 TV
TITLE: "Taters"
DATE: 01/16/09

Open on a beautiful winding mountain highway. A yellow convertible sports car is going through its gears. You can tell the driver is an expert by seeing the way the car corners and moves along the road.

It's a gorgeous day. Above the sweet sound of engine noise, we hear a voice nagging.

MRS.:   *Slow down! Slow down! What's the hurry?*

Cut inside the car to reveal a life-size Mr. and Mrs. Potato Head. He's driving intensely; she's nagging.

MRS.:   *You're driving like a maniac. Are you listening? Are you listening?*

I can't stand it when you ignore me. This wind is messing up my hair! Oh, don't give me that look. Watch the road.

Just then, they round a corner and see a herd of sheep crossing the road, right in front of them.

Mr. Potato Head slams on the brakes. Cut to the tires, which stop perfectly, just before hitting any of the sheep.

Mrs. Potato Head screams.

MRS.:   *Sheeeeeeep!*

As the car stops, we hear a loud POP. Mrs. Potato Head's mouth flies off her face, bounces off the windshield, and rolls down the side of the mountain. It's still screaming and talking.

MRS.:   *Great. Now look what you've done. I told you not to drive so . . .*

Cut to a sheep eating grass on the side of the cliff. The mouth flies by, still talking and screaming. The sheep turns to look at it, still chewing. The voice trails off as the mouth tumbles below.

Cut back to the car. Above the idling engine, there's an awkward silence in the crisp mountain air. Mrs. Potato Head blinks her big eyes at Mr. Potato Head. He stares back blankly. She has no mouth, just a hole now. She reaches into her purse and grabs something. She looks at her husband, removes her regular eyes, and pops in her "angry eyes." They're large, with flared eyebrows and red veins. You can tell she's really mad.

Mr. Potato Head raises an eyebrow ever so slightly.
He's got a slight grin on his face. He's satisfied with his good fortune.
It's his lucky day. He shifts into gear. The engine revs, and the car peels off again
down the mountain.

VO: *For drivers who want to get the most out of their cars,*
        it's Bridgestone or nothing.

CARD: Bridgestone logo

(*This "Taters" :30 TV spot was created by The Richards Group for Bridgestone Americas Tire*
Operations. Script courtesy of The Richards Group and Bridgestone Americas Tire Operations.
MR. POTATO HEAD and MRS. POTATO HEAD® & ©2010 Hasbro, Inc. Used with permission.)

Jack Westerholt, the copywriter of this spot, carpools with his wife who works at The Richards Group agency, and who helped write some of the lines. Here's how he explained why the spot sounded so real.

> *Funny, I was writing late one night and I asked my wife, "Would you say this or something like that?" She said, "You modeled her after me, right?" I said, "No, no!" We both laughed.*[6]

The agency didn't want the client to get stuck in the details of what would be the actual script. So, they only presented a concept with this line: "Slow down, slow down, you're driving like a maniac!" For the rest of the spot, they just said she kept pestering him, which they represented with "Blah, blah, blah." He said, "They wanted to connect to the truth of the backseat driver."[7] Notice the casual, conversational language in the script. Also pay attention to how the scenes are explained in this type of script format. Every frame is singled-spaced, with a double space between each one. The spoken lines are in italics to draw attention to these lines for the actors. See how the word "*Sheeeeeeep!*" is extended to indicate the actor's emphasis of the word (text box 7.2).

This script differs from the standard script format with two main columns (Video and Audio) and an additional central sub-column to indicate who's speaking, sound effects and music. See text box 7.5 later in the chapter.

There is no use of caps or two columns (video and audio). This is another kind of TV script. Be sure you compare the script and storyboard for each of the three Bridgestone spots, (1) "Taters," (2) "Scream," and (3) "Hot Item." These examples will familiarize you with the different formats to present your ideas to clients.

The next spot portrays a common emotion: instant panic just before a car accident. The universal truth is "We all scream when we're scared to death." The "Scream" spot starts with an acorn that falls in the middle of the road, quickly retrieved and enjoyed by an unsuspecting chipmunk. A car approaches and instantly the chipmunk's in danger of being hit. Everyone is screaming because they believe a seemingly inevitable accident is about to happen. The passenger in the car is screaming, the little chipmunk in the middle of the road is screaming, and all the animal witnesses in the forest are screaming. Each scream replicates the sound of that particular animal, so a teeny grasshopper has an appropriate voice: a tiny, high-pitched whirr. The attention to this kind of detail makes the spot even funnier. Of course, the car was able to swerve sharply and avert the accident, all thanks to Bridgestone Tires.

What makes the universal truth humorous is how they used anthropomorphism to show the animals reacting to danger, not as they might normally respond by fleeing or freezing in fear, but by screaming as people do (Figure 7.4). Notice how the script actually indicates a tiny chipmunk voice for the scream in line two of the first music insert (text box 7.3).

In the next Bridgestone spot, the universal truth is "You're not safe anywhere." Who would believe your tires would be stolen on the moon (Figure 7.5)? It's an exaggeration, of course. But exaggerations are often what make spots so funny. Think back to the 2010 Super Bowl "Betty White" spot for Doritos. No elderly woman could possible play a rough game of football, get tackled, and not get hurt. The idea there was that Betty White was really a guy who was "playing like a girl." So the exaggeration really worked, as it does in the "Hot Item" Bridgestone spot below. Here the astronauts are enjoying themselves, grooving to music, and gathering moon rocks. As they return to the moon buggy, they realize their Bridgestone tires were stolen (text box 7.4).

Discovering more about universal truths

Notice how strong campaigns express what many people feel. In the following Angie's List commercials, the entire premise is based on lousy home-repair workers. How often have you seen people hire workers who make a mess and don't clean up, do shoddy work, or take longer than expected? These commercials portray the universal truth "It's hard to find good help."

Of course there are other universal truths that could apply to all of these spots. See if you can come up with another one for the "Pay Per View" spot below. Here are two suggestions: "You don't always get what you pay for" and "Seeing is believing." Remember, with universal truths, you're looking to identify a common expression that is culturally and generationally neutral, meaning it resonates as true with most people.

What you really want is to entice the audience to at least listen to what you have to say. Charlie Hopper, creative director/copywriter at Young & Laramore, explained that you need to offer the audience something new, maybe even tease them into paying attention, because they might actually want to hear this. He recognizes that most people are trying to avoid advertising, as much as insurance sales people.

You're not teasing them in order to just torture them or be obscure. But, you're teasing them a little bit with something to say, "You would be interested in this if you would give it half a second."

The audience is trying to eject from everything you write, like James Bond's car. Your reader is trying to get away from you.[8]

Below are the two Angie's List TV spots as scripts. You'll see in Exercise 8, two versions of the spot. The first one was the client-approved spot. The second one shows the script after production revisions. The revised spot became the "as-produced" or "final spot." It's important to realize that some changes happen during production. Take a quick look at Exercise 8 and compare the "before" production versus the "after" production copy. What

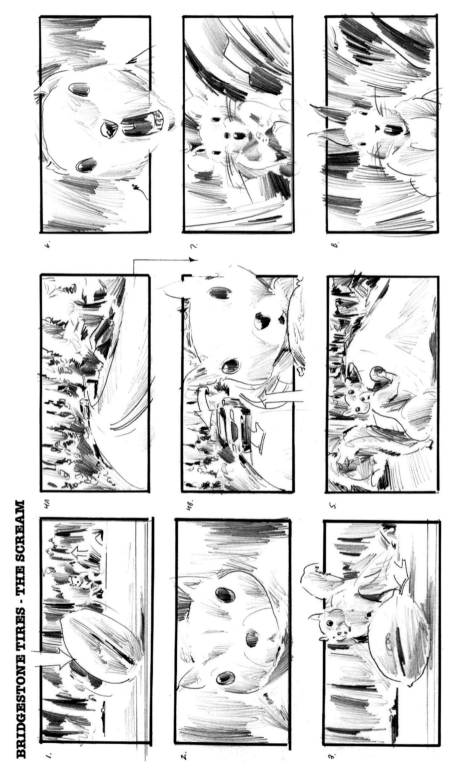

FIGURE 7.4 This "Scream" :30 TV spot was created by The Richards Group for Bridgestone Americas Tire Operations. Storyboard courtesy of The Richards Group and Bridgestone Americas Tire Operations.

FIGURE 7.4 *(Continued)*

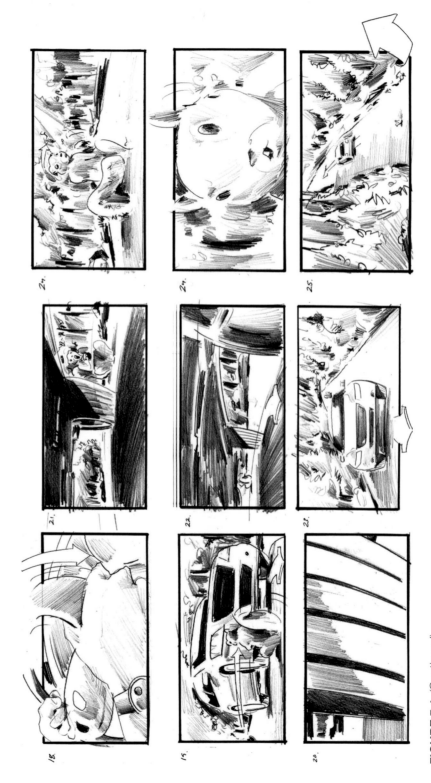

FIGURE 7.4 (Continued)

SCRIPTS AND EXAMPLES 7.3 Bridgestone TV script: "scream"

CLIENT: BRIDGESTONE
JOB: :30 TV
TITLE: "Scream"
DATE: 1/21/08

Open on a little chipmunk crossing a rural mountain road.

SFX: (Approaching car)

The chipmunk turns suddenly and dramatically.

MUSIC: BOMP-BOMP-BAAAAAAAAH . . .
The chipmunk looks at camera. As his jaw drops, he screams in a tiny chipmunk voice.

Next, we see quick cuts of different woodland creatures all screaming in one long, continuous scream in all different pitches and volume levels as they prepare to witness the carnage.

We cut to the interior of the approaching car, and the woman passenger joins the scream. The man, annoyed by his overreacting wife but in no way frightened, deftly steers around the chipmunk. We see the maneuver in dramatic, low-angle tire cam shots.

The car passes, and we see the chipmunk's relief.

VO: *For drivers who want to get the most out of their cars . . .*

Cut to the Bridgestone logo

VO: *. . . it's Bridgestone or nothing.*

(*This "Scream" :30 TV spot was created by The Richards Group for Bridgestone Americas Tire Operations. Script courtesy of The Richards Group and Bridgestone Americas Tire Operations.*)

changed in each spot? Also observe the difference in formats. See the way this script is written compared to the Bridgestone scripts above. Here each frame is labeled and numbered for clarity.

Again, compare the scripts and the storyboards. Pay attention to how the storyboards highlight ("billboard") the action in the spots. Storyboards allow clients to simultaneously see the spot visually, while reading the actors' lines. Few storyboards can capture every single frame. The point of the storyboard is to portray the main points in as few frames (and boards) as possible. One presentation board per spot would be ideal. Some spots may require more than one board. Ultimately strive to have as few as possible. This will help you eliminate depicting unnecessary frames.

Below are the storyboards for the above two Angie's List scripts. Notice how the action in the frames moves the story along.

HOT ITEM

Out on the ride of their lives, astronauts discover that
Bridgestones are everyone's favorite performance tires.

It's the future on one of Saturn's moons. Off on the horizon, a
space vehicle drives toward us. Music begins to play.

We see that Bridgestone tires are on the vehicle and two
astronauts are dancing to the music.

Astronauts are enjoying high-performance action:
cornering around the edges of craters and maneuvering
around lunar rocks.

FIGURE 7.5 This "Hot Item" :30 TV spot was created by The Richards Group for
Bridgestone Americas Tire Operations. Storyboard courtesy of The Richards Group and
Bridgestone Americas Tire Operations.

A slow-motion close-up shot shows off Bridgestone tires as the vehicle jumps through the air.

FIGURE 7.5
(Continued)

The astronauts are having fun collecting moon rocks, dancing like robots, goofing around, and enjoying partial weightlessness.

The astronauts are stopped in their tracks when they return to their vehicle. To their surprise, they discover that the vehicle is on blocks and the Bridgestones are gone.

In one astronaut's mirrored face shield, we see a reflection of light flashing across the night sky. They watch it disappear in the star-filled sky.

VO: *For drivers who want to get the most out of their cars…*

Cut to Bridgestone logo.

VO: *…it's Bridgestone or nothing.*

 SCRIPTS AND EXAMPLES 7.4 Bridgestone TV script: "hot item"

CLIENT:	BRIDGESTONE
JOB:	:30 TV
TITLE:	"Hot Item"
DATE:	07/10/08

This spot takes place on one of Saturn's moons. It's silent. Open on a wide, beautiful landscape shot of an otherworldly moon. Off on the horizon, a space vehicle drives toward us. A familiar track begins to play and gets louder as the vehicle nears camera.

MUSIC: House of Pain, "Jump Around"
Cut to a couple of astronauts groovin' to the music while driving their lunar vehicle. The astronauts' mirrored face shields are down throughout the spot. The windows are down. The music is blasting. And they're enjoying the ultimate drive – fishtails, jumps, high-performance action on moonlike terrain. The vehicle is equipped with Bridgestone tires, and we pick up killer shots of the vehicle and tires (low, tight, overhead, cornering, slow-mo, etc.).

The astronauts stop and get out of their vehicle. While they collect moon rocks, they dance to the music – doing the robot, etc. They're having fun and taking full advantage of being on another planet, tossing moon rocks into buckets, underhand, behind the back, etc. As they make their way back to the vehicle, they stop in their tracks. Their buckets drop, sending up a small cloud of moon dust.

We reveal their space vehicle, now jacked up on cinder blocks with all four tires stolen. Ripped off, as if we were in the hood.
Cut to the astronauts' mirrored face shields. We see the reflection of a flash of light zipping away across the night sky as they look up and watch the trail of light flash beyond the starry sky.

VO: *For drivers who want to get the most out of their cars, it's Bridgestone or nothing.*

SUPER: Bridgestone Logo

(This "Hot Item" :30 TV spot was created by The Richards Group for Bridgestone Americas Tire Operations. Script courtesy of The Richards Group and Bridgestone Americas Tire Operations.)

Portraying common goals

TV spots can also exemplify team spirit, group goals, and organizational missions. The **Kellogg's Frosted Flakes® "Earn Your Stripes®"** campaign uses marching chants to build team spirit, a goal of many young teams. This spot is just one example of many **Tony the Tiger®** campaigns created since his introduction in 1952. Kevin Moriarty, vice president and creative director on the account at Leo Burnett, explained the use of the team chant this way:

> *When you go out on training runs in the Army – and a lot sports teams do this, too – to make the training a little easier to take and to create this spirit of camaraderie and esprit de corps, sometimes the leader of the group will yell out something and everybody else answers. It's all for one and one for all.[9]*

The Kellogg chant was similar to the familiar Army one: "Everywhere we go-oh, people want to know-oh who we are-ar, so, we tell them. We are tigers!" In your mind, you can hear

SCRIPTS AND EXAMPLES 7.5 Angie's List TV script: "pay per view"

:30 (as produced, final spot – see exercise 8)

FRAME ONE:
WOMAN (VO): "When I wanted hardwood floors installed, I hired (SFX: BEEP TO OBSCURE BUSINESS NAME)."

FRAME TWO:
WOMAN (VO): "His work was okay, but the job took twice as long as he'd originally estimated."

FRAME THREE:
WOMAN (VO): "One month later, I opened my cable bill and found out why. He'd been . . ."

FRAME FOUR:
WOMAN (VO): ". . . watching pay-per-view movies on my TV, when he was supposed to be working!"

FRAME FIVE:
WOMAN (VO): "Don't let this guy anywhere near your house. Or, for that matter, your remote control."

FRAME SIX:
ANNCR (VO): "Angie's List uses homeowner experience . . ."

FRAME SEVEN:
ANNCR (VO): ". . . to help you learn which companies to . . ."

FRAME EIGHT:
ANNCR (VO): " . . . trust, and which to avoid."

FRAME NINE:
ANNCR (VO): "Get the power of the list . . . "

FRAME TEN:
ANNCR (VO): " . . . at Angie's List."

(This "Pay-Per-View" TV script was created by Young & Laramore for Angie's List. Image courtesy of Young & Laramore.)

the chant continuing with, "mighty, might tigers," even though the script moves forward with this message: "Tigers aren't afraid to get dirty . . . but they always play clean. They work hard. And eat right" (Figure 7.8). Now, what's the universal truth in this spot? Think about doing your best, giving something your all, and playing fair. Perhaps, "Hard work pays off," "Win fair and square," or "May be the best team win."

FIGURE 7.6 This "Pay-Per-View" :30 TV storyboard was created by Young & Laramore for Angie's List. Image courtesy of Young & Laramore.

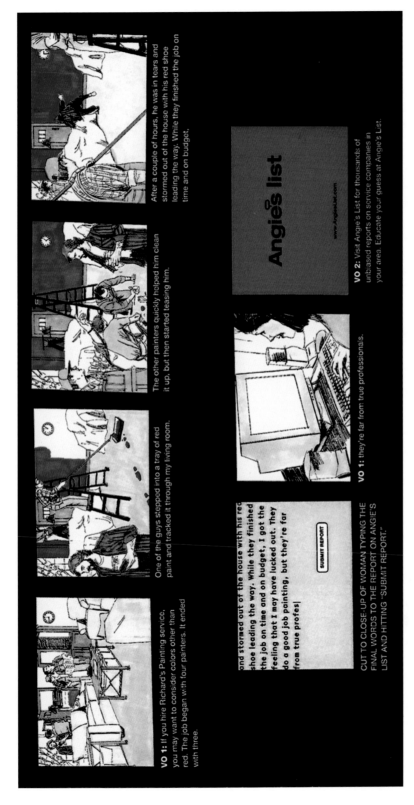

FIGURE 7.7 This "Red Paint" :30 TV storyboard was created by Young & Laramore for Angie's List. Image courtesy of Young & Laramore.

SCRIPTS AND EXAMPLES 7.6 Angie's List TV script: "red paint"

:30 (as produced, final spot – see exercise 8)

FRAME ONE:
VO 1: "If you hire (SFX: BEEP TO OBSCURE BUSINESS NAME) Painting, you may want to consider colors other than red. The job began with four painters, but ended with three."

FRAME TWO:
VO 1: "One guy stepped in red paint and tracked it across the living room."

FRAME THREE:
VO 1: "And after some teasing from the others . . ."

FRAME FOUR:
VO 1: " . . . he stormed out, his red shoe leading the way. They may have finished on time and budget . . ."

FRAME FIVE:
CUT TO CLOSE-UP OF WOMAN TYPING THE FINAL WORDS TO THE REPORT ON ANGIE'S LIST AND HITTING "SUBMIT REPORT."

FRAME SIX:
VO 1: " . . . but they're far from true professionals."

FRAME SEVEN:
VO 2: "Visit Angie's List for thousands of unbiased reports from members in your area. Get the power of the list, at Angie's List."

(This "Red Paint" :30 TV script was created by Young & Laramore for Angie's List. Image courtesy of Young & Laramore.)

The message was so strong, it was used in spinoffs on websites, including two online competitions at http://www.frostedflakes.com. First, there was the "ESPYS/ESPN Sports Page," where one young athlete could win the Youth Achievement Award and attend the 2010 ESPYS, and six finalists could go to the 2010 ESPYS Breakfast in L.A. Second, was the "Plant-a-Seed" contest, which invited teams to compete to win one of 30 **Kellogg's®** Athletic Field Makeovers™, each worth up to $15,000. It continued to be used in a radio campaign that supported girls' running to build self-esteem. The "Training Run" spots reminded girls of upcoming races and drove them to the website for more information, as discussed in chapter 6.

Moriarty said, "We wanted to make kids want to earn their stripes, which is our way of saying they want to be their best and do their best." He added:

> What we wanted to do was not try to highlight that one kid who is the superstar of the team and all that, because most kids aren't. But to want kids to participate, to be part of the bigger program and to ultimately be part of what, for lack of a better term, Tony Nation, let's say. And so hopefully it's done a little bit of that.[10]

In another **Kellogg's® Tony The Tiger®** campaign, the same marching chant is sung in English, Spanish and Japanese, representing one global message. One multilingual "Small World" TV spot celebrates young athletes everywhere and, as a proud sponsor, **Kellogg's Frosted Flakes®** salutes the sixtieth anniversary of Little League baseball around the world. The script interjects into the chant, "They come from Asia, and Europe . . . and Latin America. From half way around the world, and right here at home. And they all arrive sharing a common goal. **Kellogg's Frosted Flakes®** salutes the hard work and passion of Little Leaguers everywhere. And is proud to sponsor the sixtieth anniversary." The logo appears against a black background: Little League Baseball World Series 2007. Look at the storyboard and follow exactly where and how the chant is interrupted with the above message. Notice where **Tony the Tiger®** trademark line **"They're Gr-r-reat!®"** appears (Figure 7.8).

As is evident in all these campaigns, interactivity and engagement with the audience not only reward participants, but also strengthen their emotional connection to the brand and to the more than 58-year-old icon **Tony the Tiger®**.

Remember, you're looking for a familiar expression that is commonly accepted as true. It crosses cultural, geographic, and generational barriers. It's universally adopted; although it may be modified slightly in different languages, it still carries the same idea.

Seeing how exaggeration, humor, and strong copy drive home benefits

Many spots use exaggeration to feature consumer key product selling points and/or clear consumer benefits, as in the "Hot Item" spot we just examined. Taco Bell used humorous exaggeration in several of its commercials. One spot, Taco Bell's "Grande Quesadilla," showed a pregnant girl struggling to get on the bus and waddling down the isle because of her big belly. She sat down next to a young guy with an extended stomach. He turns to her, looks at her belly and says, "Grande Quesadilla?" assuming she was overstuffed like he was, missing the obvious. The announcer says, "So filling, it's like you're eating for two," emphasizing the abundance strategy discussed in chapter 2.

The closing line restates the clever play-on-words slogan "Think outside the bun."

Teddy Brown, senior vice president, executive creative director of the Orange County office at Draftfcb, who heads the Taco Bell account, explained that this spot fits into the agency's overall creative direction for the TV spots. In addition to exaggeration and humor, descriptive, mouth-watering copy drives home the product-centric TV messages.

A lot of our commercials end up being situational, dialogue-type commercials. The hardest thing to do is to write about, in a really natural way, people talking about a product. If you really want to get across that ooey-gooey meltness of this product is really delicious, you've got to somehow force-fit those words into an actor's mouth. You've got to really try to figure out a way to do that, particularly with Taco Bell. It has a lot of product names that are three- and four-words long.[11]

You can see how the writers strive to make an item sound scrumptious through their use of language. It's not just about naming the products and listing the ingredients. It's about making consumers almost taste the items as they hear them being described. See how he talked about the "ooey-gooey meltness?" You actually want to excite consumers' appetites and tempt their taste buds.

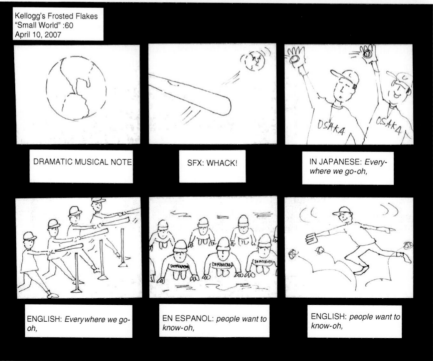

FIGURE 7.8 This "Small World" :60 TV spot was created by Leo Burnett, USA for **Kellogg's Frosted Flakes®**. Storyboard courtesy of Leo Burnett, USA and the Kellogg Company.

FIGURE 7.8
(Continued)

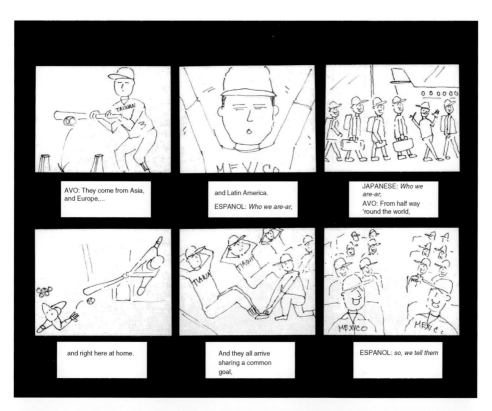

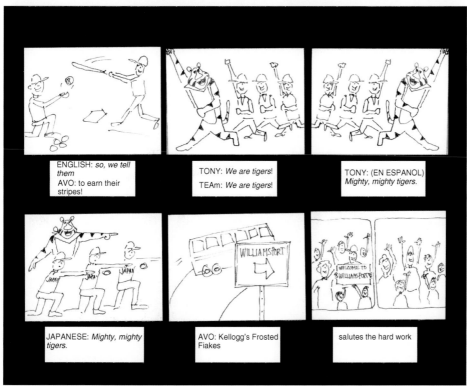

FIGURE 7.8
(Continued)

and passion	of Little Leaguers everywhere,...	TONY: *We are tigers!* ENG: *We are tigers!*
VARIOUS OVERLAPPING LANGUAGES: *Mighty, mighty tigers,*	*Mighty,*	*mighty*

tigers,...	TONY: They're gr-r-reat!	AVO: And is proud to sponser the sixtieth anniversary
Little League World Series. ENG: *Mighty, mighty*	*tigers,...* SFX: SLAM!	

FIGURE 7.9 This "True Grit" :30 TV spot was created by Leo Burnett, USA for **Kellogg's Frosted Flakes®**. Storyboard courtesy of Leo Burnett, USA and the Kellogg Company.

FIGURE 7.9
(Continued)

FIGURE 7.9
(Continued)

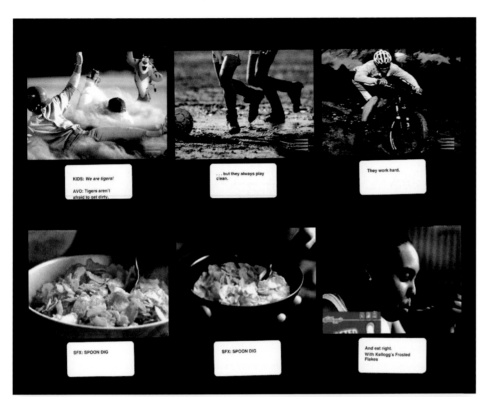

Brown continued, explaining that all humor should be smart humor, not "whacky or goofy or really radical or different just for the sake of being different." The work, he said was divided into "our situation versus our product." He went on:

> It's always going to be product-centric advertising. The situation, in more cases than not, has a hero character that more or less represents and embodies the brand.[12]

Each spot speaks about what the brand has to offer and integrates that message into a situation that emphasizes the main brand qualities. In another spot, the "Roosevelts," writers drove home the value strategy, which was restated as the "Why Pay More" campaign message. Brown explained that this particular spot was an anomaly because it was for a value-based menu, not one particular item. Usually Taco Bell's campaigns are product-centric, or focused on one key benefit it wants to communicate. "Why Pay More!®" is the campaign; "Unleash Your Power of Change" was the strategy behind the campaign as it distinguished the Taco Bell value menu from typical dollar value menus. The entire "Why Pay More" campaign was the second year of a specific menu launch, created in 2007, called "Unleash the Power of Your Change." Brown said it was a rebranding of one of the original value menus, designed "as a way to underpin the competition." McDonald's was concentrating on its dollar menu at the time. He went on:

> So, if everything on the dollar menu was a dollar, we came in and everything on our menu was 79, 89, and 99 cents. We rallied around this idea of change as a visual device and as a point of difference that we'd be able to leverage as no other QSR can leverage.[13]

He said it wasn't important to extol the benefits of value. The audience knew that 89 cents was a great deal. You don't need to focus on that. They understand the benefits of saving money. They realized that. He said, "You just have to tell them that it's 79, 89, 99 cents. And then, they'll figure out that it's a good deal."

One of the Draftfcb Orange County writers created a music video, and a music house in London composed the music.

The Taco Bell video had a very contemporary sound and feel to it and had a touch of humor. There were two online versions: the two-minute one (http://www.youtube.com/watch?v=jnl27kAK9yM) and the one-minute video (http://www.youtube.com/watch?v=MXngi6tUma0). When you watch it for the first time, notice how the price, shown in large "79," "89," and "99" numbers, was highlighted to reinforce the price (value) of the products. See how the flamboyance and excess of the Hip Hop culture was depicted, like the "blinged-out" piggy bank and the rhinestone-studded Pepsi cup. Brown said, "They're basically taking a smarter approach to celebrating the power of the change. Sometimes if you can't say it, you sing it. You just do that in a way that's going to break through." He explained that the spot leveraged the Hip Hop culture, but did it in a way that was "very tongue-in-cheek and celebrated the power of change by turning it on its head."[14]

Be sure you're observant when you watch the video(s). Notice how often Taco Bell did the following:

- Showed dimes.
- Mentioned "it's all about the Roosevelts, Baby."
- Highlighted the price.

- Talked about change (coins).
- Visually depicted dimes (as spinning tires, diamonds, etc.).
- Spelled out T-A-C-O B-E-L-L.

Pay attention to the casting. Did you find this video amusing? Watch both videos one after the other to see what was edited out. How many times did you see the Taco Bell logo? Watch again and count this time. You'll be surprised how often it was shown, but you might have missed it.

Realizing a great tip for TV spot length

As you watch commercials, pay careful attention to the writing. You'll learn how to create tighter (more concise) spots by having exceptionally well written references. Sometimes new writers wonder how much copy should be in a 30-second spot. Kevin Moriarty at Leo Burnett said that a previous creative director gave him some great advice when he worked at BBDO in New York. He told Moriarty to keep his 30-second TV spots to 70 words or less. When Moriarty presented him with a 71-word script that he thought was perfect, the "CD" told him to keep working until it could eliminate one word. He struggled with this editing assignment, asking:

> How important could it be? And he made me do it. But, it made me think ever since about that. I went to the award books from the previous year and I went through every award-winning commercial and none of them were more than 70 words. In fact, most of them were a lot less than that. So there really was something there.[15]

Moriarty's desire to better understand his creative director's TV word-length rule drove him to closely examine commercials in award annuals. He sat and counted the number of words in each award-winning TV spot. How many writers would have had the initiative to disprove or confirm this unwritten rule? He found out that all the winning spots were 70 words or less.[16] Just as billboards should be as few words as possible, preferably around seven to ten words or less, TV spots also have a word count that makes them most effective. The next time you're writing a 30-second spot, try keeping it under 70 words. Then, ask yourself if the spot seems "tighter," more concise, more focused?

Investigating ways to present TV ideas

After you examine the word count, you need to think about how you're going to present your idea to the client. Each agency has its own presentation techniques. Some use storyboards. Others show scripts. And others create stories. Sara Rose, a senior copywriter at Goodby Silverstein & Partners, who works on the Hewlett-Packard account among others, said that sometimes she doesn't write copy for global clients. She said, "We tend to *not have* dialogue in that ad, and that doesn't mean that there isn't writing involved."

It means that she and her creative partner, senior art director Lea Ladera write a story and a script to communicate the basic idea in a client presentation. She said, "What we're doing is trying to get them to understand what message we're trying to create and what our vision is."[17] The creative team writes this out in a few paragraphs. Sometimes it requires a little longer explanation.

She went on to clarify that a lot of people are under the misconception that writers only write and art directors only design. The truth is that together they create a story and a larger concept behind it. She elaborated on this point:

> I like to think that what I do is that I'm a conceptual person who specializes in writing and my art director is a conceptual person who specializes in art direction. Our titles don't necessarily limit what our contributions are to a project.[18]

For TV spots, copywriters and art directors write a script and a short story about what takes place. As a team, they're drawing a picture in the minds of their clients. They need to convey an idea in a visual way. They need to make the idea understood by everyone: both the visual and non-visual clients.

Likewise, a concept for a global client needs to be grasped by audiences around the world. The idea must be instantly understood without a need for cultural clarification or explanation. One example of a universally understood concept was the "Live Wirelessly Print Wirelessly," created by Goodby Silverstein & Partners for Hewlett-Packard. Rose came on board after the concept was developed. She explained how the "In the Air" spot, which she produced with Ladera, demonstrated wireless printing.

Rose explained that the spot dramatized how the product worked, which is an example of a "product demonstration" commercial (strategy 7 in chapter 2). It showed that printers didn't have to be attached to people's computers. That meant they didn't have to be attached to their desks. With so many people working on laptops, all over the house, now they can send a print command from any room. Colorful drawings on sheets of paper suddenly popped up all over the house, portraying the printouts that were sent wirelessly.

When the spot needed to be aired in other markets all over the world, partner agencies arranged to have the voiceover recorded in the native tongue. With such a direct and clear message, copy modifications were not necessary to "*transcreate*" (recreate or rewrite the spot in a new language). She explained the visual and copy had to work together. The concept was very direct:

> I think the announcer copy was "Print from anywhere in the house," which is what the product does because the visual was more over-the-top, metaphorical and very intriguing. We wanted the copy to be a bit more straightforward.[19]

Her creative team had multiple executions before deciding on this one. How did they pick this one? She answered:

> I think this one was just a really simple visual. There's a lot going on, but at the heart of it, it's a very simple message.[20]

As with many TV spots, one key component was to tie into the main slogan of the account: "Live Wirelessly Print Wirelessly." That way wherever consumers see the message, all the various "touch points," or places the audience encounters the campaign, like TV, online, in print, and in-store, reinforced the campaign and enhanced overall memorability with the use of one consistent line.

SCRIPTS AND EXAMPLES 7.7 Story script example: Hewlett-Packard, :30 TV, "Live Wirelessly. Print Wirelessly."

We open on a monkey flying through mid air. It acts as if this is nothing out of the ordinary. It suddenly lands on the roof of a small, Indian style Taxi that is also traveling through the air.

The driver inside shoos the monkey off of the windshield. As the monkey jumps off, the camera pulls back a little further to see other things moving through the air such as a street vendor and his fruit cart, a street sign and someone on a bicycle, etc.

We also see several people carrying brightly colored umbrellas. Suddenly, it begins to rain on them. An elephant charges through the air behind them, spraying water with its trunk. As the camera pulls back we see that all of this was happening inside of a house.

We then see an astronaut emerging from another room in the house. He flies into the hallway. He is as big as the elephant. We see the reflection on the India stream in his helmet. He grabs onto the elephant's tail and holds on for the ride.

The India images the astronaut fly down the hall. They take a turn into another room in the house. We cut inside the room; the only sound we hear is the hum of a HP Wireless Printer in action. A vacation photo of India has printed out. All the elements in the stream are present in the photo: the taxi, the monkey, the elephant, the people with umbrellas, etc.

A woman comes into the room and picks up her picture from the printer. She gives it a look as we see another print out on the printer tray. This one is a child's school report on astronauts.

COPY: Print anything from anywhere in the house with HP Wireless Printers.

SUPER: Live Wirelessly. Print Wirelessly.

We cut to a shot of an HP Wireless Printer and a laptop. Participating retailer logos also appear on the screen.

SUPER: HP Logo. HP url.

COPY: A great notebook deserves a great wireless printer. Now buy both and save $70.

(This "Live Wirelessly. Print Wirelessly" :30 TV script was created by Goodby, Silverstein & Partners for HP (Hewlett-Packard). Script courtesy of Goodby, Silverstein & Partners.)

When asked who handles what when working on a TV spot, Rose said that when it comes to production, each team is different. In her partnership with Ladera, Rose usually handles the music, sound, and final mixing of the commercials. It's important to realize that oftentimes the writers' work isn't finished when they complete the copy. Next, they may need to edit the spot, and then go into the studio to produce it. They're usually expected to handle words and sound in commercials. They must read every script out loud with a stopwatch and remember to count a slow "one-two" for each sound effect to ensure accurate script length before going into production.

Learning from beloved Super Bowl spots

The best way to improve your TV writing skills is to examine excellent commercials. This is why you should immerse yourself in award-winning spots in annual award books and review top-ranked Super Bowl spots each year. At least familiarize yourself with the *Advertising Age* list: "Top 20 Super Bowl Ads Ever" (http://adage.com/superbowl/top20).

Then, take a few minutes to view the spots. See if you can deconstruct them to determine why they created such a strong response in viewers. Try to determine what was it that created the most prized result: "talk value," also known as buzz or water-cooler chatter. When a commercial causes people to talk about it and they remember the advertiser, the spot raises awareness, heightens brand recognition, and strengthens retention.

For example, Apple's "1984" spot, which introduced the Apple Macintosh personal computer, aired one time during the Super Bowl of that year and is ranked as the number one commercial in Top Twenty Super Bowl Ads Ever list. Can you understand why it claimed first place? Part of its success was its literary reference to George Orwell's *1984*, a book often seen on high school reading lists. Many students grew up believing that the government, "Big Brother," would monitor, supervise, and control everyone's life. The spot shows a female athlete tossing a brass-headed hammer through a large screen as a breakthrough moment that defied this kind of control, explaining in the copy why "1984 won't be like 1984."

Look at the monster.com spot "When I Grow Up" and notice the intelligent copy that lets young children describe what their career goals might be if they grew up without sports. Here's one line: "When I grow up I want to file all day long." Of course, no one wants that job. That's what makes the message so compelling. How many people settle for a job they hate because they believe they can't succeed? Although not stated, playing sports can help build self-esteem and confidence, enabling children to seek more satisfying jobs. The universal truth is people settle for less because they think they can't achieve more. Sports challenge kids to try harder and give them a vehicle to stretch their self-limiting beliefs.

Although universal truths are a powerful way to connect to the audience, selecting the right type of commercial is another vehicle to drive home the message.

Identifying types of TV commercials

As you can see in the box below, there are many kinds of TV formats. Think of these as packages that contain and then deliver the concept. You're probably already familiar with many of these. You may not have known what the spots were called, but if you've watched TV, you've seen them. Think back. Do you recall viewing any *product demonstrations* (examples of how products work), *testimonials* (people talking about products they use), *talking heads* (actors talking into the camera, shot from the chest up), and *vignettes* (mini plays)? Look over the list in text box 7.8 and see how many other examples you've already watched.

> "
> The best copywriters are not always the ones with the highest ability but the ones with the highest standards. **JAMES LOWTHER, FORMER DEPUTY CHAIRMAN, SAATCHI & SAATCHI, LONDON**[21]

The sooner you're able to identify the kind of spots you're seeing, the quicker you'll develop a library of TV commercial references. Ask yourself what spots used *animation*? Which campaigns used continuing characters? What other brands have instantly recognizable *icons*? Have you seen other spots that don't fit into any of these categories? If so, start making an ongoing list of new categories. See how many more you can find.

USEFUL INFO 7.8 Some popular types of TV spots

1 *Demonstration* (like detergent spots, including Clorox 2 "Stain Research Facility" spot: http://www.youtube.com/watch?v=djDBMryseB0)

2 *Testimonials* (like the L'Oréal "Because you're worth it," spots, for example: Charlize Theron in the L'Oréal "Anti-Fade Hair Color" commercial: http://www.youtube.com/watch?v=gam3WJlKDoU&feature=related)

3 *Talking Head* (like a news anchor delivering the news, as in the Nike "Football" spot: http://www.youtube.com/watch?v=9BR6YoFv_NQ)

4 *Slice-of-Life* or *Vignette* (A little story like a TV episode where productsolves problem, like the three "Parisian Love" spots by Google: http://www.youtube.com/watch?v=nnsSUqgkDwU)

5 *Lifestyle* (how product fits into someone's lifestyle like a mini vanpacked with kids, dogs, and sports gear. It's not a story, just a snapshot. This is like the diamond ring commercial by Tacori "Cupid's Arrow: http://www.youtube.com/watch?v=f1yT6mpV3wg&NR=1)

6 *Animation* (like the Keebler Elves "Magic Middles Cookies" spot: http://www.youtube.com/watch?v=EullpM3TKuw&playnext=1&list=PLC17A60D399A1A37B&index=26 or the Coke "Beautiful" spot: http://www.youtube.com/watch?v=R1NnyE6DDnQ)

7 *Jingles* (like the Christmas spots by De Beers, such as 2006 "Morning Surprise": http://www.youtube.com/watch?v=q-jOjK003Yk and 2007 "Falling for You," or the Smirnoff "Tea Partay" Ivy League East Coast Rap: http://www.youtube.com/watch?v=PTU2He2Blc0&feature=&p=153B819AE4B0A5FE&index=0&playnext=1, which was matched by the West Coast Rap: "Green Tea Partay": http://www.youtube.com/watch?v=qGKVQeU4SXE&feature=related)

8 *Visual as Hero* (Coke "Happiness Machine": http://www.youtube.com/watch?v=lqT_dPApj9U)

9 *Humor* (like the Budweiser "Beer House" http://www.youtube.com/watch?v=Hyg3KeZchSs and the classic Pepsi "Cindy Crawford New Pepsi Can" http://www.youtube.com/watch?v=jgK40bxAdYg spots)

10 *Continuing Characters* (like the "Mac versus PC" spots as in this series grouped together: http://www.youtube.com/watch?v=siSHJfPWxs8)

11 *Reason Why* (like the De Beers "A Diamond is Forever" commercials, such as http://www.youtube.com/watch?v=4vXHm8TzLzE)

12 *Emotion*[22] (like the Hallmark card commercial, for example "Butterflies Going Back to School" spot: http://www.youtube.com/watch?v=pNFOQgVQ4KU&feature=related)

13 *Before and After* (like weight-loss programs often with a "split screen," such as "Sharla Pincock LA Weight Loss" spot: http://www.youtube.com/watch?v=QCr0S_Eh6x, sand "Becky's LA Weight Loss" spot in Spanish: http://www.youtube.com/watch?v=Q4PJh7RpfJo&feature=related)

14 *Anthropomorphism* (when animals take on human emotion, like the Budweiser Clydesdale "Hank" spot: http://www.youtube.com/watch?v=XWbO-oq6ZPw)

15 *Emotional Blackmail* (makes you feel guilty for not using the product, like the Michelin Tires "There's so much riding on your tires" TV campaign: http://www.youtube.com/watch?v=FDWHWfJq6BE&NR=1)

16 *Consumer-Created Content* (like the Doritos "Anti-bark Collar" commercial: http://www.youtube.com/results?search_query=Doritos1anti-bark1spot&aq=f)

17 *Truth* (like the Dove "Real Beauty" campaign, like the "Through Her Eyes" spot: http://www.youtube.com/watch?v=x8ukDRAuHPk&feature=related and the "Truth" anti-smoking campaign, including the "Tobacco Kills" spot: http://www.youtube.com/watch?v=Y_56BQmY_e8 and the "Body Bag" spot: http://www.youtube.com/watch?v=c4xmFcrJexk)

18 *Celebrity Spokesperson* (like the T-Mobile campaign with Catherine Zeta Jones, such as the "Families Talk Free" spot: http://www.youtube.com/watch?v=yiQEkVZ8DOg) and then Carly Foulkes for T-Mobile: http://www.youtube.com/watch?v=sPk8QB5Tg4M

19 *Celebrity Endorsements* (like the weight loss commercials for Jenny Craig with Valerie Bertinelli "Bikini" spot: and Valerie Bertinelli for http://www.youtube.com/watch?v=Hmph24uZ6Dk and the Jennifer Hudson "Me Power" spot for Weight Watchers: http://www.youtube.com/watch?v=X484yZ7NSMl)

20 *Sexy* (like the GoDaddy.com spots and buxom girls as in the "Hitchhiker" spot: http://www.youtube.com/watch?v=zFcF6ysDvQs)

21 *Cultural Impact* (like the Budweiser "Whassup!" spot: http://www.youtube.com/watch?v=W16qzZ7J5YQ or Wendy's classic "Where's the Beef?" spot: http://www.youtube.com/watch?v=Ug75diEyiA0)

22 *Role Reversal* (like the e-Trade "Talking Baby" campaign, such as the "Time Out" spot: http://www.youtube.com/watch?v=x0GsNhLt9Ds and the Doritos "Keep Your Hands off My Mama" spot: http://www.youtube.com/watch?v=r0EVSP_6XZA)

23 *Holiday Greeting* (a few classics: Hershey's Kisses as bells playing "Wish You a Merry Christmas" in this spot: http://www.youtube.com/watch?v=4HtSLF4vlrk and the Budweiser Clydesdales in a retro "Holiday Greetings" spot: http://www.youtube.com/watch?v=sXvAVtwbemE)

24 *Product Icons* (like the classic Coca-Cola "Polar Bears" campaign, such as the "Arctic Beach Party" spot: http://www.youtube.com/watch?v=xL4DbMAe-d0&feature=related, and the famous **Kellogg's® "Tony the Tiger®,"** and "Energizer Bunny" campaigns)

25 *Product as Graphic Visual* (like the "Milk Mustache" spots like this behind-the-scene with Usher: http://www.youtube.com/watch?v=GcdCDvZZtUg&playnext=1&list=PLF1D2B6C6686F87BD

&index=47, the recognizable Charles Schwab "Talk to Chuck" talk bubble, and the Apple's iPod white ear bud cords against a silhouetted image product-introduction campaign)

26 *Visual as Benefit* (like the Axe deodorant and hair product campaigns that promise to create animal magnetism, such as "Billions of Women" spot: http://www.youtube.com/watch?v=I9tWZB7OUSU &feature=related)

27 *Public Service Announcement* (focuses on a particular cause or charitable organization, usually created pro bono – without creative and/or production fees – by the agency, production house or broadcast station, like the M.A.D.D., Mothers Against Drunk Driving campaign, such as the "Drinking and Driving" spot: http://www.youtube.com/watch?v=Sp-ly-MMquc&feature=related)

Writing TV scripts

After reviewing the list did you notice how the visual drives home the message? The next time you're writing for TV, think visually. Try to let an image move the story or action along. How can your idea be projected in a visually compelling way? What graphics could stop the viewer? What scenarios could draw the audience in? What characters could become part of everyday culture? Consider all the commercials you loved. What part did the visual play? Here are a few familiar examples, in addition to the above-mentioned ones: milk mustache (California Milk Processor Board), Clydesdales and Dalmatians (Budweiser), cool guy versus geek (Apple), the bottle (Coke "Open Happiness" and "Absolut Perfection"). What other images or characters can you name?

Next, think about production. Will this idea be executable or is it so complex, it would require an entire film cast and crew? If that's in the budget, fine. If not, how else could you get this message across? If you're struggling to execute your idea, remember some of the most powerful commercials are simple. Here's one example. For a public service campaign promoting AIDS prevention, the script used two actors, one indoor location (setting), one scene, three frames, and four superimposed words. Take a moment and see if you can come up with an idea. Any luck? Okay. Here's how the spot went.

Frame one (scene one): A young couple are holding hands while walking toward double doors in a beautiful hotel room. The doors open, a luxurious king-size bed appears. They walk through the door.

Frame two: Fade to black. White text appears in two parts, one line at a time. BANG! BANG! YOU'RE DEAD!

Frame three: Logo of AIDS prevention association

So simple. So clear. So unforgettable. So affordable. It didn't lecture or preach. It just demonstrated the risk of careless behavior. One reckless moment of passion could cost you your life. It doesn't get more direct than that.

Simplicity can sometimes create a stronger response than a complicated, expensive shoot. Even fascinating, high-tech imagery doesn't have to produce high-impact reactions. How many times have you marveled at the visual techniques in a spot, but couldn't remember

TIPS AND RULES 7.9
Basic TV writing rules for scripts

1   *Concepting*

- Review the brief, any product/brand research, and consumer insight.
- Think about the audience. See them three-dimensionally, as real people, not a list of statistical data. Which *VALS category* or categories would they fit into?
- Analyze the creative strategy statement to determine the strategic creative direction.
- Reread chapter 1. Examine the handy list of strategies in chapter 2. What strategy would work for this brand? Think about several, or blending several strategies, before deciding.
- Consider the *brand personality* and how best to depict it.
- Think visually.
- Think about the kinds of talent you will be *casting*, so you have their voices and images in your mind.
- Decide what kind of programs or channels the spot would air. Are these skewed more to female or male viewers?

2   *Writing*

- Write for the ear and eye.
- Imagine the finished spot.
- Tell a complete story.
- Present an instantly comprehensible version of the spot in script or storyboard format.
- Grab viewers' attention.
- Have on- and/or off-camera actor(s) in mind from the beginning. *On-camera* actors appear in a scene or frame. *Off-camera* actors are heard as "voice only" talent.
- Start with act two. Jump right into the action. Notice how the "Broker's Kids" spot for Charles Schwab begins with the word "so."
- As in radio, use contractions like "you're" and "they're."
- Use *vernacular* (everyday speech like "gotta" and "gonna") when appropriate for the brand.
- Write in phrases, the way you speak, not in full sentences.
- Make dialogues sound natural and conversational.
- Consider various TV formats like *product comparison, animation, testimonial, vignette, product demonstration* (before and after), *celebrity spokesperson*, etc.
- Write around the setting like on location or in the studio.
    Allow a few seconds of time for visual effects like: *morphs, slow dissolves, page turns, scrolls* or *crawls, fades to black.*
- Count aloud, slowly "one, two" for a full two seconds for each sound effect and music cut.
- Remember to use the appropriate *tone of voice* for the brand.
- Analyze the pace of a celebrity's delivery if one is being cast in the commercial. Write to that specific talent's rhythm.
- Ask yourself if you want to close with a super, logo, sig, wrap up, button, and/or call to action.

- Read all scripts aloud for correct timing and copy flow.
- Time your spot with a stopwatch and allow one second of silence at the end to ensure the ending won't be cut off, so a :30 is :29 closing with a *beauty shot*, *logo* and possibly a *fade-to-black* close.

3 *Formatting*

- Set up two columns, left side for video directions, right side for audio (music, sound effects, spoken lines). Music, sound effects, and actors create an aligned middle (third) column. (See TV script format below.)
- Double space between "frames" (separate visual ideas and scenes).
- Use single space within each "*frame.*"
- Break key ideas into selected frames.
- Make sure frames move the story along.
- Decide and indicate where music comes in and out.
- Determine where to place *supers* (superimposed words like easy-to-remember phone number, website, other information).
- Break lines correctly for *voice-over* and on-camera talent.
- Think about what sound effects to use and where to place them.
- Use industry standard abbreviations and terminology like *SFX* and *CU*.
- Say client name at least twice and *superimpose* it at least once.

4 *Production*

- Consider production while you're writing. What *camera angles*, shooting techniques, and visual effects will enhance the spot?
- Think about the kind of "read" you want (how the actors should interpret the script when they read their lines).
- Select key frames to create the storyboard. Not every image will be shown.
- Select appropriate music cuts and decide where they post (are inserted).
- Select the most accurate sound effects and insert them in the appropriate places in the spot.
- Decide where to place supers on the screen (superimposed words like easy-to-remember phone number, website, other information). Do you want any information crawling along the bottom of the spot or scrolling down from the top of the screen?
- Choose where you might include a *beauty shot* (close-up) of the product.
- Consider post-production modifications like *scene edits*, *visual effects*, and *music posts*, and *sound levels*.
- Remember when producing:
  - Listen to sound levels
  - Determine if you need to color correct a frame because of a lighting or other issue.
  - Watch for picture safety, so you don't place any supers to close to the screen edges.
- Select key frames to use as "*screen grabs*" or "*screenshots*" as images that represent the main action or concept in the spot.

the product? That spot could have represented tens or hundreds of thousands, possibly even millions of dollars spent with no brand recognition. Always keep in mind that you want the viewer not only to remember the spot, but also to recall the brand.

See the above list of basic rules for writing TV scripts (Tips and Rules 7.9). Review them each time you start to create a commercial. They will help guide you toward developing successful commercials.

Absorbing key copywriting tips

Nothing replaces experience and the wisdom of seasoned writers. Sometimes just reading a few tips will help you grasp the specific writing techniques needed for great TV copy. Look at the tips below from copywriting masters, Tom Amico, Sara Rose, and Vinny Warren. Amico is a creative director/copywriter at the Kaplan Thaler Group and co-creator of the Aflac Duck with Eric David, creative director/art director. Sara Rose, as mentioned above is a senior copywriter at Goodby, Silverstein & Partners, who works on Hewlett-Packard and other accounts. Vinny Warren is the founder and creative director of The Escape Pod and one of the creators of the Budweiser "Whassup!" campaign while at DDB. Here are some important points that will fine-tune your writing.

Tom Amico's tips (Kaplan Thaler Group)

Tip 1. Make sure your writing has attitude. When we created the Aflac Duck campaign, we made sure the client bought into the fact that we didn't want a cute cuddly spokesanimal. A little attitude goes a long way in copywriting, and too much attitude is sometimes, well, just too much attitude and a turn-off. But a little can be just the right amount.

Tip 2. Saturate yourself with great advertising from around the world. The best work is coming from all over. Brazil. Iceland. Singapore. Thailand. Because they are havens for the hottest art direction, the writing is kept to a minimum. If the story can best be told in pictures (visually), be a good enough writer to leave the writing out.

Tip 3. Three words: "Kills Bugs Dead." Your English teacher might say it's redundant. The Raid client might have said we don't want to say "dead" let alone "kill" and dead in our theme line. But writing doesn't get anymore succinct or to the point than "Kills Bugs Dead." Plus it's persuasive and tells me everything I need to know about the product.

Tip 4. Read *Catcher in the Rye, Catch-22* and *The World According to Garp.* They are not necessarily the best-written books, but any page you open to, the writing is engaging enough for you to want to read more. Any place in a block of copy you write or on a script, should have the same power.[23]

Sara Rose's tips (Goodby Silverstein & Partners)

Tip 1. Well, I read this somewhere once and it always helped me, is that you need to sort of throw out your first 20 or so ideas. Write them on your first day ever working on a project because that's when you just get the bad stuff out, for lack of a better word. The most obvious solutions to a problem usually come out first. There are exceptions to that rule. You just can't be too self-satisfied with yourself. So that's a big thing. I'm never exactly happy with everything I do. I'm always willing and open to continue to work on it until I get it right.

Tip 2. Don't overwrite. A lot of people really, really overwrite. You need to learn how to make an impact with the fewest words possible. And that's even in a dialogue spot.

Tip 3. You have to be hard on yourself. You have to be really, really hard on yourself. Whenever Lea and I do a project and we work on a script, or work on an Internet idea, before we even show it internally, we talk to each other and say, "Is this something that I would want to produce? Is this something I would want to spend a lot of time on? Do I feel good enough about it? Do I feel proud of it? Could it be better?" And if we say, "Oh, no I don't really think I would be happy if it was produced," then we just don't show it. But that also means trashing 90% of our ideas. I think you have to be really hard on yourself.

I think that some young writers, juniors, think everything that they come up with is going to be amazing. There are some people where that's the case. But I think for a lot of people, you have to be hard on yourself.[24]

Vinny Warren's tips just on screenwriting (The Escape Pod)

If you're talking about TV, film, video, or whatever it is, there's an old saying if you ever saw it, it was: You write film three times. You write it when you write it. You write it when you shoot it. And, you write it when you edit it. That's the truth, right? You start out with a script when you present it, or when you sell it. That, of course, is done in isolation because you have no idea what the filming is going to be like, who is going to be directing it, any of that stuff. You have no idea of that.

Then, when you get into filming it, things will change. You think, "Oh I was thinking of it this way, but now that I thought about it more, in reality in terms of shooting, it'll change a bit, and the words will change, and things will change." Like for example, the Budweiser "The Out-of-towner" spot [www.theescapepod.com, under "Older Work"]. The script that we presented was radically different than what we shot. It had to be because the words had to change to suit this actor who wasn't terribly experienced. So, if we had adhered to the original script, it would have been insane because it wouldn't have worked.

Then, of course, you rewrite it again when you edit it, by virtue of what you choose to go on the film. So that's the way I look at writing for film. When you start out, you have no idea of this. You can't. That's something you've got to experience. When you start out everyone has the same idea. It's basically, "You get to shoot exactly what's on my page from my script because it's perfect and brilliant and I've thought about it," which is exactly wrong. When you go about it, then you realize, "Oh no, hang on, that's not right."

Then, you get more open and then, of course, that predisposes that you have the freedom to do it. When we came back to Anheuser Busch with our "The Out-of-towner" idea they weren't going, "Wait a minute. That's not the script you sold us." But, that was the general idea we sold them. And, it was funny. That's all they cared about.[25]

Just for clarification, "The Out-of-towner" spot has a guy from Texas in a cowboy hat in a bar in New York. Everyone who comes in casually says, "Hi, how 'ya doin'" as a standard greeting. The out-of-towner thinks people are really asking him how he is. So, he answers each person with the same response, drawn out in his Texan drawl, "Thanks for asking. I'm doin' just fine. I just got in today. My brother-in-law just picked me up from the airport. Mighty fine airport you got here. The people here are real friendly." Obviously, the out-of-towner doesn't understand that no one really cares and that's just how everyone says hi. It's a very comical scene. Try to watch it so you can hear how humorous his repetitive response is and how it's another example of exaggeration.

Casting TV talent

Just as in radio, you should think about the kind of talent you want as you're writing the spot. Are you looking for an *announcer*, an *actor*, or a *character actor*? What's the difference? Announcers can present a dramatic or straightforward read. Think of one-voice retail commercials or trailers for movies you've seen. They're often voiced by announcers. These voice talents don't act a part; they deliver the information about the film or brand. Actors, on the other hand, are cast for various types of spot, including vignettes, lifestyle with dialogue, or other commercials with scenes. Character actors are selected for their ability to create different and authentic-sounding regional accents and specific personalities or professions.

Try to hear the kind of read you want before you start casting. Be sure you see the talent live or on a video demo (demonstration or "demo" tape). This way you can cast the actor(s) with the appropriate look and delivery and see how well they take direction. If you're casting for a spot with a family, you may need to spend extra time to find actors who are playing various family members. You may want them to resemble each other and look related. At the casting audition ask the talents to read the script so you can hear their style of delivery. If you hire a casting agent, be sure you can view a few additional talents even if she or he has selected the key actors. In case there's a last-minute cancellation, you will have some other talent options.

Becoming familiar with TV terminology

Now let's examine how important it is to speak the lingo. If you're at a shoot, casting talent or finalizing the spot in post-production, people around you are going to expect you to understand what they're saying and to use the language of the industry. If you want to refilm a scene, you'd say, "Let's retake that shot," or "Let's reshoot that scene." If you wanted to superimpose words on the screen in *post-production*, you'd want to check for screen safety. If you need to fix the actor's collar, you'd need to call out "*wardrobe*" to alert the wardrobe person. Take some time to completely familiarize yourself with all the words listed below. Then, when you're on the set, you'll be comfortable with the language of TV writing and production.

Pay attention to how each frame is single-spaced, but is separated from the next frame by a double space. This format helps the actors and the camera crew to see the spot in a progression of actions. Here are a few links to some very effective TV spots. See how the Weight Watchers orange "Hungry Monster" icon is used in the campaign. It depicts

USEFUL INFO 7.10 Common TV terms

Animation	Cartoon-like images for special communication (Aflac Duck)
AFTRA	American Federation of Television and Radio Artists (union that represents performing talent: actors, singers, dancers, singers and broadcast announcers)
ASCAP	American Society of Composers, Authors and Publishers (organization that provides licenses and royalties for members' performances)
Beauty shot	Close-up of the product by itself
Camera angle	Position of camera in relation to the subject (object, person, or scene) when filming or photographing
Camera person	Films all the scenes and beauty shots
Casting agent	Person who auditions and selects the talent
Chyron	Character generator that creates the supers (on-screen text)
Color bars	Striped bar of test colors precedes the commercial are used as a reference point to allow for color adjustments to ensure playback will match recorded spot
Clap board	Chalkboard used to identify the "take" number for post-production (camera assistant holds the clap board up to be filmed, announces the take number, and closes the hinged top bar, producing a "clap")
Crawl	Words or images move along the screen horizontally, like a baby crawling across the floor
CU	Close-up, camera is near object or actor
Demo	DVD demonstration of talent's range of abilities or production house's samples of best commercials
Director	Person in charge of supervising the production
Dissolve	One image fades as another one comes up, if done very slowly, it's called a "slow dissolve"
Dolly	Camera is mounted on a small truck that smoothly moves across tracks to follow action in scene and carries the camera crew and director
ECU	Extreme close-up, camera is right beside object or actor
Flow	How smoothly and effortlessly the copy reads
Frame	One scene or shot in the commercial
Freeze frame	Action is completely stopped
Gaffer	Head electrician who oversees lighting apparatus
Grip	Carpenters who build and repair the set during production
Hair stylist	Person who styles the actors' hair for the shoot
Humor	Uses comedy for entertainment and retention

Icon	Drives brand recognition (Geico's gecko)
In sync	Sound track and actors' mouth movements (sound and action) are synchronized
Insert	(1) Image showing a specific detail is inserted on screen, sometimes in a box; (2) another shot is inserted into the spot
Key frame	A single, instantly recognized image from a spot
Lifestyle	Shows product in everyday use (mini vans)
Make-up artist	Person who applies and checks actors' make-up throughout the shoot (Person may also be the hair stylist on the set.)
Morph	When one image slowly becomes (blends into) another
MS	Medium shot of scene (camera's not close or far away)
Music	Helps reinforce message like an auditory punctuation mark
Music post	Where the music comes in and punctuates spot
OS	Overhead shot
PA	Production assistant (handles details of the shoot)
Page turn	An effect that changes one scene to another, resembling someone turning a page in a book
Pan	Camera moves slowly to give a wider (panoramic) view
Picture safety	During post-production, check that images and text within a preset area on the screen will appear on at-home TVs (the "safe zone")
Pre-production	Everything that needs to get done before filming (casting, booking studio, choosing location or studio, creating props, hiring production team and caterers, attaining script approval, etc.)
Post-production	Finalizing the spot (putting the scenes together, editing out superfluous copy or images, correcting colors, adding music, superimposing text, etc.)
Product	Features product advantages and how it works (detergents)
Product comparison	Highlights product's advantage (spot removers)
Props	Objects on the set to help create the scene (lounge chairs, seashells, sand for a beach scene)
Public service	Illustrates a charitable cause or organization, usually created pro bono – without creative and/or production fees – to showcase a need to the public
Quick cut	One image is replaced by another, without a transition
SAG	Screen Actors Guild (association of union talent)

Screenshot (screen grab)	Key image from one TV frame
Scroll	Words or image move vertically from the top down or from the bottom up
Sex appeal	To make products seem sexy, to create the cool factor (Axe), or to include sexy celebrities for attention
Shoot	Production of a TV spot or infomercial
Slice of life	Emotional sell (Hallmark)
Slo-mo	Slow motion (of camera)
SFX	Special effects designed to create an illusion
Split screen	Screen is divided with side-by-side images usually for a comparison
Snipe	Type on the bottom of the screen like promos for TV shows
Spokesperson	Creates awareness (Catherine Zeta-Jones or Carly Foulkes – T-Mobile)
Storyboard	A visual representation of a spot that shows the action and spoken lines in a frame-by-frame portrayal
Super	Superimpose text or image on screen
Tags	Closing lines that are recorded and inserted at the end of a spot to announce different locations, sale dates, and special offers
Take	A specific shot in a commercial, numbered and recorded on the clap board for future reference
Talent release	A written agreement with a talent as legal proof of payment, indicating a buyout that is signed by the talent, stating the amount paid, client name, title of spot, date of spot, name and location of studio
Talk value	Spots that generate consumer conversations about them
Talking head	Focuses attention on what's being said about product
Testimonial	People talk about the product to establish credibility
Tone	1,000 hertz tone plays before commercial as a pretest for audio track levels
Union signatory	Authorized union representative who completes, signs and sends in paperwork for each spot using union talent
Union talent	Actors who are union members of SAG or AFTRA
Vignette	Presents a little story like a short play
Voiceover (VO)	Off-camera actor
Wardrobe	Person in charge of selecting (styling) and maintaining the actors' clothing during filming
Wipe	Image is swept off screen as if it's wiped away
Wrap	The word to describe the completion of a spot, "That's a wrap"

TEMPLATES 7.11 Basic TV copy format

Remember only double space between frames. Also, allow the music, sound effects and actor names to create an aligned column between "Video" and "Audio."

VIDEO		AUDIO
	SUPER MODEL:	Humming along to song.
MS SUPER MODEL ON		
HAMMOCK AT OCEAN	MUSIC:	ROMANTIC BRAZILIAN UP AND UNDER
	SFX:	(OCEAN WAVES)
CUTE GUY WALKS BY	GUY:	Room for two?
	SUPER MODEL:	Maybe . . . that depends.
	SFX:	(SEAGULLS)
	GUY:	On what?

temptation as an almost irresistible, three-dimensional character. Notice the common elements from spot to spot like (1) the use of the icon, (2) the monster's whimsical personality, (3) the color orange, (4) the repeated phrases like "Show hungry who's boss," (5) the superimposition of the phone number, and (6) the inclusion of the slogan, "Stop dieting. Start living," which uses two techniques: *imperative* and *parallel construction*. The more spots you view in a campaign, the more you'll understand how to create spots that relate to each other. Look for excellent visual references that you can keep in mind when you're writing.

SCRIPTS AND EXAMPLES 7.12 Weight Watchers "momentum" campaign examples

1   Weight Watchers Momentum Program **"Hungry"** :60 TV spot: http://www.youtube.com/watch?v=K1 ytP9oazCo&feature=PlayList&p=19F844809DDE4FB0&playnext=1&playnext_from=PL&index=19 (accessed March 14, 2010)

2   Weight Watchers Momentum Program **"Hungry"** :30 TV spot (shorter version – notice what has been edited out): http://www.youtube.com/watch?v=LmXgkS3beFg&feature=PlayList&p=19F844809DD E4FB0&playnext=1&playnext_from=PL&index=16 (accessed March 14, 2010)

3   Weight Watchers Momentum Program **"Hungry in the Office"** :60 TV spot: http://www.youtube. com/watch?v=49WjrRJ_DLw&feature=PlayList&p=19F844809DDE4FB0&playnext=1&playnext_ from=PL&index=17 (accessed March 14, 2010)

4   Weight Watchers Momentum Program **"Hungry Online"** :60 online video: http://www.youtube. com/watch?v=nrwTB_yPuKc&feature=PlayList&p=82E5F609D9AE6F84&playnext=1&playnext_ from=PL&index=48(accessed March 14, 2010)

Creative TV exercises

Exercise 1: watch two of the above Weight Watchers Momentum Program "hungry" spots

Compare a :60 with a :30. How did the writer edit down the spot? What's been eliminated? Now, edit this spot down to a :10 (10-second spot).

Exercise 2: choose one of your favorite Super Bowl spots

You can go to this site http://www.spike.com/superbowl, http://www.myspace.com/superbowlads, or http://youtube.com to view them before deciding. This YouTube page has the top ten of the year: http://www.youtube.com/watch?v5_6Ce-SJreIA.

How could you extend the campaign creatively?

Exercise 3: write a 30-second TV spot to *spin out* the campaign using the same *strategy* of the main campaign

Be sure you create a campaign and use the same talent, characters, visuals, music, typography for supers, and placement of elements. Consider what sound effects would place the listener in the same scene.

Now write the same commercial as a 15-second spot. What copy could you eliminate and still deliver the same message?

Exercise 4: find one TV spot that uses one of these techniques

a Unusual visual

b Compelling sound effects

c Humor

d Vignette

Exercise 5: write a humorous :30 radio spot and a :30 TV spot

The TV spot should be for an unusual flavor of Jones soda like the following:

a Turkey & gravy

b Broccoli and cheese

c String bean casserole

d Pumpkin pie

Go to these and other websites for more information about Jones soda: http://www.jonessoda.com/ and http://en.wikipedia.org/wiki/Jones_Soda_flavor_list.

Exercise 6: Lavakan Automatic Dog Wash

Write a convincing :60 radio spot and a :30 TV spot for Lavakan Automatic Dog Wash or any other perfect pooch automatic doggie wash. You can use any technique like product demonstration, testimonial, celebrity spokesperson (can be a canine film star), vignette, product comparison, or slice of life. It's your choice. Check out these websites to see how the machine works: http://www.youtube.com/watch?v=MWR8K_RKZOo and http://www.youtube.com/watch?v5fKkYcSXJwbY&feature5related.

Exercise 7: two parodies: the Smirnoff Parody and the Sienna Swagger Wagon

Watch the Smirnoff spoof on Hip Hop culture, "Tea Partay," http://www.youtube.com/watch?v5PTU2He2BIc0. Why did this work? Why was it not offensive. Hint: Who does the spot mock? Is everything true in the spot?

Now look at the Sienna Swagger Wagon at http://www.youtube.com/watch?v=ql-N3F1FhW4. Did you find it a playful exaggeration of the Hip Hop culture? Did you find it funny when they asked, "Where my kids at?" Or when they break the rap when the little girl says, "I gotta potty."

Compare the two spots. Look at the casting, the music, the dancing, the visual references like the body language and hand gestures of the Sienna commercial and the finger sandwiches and chocolate Labs in Smirnoff spot. Did they both work? Consider the courage it takes for a client to approve these kinds of spots.

Work on developing a non-offensive parody. You can use Sienna, Smirnoff, or a brand of your choice.

Exercise 8: review the *Advertising Age* "top 20 super bowl ads ever" (http://adage.com/superbowl/top20)

Pick your favorite spot. Why did this one resonate with you? Why was it ranked so high? What made this spot work? What was the strongest part of the spot: (1) the concept, (2) the visual treatment, (3) the excellent copy, or (4) the combination of all the above?

Exercise 9: two versions of the same script for Angie's List

Look closely at the two scripts below (1) "Pay Per View" and (2) "Red Paint." The first one of each spot is "as scripted." The second one is "as produced." Can you spot the rewrites? The little changes make the scripts sound more conversational. For example, in the "Pay Per View" spot, this line, "When my hardwood floors needed refinishing," was changed to "When I wanted hardwood floors installed." It's less wordy and easier to understand. By comparing the changes (highlighted in blue), you'll see how subtle rewrites can greatly improve a spot.

Angie's List TV scripts: script 1 – "Pay Per View" :30 (as scripted – before or "preproduction")

FRAME ONE:
WOMAN (VO): "When my hardwood floors needed refinishing, I hired (SFX: Beep to obscure business name)."

FRAME TWO:
WOMAN (VO): "His work was okay, but the job took twice as long as he'd originally estimated."

FRAME THREE:
WOMAN (VO): "One month later, I opened my cable bill and found out why. He'd been . . ."

FRAME FOUR:
WOMAN (VO): " . . . watching pay-per-view movies on my TV, when he was supposed to be working!"

FRAME FIVE:
WOMAN (VO): "Don't let this guy anywhere near your house. Or, for that matter, your remote control."

FRAME SIX:
ANNCR (VO): "Angie's List helps you . . ."

FRAME SEVEN:
ANNCR (VO): " . . . decide which local service companies to . . ."

FRAME EIGHT:
ANNCR (VO): " . . . trust, and which to avoid."

FRAME NINE:
ANNCR (VO): "Get the power of the list . . ."

FRAME TEN:
ANNCR (VO): " . . . at Angie's List."

Angie's List TV – "Pay Per View" :30 (as produced – or after revisions)

FRAME ONE:
WOMAN (VO): "When I wanted hardwood floors installed, I hired (SFX: Beep to obscure business name)."

FRAME TWO:
WOMAN (VO): "His work was okay, but the job took twice as long as he'd originally estimated."

FRAME THREE:
WOMAN (VO): "One month later, I opened my cable bill and found out why. He'd been . . ."

FRAME FOUR:
WOMAN (VO): " . . . watching pay-per-view movies on my TV, when he was supposed to be working!"

FRAME FIVE:
WOMAN (VO): "Don't let this guy anywhere near your house. Or, for that matter, your remote control."

FRAME SIX:
ANNCR (VO): "Angie's List uses homeowner experience . . ."

FRAME SEVEN:
ANNCR (VO): " . . . to help you learn which companies to . . ."

FRAME EIGHT:
ANNCR (VO): " . . . trust, and which to avoid."

FRAME NINE:
ANNCR (VO): "Get the power of the list . . ."

FRAME TEN:
ANNCR (VO): " . . . at Angie's List."

(*This "Pay-Per-View" TV script was created by Young & Laramore for Angie's List. Image courtesy of Young & Laramore.*)

Angie's List TV scripts: script 2 – "Red Paint" :30 (as scripted)

FRAME ONE:
VO 1: "If you hire Richard's Painting service, you may want to consider colors other than red. The job began with four painters. It ended with three."

FRAME TWO:
VO 1: "One of the guys stepped into a tray of red paint and tracked it through my living room."

FRAME THREE:
VO 1: "The other painters quickly helped him clean it up, but then stared teasing him."

FRAME FOUR:
VO 1: "After a couple of hours, he was in tears and stormed out of the house with his red shoe leading the way. While they finished the job on time and on budget . . ."

FRAME FIVE:
CUT TO CLOSE-UP OF WOMAN TYPING THE FINAL WORDS TO THE REPORT ON ANGIE'S LIST AND HITTING "SUBMIT REPORT."

FRAME SIX:
VO 1: " . . . they're far from true professionals."

FRAME SEVEN:
VO 2: "Visit Angie's List for thousands of unbiased reports on service companies in your area. Educate your guess at Angie's List."

Angie's List TV scripts: "Red Paint" :30 (as produced)

FRAME ONE:
VO 1: "If you hire (SFX: Beep to obscure business name) Painting, you may want to consider colors other than red. The job began with four painters, but ended with three."

FRAME TWO:
VO 1: "One guy stepped in red paint and tracked it across the living room."

FRAME THREE:
VO 1: "And after some teasing from the others . . ."

FRAME FOUR:
VO 1: " . . . he stormed out, his red shoe leading the way. They may have finished on time and budget . . ."

FRAME FIVE:
CUT TO CLOSE-UP OF WOMAN TYPING THE FINAL WORDS TO THE REPORT ON ANGIE'S LIST AND HITTING "SUBMIT REPORT."

FRAME SIX:
VO 1: " . . . but they're far from true professionals."

FRAME SEVEN:
VO 2: "Visit Angie's List for thousands of unbiased reports from members in your area. Get the power of the list, at Angie's List."

(*This "Red Paint" :30 TV script was created by Young & Laramore for Angie's List. Image courtesy of Young & Laramore.*)

Notes

1   Denis Higgins, *The Art of Writing Advertising: Conversations with the Masters of the Craft* (Chicago, IL: NTC Business Books, 1965), 85.

2   Drummond Berman and Simon Nickson, personal communication, April 8, 2009.

3   Drummond Berman and Simon Nickson, personal communication, April 8, 2009.

4   Sheena Brady, personal communication, May 8, 2009.

5   Sheena Brady, personal communication, May 8, 2009.

6   Jack Westerholt, personal communication, August 14, 2009.

7   Jack Westerholt, personal communication, August 14, 2009.

8   Charlie Hopper, personal communication, November 26, 2008.

9   Kevin Moriarty, personal communication, August 24, 2009.

10   Kevin Moriarty, personal communication, August 24, 2009.

11   Teddy Brown, personal communication, October 26, 2009.

12   Teddy Brown, personal communication, October 26, 2009.

13   Teddy Brown, personal communication, October 26, 2009.

14   Teddy Brown, personal communication, October 26, 2009.

15   Kevin Moriarty, personal communication, August 24, 2009.

16   Kevin Moriarty, personal communication, August 24, 2009.

17   Sara Rose, personal communication, April 24, 2009.

18   Sara Rose, personal communication, April 24, 2009.

19 Sara Rose, personal communication, April 24, 2009.

20 Sara Rose, personal communication, April 24, 2009.

21 The Designers and Art Directors Association of the United Kingdom, *The Copywriter's Bible* (Mies, Switzerland: RotoVision SA, 2000), 109.

22 Robert Bly, *The Copywriter's Handbook: A Step-by-Step Guide to Writing Copy That Sells* (New York, NY: Henry Holt, 2005), 232–237.

23 Tom Amico, personal communication, June 30, 2009.

24 Sara Rose, personal communication, April 24, 2009.

25 Vinny Warren, personal communication, September 4, 2009.

8

THE DELIVERED AND ABRIDGED WORD

Direct mail, mobile, and small-space writing

When you write, always try to win their hearts. Their minds will tag along.

JUAN SANTIAGO LAGOS, ASSOCIATE CREATIVE DIRECTOR ALMA/DDB [1]

Exploring direct mail

Grasping why direct mail?

Learning a few pointers about writing self-promotion letters

Creating messages for mobile e-mail marketing

Writing copy for product packaging

Examining examples of creative package copy

Learning some tips for small-space writing from Charlie Hopper

Creating coupon copy

Examining online banner ad copy

Understanding catalog copywriting

Creative abridged writing exercises

In the following pages, you'll learn the difference between direct mail and direct response. And why, with direct mail, you need think about creating the outside message before the inside one. You'll realize that even the most mundane assignments can be creative, like the Orkin postcards. You'll find out why direct mail is still being used and how to make it fun, effective, and strategic. You'll be referred back to chapter 2, so you can review the 50 types of strategies.

You'll also read about writing sales letters. If you're thinking, "Who cares?" You do. You may be writing a letter of introduction to a prospective employer or as a follow up e-mail after an interview. Yes, they're sales letters. And, they need to be persuasive.

You'll be reminded to think about other direct methods of reaching your audience, such as e-mails, mobile coupons, product-related apps, interactive (online) banner ads, and so on. You'll read about tips for creating successful e-mail marketing campaigns. You'll discover the importance of editing down your writing for small-space messages like coupons, catalogs, and product packaging. Best of all, you'll examine some exciting examples of humorous package copy, including Ugly Mug Coffee and Red Brick Beer.

Okay, enough said. Now let's begin our investigation of the delivered word through direct mail, mobile, and small-space messaging.

Exploring direct mail

No matter how many people believe direct mail is an ancient marketing tactic, it still exists. Therefore, well-rounded copywriters need to be equally comfortable in this in other small-space media vehicles. We will now examine the writing techniques that create powerful direct marketing communication. So that the received material is read and saved, not ignored and tossed. What's unique about direct mail is that there two parts to consider when writing: (1) the outside and (2) inside (or reverse side). Writing a compelling message for the outside of the piece instantly captures the recipient's attention. That is true whether it's on the envelope of an inserted piece or on the front side of a self-mailer, (marketing materials sent without an envelope). For example, if a headline on the envelope reads, "Ummm . . . there's an ice-cream cake inside," you might open it. Inside could be a coupon from Carvel or Dairy Queen.

Here are a few points to remember when creating copy that will be delivered as a *direct mail* piece in the mail. This is often confused with *direct response* mechanisms. Those are messages with a call to action, not necessarily delivered by the post office. These cover a wide range of media from printed pieces like door hangers, magazine sleeves, messages on dry cleaning bags, coupons; *out-of-home* ads like billboards with 1-800 numbers; digital coupons on websites, mobile devices or sent by e-mail, and so on. Let's get back to direct mail. Here's a short, useful list of considerations.

The last example (e) is called an "*eyebrow*" in a print ad. We discussed this in chapter 5 As a reminder, it's a line of copy that sits about the headline and targets a specific audience.

Media change; customers don't. **DRAYTON BIRD, WRITER, SPEAKER, MARKETER AND AUTHOR OF** *COMMONSENSE DIRECT & DIGITAL MARKETING*[2]

Grasping why direct mail?

Before you write anything that's going to be mailed, you must clearly understand why this particular format was chosen as the medium.

CHECKLIST 8.1 Direct mail handy checklist

1   Consider the outside first.

    a How can you get the recipient to read a self-mailer?

    b What could you say on an envelope or box to entice the addressee to see what's inside?

        i Ask an intriguing question.

        ii Make a seemingly outrageous, yet true, statement.

        iii Deliver an important and relevant fact.

        iv Offer a savings or coupon.

        v State there's a product sample inside (a small consumer tester, like a tiny bottle of shampoo, a mini bar of soap, or a little box of cookies).

2   Know how this piece will be sent.

    a To occupant through bulk mail?

    b To a specific, named recipient through standard mail?

    c To a targeted and restricted audience through a priority or rush delivery?

3   Think about how to personalize the message.

    a Feature how the company, product, or service solves problems.

    b Demonstrate why readers need to act now.

    c Propose a limited, time-sensitive offer.

    d Present an immediate or frequent-user discount.

    e Address the consumer as a product user. For example: "Attention eyeglass wearers" or "Cookie lovers."

Look at these questions and be sure you can answer them before you start developing the copy:

- What benefits are there in direct mail?
- What's the purpose of the piece?
- What needs to be said first?
- Who's your primary audience?
- What do they need to hear?
- How will this product help them?
- What do you want them to know?

Even if you throw out all the junk mail you receive, you should start looking at the pieces that you at least glanced at. If you receive or discover a great direct mail piece, keep it and start a "clip" or "swipe" file with great examples. This way you'll always have a reference. Also, be sure you're reading award annuals like the *One Show*, going online to see industry award show winners like the Cannes Lions International Advertising Festival, Webby, D&AD, Clio, and the Art Directors Club, or trade publications like *Advertising Age*

(*Ad Age*), *Adweek, CMYK, HOW, Communication Arts, Print,* and more. Some publications have related magazines like Ad Age's *Creativity.*

Drayton Bird, writer, speaker, marketer and author, who ran Ogilvy & Mather Direct in London, has written several advertising and copywriting books. His classic, written 25 years ago, *Commonsense Direct & Digital Marketing* is in its fifth edition. There's a quote on the cover by David Ogilvy that reads, "Read it and re-read it. It contains the knowledge of a lifetime." The inside cover added another Ogilvy quote: "Drayton Bird knows more about Direct Marketing than anyone in the world. His book about it is pure gold." On his blog site http://drayton-bird-droppings.blogspot.com/ he lists "51 Helpful Direct Mail Ideas." I've selected the following dozen tips and included in parenthesis their original numbers.

1 *(#1) Communicate more than your competitors.*
2 *(#2) Do what a salesman would do.*
3 *(#9) Write from me to you – never from a "team."*
4 *(#14) Online marketing is just accelerated offline marketing.*
5 *(#16) Use "reason why" copy.*
6 *(#21) Always make it easy to respond.*
7 *(# 26) Read your copy out loud.*
8 *(#27) Use research for illumination. Not support.*
9 *(#29) Leave well enough alone if tests prove something new won't be better.*
10 *(#32) Search the world and steal the best.*
11 *(#38) Spend 90% of your time thinking about how to single out your prospect.*
12 *(#47) Until you know how to do better, copy.*[3]

From his website (http://www.drayton@draytonbird.co.uk) you can read several helpful articles. Here's an excerpt from "7 Deadly Sins and How to Improve Results."

Why do many people call direct mail "junk"? Because most is.
But sending sloppy junk to people is really a form of personal insult. It says you don't care.
Here's where people go wrong – and how you can make your messages work much, much better.

1 *Not taking it seriously.*
2 *Failure to test.*
3 *Not aiming at the right people.*
4 *Trying to be clever.*
5 *Being too brief.*
6 *Omitting essentials.*
7 *Not having a letter.*[4]

Bird was asked how often a marketer should write to a consumer. Here was his answer: "The question is not how often do you write, it is what you say when you write." He continued saying, "The aim is that people should look forward to getting it, not "more bloody sales stuff from them."[5]

Direct mail is not a hit-and-miss medium. Each piece that's sent out can be tested for its effectiveness by tracking the call to action. For example, how many coded (for tracking

FIGURE 8.1 This "Beach" postcard was created by The Richards Group for Orkin. Image courtesy of The Richards Group and Orkin.

purposes) coupons were redeemed? How many calls came in to a designated toll-free number? How many people entered a code online to make a purchase? And, so on.

Writing for a direct mail message means being pithy. Get to the point and have a benefit. Before approving the copy ask yourself: "Would I read this or ignore it?" If it's in an envelope, ask, "Would I open it or toss it out?" Be honest. Be painfully truthful with yourself. If it bores you, it will bore the reader. It doesn't matter what the medium. The message is still about being relevant, *on- strategy*, *on- target*, and engaging. So, the audience will respond.

Even if you rarely ever write direct mail, you still need to be versed in the medium. Although his agency doesn't create a great deal of direct mail, Vinny Warren, founder and creative director of The Escape Pod, explained his agency's approach this vehicle like this:

> *Obviously, it's a cousin of print. Basically, with direct mail what you're doing is hoping that what you're saying is exactly what the person needs to hear. So generally speaking it's like, "Do you need a new boiler?" "Oh, I need a new boiler."*
>
> *So it's like you have to assume interest, I think. You have to assume interest in general, but in this case, in direct mail, you have to go with the assumption that it is, "Oh, this is exactly what this person needs on some level."*[6]

Here are two fun examples of direct mail postcards by Orkin (see Figure 8.1, Figure 8.2), the pest control service company. Before you look at them, ask yourself what you would do with this kind of assignment. Would you look for a concept that forced the recipient to read the postcard? Or would you just write a predictable headline? Remember, regardless of the scope of the assignment, whether it's a local or global message, it should always reflect your best thinking.

Look how the postcards used a combination of strategies discussed in chapter 2 to point out that your home is now bug free. These included *role reversal* (#22), *humor* (#25), *anthropomorphism* (#27), and *exaggeration* (#29) strategies. The homeowners received the postcards, supposedly sent from the insects that

I think what writers and creators generally have to be armed with is this: try not to take criticism personally. **MATT ZISELMAN, CREATIVE DIRECTOR, SAPIENTNITRO**[7]

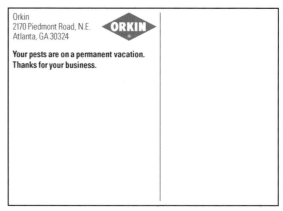

FIGURE 8.2 This "Snow" postcard was created by The Richards Group for Orkin. Image courtesy of The Richards Group and Orkin.

were shipped off to a "vacation," compliments of Orkin. It's also a way to remind customers that their homes are fully protected.

The copy has to show the audience why they want the product or service. Think W-I-I-F-Ms. Remember that means what's in it for me? If you can't clearly demonstrate the benefit, who cares? No one has time to bother reading irrelevant materials. Notice how relevant and reassuring the Orkin messages were.

Besides marketing materials that you will create for clients, you should also learn how to write strong sales letters, as well. Why? Because you probably will be writing a letter of introduction for a dream job or a global account some day. So, learning how to spark the reader's interest will always serve you well, especially if that person is your prospective employer or client. If your letter is strong enough, it could at least land you an interview or meeting.

Learning a few pointers about writing self-promotion letters

Writing a powerful letter is not a useless skill. And, no, it's not a lost art. It's a vital skill you need to develop. That is, if you want to work at your first-choice agency or company and if you want to write proposal letters that grab the attention of potential clients. Some people have arranged interviews and client pitch (presentation) invitations just from the strength of their introduction letters.

Okay, so how do you begin? By becoming the recipient and asking: "What do I need to hear to keep reading?" Creative hiring decision makers are looking to be entertained, surprised, impressed, and basically swept away by your persuasive copy.

Here are a few basic rules to keep in mind from one of the most respected direct mail marketers, Drayton Bird, whom we've mentioned earlier.

Notice how this list of points works equally well whether you're looking to be hired as a job applicant by an employer or as an agency by a client. The most important point is to remember what you can provide, not what you're looking to get, like invaluable experience. Turn the letter around in your mind and feature what you bring to the proverbial table.

ADVICE FROM THE PROS 8.2 Drayton Bird's letter writing principles

1 Only approach the right people – the ones you think you can do a good job for; those for whom your "product" – you and your talents – is right.

2 Conduct reconnaissance. Learn as much as you can about the people you want to work for. This will enable you to speak to the right people and address their needs. It also shows you have been keen enough to learn about them. Every time I get a letter from a job applicant, which refers to something my company or I have done, I read with quickened interest. Like everyone else I am interested in people who are interested in me.

3 Following that, talk about the interests of your prospect, not your own (nearly all job application letters I see talk about what the applicant wants rather than what's in it for me).

4 Then move on to your special skills, which you must relate to the needs of your potential employer, just as you must relate the needs of your customer to your product or service.

5 Put in some impartial proof that what you say is true. Hardly any letters do. Almost invariably when somebody writes to me for a job, I write back and ask them for comments from previous employers, as well as samples of their work.

6 Include a résumé, which gives every reason why you should be hired.

7 Make it abundantly clear that you're eager to work for the people you're writing to and say why.[8]

For successful sales letters, Bird lists five specific ingredients. These are (1) Know your product or service, (2) Think about your prospects (potential customers or clients), (3) Create an offer or incentive to take action, (4) Polish your writing technique, and (5) Demonstrate your writing talent. Bird pointed out that the first three ingredients, or components, don't include talent, but emphasize content.[9] As long as the content is focused on the product and consumer, and offers an incentive to buy, the letter will still succeed. You might present a trial offer or money-back guarantee (if it's a product). That gives consumers more confidence to make the purchase. You could also consider including the following when writing your own "pitch" (self-promotion) letter:

1 Select the agencies or companies you believe are a "fit" for your creative talent.

2 Show that you are highly familiar with the kind of accounts they handle and/or creative work they do.

3 Provide a glimpse into your creativity by writing in an engaging way.

4 Consider using visuals. Yes, in a letter. They're unexpected.

5 State clearly why you're a match.

6 Demonstrate your innovative thinking and unique skills.

7 Sell them on YOU!

Whatever message you're creating, whether it's direct mail, an e-mail, or mobile, you must show readers why they should respond. Paint a benefit-laden self-portrait and present an irresistible offer. Think mutual benefit and reward.

Creating messages for mobile e-mail marketing

Messages today reach consumers everywhere they are. Mobile devices have become yet another medium to speak to them. Marketers are using them to stay in touch, as reminder notices for medications, as coupon delivery systems, as product-related apps, as ad vehicles within interactive games (as mentioned in chapter 12), and more. Rather than being hesitant to develop mobile messages, jump in. You just need to realize if you have a Web-enabled phone or another mobile device, you're already playing in the arena.

Here's an article that will help you understand how to write stronger mobile copy. Realize your readers are on the go. They don't have time for vague correspondence or unclear offers. Get focused. Then, get writing. Author Shane Ketterman's blog Tablet Computer Geeks posts current information on the iPad, including accessory reviews, app reviews, and industry updates.

As you read the article, look at Ketterman's easy writing style (Advice From the Pros 8.3). Notice the short and uncluttered sentences. Look how his first sentence uses neuro-linguistic language for the visual person (discussed in chapter 3): "Picture this scene." Did you keep reading? Analyze what made you continue. Then, learn from writers that pull you in. Whether they're journalists, bloggers, novelists, non-fiction writers, or copywriters. If you can't stop until you finish what you're reading, become a student of that writer.

Look how the blogger takes you step by step through the process and wraps everything up at the end. Focus every time you're reading. Look at sentence length, organization, tone of voice, and overall writing style. Examine whatever you read. Dissect the prose or copy. Don't be a sleepy reader. Be alert and analytical. Soon you'll pick up useful techniques just by noticing them.

Writing copy for product packaging

Just as in direct mail, mobile e-mail marketing, and other direct response mechanisms, brevity is the key to product package copy. Space limitation forces writers to condense their thoughts down to the most minimal expression. Whether they're developing messages for cereal boxes or canned goods, movie DVDs or musical CDs, package writers must say more in less space. Although package design drives the consumers' eye to the product, the message must clarify what it contains to help make the sale. Let's examine the difficulties and solutions to package writing in this small-space overview.

Examining examples of creative package copy

Just as you should glance at all incoming junk mail, you should also look at every item you buy. Examine every promotional item you receive. And pay attention to the copy, even on your breakfast cereal boxes. If you pay attention, you might find some entertaining writing at the most unexpected places.

ADVICE FROM THE PROS 8.3 Five tips for better results with mobile e-mail marketing from Shane Ketterman

Picture this scene.

A reader of your blog and a loyal subscriber gets a new mobile device.

No problem: You've taken great care to make your site mobile friendly.

You've even taken the right steps to convert more mobile readers to your e-mail list.

So you feel pretty confident that all your bases are covered.

Until your subscriber gets her first e-mail from your latest marketing campaign. It's all squished up on the screen, it's impossible to click on any of the links, and the message overall is terribly hard to read.

Your loyal reader really wants to get the benefit of your great content. So she spends some time fumbling around trying to make sense of it.

But eventually frustration wins. She gives up and hits the red "delete" key.

Think this doesn't happen? It sure does. I've seen it, more than once.

Mobile e-mail marketing design is smoking hot. If you can manage to make sure your mobile readers are satisfied with those subscriber-based e-mails, then you have covered what may be the largest of your readership. And here are some tips to help you out:

1 Include a plain text version of every message

Including a plain text copy of every HTML message you send will help eliminate potential issues for those subscribers with mobile readers that do not support HTML.

Any good e-mail marketing service lets you include a plain text version, make sure you're using it.

2 Keep links uncrowded

If your e-mail message has links that you want your readers to click on, such as navigation back to your main site (recommended), then make sure those links stand out on their own.

In other words, keep them uncrowded so it's easy to click them within a very small space.

Imagine your loyal reader flicking around on a tiny screen to get to that link – and how frustrated you get when the links are so close together that you can't land on the one you want. If you want clicks, make it easy.

3 Pull the reader in with your subject line

Hop on over and read Brian's article on the three key elements of irresistible e-mail subject lines.

Now . . . actually use those three key elements for your e-mail marketing messages.

Like any headline, an e-mail subject line has to capture attention quickly and drive the reader to click through.

By the way, the current best practice for subject lines for mobile devices is to keep it within five words. That's right, you have about five words to grab the attention of your reader. Why? Because after about five to seven words, the subject line gets truncated and thus it's a lost opportunity.

4 Use the right tags for your images

If your e-mail marketing message includes images, make sure you include an alternative (alt) tag to describe what the image is. (You should be doing this for any HTML content you create – mobile readers aren't the only users who may not be able to see your images.)

Don't stuff this tag full of keywords, it doesn't work. Use it for what it was meant for – to briefly describe what the image is, in a way that lets your reader make sense of it if the image isn't visible.

Many devices can display all your images correctly, but not all of them will, so it's just smart to use alternative text to make sure every reader gets the message that image was supposed to convey.

5 Is your call to action clear?

People using mobile devices spend a little less time taking in the content due to the smaller screen sizes and the fact that they are usually on the go, so make sure your e-mail marketing has a clear call to action.

Put it either near the beginning or somewhere where it will stand out. Don't make it hard to find . . . after all, it's the key to getting the response you want.

Last thoughts

You might be wondering how to know what your e-mail message will look like on all these devices. Just because it looks great on an iPhone doesn't mean it won't be mangled on a Blackberry. There are some great simulators out there that let you see how things will appear on the various devices. A Google search for "mobile device simulator" will give you lots of options.

Whatever e-mail marketing service you use, spend some time in settings area and explore the various options they have for delivery. Now that you have some tips to keep in mind, you never know what options they have that you just didn't see before.

How about you – what experiences have you had with mobile devices and e-mail marketing?[10]

For example, when Miami Ad School wanted to develop a memorable self-promotion, it created its own brand of bottled water. Everyone who's familiar with the school knows that the owners and founders, Ron and Pippa Seichrist, bring their dogs to work and allow students to bring their furry friends to the school. One of the dog's names was Smudge. So, naturally it called the water "Miami Ad School Smudge Slobber." In this case, the school wanted to showcase its creative talent. President Pippa Seichrist was the copywriter who penned these fun lines for the water bottle label (see Figure 8.3):

Delicious! Refreshing! Authentic Smudge Slobber is collected three times daily, just before feedings to assure the most abundant flow and richest flavor. Depending on his diet, the bouquet varies from a peppery range-raised chicken (if he steals an unfinished sandwich from one of the students) to just a hint of blueberry (when he finds an unattended muffin.) Of course, the richest flavor of all is the deep taste of game after an especially ripe roadkill. Smudge is not particularly fond of cat nuggets so his slobber almost never has the telltale acidity of kitty litter. Drink this slobber knowing that you are enjoying perhaps the most extraordinary blend in the animal kingdom. Smudge Slobber is only available from the private collection of Miami Ad School. It's not sold at Walmart and cannot be found at any vineyard in Napa. Drink and enjoy! Warning: This product is highly addictive. Too much can cause ears to lengthen and grow fur. If an attraction to crotches or the desire to hump is detected, heel, sit and rollover. Good Dog![11]

Just in case you think writing copy for packaging is not exciting, think again. The most mundane writing assignments are there to test your creativity. If you were told you needed to write copy for coffee packages, you might sniff your nose at that. But, before you do, take a look at how the writers at Young & Laramore answered that challenge. The writing is

FIGURE 8.3 This "Smudge Slobber" bottled water label was created by Miami Ad School as a self-promotion. Image courtesy of Miami Ad School.

personal, fun, and whimsical. You feel as if the coffee inside is talking to you. Read through the amusing headlines and then the unexpected package copy. You might never skip reading product packages again.

Charlie Hopper, creative director/copywriter, Young & Laramore was asked about this campaign. Here's what he said about how the writers and designers created it:

> *Ugly Mug is such a wonderful launching point. That was a primo example of a team that really blurred, and even tried to eliminate, the lines between writing and designing, and work together on both aspects of it: the designer having very strong opinions about the writing and the writer having very strong opinions about the design.*[12]

Take a moment and identify the types of techniques and strategies that were used. Notice the use of *vernacular* on the second headline, "We ain't got no alibi," and the use of *imperative* or *command* in the fourth, fifth, and six. You can't help but smile over the dry humor, like number five: "We did our part. Now don't mess this up."

The back of all the coffee bags share the same copy, which is set in all caps and includes the "*sig*" or *signature* (corporate information) as we discussed in chapter 5:

UGLY MUG COFFEE CO.
  Memphis, Tennessee USA
  uglymugcoffee.com

This mandatory copy, generally referred to as "*mandatories*," gives loyalists a chance to contact the company directly and order more coffee online. (See Figure 8.4, Figure 8.5, Figure 8.6, Figure 8.7, Figure 8.8, Figure 8.9, Figure 8.10, Figure 8.11.)

CHECKLIST 8.4 Small-space writing checklist

1 Think Small.

  a Say more in less.

  b Rush to the main idea.

  c Delete all unnecessary copy.

2 Become an Observer.

  a Go shopping for examples.

  b What stopped you in the store:

    i   Package design?

    ii Colors on package?

    iii Copy on box?

3 Ask Yourself: What Would Make You Buy?

With just a few words to say, be critical. Ask, did it:

  a Create curiosity?

  b Answer an objective?

  c Provide a solution?

  d Promise entertainment?

4 Collect Great Examples.

  a Create a swipe or clip file.

  b Save packages, including:

    i   Items you purchased

    ii   Products with amazing packaging, including

    iii CDs

    iv   DVDs

    v   Unique teas

    vi   Product packaging with exciting copy

      1 Toys

      2 Books

      3 Games

      4 Cereals

      5 Digital devices

SCRIPTS AND EXAMPLES 8.5 Headlines for Ugly Mug Coffee bags (these were set in all caps on the bags.)

1 OH, WHAT A BEAUTIFUL MORNING (bag with red type)

2 WE AIN'T GOT NO ALIBI (bag with dark brown type)

3 COFFEE POWER ACTIVATE! (bag with yellow type)

4 WE DID OUR PART. NOW DON'T MESS THIS UP (bag with green type)

5 DON'T BE WAITING FOR NO APOLOGY. IT AIN'T COMING (bag with light blue type)

6 WAKE THE WAKE OF THE JUST (bag with light brown type)

7 YOU ARE NOW LEAVING SLEEPYTOWN (bag with dark blue type)

8 TICKLES THE COFFEE BONE (bag with orange type)

Back panel copy:

This Coffee . . .

Hails from Memphis. The Seattle of Southwestern Tennessee. Is purchased, roasted and packaged with a little something we like to call integrity. Reminds us of a time before the double mint mocha decaf skim latté ruled the earth. Knows good looks will only get you so far. Speaks without resorting to faux European words. Except faux. Understands you. Maybe too well. Works best with one to two tablespoons of ground coffee per 6 ounces of water. Is the latest little bundle of joy from Ugly Mug Coffee[13]

(Copy courtesy of Young & Laramore.)

FIGURE 8.4 This unexpected package display message was created by Young & Laramore for Ugly Mug Coffee. Image courtesy of Young & Laramore.

FIGURE 8.5 This unexpected package display message was created by Young & Laramore for Ugly Mug Coffee. Image courtesy of Young & Laramore.

FIGURE 8.6 This unexpected package display message was created by Young & Laramore for Ugly Mug Coffee. Image courtesy of Young & Laramore.

FIGURE 8.7 This unexpected package display message was created by Young & Laramore for Ugly Mug Coffee. Image courtesy of Young & Laramore.

FIGURE 8.8 This unexpected package display message was created by Young & Laramore for Ugly Mug Coffee. Image courtesy of Young & Laramore.

FIGURE 8.9 This unexpected package display message was created by Young & Laramore for Ugly Mug Coffee. Image courtesy of Young & Laramore.

FIGURE 8.10 This unexpected package display message was created by Young & Laramore for Ugly Mug Coffee. Image courtesy of Young & Laramore.

FIGURE 8.11 This unexpected package display message was created by Young & Laramore for Ugly Mug Coffee. Image courtesy of Young & Laramore.

Learning some tips for small-space writing from Charlie Hopper

Charlie Hopper, creative director at Young & Laramore, explained that writers need only to write enough lines to get the point across. Regardless of the advertising vehicle, small space messages must punctuate the points. Eliminate everything that's superfluous and focus on what you want the reader to know. Here are his tips for writing with space restrictions.

Charlie Hopper's tips for small-space writing

1   In every case – every single medium from banner-being-flown-off-the-back-of-an-airplane-at-the-seashore to a blog entry, the same basic rule always applies: only say what you have to say, and get out. Don't assume people are looking to fill their time by reading your wonderful writing. Say it, and get away.

2   In this age, you have to be interesting or just forget it. Even in a small space, you have to say something worth thinking about, worth spending time with. Because whether you have a Super Bowl ad or a small space, and somehow you induce the reader to spend a moment looking at your copy, they'll instantly forget it and it will be the same net result as if they didn't read it. Be relevant, and surprising, no matter

how much or how little space you have. Say it, be charming (but don't fool around using a lot of space being charming) and get away.

3   Skip the intro. Don't tell them that you're going to be interesting in a moment.

4   Short sentences help. It makes your writing a lot more muscular, and it lures in the reader. They subconsciously note that the sentences are brief. They figure, they can get in and get out. Then they're stuck. Eventually, for rhythm, you might introduce a longer sentence just so you don't sound punchy. But then, be brief again.

5   Go back and edit. In that second sentence in the previous paragraph, I'd originally written, "It makes your writing a lot more muscular . . ." By removing "a lot" I didn't lose much, and I have two words I can spend later on something else.[14]

Other product package copy only used a branded name, a slogan, or a headline. For example, when The Escape Pod developed an OfficeMax brand of "Back-To-School" items, it named the line "Schoolio Von Hoolio." It was fun, catchy, and it rhymed (a writing technique we discussed in chapter 4). It also had no copy and what agency president and founder Vinny Warren called "crazy design." It was easy for kids to ask their parents for it and it was a clever way to introduce a new product line. Vinny Warren, president and founder of the agency, explained the packaging like this:

> It was more of a brand idea that the packaging was integral to. The idea was packaging in a way. It's a "Back-To-School" brand designed to compete. It's an OfficeMax brand. It was designed to compete with Crayola. Their thinking was crayons are crayons. Most of this stuff is generic. So, basic packaging is the thing that can make the difference.
>
> And so our "Schoolio Von Hoolio," if you were a kid at age 10, "Schoolio Von Hoolio" is going to appeal to you more than Crayola, I'm guessing. Because it's more whimsical.
>
> The "Hoolio" is about all the "Back-To-School" stuff. Folders, you name it. It became their internal brand.[15]

When you're developing copy for packages, you may only need to focus on creating a sticky brand name. Sometimes the package design says everything. For example, when a plastic yellow lid was placed on top of a Heineken beer, it resembled a tennis ball container. The design said everything. It was a clear visual statement that instantly connected Heineken to a tennis tournament as a US Open sponsorship. Heineken has continued this relationship for more than 19 years, creating promotional items to increase consumer brand recall.[16]

An amusingly clever promotion was the December 2008, in-time-for-the-holidays "packaging" of Burger King's flame-broiled smell with its own cologne called "Flame." Created by Crispin Porter + Bogusky, it was the first fast-food fragrance and priced at just $3.99, it was sold out in four days. Soon it was on eBay selling for $76.00, mentioned by late-night hosts Jay Leno and David Letterman, and presented as an answer on TV's game show *Jeopardy*, hosted by Alex Trebek. You can read about the product launch and see the "Sell the Smell" video at http://melkreilein.posterous.com/. Then, in 2009, the fragrance was launched in the UK with Piers Morgan in the "The Scent of Seduction" campaign. It sold at Selfridges for £4.99. You can see the UK campaign at http://www.dailymail.co.uk/tvshowbiz/article-1193031/Piers-Morgan-beefcake-advertises-new-Burger-King-perfume-whiff-fakery.html.

One more package design and copy worthy of your full attention is Red Brick Beer, created by 22squared. Developed by Red Brick Brewery, this was a regional beer. The challenge was to reach 120 million Southern beer lovers. How? By speaking "Southernese." And, by integrating iconic Southern phrases and recognizable visuals. The unifying and catchy campaign slogan was "Beer from around here." It had a friendly, familiar and neighborly tone. It also implied a *universal truth*: "The rest of the world is crazy."

The intoxicating copy and down-home design not only produced the intended results, it also received prestigious industry awards. Red Brick's packaging was honored as one of The Dieline's Latest Top 10 Package Designs in 2010.[17] In addition, Red Brick's packaging was featured in *Communication Arts 2010 Design Annual*[18] and one of the campaign's posters received a Merit Award in the 2009 One Show.[19]

With a tiny media budget, 22squared utilized the packaging itself to sell the product. (See Figure 8.12, Figure 8.13, Figure 8.14, Figure 8.15.) The copy made interesting statements and humorous comments on each of the six-packs such as:

1   *Pale Ale* – Like a classic California pale ale, but from America.

    Best served cold. Straight from the bottle. Or a glass. Or a mason jar.

2   *Blonde* – This Blonde has a good crisp body. Stop your snickerin.

    Best served cold. On the porch. In the early evening. With a dog.

3   *Brown* – A nice, smooth ale. Says "Yes sir" and "Yes ma'am."

    Best served cold. Best served below the latitude of 39° 43′ 20° N.

4   *Porter* – As thick and stout as a BBQ line cook.

    Best served cool. On a cold day. But not "Boston" cold. That weather should be illegal.

There are also funny quotes on each six-pack from "Bob," as if consumers knew him. Here are a few examples. (See Figure 8.16, Figure 8.17.) "Bob at Red Brick says" . . .

1   "My friend started drinking Northern brews and soon he was saying the word pop."

2   "When you buy New England beer you're just giving more money to the Queen."

3   "The problem with beer from Milwaukee is that the label's all in Milwaukeean."

4   "We call it Helluva Bock. But you can call it Heckuva Bock if you're drinking it in church."

Curt Mueller, creative director and writer for the Red Brick campaign explained how he and the designer worked together, exchanging ideas back and forth:

During this project, I sat directly next to the designer and we constantly traded copy and designs back and forth. We inspired each other, and we were brutally honest with each other. As a writer on packaging design projects, you have to leave your ego at the door. Your words are only important insofar as they complement the overall design and tone.

He described the brand's uniquely Southern personality and whimsical *tone of voice* in this way:

The South has always seen itself as its own country. We leveraged this attitude and created a new enemy to fight against: the non-Southern import. Our packaging reflected Southern sensibilities and the idea that all beer from outside the South is an import. We added Southern visual references and a lot of Southern humor to make it go down easy.[20]

FIGURE 8.12 This "Beer From Around Here" Pale Ale package design was created by 22squared for Red Brick Beer. Image courtesy of 22squared.

FIGURE 8.13 This "Beer From Around Here" Brown package design was created by 22squared for Red Brick Beer. Image courtesy of 22squared.

FIGURE 8.14 This "Beer From Around Here" bottle package design was created by 22squared for Red Brick Beer. Image courtesy of 22squared.

FIGURE 8.15 This "Beer From Around Here" Southern Sampler package design was created by 22squared for Red Brick Beer. Image courtesy of 22squared.

FIGURE 8.16 This "Beer From Around Here" "Bob Says" side of Pale Ale package design was created by 22squared for Red Brick Beer. Image courtesy of 22squared.

FIGURE 8.17 This "Beer From Around Here" "Bob Says" side of Brown package design was created by 22squared for Red Brick Beer. Image courtesy of 22squared.

Once you look at the campaign carefully, you are able to see how strategically driven the message was. Mueller reduced the creative brief down to one concise sentence:

Immediately increase sales of Red Brick beer by appealing to Southern craft beer drinkers.[21]

He shared the strategic thinking behind the copy in four points:

1   *Their marketing needed a single voice.*

2   *Their budget didn't allow for a significant marketing push.*

3   *We would have to take advantage of their free media: their packaging. The packaging would have to tell the story of Red Brick, and be their "advertising."*

4   *99% of craft beer brands speak like someone you'd hate to have a beer with. We wanted to talk like an old friend – a self-deprecating, half-drunk, Full-Southern friend.*[22]

What is interesting to note is when asked if the copy changed from market to market. Mueller commented, "No, being proudly xenophobic is part of Red Brick's charm."[23]

He went on to describe how the slogan was the catalyst behind the concept, message product names, and package design, creating an instantly recognizable visual impression.

Red Brick is a craft beer made by Atlanta Brewing Company in Atlanta, GA. We redesigned not just their packaging, but their entire visual identity, using the tagline "Beer From Around Here" and the concept that all beer from outside the Southern states is effectively an import. We simplified the names of their products, added writing with Southern personality, and incorporated visual cues from Southern industrial products. With a limited ad budget, we made the packaging the advertising, and managed to turn a brand with no recognizable identity into a brand with not just an identity, but a rich cultural story.[24]

What were the objectives and results of this campaign? Red Brick wanted to increase sales by 100% at the end of 2009. Sales far exceeded that goal within a year. There's no question that this humorous package copy's success was nothing to laugh at.[25]

 ADVICE FROM THE PROS 8.6 Basic writing tips from Curt Mueller

1   Inhale writing that isn't advertising, from Tolstoy to Twilight.

2   Don't have a style. You're a copywriter, not a novelist. Be adaptable.

3   Don't work as hard as senior writers and creative directors, work harder. You're not yet adept at recognizing when you're "there." Keep going long past when you think it's time to quit.

4   Start by writing exactly what you want to say, as simply as possible. Write it at the top of the page and refer to it often.

5   At times you'll feel like a genius; at times you'll feel like an illiterate hack. Neither is true.[26]

What you should notice is how one brand-related product, like the ones mentioned above, can create buzz. It created attention because the idea was unique and unexpected. Challenge yourself to use new media (like smell marketing) in an innovative way for future clients.

Copy for all small-space vehicles requires a special kind of thinking. Writers know the space is limited, so they must begin by deleting whatever is not crucial to the message, and distill the copy down to its bare bones of necessary facts.

Creating coupon copy

Other examples of restricted-space messaging are coupons, from traditional print to digital, including online, e-mail, mobile, such as QR Codes (like coupons for smartphones), and more. When people look for coupons they want two things: savings and a great offer. When Teddy Brown, senior vice president, executive creative director of Orange County office at Draftfcb was asked to talk about Taco Bell coupons, he said:

> They'll do coupons to stimulate traffic. For instance, right now there's a Black Jack Taco spot on the air and they are running a free taco night giveaway. But usually it's this notion of free that stimulates traffic pretty decently. So it's a "Free Taco After Dark," from 6 P.M. to midnight on Halloween.
>
> They'll do things like that. They'll do tie-ins with major league baseball like America gets a free taco if someone steals the base.[27]

He was talking about the fall 2007 "Steal a Base, Steal a Taco" campaign. During the World Series, whenever a baseball player from either team stole a base Taco Bell gave away a free "Beef Crunchy Taco" to anyone who wanted one.[28]

Coupons can generate new and repeat business, traffic, interest in an everyday, special, or introductory item, and can increase sales on slow days. If your coupon has a strong offer and also uses unexpected, creative copy, they will stand out from the competitors.

Vinny Warren, founder and creative director of The Escape Pod, also commented about coupon writing. What was interesting was that the audience, in this case, really wanted to see the message, unlike other advertisements or promotions. Someone clipping coupons is looking to save. Here's what he said:

> Basically, you have to presume interest.
>
> Yes, you've got to go, "Oh, you're interested in ten cents off the frozen peas." It is what it is.
>
> Mostly, you can finesse the execution of them. Ultimately again, people aren't reading them for fun. They're like, " How much do I get off of this?"[29]

Now, let's focus on another type of small-space ad: online banners.

Examining online banner ad copy

Small print ads were one challenge. They didn't have very much physical space to make an impression, so they had to be very creative to work. Online banner ads appear on sites people are already visiting. They're right in front of consumers; yet they need to offer something valuable or they'll be ignored. Creating an impact in a tiny space is still a challenge. The difference is that digital banners can be interactive and ask viewers to click on something, play a game, answer a question, take a quiz, and so on. They can start a brief dialogue with the consumer.

Let's look at a few interactive banner ad campaigns that gained global attention. On the Innocent Drinks website, several banner ads invite consumer so to take action (http://juice.innocentdrinks.co.uk/). They can (1) Watch the TV spot, (2) Shake a tree and win prizes, and (3) Look at the product line. The copy is casual and friendly. For example above the banner ad to see the beverages, the imperative headline states, "Meet the family." It's warm and inviting, like a friendly neighbor's invitation to stop by for a cup of coffee.

Another interactive banner ad that was noticed was the "Pringles Can Hands." The copy, which started with "Love can be complicated," changed each time someone hit the "click" button next to the Pringles icon. It won a 2009 Cannes Cyber Lions Gold Award. See it at http://awardshome.com/cannes2009/pringles/can-hands.html.

Take time to visit digital agencies' websites where you'll see examples of banner ads. Look at Ovation Guitars sweepstakes to win one of 12 celebrity guitars or a $5,000 custom Ovation guitar. Contestants created then posted video guitar lessons. Consumers voted for their favorite lesson and Joe Tunan was the winner. To see the banner ads developed by Digital Surgeons go to the agency's website under "The Work." Click on "Websites," then "Launch" to see it. It's at http://www.digitalsurgeons.com/our-work/#/websites and also at http://digitalsurgeons.com/client/ovation/sneakpeek/728x90/. The first banner ad (Figure 8.18) links to the Ovation Guitars website: http://ovationguitars.com/. See how both banner ads have a call to action: (1) "Check it out" and (2) "Enter to win."

Notice in the first ad how the copy uses vernacular or everyday language as discussed in chapter three and elsewhere. "Blah. Meh. Ugh. Yawn." Then, it wakes up the audience with "Hello" and invites them to "go against the grain," using a *play on words*, as explained in chapter four.

When you think about online banner writing, think about out-of-home billboards. Writers strive to keep the message to seven words or less because people are driving more than 55 miles per hour down the highway. Well, online consumers are usually going even faster, surfing from one website to another. So, you need to stop them and engage them. Or they're gone. Remember, if you can present a good deal or a great prize for a sweepstakes, your message will be relevant to a particular target. As with all advertising, be sure you're clear on who those people are. What their needs or problems are as discussed in chapter 1.

Small-space writing also includes online and printed catalog copy. This form of copywriting is some of the briefest around. You must include all the main points because these shoppers are looking for information. And, they want it fast.

Understanding catalog copywriting

Some other catalog companies, also have retail and e-stores now. Some, like Harry & David, 1-800-Flowers, Walter Drake, and Hammacher Schlemmer (America's longest running catalog, which started out in 1848 as a hardware store with unusual inventory in Manhattan) exist via catalogs and e-stores, alone.

If you end up writing catalog copy for some clients, hop online so you can review them. Start also looking at and collecting printed catalogs wherever you find them. Pay attention

SCRIPTS AND EXAMPLES 8.7 Ovation Guitars copy

FIGURE 8.18 This "Blah-Meh-Ugh- Yawn" animated online banner ad was created by Digital Surgeons for Ovation Guitars. Image courtesy of Digital Surgeons.

1 Banner ad #1 (Figure 8.18)

Blah. Meh. Ugh. Yawn.

Hello. Go against the grain.

Unique tone. Better projection. Unmatched Playability.

The all new

OvationGuitars.com.

Check it out.

2 Banner ad #2

Ovation's Video Lesson Contest

Guitar Giveaway.

Win one of 12 celebrity guitars

or a

$5,000 custom Adams

Enter to Win!

(Copy courtesy of Digital Surgeons.)

CHECKLIST 8.8 Catalog copywriting checklist

1 Put key features first.

2 Write crisp, concise copy.

3 Sell the USP (unique selling point or proposition).

4 Be persuasive.

5 Be truthful. Do not exaggerate.

6 Capture the reader's interest.

7 Say more in fewer words.

8 Reread copy and edit superfluous words.

to how briefly and clearly each item is described. To get an idea how crisp this writing is, define yourself in a sentence of seven words or less. Make sure this one sentence could actually describe your talent to an employer or client. Not so easy, right?

Creative abridged writing exercises

Exercise 1: write an introduction letter for a prospective employer

Part 1 To start, just write three strong paragraphs.

Part 2 Now read it out loud. Ask: Would you call in this applicant for an interview?

1 Is the copy
   a Catchy?
   b Personable?
   c Informative?
   d Engaging?
   e Creative?
   f A reflection of your talent?
   g Persuasive?

2 Does the letter show:
   a Your understanding of the company?
   b What you have to offer?
   c How you could help this firm grow?
   d Why you're an ideal fit?
   e W-I-I-F-M (What's in it for "me," meaning the employer.)

Part 3 Fine-tune the letter to make you sound like the right candidate for the job. Make it tempting. Add one more paragraph to encourage the employer to call you for an interview.

Exercise 2: write an interactive banner ad

1 How can you animate it?
2 What can you ask the audience to do? (Enter a contest, write a comment, or create a video showing them using the product or service.)

Exercise 3: find two examples of great banner ads

Why were they effective? How could you continue the campaign?

Notes

1 Juan Santiago Lagos, personal communication, January 12, 2010.
2 http://drayton-bird-droppings.blogspot.com, posted January 14, 2011 (accessed January 21, 2011).
3 http://drayton-bird-droppings.blogspot.com, posted January 14, 2011 (accessed January 21, 2011).
4 http://drayton-bird-droppings.blogspot.com, posted January 14, 2011 (accessed January 21, 2011).
5 http://drayton-bird-droppings.blogspot.com, posted January 14, 2011 (accessed January 21, 2011).
6 Vinny Warren, personal communication, September 4, 2009.

7   Matt Ziselman, personal communication, January 30, 2009.

8   Drayton Bird, *How to Write Sales Letters That Sell: Learn the Secrets of Successful Direct Mail* (London: Kogan Page, 2004), 21.

9   Bird, *How to Write*, 17–18.

10   http://www.copyblogger.com/mobile-email-marketing/ January 28, 2011 (accessed January 28, 2011).

11   Pippa Seichrist, personal communication, January 30, 2011.

12   Charlie Hopper, personal communication, November 26, 2010.

13   Charlie Hopper, personal communication, November 26, 2010.

14   Charlie Hopper, personal communication, November 26, 2010.

15   Vinny Warren, personal communication, September 4, 2009.

16   Sandi Karchmer, "Heineken a Winner in the U.S. Open," *Marketing Through the Clutter*, posted October 1, 2007, http://sandisolow.blogspot.com/2007/10/heineken-winner-at-us-open.html (accessed February 29, 2011).

17   http://www.thedieline.com/blog/2010/6/21/red-brick-beer.html (accessed March 1, 2011).

18   http://www.commarts.com/SearchOn.aspx?colpg=0&col=1063&inum=376 (accessed March 24, 2011).

19   http://www.oneclub.org/os/search/?year=&id=10456 (accessed March 24, 2011).

20   Curt Mueller, personal communication, March 21, 2011.

21   Curt Mueller, personal communication, March 21, 2011.

22   Curt Mueller, personal communication, March 21, 2011.

23   Curt Mueller, personal communication, March 21, 2011.

24   Curt Mueller, personal communication, March 21, 2011.

25   Curt Mueller, personal communication, March 21, 2011.

26   Curt Mueller, personal communication, March 21, 2011.

27   Teddy Brown, personal communication, October 26, 2009.

28   http://consumerist.com/2007/10/taco-bell-to-give-away-free-tacos-if-a-base-is-stolen-in-the-world-series.html (accessed February 26, 2011).

29   Vinny Warren, personal communication, September 4, 2009.

THE AMBIENT AND MOVING WORD

Out-of-home and transit

> I don't think you should think of yourself as just a writer so much as someone part of the team trying to create an idea.

KEVIN MORIARTY, VICE PRESIDENT AND CREATIVE DIRECTOR, LEO BURNETT [1]

Starting from the medium

Noticing messages wherever you are

Looking closely at out-of-home messages

Thinking about surprising the audience

Understanding your audience's frame of reference

Being irreverent and still effective

Taking a once touchy subject into a humorous campaign

Finding new places to advertise

Creative ambient exercises

The Copywriter's Toolkit: The Complete Guide to Strategic Advertising Copy, First Edition. Margo Berman.
© 2012 Margo Berman. Published 2012 by Blackwell Publishing Ltd.

In this chapter, we'll meander through the entertaining world of ambient and transit advertising. You'll see how stimulating and rewarding it is to create innovative, out-of-home messages. You'll be inspired to think up new places to advertising and you'll start to notice "delivery vehicles" like manhole covers, retail store sliding glass doors, and pedestrian crosswalks. You'll scrutinize promotional messages and find out how to categorize them.

You'll realize how important it is to challenge yourself to come up with ingenious copy as well as novel venues. You'll understand how effective it is to surprise and entertain the consumer. You'll find you can be funny and even irreverent, as in the Legal Sea Foods and Feckin Irish Whiskey campaigns. You'll stretch yourself to think visually so you can enhance any message. You'll also learn to use traditional out-of-home vehicles in nontraditional ways. Like the Silver in the City store window stickers. And how an ordinary bus shelter can deliver a far-from-ordinary message, as in the Charles Schwab campaign.

You'll be inspired to blend technology with signage and create an interactive message that speaks to a very narrow market: New York City marathoners and their families. You'll also find an ambient checklist to help you as you're developing your own unique ideas. Now, let's take a closer look at this exciting medium.

Starting from the medium

Today, more than ever, messages are everywhere: on airport luggage carousels, mall escalator sides, sidewalks, shopping cart handles, basically you name it, and if an advertising hasn't appeared there, it will. Writers unfamiliar with these new vehicles of expression will soon find themselves bypassed or replaced by professionals with a wider repertoire of expertise. Here, we will investigate the emerging media opportunities and the kind of imaginative verbal execution they demand.

Once you know where the message will be seen, you can think backwards. The first question is always this: Where is the message going to be placed so the targeted consumer will see it? Will it be on any of these out-of-home locations? Or somewhere new?

- Sliding glass doors inside mall stores? (Static cling images of people were on both sides of sliding glass doors in malls across the world from Mumbai, India to Buenos Aires, Argentina. When shoppers approached, the doors parted with the static cling people separating. The message "People Move Away When You Have Body Odor" was for Axe deodorant. See it at http://www.hemmy.net/2006/10/15/creative-advertisements-around-the-world/.)

- Retail store windows in malls and airports? (Static cling image of a woman smashing into a sliding glass door to show how well I.C.U. glass cleaner works. See image at http://www.blogiversity.org/forums/t/4965.aspx.)

- An outdoor field? (With a section mowed by a Gillette BIC razor leaning against a billboard. See it at http://www.piculous.com/10-innovative-advertisements/.)

- Mall escalator steps? (Images of people in rollercoaster seats move with the escalator as if they were on the ride at Hopi Hari amusement park, in São Paulo Brazil. See it at http://www.gushmagazine.com/category/Edgy-and-Innovative-Ads/P20/. Click to page 3.)

- Sides of buildings, called "wallscapes"? (A giant, 3-D Spiderman crawls along a building side. See it at http://www.gushmagazine.com/category/Edgy-and-Innovative-Ads/P20/. Click to page 3.)

- Bus wheels? (A bus wheel in Japan acts as the lens of a camera, with the rest of the camera drawn on the bus side, around the tire. See it at http://www.gushmagazine.com/article/camera-bus-wheels/.)

- A Zamboni machine? (With a Gillette Fusion razor in the front of the machine, clean shaving the ice rink at a hockey game. See image at http://www.creativecriminals.com/images/gilettefusion2.jpg or at http://creativecriminals.com/tag/razors/.)

- Pedestrian crosswalk stripes? FedEx Kinko's placed an open, oversized bottle of a liquid white out product on the sidewalk with its brush lying sideways in the crosswalk, as if the lines were just painted. (See it at http://digitalartempire.com/2010/03/amazingly-creative-advertising-you-must-see/.)

- Door hangers? (*The Economist* asking guests "Would you like a wake-up call?" on hotel room doors. See it at http://www.coloribus.com/adsarchive/outdoor-ambient/the-economist-door-hanger-13356555/.)

- Subway overhead handrails? (Bar bells are place along the overhead rails in New York City to remind commuters to work out. They were advertising The Fitness Company. (See it at http://www.blogiversity.org/forums/t/4965.aspx.)

- Subway straps? (An image of a Pilot watch is on the strap, reading, "Try it here. The big Pilot's watch". See it at http://www.designenterprise.com/wp-content/uploads/2007/08/busads.jpg.)

- Power lines? (There was a gigantic, wide-tooth comb set into power lines with the Rejoice logo to publicize Asia's number one detangling shampoo by Procter & Gamble. See it at http://www.piculous.com/10-innovative-advertisements/.)

- Bendable straws? (This showed a flexible woman bending backwards to promote the Y-Plus Yoga Center in Hong Kong. See image at http://www.hemmy.net/2006/10/15/creative-advertisements-around-the-world/#.)

- Manhole covers? (A message from Folgers to New Yorkers was placed around a lifelike image of a cup of coffee, painted on top of a manhole cover. The steam floating up looked as if the coffee were piping hot. It read, "Hey, city that never sleeps. Wake up. Folgers.")

- Cocktail umbrellas? (An anti-date drug message, created by TBWALondon, "This is how easy it is to spike your drink" was placed in drinks left unattended at London bars.)

View the above three images here: http://www.adsideas.com/unusual-places-eye-catching-ads/. Be sure to check out these other exciting ambient ads at http://www.google.com/images?client=safari&rls=en&q=innovative+ads&oe=UTF-8&um=1&ie=UTF-8&source=univ&sa=X&ei=syd5TeOGGuiE0QHj8JDbAw&ved=0CCEQsAQ&biw=1239&bih=715. Look for ads in unusual places. Then, study the copy. Notice how the object stops consumers and how each message draws them in closer.

Take a moment to check out the links. These images can be found on multiple sites. The above list will give you a few places to start. Each image is well worth your attention, and will boost your creative energy.

Also take a look at Atomic Props & Effects (http://www.atomicprops.com/portfolio/index.php). There you'll see 3-D boards with hard-to-believe images, like "paparazzi" on a billboard photographing a Cadillac and two life-size billboard "workers," one the scaffold and the other jumping into an impossible-to-resist a 3-D MINI Cooper at the bottom of the board. There are many other exciting ambient ads, as well. Some are street-lined or bus shelter sculptures. Others are illuminated to replicate the product, like the 3-D, oversized vertical board for iPod. (See it at http://www.atomicprops.com/portfolio/index.php.) Wander around this site. You'll be bombarded with creative ingenuity.

Take a look out Outdoor 3D, too, for inflatable designs (http://www.3dbillboard.com/). You won't forget the 3-D monster breaking through the billboard to advertise Monster. com or the giant, one-eyed, 3-D creature wrapping around the board promoting Halloween shopping at Target.

Be aware that some 3-D billboards are expected to be such a distraction, they may cause car accidents. The first 3-D billboard for Wonderbra at the Waterloo Train Station in London created a media stir. Because Wonderbra claims to be able to make it look as if a woman's bra had increased two cup sizes, the 3-D effect only magnified the enhancement. However, without 3-D glasses, the image appeared slightly blurry, causing people to stare even more. (See the image at http://adsoftheworld.com/media/outdoor/wonderbra_3d_billboard. Read the article about distracting drivers at British Mail Online, http://www.dailymail.co.uk/news/article-1311856/New-Full-Effect-3D-Wonderbra-advertisement–distraction-drivers.html.) The idea of using 3-D in this way is effective, as you can imagine.

Check out 3-D wallscapes at Foster Media (http://www.fostermedia.com/sign.html). Make it a habit to regularly search for innovative ads on Google to keep up with the newest ambient messages. This will give you a steady diet of creative inspiration.

USEFUL INFO 9.1 Kinds of ambient media

1 Signage

   a Outdoor

      i *Billboards* (traditional or with movement, 3-D, extensions, inflatables, interactivity, etc.)

      ii *Wallscapes* (giant ads on buildings)

   b Indoor

      i Store displays

         1 *POP* – point of purchase

         2 *Shelf talkers* – messages next to products

         3 *Floor talkers* – messages on retail floors

         4 *Window messages*

            a Stickers (static cling ads)

            b Flyers (inside store windows)

            c Posters (free-standing signs in malls)

2 Transit

  a Outdoor

    i Messages on transportation vehicles

      1 Buses

      2 Taxis

      3 Subways

      4 Trains

      5 Trucks

  b Indoor

    i Stations

      1 Train

      2 Airports

      3 Subway

        a Wraps

        b Kiosks

        c Signs (inside and out)

  c 3-D objects

    i Bar bells on subway hand rails

    ii Watches on overhead subway hand straps

4 New media

  a Cocktail napkins

  b Elevators

  c Sculptures

  d Free items (with tracking devices) placed in the street for people to take

5 Movies

  a Posters

  b On-screen messages

  c Messages on candy packages, popcorn cartons, etc.

6 Other out-of-home

  a *Arenas* – posters around the stadium, concession stands, etc.

  b *Aerials*

    i Blimps

    ii Hot air balloons

    iii Banner ads on planes

  c *Island displays* – freestanding kiosks inside stores with stand-alone products like beer or soda in supermarkets

Noticing messages wherever you are

Ambient advertising, that is, messages in unexpected out-of-home locations, is everywhere. Pay attention. Be alert. And, analyze messages wherever you find them. Then, consider what would be the most effective way to use this medium. Think about the following message-influencing questions.

- Is there movement involved affecting how the copy is read? (Sometimes you see this in transit ads on cabs, bus sides, or sliding glass doors.)
- How much space do you have for copy? (Less copy says more on billboards.)
- What could you say to create an impossible-to-ignore message? (Think verbal and visual stopping power.)

Keep in mind that thought-provoking messages can appear in the most mundane places. This is why you need to stretch yourself creatively. Don't dismiss any medium as ordinary. Yes, the medium can be run of the mill, but your message can still be remarkable. Ask is the message going to be delivered via one or more of these vehicles?

- Indoors? – Like point-of-purchase signage, window posters, or shelf talkers, which are messages next to products on store shelves
- Out-of-home? – Like a lawn sign in a park (as PEDIGREE® did to raise awareness for shelter dogs with dog-shaped signs in New York's Central Park and a pleading message saying, "Wish I Was Here."[2])
- On indoor moving objects? Like shopping cart handles in supermarkets
- Intrusive? – Like videos inside elevators, pizza box tops, or gas station displays
- Interactive? – Like quizzes on websites or text messages on billboards
- In print? – Like magazine ads and inserts
- In broadcast? – Like radio or TV spots
- On mobile devices? Like QR codes on cell phones
- On transit-related objects? Like bus wraps, bus sides, bus shelters, train stations, cabs, trolleys, jeeps, boats, or trucks
- On digital displays? Like New York Times Square
- In unusual places? – Like ads in urinals (yes, urinals)

Whenever you're creating ambient messages, think about surprising the audience and reaching them when they aren't expecting it. Once you've stopped them, make sure you reward them with an entertaining, captivating, unexpected and brilliant statement. If your concept is boring, it will be ignored. If it's *off-target*, it won't be understood. If it's *off-strategy*, it's a waste of time. Focus. Ask more of yourself. Start over if you haven't created a concept and copy that are anything less than terrific.

Looking closely at out-of-home messages

Let's look at a traditional out-of-home vehicle: billboards. As mentioned in chapter 8, these messages should be as brief as possible: seven words or fewer. Sometimes you'll see ordinary, uninspired messages. Other times you'll find extraordinarily creative ones.

TIPS AND RULES 9.2
Tips for writing ambient copy

1   Less is more. Edit and reedit.
2   Develop traffic-stopping concepts.
3   Catch audience off-guard.
4   Create a surprise, verbally and visually.
5   Be irreverent when appropriate.
6   Entertain and engage the viewer.
7   Use interactivity when possible.
8   Allow humor to sell *benefits*.
9   Think visually. How can you enhance the message?
10 Don't stop concepting until you create an idea that *spins out*.

According to Vinny Warren, founder and creative director of The Escape Pod, you'll find more creative billboards in the UK and in Europe than in the US. He said:

The standards of graphic design are little higher and the medium of outdoor has a better reputation. People put more thought into it than maybe here. If you look around here, I mean I'm looking around here. It's all boring. That's the problem with outdoor.[3]

Of course, not all billboards are unimaginative. Some have extensions (with parts that go above or below the standard rectangular board). Some have moving parts. Some have actual cars, like the MINI Cooper (by Crispin, Porter + Bogusky) on them.[4] And, some even have live people on them like TBWA's Adidas board in Japan.[5] One billboard for Heineken was on a stretchable material and looked as if someone's hand were reaching from behind the fabric to grab a beer. (See this image at http://www.hemmy.net/2006/10/15/creative-advertisements-around-the-world/#.) The challenge, as a writer and designer, is to create traffic-stopping billboards, not boring ones.

Every time you're on the highway or on a street with billboards, notice that some catch your attention. What makes you look? The message? The visual? The movement? The extensions that stretch beyond the board? The special effects? If you're able to take a photo at a red light, do it. That way you can look at the board later and analyze what you liked about it. You'll also have a visual reference when you're working on billboards.

Thinking about surprising the audience

Just think how exciting it is to be stopped right where you are and notice a great message. What can you create that will not only reach the audience you want, but also surprise them? What can you do to create their attention? How could it be more powerful?

As mentioned in chapter 12, Ikea used innovative social media as discussed in the article "Ikea Facebook Tag."[6]

The Ikea campaign also displayed creative use of ambient and transit media with these brilliant and unexpected ambient messages:

* Mobile displays of Ikea rooms furnished inside see-through trucks (See image at: http://www.toxel.com/wp-content/uploads/2008/06/uad19.jpg.) Bus stops made over to look like living room seating areas (See image at http://www.creativecriminals.com/images/busstopikea1.jpg.)

"Try to learn discipline. Don't be satisfied too quickly. **KT THAYER, CREATIVE DIRECTOR, VITRO**[7]

You would think that in-store signage is a thankless assignment. You're wrong. The next time you're shopping in a store with whimsical merchandise and see creative messages snap a picture and send it to yourself. Some in-store messages are very exciting. They stop you and make you think.

Let's examine a wonderfully entertaining indoor signage campaign created by Young & Laramore for the Indianapolis boutique, Silver in the City. The shop carries a range of unique gifts, personal and houseware items. To showcase its uniqueness, the agency created an equally unusual way to draw window shoppers in for a closer look. The clever stickers are on the store windows. The reflections from the glass capture street images. Being that it's a street busy with pedestrian shoppers, strolling with their Starbucks beverages and stopping to browse. Some of these passersby can be seen in the glass as well.

Little picture frames that stick to the outside of the window surround the item being showcased for the shoppers. Browsers can read humorous little remarks. Charlie Hopper, creative director at Young & Laramore, described the entertaining messages like this:

> They create an interactive experience in the most classic sense without any online pixels, or bytes, or bits. You're having an interactive experience standing on the sidewalk with the store where it's talking to you and saying charming things, like "If it looks this good on a headless torso, imagine how great it will look on you." There's the one that says, "Oh, that is so you. Seriously. And we don't say that to just everybody." Obviously, it's on the glass and it does.[8]

Some of the jokes are not obvious. Instead, they're obscure and speak to a "hipper kind of audience." He continued:

> It kind of gives you the compliment that you would get the joke. For example, over a fun little handbag or something, it says, "We understand James Brown's father has one just like this." You have to think, "What the heck does that mean?" Two, three, four, five. "Oh, I get it. 'Papa's got a brand new bag.' I'm hip enough to get that because I know things like that." There are a lot of different kinds of humor like these light-up stars, "Don't let the stars get in your eyes. Okay, you've been warned. No lawsuits."[9]

Look at the following images and read through all the headlines and subheads. See how together they create one campaign, even though the connecting thread is witty writing and not necessarily one thematic idea. Some only had headlines because no subhead was necessary. Notice how the headline is set in non-serif type and the subhead is set in script. Also observe how Figures 9.1–9.5 have just a headline, but the second part is set like a subhead.

Not only did the campaign include outside window cling messages; it also included innovative in-stores signage, as printed cardboard cards, next to the merchandise. For example, to showcase the baby clothes, the agency created a clothesline with onesies (one-piece baby outfits) hanging on with clothespins. Right alongside them was a cardboard cutout of a onesie with the message in Figure 9.6.

Notice how whimsical the writing is. The messages play with the audience. For example, Figure 9.6 says, "Yes, we put baby in a corner. For God's sake, nobody tell Patrick Swayze." This makes the audience connect the word "baby" to the character named Baby, played by Jennifer Grey opposite Patrick Swayze, in the movie *Dirty Dancing*.

FIGURE 9.1 This exterior window cling message adheres to storefront windows and was created by Young & Laramore for Silver in the City, a unique jewelry-to-houseware boutique. Image courtesy of Young & Laramore.

FIGURE 9.2 This exterior window cling message adheres to storefront windows and was created by Young & Laramore for Silver in the City, a unique jewelry-to-houseware boutique. Image courtesy of Young & Laramore.

FIGURE 9.3 This exterior window cling message adheres to storefront windows and was created by Young & Laramore for Silver in the City, a unique jewelry-to-houseware boutique. Image courtesy of Young & Laramore.

FIGURE 9.4 This exterior window cling message adheres to storefront windows and was created by Young & Laramore for Silver in the City, a unique jewelry-to-houseware boutique. Image courtesy of Young & Laramore.

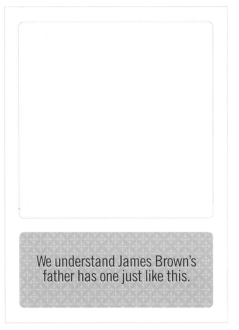

FIGURE 9.5 This exterior window cling message adheres to storefront windows and was created by Young & Laramore for Silver in the City, a unique jewelry-to-houseware boutique. Image courtesy of Young & Laramore.

FIGURE 9.6 This point of purchase display message was created by Young & Laramore for Silver in the City, a unique jewelry-to-houseware boutique. Image courtesy of Young & Laramore.

FIGURE 9.7 This point of purchase display message was created by Young & Laramore for Silver in the City, a unique jewelry-to-houseware boutique. Image courtesy of Young & Laramore.

In Figure 9.7, to accompany action figures, the line, "Some figures get more action than others," is featured. One of the funniest lines appears next to coffee mugs, shown in Figure 9.11: "Of all drugs, coffee has the wittiest paraphernalia."

How much fun were these headlines to discover as you're just peeking in the window? They're captivating. They told each window browser, "We were expecting you and we're glad you stopped by." That's what great copy does. It thanks readers for spending their time and rewards them intellectually with its cleverness.

The writing demonstrates a familiarity with the reader. It shows an understanding that the audience is in a relaxed state of mind because they're window-shopping and strolling down the street.

Understanding your audience's frame of reference

Some campaigns are so authentic in their *tone of voice* they sound as if the consumers wrote them. One that exemplifies this is the Charles Schwab "Talk to Chuck" campaign, which we've discussed in several chapters, including 5, 7, and 13. We'll reexamine the out-of-home component here and the multimedia aspects again in chapter 13.

What makes this campaign such a standout? There are several factors. It doesn't look our sound like an advertising message. It sounds like a friend speaking truthfully to another friend. It's sincere and candid. It's persuasive just because of its direct message and instantly identifiable visuals. As Simon Nickson, the account's art director and creative director at Euro RSCG, said:

FIGURE 9.8 This point of purchase display message was created by Young & Laramore for Silver in the City, a unique jewelry-to-houseware boutique. Image courtesy of Young & Laramore.

FIGURE 9.9 This point of purchase display message was created by Young & Laramore for Silver in the City, a unique jewelry-to-houseware boutique. Image courtesy of Young & Laramore.

FIGURE 9.10 This point of purchase display message was created by Young & Laramore for Silver in the City, a unique jewelry-to-houseware boutique. Image courtesy of Young & Laramore.

FIGURE 9.11 This point of purchase display message was created by Young & Laramore for Silver in the City, a unique jewelry-to-houseware boutique. Image courtesy of Young & Laramore.

It really is a classic kind of advertising campaign. It's very clear in its intentions. There's not a whole lot of the bells-and-whistles stuff.[10]

This campaign "got inside the head" of consumers. It understood their emotional stress related to financial worries. The copy reflected their concerns. Drummond Berman, copywriter and creative director at Euro RSCG, and Nickson's creative partner on the account explained the writing this way:

Whatever our client wants to put out there as a message, we'll always try and turn it around to answer a real need, or angst, or something that we've actually heard coming from someone's mouth out in the market. Because I think that's where we resonate, and where people look at our stuff and think, "They get me. I may not be interested in this right now. But when I am, at least I know there's someone who understands the way I feel." It's not just a list of products and attributes, which I think a lot of investment companies make the mistake of putting out there.[11]

Look at the headlines in these two out-of-home messages (Figures 9.12 and 9.13). The first one, a billboard (Figure 9.12) shares a commonly felt, but seldom-stated, thought, "Wow, I'm 50." When many people turn 50, they feel it's a turning point in their lives. They're now half a century old. They realize they're past the midpoint in life, which is only verified by receiving a membership request from AARP right around their birthday. Great, right? They're thinking, "Thanks for reminding me." They realize they're now in a different phase of their lives, and it may catch them off-guard. Look at the simplicity of the headline. In just three words it encapsulates all of those emotions: the surprise and the realization that they reached 50.

The second one (Figure 9.13) was a bus shelter. It reassured investors that their accounts mattered, regardless of size. Their accounts should be treated with equal care because their investments are just as important as everyone else's. The headline says it in seven words: "Big account. Small account. They all count."

When asked about writing for different media, Drummond explained how he approaches out-of-home writing, which he calls "the most disciplined writing that you ever do."

Because with out-of-home, you've got somebody speeding past at 50 mph. You've got a very limited amount of space and time. So you've got to sum up everything you need to say in let's say seven words. We rarely go beyond seven words in a headline. Also when you're writing it, you're condensing it down into the absolutely shortest form possible, but

FIGURE 9.12 This "Talk to Chuck" billboard was created by Euro RSCG for Charles Schwab. Image courtesy of Euro RSCG.

FIGURE 9.13 This "Talk to Chuck" bus shelter was created by Euro RSCG for Charles Schwab. Image courtesy of Euro RSCG.

you can't lose the charm, the wit, the intelligence, or any of that. So every single word has to work really, really hard.

And so, for us, that's probably the most challenging medium because, let's say our message is that since the crash in October, people who thought they were about to retire, now all of their retirement plans are in tatters, and they have no idea how to get back on track. There are a lot of elements to that. There's a lot of science to that, but we need to put that on a billboard.

How do you condense those thoughts down?[12]

He answered that question, explaining how the creative process and key components that develop strong out-of-home messages differ from writing print ads. He described what makes it even more challenging and also detailed the similarities between the two media.

So in out-of-home, you have to work really, really, really hard condensing, trying to find the shortest, snappiest, most memorable way of saying things. But you can't abandon any of the key pillars of the campaign: the tone of voice, the message, the truth, any of that stuff. For me with print, it's just a little easier, I guess.[13]

Berman also described what makes it even more challenging and also detailed the similarities between the two media this way:

It's all the same criteria. You want to stop people in their tracks. You don't want a headline to be banging on and going on forever. It does need to succinctly capture something that is going to resonate with someone and make them want to read on.[14]

Unlike the print medium, where people are sitting down and leafing through the pages, focused on reading, with an out-of-home message, they're not expecting it. So writers need to interrupt whatever they're doing to get their attention. He said they usually write 15 headlines. Although all would work for print, only four would work for out-of-home.

He continued, explaining how print ads, without having a limited number of words in the headlines give writers more creative flexibility, while shorter out-of-home message restrict them.

I just think the onus on writing a print headline is you have to be creative, you have to be relevant, you have to be truthful, and you have to capture the tonality of the campaign. But you don't have to do it in seven words. You can bring in word play a little more.[15]

That's the test for writers: to create powerful messages wherever they appear, regardless of restrictions. Keep a lookout for brilliant examples, and you'll find them. ASICS is another campaign, created by Vitro that mastered out-of-home messages and showed everyday athletes it understood their *point of view*. In chapter 5 we discussed several print ads and in chapter 12 we will examine interactive messages. Now, we'll look at the ASICS out-of-home campaign created specifically for New York Marathon runners and their supporters. In Figure 9.14, the ASICS ABC SuperSign in Times Square shouted encouragement to all the participants and invited their fans to cheer them on with their Twitter tweets. Look at how the language on the boards speaks directly to the runners:

Hello Central Park. Goodbye Giving Up.
Hello New York. Goodbye Uncertainty.
Hello New York. Goodbye Limitations.

Campaigns that create unexpected communication and catch viewers off guard are more easily remembered. Who would have thought to create a giant Lite-Brite (Figure 9.15) of an ASICS shoe? Vitro did. It's colorful, luminescent, and beautiful, like a work of art. It forced the audience to notice it by its bold creativity. It made an impact in the dozen locations where it was displayed, including the Winter Music Conference in Miami and a launch event at Spotlight Studios in Manhattan.

Clichés are dangerous because of that. They just say, "Oh, never mind, there's nothing new here. Move along.

CHARLIE HOPPER, CREATIVE DIRECTOR AND COPYWRITER, YOUNG & LARAMORE[16]

Being irreverent and still effective

Legal Sea Foods "Fresh Fish" transit ad campaign gained a great deal of press attention when a series of irreverent ads (Figures 9.16–9.22) appeared on taxicabs and trolley cars. Some messages developed

FIGURE 9.14 This "ABC SuperSign" out-of-home sign was created by Vitro for ASICS America Corporation. Image courtesy of Vitro.

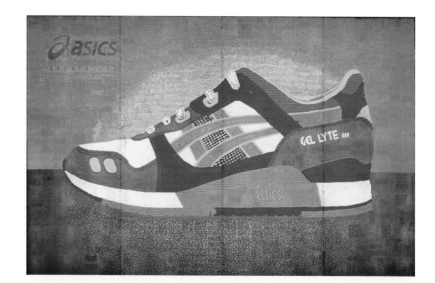

FIGURE 9.15 This "Lite-Brite" art piece was created by Vitro for ASICS America Corporation. Image courtesy of Vitro.

FIGURE 9.16 This "Kiss My Bass" out-of-home ad was created by DeVito/Verdi for Legal Sea Foods. Image courtesy of DeVito/Verdi.

FIGURE 9.17 This "Bite Me" taxi top ad was created by DeVito/Verdi for Legal Sea Foods. Image courtesy of DeVito/Verdi.

FIGURE 9.18 This "Carp" ambient ad was created by DeVito/Verdi for Legal Sea Foods. Image courtesy of DeVito/Verdi.

FIGURE 9.19 This "Halibut" taxi top ad was created by DeVito/Verdi for Legal Sea Foods. Image courtesy of DeVito/Verdi.

FIGURE 9.20 This "Blowfish" ambient ad was created by DeVito/Verdi for Legal Sea Foods. Image courtesy of DeVito/Verdi.

FIGURE 9.21 This "Movie Sucks" out-of-home ad was created by DeVito/Verdi for Legal Sea Foods. Image courtesy of DeVito/Verdi.

FIGURE 9.22 This "Your Sister" taxi top ad was created by DeVito/Verdi for Legal Sea Foods. Image courtesy of DeVito/Verdi.

by the New York ad agency, DeVito/Verdi, on the Green Line trolleys were considered so offensive, the MTBA (Massachusetts Bay Transportation Authority) banned them. The message particularly disparaging toward train conductors was: "This conductor has a face like a halibut."

1   If that's your girlfriend, I'd throw her back.

2   This cab gets around more than your sister.

3   This cab driver has a face like a halibut.

4   Darn, you smell like carp.

5   Kiss my bass.

6   Bite me.

7   Hey, Chumbug!

8   Is that a worm in your pocket or are you just happy to see me?

9   Your mother's a blowfish.

10 This movie sucks.

Legal Sea Foods CEO, Roger Berkowitz, responded on radio with what started out sounding like a "solemn" apology, but turned out to be an equally impertinent and similarly humorous answer.

> We should have never, ever said, "This conductor has a face like a halibut," when the truth is, most conductors don't look anything at all like halibuts. Some look more like groupers or flounders. I've even seen a few who closely resemble catfish. And there's one conductor on the Green Line that looks remarkably like a hammerhead shark. So we feel badly about this mischaracterization.[17]

The slogan "If it isn't fresh, it isn't legal!" uses a play on words slogan technique (#4), discussed in chapter 4 and humor strategy (#25), explained in chapter 2. The fact that the brand personality displayed a lack of self-restraint made the campaign even funnier. The line "This cab gets around more than your sister," which is at first shocking, quickly becomes too funny to take as a serious offense. If you can't laugh once in a while at a mischievous-but-not-malicious remark, you're turning into a somber sour puss.

This cheeky campaign also included print and TV, which we'll discuss, along with other humorous ads, later in chapter 13.

The Escape Pod created another almost rebellious campaign for its client Feckin Irish Whiskey. You can tell just from the bold name, the brand's personality exhibits a proud sense of defiance.

Taking a once touchy subject into a humorous campaign

Vinny Warren, founder and director of The Escape Pod talked about the Feckin Irish Whiskey campaign, which we will discuss in chapter 11. The three following posters (Figures 9.23–9.25), which appeared in many places including bars and magazine ads, highlight, in a very funny way, Irish terrorism. A topic once considered too volatile to consider using in a campaign. It was used here mostly because of the target audience's familiarity with it. As Warren explained:

> I looked at it and my thinking was what if you're a 22-year-old guy from Georgia? What are the two things you might know about Ireland? One of the things that you might know would be the film Snatch, with the Irish Gypsy background. The other thing that you might know is we have history of terrorism, right?
>
> That's all finished now, thank God. But, it was one of the things that Ireland was known for. So I figured let's key into that.

Feckin Irish Whiskey, which ran a national campaign, introduced the brand using the tagline "The Spirit of Irish Rebellion." The language was warm and familiar, as if you were having a drink with a buddy at a bar. Warren described the message, *tone of voice* and brand positioning this way:

> If you look at the tone of the ads, we were basically going after the shot whiskey market. So we were competing with tequila and whatever else people would drink as a shot.
>
> That was the idea. It was positioning in that way as opposed to the usual romancing whiskey and all that middle-aged approach. We were just like, "Hey let's just drink it."[18]

The campaign not only spoke in a bold way, with language like "arse" and "piss off"; it also went head to head with an unexpected market: not other whiskeys, but with other alcohols used in shots.

FIGURE 9.23 This "Arse" poster was created by The Escape Pod for FECKIN Irish Whiskey. Image courtesy of The Escape Pod and FECKIN Irish Whiskey.

FIGURE 9.24 This "Piss Off" poster was created by The Escape Pod for FECKIN Irish Whiskey. Image courtesy of The Escape Pod and FECKIN Irish Whiskey.

FIGURE 9.25 This "Abruptly" poster was created by The Escape Pod for FECKIN Irish Whiskey. Image courtesy of The Escape Pod and FECKIN Irish Whiskey.

Before we move on, look again at the copy in each poster. See how the art director emphasized certain words to draw in the reader. Also pay attention to the slogan and how it makes a direct statement: "The spirit of Irish rebellion."

"After months of negotiations, *Ireland's* hottest rock group agreed to appear in this ad for *Feckin* Irish Whiskey: The next day, however, they called and told us to shove the contract up our *arse.*" (Figure 9.23)

"Ireland's most famous movie star agreed to appear in this ad for *Feckin* Irish Whiskey: But at the very last minute, he cancelled and told us to *piss off.*" (Figure 9.24)

"Ireland's leading soccer player said he'd be happy to appear in this ad for *Feckin* Irish Whiskey: But alas never turned up to be photographed. When we called to ask him why *he just swore* at us and hung up *abruptly.*" (Figure 9.25)

There was a fourth poster that continued in the same irreverent *tone of voice.* It demonstrated campaign continuity and read: *Headline*: Go Ahead Drop the F-Bomb. *Subhead*: 1.5 oz. of Feckin Irish Whiskey 16 oz. Beer (Any Kind).

This just shows how you can use potentially offensive language because you know you're speaking to an audience that wouldn't be offended. Realizing that these posters would be read in bars, made the verbiage all the more appropriate.

Sometimes the location of the ad could be considered annoying, like commercials on commercial-free radio or messages in bathrooms. People may be tired of seeing messages everywhere. But, now some unexpected locations have become commonplace, like airline tray tables and quick-service restaurant tray liners. We'll look at one great example of a tray liner next.

Finding new places to advertise

Just because your audience is already a customer doesn't mean you can't still market to them. In fact, they're the best ones to reach to strengthen the brand–consumer relationship. That's why you'll see creative messages in practical places like the playful Chick-fil-A tray liners (Figure 9.26). Here is a perfect opportunity to invite the target audience to come in for breakfast. They're already fans, so you're not convincing them to try Chick-fil-A, only to return in the morning. Look at how the type is set in the headline and notice the deliberate spelling errors as the cow invites you to come over to eat:

"Therz only one way 2 a great brekfust."

You couldn't expect more from a cow, could you?

When you're creating fun headlines, think about where else the message will appear. Make sure it's portable. Ask yourself:

- Can your message work in another locale?
- Can you create an idea that *spins out*?
- Can it illicit audience participation?
- What other ideas could you use?
- Did you consider an alternative message:
  - For a different audience?
  - In another *tone of voice*?
  - With different benefits?

So, to me, the more you read and the more you fill your mind with different types of writing styles, I think that gives you more bows in your quiver, if you will. **MATT ZISELMAN, CREATIVE DIRECTOR, SAPIENTNITRO**[19]

Good Ingredients Prepared Fresh.
It's The Chick-fil-A Way.

Every Chick-fil-A restaurant starts with quality ingredients, preparing all foods fresh daily. First and foremost, we use only 100% whole-breast chicken that's hand-breaded and cooked in peanut oil, which is naturally trans fat and cholesterol free. The cabbage for our Cole Slaw is chopped fresh daily, along with the carrots for our Carrot & Raisin Salad. Our wraps and salads are handcrafted daily with freshly cut vegetables. And it doesn't stop there. Even our delicious Iced Tea is brewed each day with our own special tea blend, and our Chick-fil-A Lemonade is freshly squeezed daily by hand. Freshness: it's key to our famous Chick-fil-A taste, and it always will be.

For complete nutritional details and dietary information, please visit chick-fil-a.com.

	Calories	Total Fat (g)	Saturated Fat (g)	Trans Fat (g)	Carbohydrates (g)	Protein (g)
Entrées						
Chick-fil-A Chicken Sandwich	430	17	3.5	0	39	31
Chargrilled Chicken Sandwich	260	3	5	0	33	27
Chargrilled Club Sandwich	380	12	5	0	34	36
Nuggets (8-count)	260	13	2.5	0	10	27
Chick-n-Strips (3-count)	350	17	3.5	0	17	33
Chicken Salad Sandwich	500	20	3.5	0	53	29
Cool Wrap						
Chargrilled Chicken Cool Wrap	410	12	4	0	49	33
Spicy Chicken Cool Wrap	400	12	4	0	47	35
Chicken Caesar Cool Wrap	460	15	6	0	46	39
Salads						
Chargrilled Chicken Garden Salad	170	6	3.5	0	10	22
Chick-n-Strips Salad	450	22	6	0	26	39
Southwest Chargrilled Salad	240	9	4	0	17	25
Chargrilled Chicken & Fruit Salad	220	6	3.5	0	21	22

	Calories	Total Fat (g)	Saturated Fat (g)	Trans Fat (g)	Carbohydrates (g)	Protein (g)
Sides						
Fruit Cup (medium)	70	0	0	0	17	0
Yogurt Parfait (no topping)	180	3	1.5	0	37	6
Waffle Potato Fries (small)	280	16	3.5	0	31	3
Cole Slaw (small)	360	31	5	0	19	2
Carrot & Raisin Salad (small)	260	12	1.5	0	39	2
Side Salad	70	4.5	3	0	5	5
Hearty Breast of Chicken Soup (small)	150	4	1.5	0	19	9
Desserts						
Icedream Cone (small)	170	4	2	0	31	5
Fudge Nut Brownie	370	19	6	0	45	5
Cheesecake (slice)	310	23	13	0.5	22	5
Vanilla Milkshake (small)	540	23	13	0	74	13
Chocolate Milkshake (small)	600	23	14	0	88	13
Strawberry Milkshake (small)	610	23	13	0	92	13
Cookies & Cream Milkshake (small)	570	26	14	0	80	14
Lemon Pie (slice)	360	13	6	0	58	6
Breakfast						
Chick-fil-A Chicken Biscuit	450	20	8	0	48	19
Chicken Breakfast Burrito	420	18	7	0	41	22
Sausage Breakfast Burrito	480	27	11	0	38	21
Chicken, Egg & Cheese on Sunflower Multigrain Bagel	500	20	6	0	49	30
Chick-n-Minis (3-count)	260	10	2.5	0	29	13
Cinnamon Cluster	400	15	6	0	61	8
Beverages						
Iced Tea – Sweetened (small)	90	0	0	0	24	0
Freshly Squeezed Lemonade (small)	170	0	0	0	46	0
Freshly Squeezed Diet Lemonade (small)	15	0	0	0	6	0

Chick-fil-A uses 100% refined peanut oil. Nutritional values do not include condiments or dressings. This item is printed on 100% recycled paper that contains at least 26% post-consumer content.

FIGURE 9.26 This "Chikin Maze" trayliner was created by The Richards Group for Chick-fil-A, Inc. All trademarks shown on the trayliner are the property of CFA Properties, Inc. Image courtesy of The Richards Group and Chick-fil-A, Inc.

- Can you inspire user-generated content and:
  - Show photos of consumers?
  - Exhibit children's artwork?
  - Create an open dialogue among users?

Whatever the medium, think beyond it. See what other ways you can use the message. If it's limited to just one particular medium, can you create a related concept for a different vehicle? Be sure all of your communications show a unified idea before settling on the campaign concept. If it's a *big idea*, it's not limited by medium because it's flexible. It's bendable. And it lends itself to adaptation.

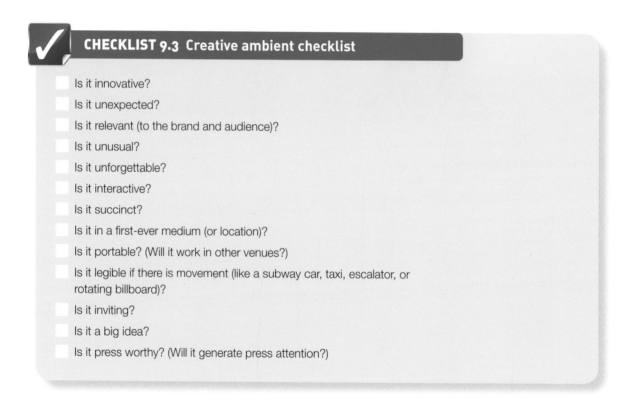

CHECKLIST 9.3 Creative ambient checklist

- Is it innovative?
- Is it unexpected?
- Is it relevant (to the brand and audience)?
- Is it unusual?
- Is it unforgettable?
- Is it interactive?
- Is it succinct?
- Is it in a first-ever medium (or location)?
- Is it portable? (Will it work in other venues?)
- Is it legible if there is movement (like a subway car, taxi, escalator, or rotating billboard)?
- Is it inviting?
- Is it a big idea?
- Is it press worthy? (Will it generate press attention?)

Creative ambient exercises

Exercise 1: make a list of ambient messages in places you've never seen before

Exercise 2: think up two new places for new ambient messages

- What kind of product or service would work in these locations?
- How could you make it more engaging and entertaining?
- Could you use animation? Illumination? Movement? 3-D? Interactivity?

Exercise 3: write stop-'em-in-their-tracks headlines for each of the two ambient messages

Check that they're appropriate for the brand and they'll target the audience.

Exercise 4: create a humorous, *on-target*, *on-strategy* message for one of the messages

Exercise 5: spin this message out and created related concepts to use in two other ambient locations

Notes

1   Kevin Moriarty, personal communication, August 24, 2009.

2   Margo Berman, *The Brains Behind Great Ad Campaigns: Creative Collaboration Between Copywriters and Art Directors* (Lanham, MD: Rowman & Littlefield, 2009), 200.

3   Vinny Warren, personal communication, September 4, 2009.

4   Margo Berman, *Street-Smart Advertising: How to Win the Battle of the Buzz* (Lanham, MD: Rowman & Littlefield, 2010), 13.

5   Margo Berman, *Street-Smart Advertising: How to Win the Battle of the Buzz* (Lanham, MD: Rowman & Littlefield, 2010), 109.

6   http://viralingoutofcontrol.wordpress.com/page/2/ (accessed February 20, 2011).

7   KT Thayer, personal communication, September 26, 2010.

8   Charlie Hopper, personal communication, November 26, 2008.

9   Charlie Hopper, personal communication, November 26, 2008.

10   Simon Nickson, personal communication, April 8, 2009.

11   Drummond Berman, personal communication, April 8, 2009.

12   Drummond Berman, personal communication, April 8, 2009.

13   Drummond Berman, personal communication, April 8, 2009.

14   Drummond Berman, personal communication, April 8, 2009.

15   Drummond Berman, personal communication, April 8, 2009.

16   Charlie Hopper, personal communication, November 26, 2008.

17   Roger Berkowitz, personal communication, March 17, 2011.

18   Vinny Warren, personal communication, September 4, 2009.

19   Matt Ziselman, Creative Director at SapientNitro, personal communication, January 30, 2009.

10

THE ONLINE COMMUNAL WORD

Digital dialogue, virtual community, blogging

 Idea is king, not the media.

ALESSANDRA LARIU, SENIOR VICE PRESIDENT, DIGITAL GROUP, MCCANN ERICKSON [1]

The Copywriter's Toolkit: The Complete Guide to Strategic Advertising Copy, First Edition. Margo Berman.
© 2012 Margo Berman. Published 2012 by Blackwell Publishing Ltd.

In this section, you'll understand how to write for the Web by being an observant user. You'll find out how to best talk to site visitors and blog followers. You'll see the easiest ways to engage them and draw them into an open conversation. In addition, you'll be reminded to (1) think about the *tone of voice* for your site and blog, (2) notice website and blog headlines, (3) read ad agency blogs, (4) review techniques in chapter 4, (5) edit out all superfluous copy, and (6) fine-tune your digital writing skills. You'll add to your toolkit with the 10 basic rules of copywriting.

By following top copywriting blogs you'll find new tips, learn how to create a successful blog, and find out the golden rules to being a great guest blogger. Most importantly, you'll realize how to avoid unethical and bad social media manners.

All in all, you'll walk away a more expressive digital writer, a more effective online communicator, and a more interactive evaluator.

Interacting with your online audience

Popular online campaigns like the earlier mentioned Elf Yourself or M&M'S are interactive vehicles that allow people to play. On both these sites, people can create their own characters with words, faces and new colors at (www.elfyourself.com and www.mymms.com), or their own avatars http://www.mms.com/us/becomeanmm/create/. Other equally entertaining interactive campaigns were accessible at: www.madmenyourself.com

Product comparison sites like www.consumersearch.com first collect and evaluate brand reviews, then recommend products. Smart brands have created interactive websites, which allow consumers to compare products for themselves. For example, BLUE pet food lets pet owners compare the ingredients in some popular dog and cat food with BLUE ingredients at http://bluebuffalo.com/true-blue-test. Consumers who participate in the "True Blue Test," receive an online $5.00 coupon toward their purchase of BLUE pet food products. This shows that interactive sites can be informative and not just entertaining. The most important thing to remember is that digital communication allows for a conversation with the consumer unlike any other medium before it.

Writing for the Web

Writers today realize they cannot just take printed collateral pieces or broadcast work and apply them online. Writing for the Web requires clear and immediate communication with the audience, who, like the radio listener or TV viewer, is just a button or click away from leaving. Web surfers are looking for instant information and are impatient if the navigation is slow or the language is confusing. Keeping the visitor on a site long enough to describe the company's services or benefits requires brevity of expression paired with an uncanny insight into consumers' needs. The best way to write engaging online copy is to become the consumer yourself.

Surfing the Web

Each time you visit a site, analyze what worked and why. Notice what you liked or disliked about how the information was presented. Find excellent site examples that serve as copy guides. What would you borrow? What would you change? Be sure to consider the following:

- The choice of language.
- The way the sites are organized.
- The images and visual references that support the copy.
- The ease or difficulty of navigation.

Did you find everything you were looking for? Could you understand the message of each page? Was there information flow or was it disorganized? If you were writing the web copy, how would you modify it?

Talking to the reader

Any time you write for online or any other medium, you must imagine your audience. See them as individuals, not a sea of blurred faces. Think about these people before you write your first phrase for a website, blog, or online article. Ask yourself each of these questions as you're thinking about your message:

- What would you say if the person were in front of you?
- How can you personalize the language?
- Where can you initiate a dialogue (when appropriate)?
- How can you make the site interactive? Think about using
  - questions and answers
  - quizzes
  - puzzles
  - forums
  - games
  - contests
  - comments
  - engaging activities (like creative recipes or other how-to tips).

Evaluating the copy's tone of voice

How do you want your website to sound? What is the brand or company's personality? Does this site have scientific, medical, or legal advice? Is it a site that explores new technology? Does it present new cocktails or review restaurants? Does it list exciting places to go and famous sites to see? You can see how different the copy would be for each of these sites. Just like all copy, you must always decide the following:

- Is it company appropriate?
- Is it audience appropriate?
- Is it compelling?

- Is it understandable?
- Is it relevant?
- Is it informative?
- Is it concise?
- Is it persuasive?

Online audiences are especially time-conscious. They might be accessing the Web on a mobile device, not necessarily on their computer. How quickly can they find what they're looking for and how easily is the message received? If key information is buried far (several clicks away) from the main site, they may not bother to search for it.

Digital communication is instant delivery. Any delay is a deterrent. Lengthy, complex sentences are a no-no. Simple, get-to-the-point are a go. Less is more. And faster is better. See how easy that was to read? That's the idea. Keep them reading. So you won't lose their interest.

Including clever headlines

Powerful headlines work equally well online, mostly, because they're unexpected. How often do you read a headline that makes you stop and smile when you're surfing? Not too often. Look at these fun examples of headlines at www.uglymugcoffee.com.

Of course, not every website needs to create catchy headlines, but for those products or companies where it would work, you should consider this. Why? Because it engages and entertains the audience. It raises their interest and directs their attention, so visitors keep reading a few minutes longer.

One online article by Brian Clark, founder of the CopyBlogger (www.copyblogger.com) addressed five "magnetic headlines" in his blog, "Warning: Use These 5 Headline Formulas at Your Own Risk." He explained that even though these headlines date back more than 80 years and some are attributed to Maxwell Sackheim, they might still work well. Clark, who used one of the following headline "formulas," credited more than 1,600 Diggs (www.digg.com, a

 SCRIPTS AND EXAMPLES 10.1 Fun website headlines

Headline: We Ain't Got No Alibi (About Us page)

Headline: Tickles the Coffee Bone (About Our Coffee page)

Headline: You Are Now Leaving Sleepy Town (Shop page)

Headline: Coffee Power Activate (Locations page)

Headline: We Did Our Part Now Don't Mess This Up (Contact page)

(Headlines courtesy of Young & Laramore.)

site where people can share something they like or "Digg."). That particular blog post was also mentioned on numerous social media news sites and drove 70,000 unique new visitors to his site. Not bad, for an "ancient" headline technique. Read the article at www.copyblogger.com/headline-swipe-file-3/.

Here is the list of these five tried-and-true headlines. You can use them as a reference. Modify them. Try them. Or even discard them. At least you've familiarized yourself with them. As you read them, try to see why you think they can still work. You would fill in the "blank" with appropriate, product-related copy. The blog post has been edited down. Please refer to the original article for the full content: www.copyblogger.com/headline-swipe-file-3/.

Clark offers the following warning:

If you don't match up an appropriate headline structure with your content, you might crash and burn worse than if you just came up with a headline off the top of your head.[2]

 ADVICE FROM THE PROS 10.2 Warning: use these five headline formulas at your own risk

Magnetic Headlines.

1 *Warning: [blank].* Starting a headline with the word *warning* will almost always catch attention, but it's what you say next that will determine how well it works for your particular content.

- Warning: If You Depend on Google for Both Traffic and Advertising, You Pretty Much Work for Google

2 *How [blank] Made Me [blank].* Use this structure when relating a personal story. The key to the most effective use of this template is for the two blanks to dramatically contrast, so that the curiosity factor goes way up and people feel compelled to read more.

- How a "Fool Stunt" Made Me a Star Salesman

3 *Are You [blank]?* A nice use of the question headline, designed to catch attention with curiosity or a challenge to the reader. Don't be afraid to be bold with this one.

- Are You Ashamed of Smells in Your House?

4 *[Blank] Ways to [blank].* One of the best list structures, because it's really a "how to" headline enhanced by specificity that either impresses the prospective reader with how many tips you've got, or at minimum let's them know exactly what to expect.

- 101 Ways to Cope With Stress

5 *If You're [blank], You Can [blank].* Another great use of specificity, this headline addresses a particular type of person with the first blank, and the beneficial promise to that person in the content or body copy with the second.

- If You're a Non-Smoker, You Can Save 33% on Life Insurance.[3]

(Headline list and comments courtesy of Brian Clark, founder of Copyblogger and co-founder of Scribe.)

Analyzing the message

As with print, broadcast, out-of-home, and ambient ads, digital messages have the same set of criteria. "The 10 Basic Rules of Copywriting" from *Phrases That Sell*, written way back in 1998, still hold true today.

It's amazing how these same 10 rules are applicable to traditional and emerging media. That's because they're the key to good copy. Of course, strategic thinking must be present. It's not just about strong writing. It's always about innovative thinking. It's also about double-checking that you can say "yes" to these questions and points mentioned in earlier chapters, like correct *tone of voice*, relevance, and so on:

- Does it showcase the firm's *benefits*?
- Is the message *on-strategy*?
- Does it keep the visitor reading?

Look at all new and emerging media every opportunity you can. Pay attention to how the messages are presented. Look at the length of copy, the kinds of headlines being used for blogs, online articles, websites, ambient, and all other media.

TIPS AND RULES 10.3
The 10 basic rules of copywriting

1   Know your audience.
2   Understand your product or service.
3   Find your principal selling point (PSP).
4   Write benefit-oriented copy.
5   Chose active versus passive words. (It *creates* perfect cappuccino, not the cappuccino *was created* perfectly.
6   Short sentences and short words can add up to big ideas.
7   Use formats that promote. (Today online and mobile reach the audience.)
8   Use offers that sell.
9   Tell your readers what to do. (Use a call to action.)
10 Tout your name. (If readers don't know who's advertising, they can't order.)[4]

Creating a successful blog

Before you create a blog be sure you consider all six types or categories of blogs. That way all of your posts will be relevant or "granular." Review this source list of niche topics from *ProBlogger* and see which one best fits the brand. If you're the brand, be just as critical. Here are a few places to look for a topic:

1   *AdWords Keyword Tool* (https://adwords.google.com/select/KeywordTool) – Join Google AdWords and, without having to place an ad, you'll find research tools to see the number of people searching for certain keywords.

> Here's one of the reasons I love blogs is because they're great for practicing writing.
>
> **VINNY WARREN, FOUNDER AND CREATIVE DIRECTOR, THE ESCAPE POD**[5]

TIPS AND RULES 10.4
10 steps for a successful blog series

1   Select a subject (topic).

2   Create a list of post ideas to make sure your topic is broad enough.

3   Establish goals. Decide how often you'll blog and how long each post will be.

4   Develop drafts for future posts. Give them a headline and a few lines to remind you about the topic. Post on your blog site and finish it later.

5   Select a title for your blog topic. Choose something catchy with well-chosen keywords for the search engines.

6   Publicize your new blog series. Get the word out via your social networks. Let your audience know how many posts to expect in this particular series.

7   Write an explanation to introduce your topic to your readers.

8   Blog every day. Some writers create future blogs. Some prefer daily posts.

9   Connect your posts with links to one another. That way readers can see the entire series and read them in any order.

10   Finish your blog series so it has a sense of completion for the reader. Sum up main points.[7]

2   *Google Trends* (www.google.com/trends) – This reveals the most popular search terms so you can learn if that topic is gaining or losing interest.

3   *Google Blog Search* (www.google.com/blogsearch) – See who's writing about what.

4   *Wordtracker* (www.wordtracker.com/) – With a free trial you can discover which words come up more often in searches and which sites already exist.

5   *Yahoo! Buzz* (http://buzz.yahoo.com) – This summarizes the types of subject matter surfers are searching on Yahoo.[6]

I recommend you read *ProBlogger* cover to cover. You'll discover 20 types of blog posts: (1) instructional, (2) informational, (3) reviews, (4) lists (of suggestions or tips), (5) interviews, (6) case studies (of writing examples), (7) profiles (of people), (8) link posts, (9) "problem" posts (of product issues), (10) comparison posts (of similar products), (11) rants (of controversial topics), (12) inspirational, (13) research, (14) collation posts (of collected opinions), (15) prediction and review posts (of what will and then did happen), (16) critique posts, (17) debate, (18) hypothetical posts (of "what if" speculations), (19) satirical posts, (20) memes and projects (topics that go viral).[8] It is packed with rich content, informative lists, and callout boxes that deserve your attention if you plan to become a professional blogger.

Reading blogs for digital writing tips

Become a student of good online writers. The best way to learn how to write from a particular medium is to read copy by some masters. Some copywriters who have mastered one medium can easily transfer those skills to another similar one. For example, Drayton Bird, a direct marketing expert, formerly at Ogilvy & Mather, has written numerous books on writing and marketing. Now, a blogger (http://drayton-bird-droppings.blogspot.com) with more than 10,000 followers, he said the following about digital communication:

Media change; customers don't. Apart from a few technical details – like the difference between paper and screens, and the limits imposed by spam filters there is no reason to believe you should change your writing that much for the Web.[9]

On his many sites are helpful writers tips, like the "51 Helpful Direct Mail Ideas," some of which are listed in chapter 9.

Another blogger you should be reading is Andy Beal, founder of Marketing Pilgrim, and coauthor of *Radically Transparent: Monitoring and Managing Reputations Online.* He has been blogging for more than 10 years. His blog, www.marketingpilgrim.com, which he started in 2005, was named #11 (on January 21, 2011) by *Ad Age Power 150*, a daily ranking of English-language, global blog sites. He started blogging "to share his thoughts and opinions on marketing news" that came across his desk. He added, "I wanted a place where I could carefully construct my thoughts on what I was reading. When you're forced to break it down in a blog post, you really get an understanding of it for yourself."[10]

This allowed him to explain his thoughts to his inquisitive staff on the latest media announcements. Another benefit was each blog post or article created a strong online presence that increased his credibility, and led others to consider him an Internet marketing expert, hire him as a speaker, and become his marketing clients. Ultimately, his Marketing Pilgrim posts attracted the attention of Wiley & Sons, which resulted in the release of his first book (mentioned above) in 2008.

He has mentored several copy bloggers and is often asked how long a blog should be. He said length was less important than consistency. If you normally write 250 to 300 word posts, don't suddenly switch to 2,000 words. The change in length confuses your audience, who's expecting a shorter entry. When asked how long his blog posts usually were, he said around 400 to 500 words.

Here are a few more of Beal's writing insights:

You can see how seasoned bloggers think about how to engage their audience. They think about creating a brand personality, about being personable, open, and inclusive. They ask their readers to participate by leaving bits of information out, by creating opposing opinions, and by posing a question. All of these techniques are similar to a *call to action.* They tell the reader what they should do: state an opinion, take a different position on a topic, or answer a question. The key is to create that dialogue with your audience.

If you find yourself longwinded as a writer, editing is crucial for crisp, concise digital content. Learning what to leave out is as important as deciding the right content to put in for your audience. Next, we'll look at some tips to cut copy.

Editing: Charlie Hopper's tips to cut copy

Most seasoned writers have learned that less really is more. As impossible as it may seem to cut some copy out, those edits usually tighten up the writing. Eliminate adjectives, unnecessary words, and superfluous or qualifying phrases (like those that begin with

> On some blogs, there's just too much content. People just want to get a sound bite really fast. **PETER SENA II, FOUNDER AND CHIEF TECHNOLOGY OFFICER, DIGITAL SURGEONS**[12]

ADVICE FROM THE PROS 10.5 Andy Beal's top blogging tips

1 I think the biggest thing is personality. The readers are going to be drawn to you as the author. They want to know what you feel about it. They're interested in your opinions. Inject some humor. Inject some cynicism. Inject whatever you feel about the topic you're writing about.

2 Be a little more concise than if you're writing something like a white paper or a book. You're fighting for limited attention on the Internet. Use same basic structure of journalism:

- Write a good headline.
- Try not to bury the lead too much. Try to summarize the *point of view* right at the beginning.
- Dive right into it.
- Make sure that we finish with some kind of analysis, commentary, or some kind of personal insight.
- Try to keep it concise.
- Use a lot of bullet points.
- Use a lot of lists.
- Make sure we bold key things that you don't want the reader to miss.

3 Ninety-nine percent of the time, I include an image in something I'm going to publish. Just as you try to make your title interesting, don't underestimate the power of some kind of image that relates to the article or the story.

4 The reason why blogs are successful is that there is some level of interaction there. You're not writing articles or reports that are being published in the paper, where there's no area of feedback from your readers. Blogs strive to encourage comments. They encourage sharing. One of the things I always advise is to never be complete. If I covered every aspect of it, there's really no opportunity for discussion. Most of the time, I try to be a little bit polarized. So, I'll take one stance on an item, one side of the story and leave it open for other people to come in, take the opposite stance and create a debate over it.

5 I always try to introduce a question of some sort. Don't think that your readers are going to be really willing to jump in and leave a comment. They'll read your article. They'll think, "Well, that's really good." If you don't give them a jumping-off point, you're not going to get that much interaction. I always try to finish my posts with a question where I'm encouraging their participation and getting them involved.[11] Blogging tips courtesy of Andy Beal, founder of www.marketingpilgrim.com.

"which" or "that.") To help you "squish it down," as Hopper says, you can use one of his secret little tricks:

> *You can almost always do this: It's one of my magic tricks when I do it. If somebody gives me copy, especially Web copy, because people think the Web is elastic. They think they can write and write and write and they can't. No one reads it. You can almost 100 percent of the time cut off the first paragraph, no matter what you're writing. Just cut off the first paragraph. That always works.*[13]

It's just like in TV and radio copy, where you start with act two. So, you jump right into the main storyline, without the introduction. Just be sure the copy you're writing is appropriate for that site and will draw readers.

Writers eager to learn to blog should be aware of which writers are the top copy bloggers. Great writers are forever students. So, all serious copywriters should add to their reading list the following top copywriting blog sites. Then, look for others to add to this list. Sites change frequently. It's your job to keep up. Don't feel overwhelmed. Instead, feel as if you're at a giant candy store with fun, new inventory whenever you return.

 USEFUL INFO 10.6 Top copy-specific blogs from "top copywriting sites"

1   Clayton Makepeace Total Package

2   Daniel Levis Presents

3   Michael Fortin on Copywriting

4   The Copywriting Maven

5   Copyblogger

6   John Carlton Marketing Rebel

7   Copy Ideas by Robert Stover

8   Ben Settle

9   Bob Bly

10   Info Marketing Blog

11   Ryan Healy

12   Ink Thinker Blog

13   Eric Graham

14   David Garfinkel

15   Copywriter Underground

16   Matt Ambrose

17   Ray Edwards

18   American Copywriter

19   Futurenow

(List courtesy of John Kirker, http://topcopywritingsites.com.)[14]

Looking into blogs for ad agencies

Vinny Warren, founder and creative director of The Escape Pod, confirms that successful blogs are an open forum rich with interaction. Many agency blogs are used to speaking with their audience as well as showcasing their work. Warren talked about the kind of writing for the posts on his firm's blog. Unlike bloggers, agency blog writers can talk about whatever they want. Their posts don't have to have a topic or a specific train of thought. One thing they both have in common, though, is the length of time it takes to attract a loyal following.

> You can be a lot more liberal and lot more indulgent because "Hey, if you're reading our blog, God help you, number one. But, number two, you know it's our blog and it's our forum for what we think." So that's a bit more one-sided in favor of us because no one's forcing you to read it. It's for fun, and it's for promotion, and it's for a lot of things. It doesn't really have a focus.
>
> Here's one of the reasons I love blogs is because they're great for practicing writing. That's a good thing in general, and thinking, and you get to meet new people. But, it's kind of sobering, too, in that you realize you know how hard it is to get an audience online. You know because you're not going to get thousands of people going to your blog. It will take a while. It works slowly.[15]

Learning blogging tips

Another blogger, Hesham Zebida, founder of FamousBloggers.net (ranked #28 on Ad Age Power 150, October 12, 2010, suggested the following tips from his article "How to Cook an Irresistible Blog," January 3, 2011). Here is a summary of some helpful suggestions gleaned from this article.

1 Spread the word by sharing your ideas.
2 Integrate your blog with social media for optimal search results.
3 Become active on social networking platforms. These help spread the word for your blog in no time, like: Tweetdeck, GoogleBuzz, and foursquare.
4 Make sure you write regularly and make your blog niche that can arouse interest, called "nicheworking."
5 Connect with other blogs via Blog Catalog, MyBlogLog, BlogFrog, and others.
6 Start a forum for your blog so that your readers can participate (http://forums.com/).
7 Integrate social media buttons in your blog, so readers can share it on Twitter, Facebook and other social networking/bookmarking platforms. (Just a "Like" button can work wonders.)
8 Hang out with your readers on Facebook, Twitter, and other similar places.
9 It is essential that when you are blogging, you are consistent.
10 If you have an impressive number of visitors in your blog, love them. Post articles on a regular basis, which your readers might find interesting.
11 Offer them something that makes them come back.[16]

Most bloggers don't just blog. They're an integral part of the online community. They share their ideas. Comment on other blogs. Ask and answer questions. Most importantly, they participate on a regular basis. However, if you can't keep a blog going, you could guest blog as long as you know the "rules of the online road."

Learning the rules of guest blogging

If you're invited to guest blog, be sure to review David Leonardt's January 4, 2011, blog post "The Golden Rules of Guest Blogging." The following points are a shortened version of this post.

1   *Know Thy Blog.* That's right, take time to study the blog you want to guest post for. What topics do they cover? What topics do they avoid? Are posts serious? Fun? Are posts very professional or very informal? Very carefully worded? Or anything goes? Are posts one-sided or well balanced? Are all the posts long? Short? All different lengths? These are just some of the points to look for.

2   *Don't Bore Thy Audience.* Keep in mind what you learned about the blog you wish to write for. Even if it is a very serious blog, you don't have to be boring. For instance, how to eat frugally has been written all over the blogosphere, but how animals can teach us to eat frugally has not been covered very much. Get creative.

3   *Bring Value to the Table.* Why on earth would I want you to write for my blog? Here are a few that I would consider worthwhile . . .

- You have an amazing idea that captures my imagination.
- You have superstar credentials.
- You have an amazingly strong account at Twitter or StumbleUpon or other places that can drive traffic and links to my blog.
- I can't write for the life of me and I need good writers that will impress people with the quality of the post.
- I have a far too ambitious publishing schedule to cover it all myself.

What do you have to offer?

4   *Approach Bloggers Who Welcome Guests.* Try searching Google for your keywords along with "guest post" or "guest blog." Or head over to Ann Smarty's guest blogging forum where many of the more eager hosts are already waiting for you.

5   *Write Well.* If you write trash, your post will be accepted on a trashy blog. You get what you pay for. Or what you write for. Or what you scribble for. This falls under the heading of "when is an opportunity not an opportunity?"

There are also some guest blogging tips to consider at About.com (http://weblogs. about.com/od/marketingablog/tp/GuestBloggingTips.html).[17] (Read more: http://www. seo-writer.com/blog/2011/01/04/the-golden-rules-of-guest-blogging/#ixzz1AJ2nHH3f.)

Revealing more bloggers' observations

There are distinct differences between writing blogs for advertising, publicity, news, or promotions. Many bloggers write articles and shape their messages differently depending on the communication vehicle. Lena L. West, founder, CEO and chief strategist of xynoMedia

Technology and blogger for www.entrepreneur.com and other business e-publications, explained how writing for a blog is different. Although she states that most blogs are 250 to 350 words, we have seen that the "average" length varies. Many write 450 to 500 words. Other, lengthier posts are 2,000 words. Here is what she had to say when comparing blogging to other kinds of writing:

1   *The differences between writing a blog and other forms of writing like publicity, advertising, journalism, promotions, and so on* – Writing a blog is distinctly different from many other forms of written communication. Good blog posts are conversational in tone and are not designed to persuade the reader to purchase anything, but rather to engage the reader in a dialogue about or generously educate the reader in a particular topic.

One of the problems that many people have with bloggers is they say they don't fact check their content. To that, I say, yes and no. Many blogs, like the Huffington Post, are written in a decidedly journalistic style so it would make sense that they would check their facts as a traditional media publication might.

However, there are many blogs that are the sole musings of one expert or a group of people who work at a company. They are based on opinion or experiences gleaned while working in their industry and many times people agree or disagree – and therein lies the conversation that can spontaneously erupt on blogs.

2   *Specific writing tips or techniques for this medium* – The average blog post is 250–300 words, so this is not the time to write War & Peace. However, everyone has different blogging preferences. There are many people who write short, pithy blog posts several times per week and there are other people, like personal development guru, Steve Pavlina, who write *very* long blog posts once or twice a week.

The main things are to keep it interesting and make sure the content engages the people you know your audience to be. In other words, if you know they like to talk about red hats, why start a conversation about green hats – unless, of course, it's to compare them to red hats.

It's OK to be personable without being personal. Sometimes even business people go overboard and write about personal things like pets or family illnesses. Now, if that level of transparency is part of your brand, that may work, just be mindful of how much you share; TMI [too much information] is alive and well.

3   *Your secrets to keep blogging under control* – Part of the reason that many people don't realize success with blogging – or social media in general – is the complete and utter lack of focus. They don't know why they're blogging, how often they should blog, what they should blog about or how to measure their success – or lack thereof.

We teach our clients a new concept called: flexible structure and it involves us helping them outline a plan of attack for their blog that includes goal setting, content selection and their calendars.

4   *How blogging can create a relationship with the reader* – Social media and its tools are simply human communication with very thin layers of technology applied so it's only natural that when you, the blogger, initiate a conversation through your blog posts that people will want to create a deeper relationship with you. That's just human nature.

5   *In what ways blogging can increase press and profits* – Clients and potential clients aren't the only people who read blogs – reporters read them too. I've gotten a lot of media coverage because in either a blog post or a podcast I've been able to provide a different point of view that the journalist needed to balance out his story.

There's also money to be made by playing the offense as well. A company can monitor what's being said about both their brand and their competitors' brand, and leap in to the rescue when they fall short.

A prime example of this in action is when FTD.com let me down in a major way one Mother's Day. I ordered the Laura Ashley Deluxe – that means extra roses. When my mother called to thank me for the flowers, I had her describe them and she told me she had received daisies. Ummm . . . not roses at all. I didn't pay for daisies, I paid for roses – and deluxe roses, thank you. After calling their toll-free number and being on hold so long their telephone system disconnected me – this happened three times by the way – and emailing them, I had no choice but to take my complaints to Twitter. 1-800-FLOWERS came to the rescue. They had a search alert for the letters "FTD," read my complaint and offered me a coupon and to make it right by sending my mother flowers. Not only does 1-800-FLOWERS have a customer for life, but I tell this story to anyone who will listen.[18]

The last point above is especially important. It shows the power of the Web to disseminate information quickly. Disgruntled customers today can instantly tweet their complaints to thousands, and even more, followers. Some companies have actually hired people and/or assigned staff members to monitor Twitter to try to quickly handle complaints. Airlines have been known to try to resolve complaints for passengers who are tweeting about their negative experiences while at the airport. In a matter of moments, people can hear and share the headaches of weary travelers. With the power of the media in the hands of the consumers, one bad experience can create a ripple of damaging impressions.

What marketers today want to do is find quick solutions to consumer issues that can escalate out of control. Articles about company success stories can bolster public opinion. Online marketers often write informative articles and post useful tips on blogs to establish themselves as experts, as we've already seen. How does writing articles differ from blog writing? Let's take a look.

Looking at online versus print articles

Deltina Hay, author of *A Survival Guide to Social Media and Web 2.0 Optimization* and president of Dalton Publishing, writes blogs and series of articles about the power of social media, which were published in IBPA's *Independent* (formerly PMA). They were also posted online. Here's what Hay also said about the difference between writing articles for the Internet and for print.

Writing for print media should typically be more formal, since readers tend to peruse the entire article or spread more thoroughly. One benefit to this is that including sidebars of information, like the resources in these pieces, are more likely to be taken in by the reader.
It tends to be more difficult to hold the attention of digital readers – they are even inclined to block out sidebars while focusing only on the body of the article itself. Consequently, PMA's online versions of the same articles, simply list the sidebar items at the end of each article.

She added that instead of using sidebars, they could be shown as links to references or resources that could expound on the article content. Some services don't want to include links in their featured articles. Hay pointed out the different *tone of voice* between the blog post and the online article this way:

> *The Social Media Power blog post is more casual, personable, and conversational, while the SiteProNews article is more formal and to the point. Adhering to a specific word count is one reason the SiteProNews article is more succinct, but another reason is that it is meant to appeal to a broader readership. When I write a blog post, I am "talking" directly to my readers, so the style tends to be instructional, as opposed the more informative tone I would use in an article.*
>
> *Whether I am writing an article for print media, for online media, or for a blog, the content is always edited and proofread. Like all media – old and new – readers will weed out the crap, and regularly return to quality.*[19]

She went on to say that most of the articles had a blog post related to it. She added that nonarticle posts should be more casual and shorter in length. They could have top nine list or tips or useful tools. Interested readers can search the article's title in blog categories to see them posted or to see if it has been syndicated somewhere else. For example, this online article and the blog post are the same with only the intro and title changed. The only things missing in the article are the links that would appear in the blog.

Authors can use blogs to reach out to their audiences while they're writing their books and do so by presenting sections online. She wrote an article explaining why authors should build a social media newsroom (http://www.ibpa-online.org/articles/shownews.aspx?id=2573) for the Independent Book Publishers Association.

Some blogging authors ask their audience for suggestions and comments. This interaction with the audience strengthens the bond between the reader and the author, and heightens fan loyalty. If you're blogging and writing articles that you intend to use in a book, you may want to consider engaging your audience by asking them to share their opinion as you're writing your manuscript.

If you're writing website copy for an author think about how you would get the reader involved. Would you ask for story suggestions? Would you leave clues to solve a mystery or have an online scavenger hunt to find an answer? What kind of writing would be enticing enough to pique the reader's attention?

You can gather some valuable advice from bloggers who are no longer active. One former blogger is Gary Bencivenga who, before his retirement, offered his suggestions in Marketing Bullets. They're still available via this link: http://www.marketingbullets.com/archive.htm. One post talked about the two most powerful words in headlines. Surprisingly they weren't "free" or "new." The blog explained how "free" and "new" garner a "Yeah, right" skeptical response in the reader who's heard those words a zillion times before.

Instead, the two magic words were "If . . . then." The idea is this: "If you could manage to read this line, then you'd see that I kept your attention." Or "If you could give me 10 minutes

> **"** Because in many ways we are being tasked with the same goal, we have a limited amount of time, a limited amount of space, and we want to form an emotional resonance between the reader and the brand. **MATT ZISELMAN, CREATIVE DIRECTOR, SAPIENTNITRO**[20]

a day, I promise you'll see a better body in a month." The headline forces the reader to commit some effort to gain the result. Of course the 10-minute guarantee has to really work. It could be resistance band exercise, or an easy-to-follow diet plan. Whatever it is, it has to be doable.

(See this particular article at http://www.marketingbullets.com/bullet03.htm.)

As with all media, the best thing you can do is jump right in. Replace apprehension with a sense of exploration. Then, think about how you could expand your or your client's digital footprint (presence on the Web). The most important thing is to be a dedicated observer. Don't just read blogs. Analyze them. Don't just visit websites. Scrutinize the copy. Don't just sit there. Participate in online discussions. Always ask yourself:

- What kind of clients would work well in this medium?
- How can I use it in a new way?

Constantly look for new examples of great blogs and innovative, digital marketing. Also pay attention to some unethical uses of blogs like luring visitors to other sites by posting criticisms of companies or bloggers. The following is a list of words that describe some objectionable blogging behavior. You don't need to resort to any of these actions to improve your search engine rankings. Just write useful and informative posts that are relevant to your followers.

USEFUL INFO 10.7 Social media ethical issue terms

Blogola – Getting paid in free merchandise to promote a product (the updated version of "payola" when radio station hosts were paid "under the table" to play certain songs on air).

Brandjacking – Creating sites, blogs, and social media sites to trick consumers into thinking they're reading about a certain brand through the illegal use of hijacked corporate identities like logos, slogans, URLs (website addresses), etc.

Comment Spam – Posting negative comments on blogs or social networking sites that drive traffic to a third-party site.

Flog – Establishing a fake blog created to appear as unbiased comments, but actually paid bloggers representing a company (made famous by a WalMart fake blog, "Wal-Marting Across America," which looked as if it were created by an ordinary couple traveling the country stopping at WalMart parking lots and chronicling their journey. WalMart has deleted the hyphen in its name.)

Link Baiting – Attempting to generate more traffic to sites and raise search engine rankings by posting outrageous blog headlines like "Bloggers are Fools" or offering cash incentives to lure people to click through to the site.

Pay per post – Working through a pre-agreed arrangement, bloggers receive payment to write positive reviews about various products or services.

Screen Scraping – Committing digital plagiarism, where people steal or "scrape" other people's blog posts and repost them without permission or citing the source.

Splog – Setting up a spam blog to reroute search engines to another site or blog in order to increase a site's search rankings.[21]

Reviewing digital writing

As we discussed, digital writing needs to be focused, targeted, succinct, and easily digestible. If your copy is too complicated, no one will read it. If the website is disorganized and tough to navigate, your audience may not find the information they seek. If your blog lacks focus, your readers will wander away. Once again, you must picture your audience and think about why they're reading your blog or visiting that site. Make sure you remember to reward your readers for their time by making it an easy read.

CHECKLIST 10.8 Blogging checklist

1   Read other bloggers.

2   Research popular blog posts. See what topics are gaining and losing interest.

3   Decide your niche.

4   Pick the kind of blog you want to write, like inspiration, debate, critique, etc.

5   Select a blog series. Make sure it's broad enough for ongoing posts.

6   Create a catchy title for the series.

7   Write attention-getting headlines for each post.

8   Show your personality in your writing. Have a *point of view*.

9   Create a relationship with your reader.

10 Keep each post the same length.

11 Blog with regular frequency: daily, weekly, monthly, etc.

12 Sum up key ideas.

13 Leave out a few points to invite audience in to add their thoughts.

14 Ask a question to encourage participation.

15 Summarize the entire blog series.

16 Create interlinks to all posts in the series.

17 Spread the word about your blog.

Creative blogging exercises

Exercise 1: what kind of blog could you create that would share professional insights in your industry?

Write a short 250-word blog. How would you engage your audience to participate?

- What would you leave out to allow readers to share their wisdom?
- What kind of question would you ask to encourage their response?

Exercise 2: what blog could you develop for a local business?

Pick a florist, a bakery, a home improvement store, a kitchen appliance store, or any other retailer. Determine your audience. Then, decide what you could write about that would be unexpected, entertaining, and helpful.

- What kinds of topics can you come up with to discuss?
- Could you create a contest?

For example, ask for the best family recipe for pumpkin pie for a bakery. Or the easiest table arrangement for a particular holiday for a florist.

Exercise 3: find a blogger you really enjoy reading.

Write a blog that would fit into the range of topics. Write a blog with a catchy title. Later, after you've posted a few comments on this blog, ask if he or she would like to post your article. Be sure you spell-check it before it goes out for submission.

Notes

1   Alessandra Lariu, personal communication, October 16, 2010.

2   http://www.copyblogger.com/headline-swipe-file-3/ (accessed December 6, 2010).

3   http://www.copyblogger.com/headline-swipe-file-3/ (accessed December 6, 2010).

4   Edward Werz and Sally Germain, *Phrases That Sell: The Ultimate Phrase Finder to Help You Promote Your Products, Services, and Ideas* (Chicago, IL: NTC/Contemporary Publishing Group, 1998), 2.

5   Vinny Warren, personal communication, September 4, 2009.

6   Darren Rowse and Chris Garrett, *ProBlogger: Secrets for Blogging Your Way to a Six-Figure Income*, 2nd ed. (Indianapolis: Wiley Publishing, 2010), 36.

7   Rowse and Garrett, *ProBlogger*, 36.

8   Rowse and Garrett, *ProBlogger*, 85–88.

9   Drayton Bird, personal communication, January 14, 2011.

10   Andy Beal, personal communication, January 12, 2011.

11   Andy Beal, personal communication, January 12, 2011.

12   Peter Sena II, personal communication, February 1, 2011.

13   Charlie Hopper, personal communication, November 26, 2008.

14   http://topcopywritingsites.com (accessed January 5, 2011).

15   Vinny Warren, personal communication, September 4, 2009.

16   http://www.famousbloggers.net/blogging-social-media.html (accessed January 6, 2011).

17   http://www.seo-writer.com/blog/2011/01/04/the-golden-rules-of-guest-blogging (accessed January 6, 2011).

18   Lena L. West, personal communication, October 25, 2009.

19   Deltina Hay, personal communication, June 22, 2009.

20   Matt Ziselman, personal communication, January 30, 2009.

21   Joel Postman, *SocialCorp: Social Media Goes Corporate* (Berkeley, CA: New Riders, 2009), 120–123.

THE ONLINE WORD

Websites

"" The readers can sense that you are talking to them, and only them, at that particular moment. ""

MATT ZISELMAN, CREATIVE DIRECTOR, SAPIENTNITRO [1]

Considering different types of digital directions

Examining a site with straightforward copy

Looking at copy on two digital agency sites

Examining a humorous site

Understanding SEO as a writer

Staying current about SEO

Learning digital media from online experts

Creative online writing exercises

Even if you are the most adept Internet user, surfing is not the same as creating content online. In this chapter, you'll become more aware of the techniques and terminology behind the web pages. You'll discover types of digital directions you can choose from, including hard sell (like landing pages that scream, "Buy me"), product-based sites (that resemble print catalogs), information-based sites (like disease symptoms on medical sites), self-promotion sites that showcase a company's best work (like agency websites), and more.

You'll realize why you should start thinking about smaller screens that display web pages and how a site should be reduced into a microsite so it can be viewed equally well in a miniaturized version. You'll begin to see how important easy site navigation is when you're developing the web page. You'll also notice that content, language, and targeted keywords will boost its search engine rankings, help the site's traffic, and optimize its online exposure.

You'll start to communicate with website visitors and think about their values and how you can showcase relevant benefits. You might even consider using humor on your site.

Most importantly, you'll recognize that you would be more marketable as a "T" talent. That is someone who brings a breadth of understanding about many topics and a depth of knowledge and talent in one key area. You'll see that it's necessary to learn to work in teams. And you'll become even more familiar with terminology through the list of common Internet words at the end of this chapter.

To begin, we'll look at various kinds of websites, so you'll be able to create the most appropriate type for yourself and your future clients.

Considering different types of digital directions

You've probably noticed some websites are news or information sites. Others are entertainment sites. Some are corporate or association sites. Many are social media sites. There are numerous other types, for example, sales or "retail" sites.

If you haven't yet run into a site that screams BUY NOW, you haven't wandered around looking for what appeared to be an information site. Some sites practically bark at the audience, much like the old barkers at the circus: "Step right up! Step right in! What you'll see will amaze you!" The site might ask for your name and e-mail address before sharing the information. Then, if you ignore the request and try to wander around, the same message will reappear over and over. If the message had a disclaimer stating it would not share this information, you might feel more comfortable giving it. What you don't want is to be digitally harassed with endless offers. You also want the assurance that you can easily get out ("opt out") of or "unsubscribe" from unwanted correspondence.

Writers who are trying to build an audience should guard against just gathering a "list" of e-mail addresses instead of building a loyal online following. Visitors shouldn't feel pressured to offer contact details in order to receive the material. They should believe that they would enjoy reading the information and not be worried about endless follow-up correspondence.

Some direct response "experts" have mastered the hit-them-over-the-head-with-offers approach. Then, they applied that technique online. Depending on the audience, it can appeal to or alienate the market. Many people find it as offensive as screaming car commercials, high-pressure sales people, and weekend phone solicitors.

Some sales-driven sites have become experts in offering advice or suggestions without barraging the audience and have succeeded in gathering a loyal following. These include the following examples and endless others: book-buying-and-more sites like www.amazon.com, medical sites like www.webmd.com or www.mayoclinic.com, travel sites like www.hotels .com or www.orbitz.com, office supplies sites like www.officedepot.com or www.officemax .com, and high-end fashion sites like www.gucci.com and www.neimanmarcus.com. Some specialty e-stores with a bricks-and-mortar locations require visitors to make an appointment to see their entire inventory, like www.kleinfelds.com, the bridal shop on the TV reality series *Say Yes to the Dress*.

Notice the copy in all the sales sites focuses on product details and price. This writing is very similar to printed catalog copy of direct-mail books like Victoria's Secret, JCPenney, HoneyBaked Ham, and others. If you're writing "catalog" (product and price) copy, be sure you're reading examples to familiarize yourself with the style. This succinct copy looks easier to write than it is. Everything is stripped away except the essential content.

When you write for the digital medium think the same way: Delete everything that's extraneous. Stick to the facts. But, keep the brand personality.

Other sites solely provide information free of solicitation. Here are a few examples: www .Wikipedia.com an open-source, consumer-created encyclopedia, http://medical.nettop20 .com, a content-rating site to guide consumers to the best medical advice online by naming top twenty sites, and www.merckvetmanual.com, which discusses pet health problems. Other sites cover less serious subjects; like www.catalogsfroma-z.com, which presents a list of direct mail and online shopping catalogs. These types of sites are purely fact-sharing sites, not those posing as information sites, which then attempt to sell you something.

Examining a site with straightforward copy

I'm a big believer in the fact that while the Internet is an information resource, I think that information can, and should be conveyed, in a compelling, entertaining, aesthetically pleasing way. **MATT ZISELMAN, CREATIVE DIRECTOR, SAPIENTNITRO**[2]

One information site that features simple, direct, and clear copy is that of DDB (http://www.ddb .com/who-we-are/roots.html). Just reading the "Who We Are" section easily walks the reader through the agency's philosophy and lineage. Concisely explained, each section is introduced with a lucid subhead. Look at the copy below from the www.ddb.com "Roots" page in this section and see how it succinctly describes the agency.[3]

SCRIPTS AND EXAMPLES 11.1 Where we come from

In 1949, three enterprising gentlemen, Bill Bernbach, Ned Doyle and Maxwell Dane gave the advertising industry a wake-up call. They introduced a new approach to marketing that relied on insight into human nature, respect for the consumer, and the power of creativity. In short, they said: Let's stop talking at people and instead start conversations that lead to action and mutual benefit.

This heritage tells us who we are, what we believe and how we should behave. It inspires us to continually challenge standard convention. From Bill Bernbach to Keith Reinhard to the present generation of DDB leaders, we continue the revolution.

Ideas are the fuel of DDB. Throughout our evolution we have been guided by a series of relevant and related ideas:

Creativity is the most powerful force in business

DDB's pursues collaborative relationships with clients and partners to find the hidden potential of people, brands and business through creativity.

Insight into human nature

We believe that great ideas come from keen insights and one good idea can propel a brand for years.

Respect for the customer

DDB has long led the way by recognizing that brands are in the hands of consumers, not brand managers. Nothing is more important and relevant today.

Respect for our world

As influential communicators, DDB is in a position to use creativity as a force for good. As Bill Bernbach so eloquently put it, "All of us who professionally use the mass media are the shapers of society. We can vulgarize that society. We can brutalize it. Or we can help lift it onto a higher level."

(Copy courtesy of DDB.[4])

Although this looks like very straightforward copy, don't underestimate its directness. This kind of carefully constructed copy on the agency's website reflects a clarity of thinking that reaches across all levels of client work, from strategy through concept and execution. The point is if the agency writes this well for itself, it will do no less for its clients.

Watch that you always carefully structure your agency's as well as your clients' website copy to reflect the brand's or company's personality in an appropriate *tone of voice* for the audience. Be diligent in polishing your communication skills. Brush up on your digital writing style by reading copy from those who spend their days creating this kind of content.

Looking at copy on two digital agency sites

Website #1: Digital Surgeons

Digital Surgeons, an award-winning, Connecticut-based interactive agency, has received Promotion World's Reader's Choice Best Search Engine Marketing (SEM) Company Award. With a fresh-thinking, inventive approach to digital communication, the agency's work stands out. A recent infographic comparing Twitter versus Facebook received more than 100,000 online mentions. Experts in interactivity, social media, data visualization, and more, the Digital Surgeon website speaks in an informal way. Unstuffy and unpretentious, the copy on the site demonstrates the agency's personality with humor and engaging self-description. Here's one paragraph from the website's "About" page.

> Have a one-on-one conversation with someone. Having a one-on-one conversation entails having your *point of view* on the world. **SHEENA BRADY, CREATIVE DIRECTOR/COPYWRITER, WIEDEN+KENNEDY**[5]

Next to a visual of a cup of Starbucks coffee, the stacked headline reads as a boxed checklist:

- *Caffeine Fueled.*
- *Kid Tested.*
- *Mother Approved.*

The first paragraph of copy follows answering the headline "Who."

Who are we? An entrepreneurial, energetic, agile, curious, close-knit band of award-winning new media junkies; a mashup of creative technologists, designers and brand strategists with a surprising depth of experience and an equally surprising lack of ego. We stay one step ahead of the ever-changing intersection of marketing, advertising and technology, and take a huge amount of pride in the work we create and in the results our clients enjoy.

Just calling their team a "mashup" of various talent and saying there is a "surprising lack of ego" is humbling and disarming. Sometimes when there are creative "stars" there are also creative star egos. This tells prospective clients we're not a headache to work with, yet we're bright and multitalented. Something every client wants to hear without listening to a plethora of boastful language.

In the section called "What We Do," the language clearly states the agency's competencies. It starts with a simple, paradoxically understated yet bold headline: "We know digital." The copy explains:

The media ecosystem is evolving daily. Since we consider ourselves contributors to this evolution, we've amassed an incredible arsenal of services to help you build your brand. Seriously, by the time you get to the end of this list some new buzzword will have emerged, and every blog and social network will be cluttered with chatter about it. We'll help you navigate around the useless and keep you heading towards the useful.[6]

The first sentence shows that the talents realize they must stay ahead of the next emerging media. It promises a commitment to not only take the pulse of the industry, but also to contribute to new trends. Once again, the language shows self-confidence without conceit.

Website #2: Fi (Fantasy Interactive)

Right from the start, Fi's home page is welcoming. First there's the greeting, set at an angle to give it movement and catch your attention. It's personable and engaging:

Hello there! We love meeting happy designers, producers, and developers.[7]

You'd never guess that they have been named the Global Digital Agency by HTC, which we'll discuss in a moment. On the bottom of this and some successive pages, the firm reminds readers who they are and what they do, like this:

Fi is a multi-award-winning and global full-service digital agency. We believe in quality over quantity.[8]

The last line is the company slogan. Do you remember what kind of tagline (or slogan) this is? Think for a moment. Don't rush yourself. Refer back to the list of 16 *slogan techniques* in chapter 4. That's right. It's a *statement of use or purpose* (#6) type of slogan. What's the *point of view* of this line, as explained in chapter 3? Yes, it's *self-serving* (#1). It's delivered from the company's perspective.

Throughout most of the site, client projects are explained in brief statements like these below. There's no superfluous copy. Each block of copy is reduced down to its pure essence. Clear and uncomplicated, like this:

- *Google and Fi worked together to educate the public about the Web and browsers. Using the latest HTML5 technology, we created an interactive reading experience.*

- *All New Fox.com. How do you design and develop the ultimate video experience for millions?*

- *"Pulse of the City." A revolutionary, multiplatform campaign to introduce the new Range Rover Evoque.*

- *"Life is Amazing." A stunning natural history showcase for BBC Worldwide.*[9]

If you get a chance, be sure to check out the interactive book, created by Google and Fi, with pages you actually turn, one by one. It's listed under "20 Things I learned about Browsers and the Web."

Under "Work," there are five categories to explore: (1) All, (2) Portals, (3) Applications, (4) Microsites, and, (5) Mobile. The selected client list presents each with one succinct and descriptive line of copy and a "View case study" link. The key point here is how the copy is clearly written. Think about how much effort it takes to summarize an entire project in one sentence. Here are two examples.

On the "Work" page, under "All," some clients have both the case study link and a second link to launch the site. These "call to action" links allow visitors to see the work firsthand. Although all sites are interactive, inviting the reader to scroll up and down, go to different pages, make a purchase or go to other links, Fantasy Interactive cuts down on the reading time and maximizes the viewing time. Below are two examples.

a BBC "life is"

Line of descriptive copy: Fi creates a unique showcase for the BBC's natural history footage.
   Choice of two actions: (1) View case study and (2) Launch the site.
   Line of call to action copy: Dive into Life Is and explore the rich content.

b Google "Zeitgeist"

Line of descriptive copy: Fi and Google created innovative, online data visualizations for "Zeitgeist," Google's end-of-year search reports.
   Line of call to action copy: View case study[10]

On the "About" page, under "About Us," to explain who Fi is, the agency has managed to bring the copy down to a few seconds of reading. The headline promises, "Fi in five Seconds." The copy delivers the promise. Then, gives this super short answer, packed with content:

Fi is a world-renowned, full-service interactive firm with 11 years' experience, 3 offices, 55 Industry Awards, 90% Direct-to-Client relationships and 10% Agency Partnerships. We believe in quality over quantity.[11]

Notice, in those five seconds, the tagline wraps up the introduction. Once again, there are two calls to action or invitations (1) to follow Fi on Kontain (www.kontain.com) for the "latest news, events and tutorials from the Fi employees"[12] and (2) to check out its blog. Kontain allows users to see up-to-the minute images or "snapshots" of what Fi is doing right now or in "real time."

Pay close attention to how fast visitors can find what they're looking for in just a few short lines. Brevity is key to the fluidity of this site. For example, under the "Services" page, there are four sections: (1) Strategy, (2) Design, (3) Technology, and (4) Process. Look at the short description "Strategic Thinking" under Strategy:

> *Fi is a global interactive firm. We deliver interactive services and media platforms: web-based applications, microsites, mobile experiences, portals, and interfaces for games and TV.*[13]

On the "Services" page, under "Technology," the hyphenated, one-word headline sums up perfectly what they do: "Cutting-Edge" work. The language is not vain or self-congratulatory; it's modest and genuine. *Tone of voice* is crucial when agencies are talking about their work. If they sound too self-impressed, they may give the impression they're prima donnas to work with. Here, Fi is sharing its ambitious goals and explaining how it realistically plans to execute them. Most importantly, it promises to deliver an inventive design solution that's both functional and powerful.

> *Fi is committed to achieving a perfect balance of world-class engineering and inspiring design. Our technologists have the desire and skill to push boundaries and innovate – without losing sight of usability and robustness.*[14]

Even on the homepage, it simply states its worldwide creative stature in more of a low-key press release announcement than a high-and-mighty-are-we headline, summed up in a few short phrases, so upfront and unfussy. More disarming than that is that the headline is presented in a cartoon as a plane banner ad being flown in the sky:

> *HTC Appoints Fantasy Interactive as Global Digital Agency*[15]

Not bad, considering *Fast Company* (March 2010, issue) recognized HTC as (1) number 31 in its list of "50 Most Innovative Companies" and (2) number two in the consumer electronics company category.

Take a moment to examine the copy on the HTC site: http://www.htc.com/www/htcsense/index.html. You'll find it whimsical and fun, like the animated cartoon images that accompany the copy. Here are a few lines that quickly draw in the reader:

> *HTC Sense is an experience . . . designed around little insightful ideas. Ideas so simple . . . you think, "Why hasn't anyone else thought of that?"*

Click through the three green thought bubbles (1) "Preview Your Drive," (2) "Flip to Silence," and (3) "Map With Compass." You'll find the copy just as entertaining as the playful images.

Then go back to the Fi website copy. Explore the projects and read the case studies so you'll have a deeper comprehension of how digital problems and client goals are being addressed. Start to develop a high personal standard so you won't settle on the first creative concept or digital solution that occurs to you. Dig deeper. Think broader. Ask yourself how you can create a bigger digital footprint (stronger presence on the Web) by tying digital work into existing or future campaigns.

Let's take a look at an agency that used a humorous strategy in its multimedia campaign to reach a young male market in the US. We'll look at the website first and out-of-home messages in chapter 12.

Examining a humorous site

There's always a fine line when you're creating irreverent copy. It's bound to offend someone somewhere. Then, imagine being brave enough to post it on a website for a client! That takes real courage. That's exactly what The Escape Pod did for Feckin Irish Whiskey. Vinny Warren, founder and creative director of The Escape Pod, being Irish himself, felt it was okay to depict the IRA. The client was nervous, thinking it could be offensive.

Warren defended the copy by saying, "I think people get offended on other people's behalf, sometimes."[16] Warren assured him that anything could be humorous, explaining that he personally said he thought IRA press conferences were hilarious. "And, the constant splitting within the factions was another source of comedy to me."[17] Warren said terrorist and national organizations are always splitting and that there are always internal disputes.

He said the tagline for one of the campaign's posters, which we discussed in chapter 9, was "The Spirit of Irish Rebellion." That became the idea behind the website. Here's how Warren explained the site's creative direction.

> We had a website, which basically looked like an IRA press conference from the 1980s.
> A guy talking to camera. He's basically announcing that there's been a split within the
> Feckin Irish Whiskey organization. There are now two separate fractions and you should
> choose which one most reflects your feelings. Then, when you clicked on one of them,
> you were told that there was a further split within this Feckin Irish community faction,
> and there are now two new ones. And so, in essence, you keep going and keep going and
> keep going until it got ridiculous. But, everyone was the same. So, it was a joke on Irish
> terrorism pretty much, right?
>
> I thought, well I can do that because I'm Irish. We did it and the client looked at it and
> was nervous about it.[18]

Regardless of what kind of website copy you're writing, whether it's informative, serious, humorous, and so on, ultimately you want also to have some understanding of how to increase traffic through search engine optimization.

Understanding SEO as a writer

To help elevate websites' positions in search engine rankings, writers need to understand how to create language that speaks to the audience while positively impacting search engine results.

Look for helpful articles, especially those that list expert sites where you can learn the ins and outs of digital marketing. The term SEO (search engine optimization) is often used to explain how to maximize the impact and traffic of your site.

Before we look at some writing tips from Derek Cromwell, a self-taught content manager and founder of Thunder Bay Media, we need to understand some words that appear frequently in SEO discussions. The first is "keyword density," which appears in his first tip.

That refers to the frequency of important words or phrases, called "keywords," compared to other words that appear on the same web page. Back in the 1990s, search engines used to analyze that percentage to help rank sites. When writers overloaded their clients' pages with keywords, called "keyword stuffing," that backfired with penalties that negatively affected their rankings. Keyword usage should safely stay 3% or lower to avoid "search spam" labeling, which creates a higher, but false web ranking. Just watch when you're writing for a site that you don't overuse keywords.

Another mentions "podcasts." These are audio-digital recordings that can be created as a series or an independent file, which are downloaded by listeners online, via an mp3 player (like an iPod), or other mobile devices. If they're lengthy (such as half-hour long) audio presentations, think of them like online radio shows. Some people create podcast interviews or informative programs. Unlike podcasts, "webcasts" can be audio or video digital messages. Both can be delivered after they've been recorded or distributed live, as streaming simulcasts, like radio and/or TV shows, as well as Internet-only radio shows.

Here are Cromwell's main writing tips.

ADVICE FROM THE PROS 11.2 Derek Cromwell's website copywriting tips

1 *Remove the phrase "keyword density" from your vocabulary.* When you're writing content, you're not thinking about search rank; you should be thinking about whether or not you're connecting with your target audience. If you write good, authoritative, informative, entertaining and/or education content then in many cases the SEO will come naturally. If you do need specific keywords to be emphasized, apply them last only after you've written a piece that targets people.

2 *Writing content for marketing purposes is about more than just writing 50 articles tightly focused on a few random keywords in order to gain search visibility.* That is not a strategy. Writing content for the Web is about bringing various pieces of content together (blogs, articles, white papers, eBooks, podcasts, videos) to educate, to tell a story and to entice the reader to want to learn more from you and you alone.

3 *When you're writing for the Web, headlines are vital to the success of content whether it's a web page, an article or a video.* Learn to write compelling headlines and understand that you should spend nearly as much time crafting a compelling title as you do writing an entire piece of content. While studying to create better content, pay attention to the headlines around you in print ads, magazines, newspapers, etc.

4 *Solve, don't shill:* When you're writing content outside of ad copy for the purposes of branding or thought leadership, your content should provide a solution or the path to a solution. Articles, blogs, and press releases – these are not the place for hyped up sales.

5 *Know who you're writing for.* Your connect needs to identify the target audience, empathize with them, connect with them, engage them and provide a solution (or a path to it). If you haven't researched the target audience then you won't know their likes, dislikes, hot buttons, spending habits, psychographics, the problems they face, the questions they have and the solutions they're looking for. Do your homework.[19]

Some other key points Cromwell mentioned in "Website Copywriting," an article posted in 2010, emphasized the importance of keyword context, meaning that themed words needed to be set around your keywords, rather than stuffing the article with misplaced keywords. That is as bad as repeating five or six keywords instead of creating a specific phrase. He also mentioned that online articles require in-depth research and should not just be tossed out onto the Web without careful attention to detail. He reminded readers that web copy that engages and relates to the visitor increases the blogger's credibility and chance of a sale. If you don't create content-appropriate copy, you'll create high bounce rates and low conversion-to-sale rates. That means people will visit and then quickly leave without making a purchase.

Staying current about SEO

In addition to reading copy blogs as discussed in chapter 10, online content writers should be following SEO blogs. Learning to drive traffic to a website can help develop an audience. When you add interactivity to the site, you already have a built-in audience with the potential for response. See what the online experts are recommending and add those blogs to your reading list. The following is a list of informative blogs that talk about guidelines to increasing web traffic. Even if you read only one or two on the list, you're at least familiarizing yourself with SEO content.

Here is an article listing the top 24 SEO blogs according to HubSpot. Pay attention to how the article starts: with a short sentence and a brief paragraph. Then, it gets right into the heart of the message, offering the list of websites. This allows readers to quickly find the information they were seeking. A longer introduction might have annoyed the audience. In fact, readers may have skipped it all together. See how it ends: (1) with a suggested site from a reader and (2) with an invitation for visitors to send in other links and a reference to more information.

> It [the Internet] is a near-perfect direct marketing medium because it involves a two-way exchange between user and provider of a service or a product. **DRAYTON BIRD, WRITER, SPEAKER, MARKETER, AND AUTHOR**[20]

USEFUL INFO 11.3 24 awesome SEO blogs everyone should read

(Posted by Kipp Bodnar, Tue, Aug 24, 2010 @ 01:20 PM)

Search engine marketing is constantly changing. Like social media and other aspects of online marketing, search engines are working to deliver better results for their users. To do this, they are focusing on new areas like localization and social search. As a marketer, it is important to keep up with all of this news, so here is our reading list of search engine optimization (SEO) blogs that will help make you a better marketer.

1   *SEOmoz Blog* (www.seomoz.org/blog) – SEOmoz has become the gold standard for SEO information and how-to articles. Its team of contributors offers an article per day to help expand your SEO knowledge.

2   *Marketing Pilgrim* (www.marketingpilgrim.com) – Andy Beal and his team of talented writers break search engine and Internet marketing news and discuss major industry trends impacting marketers.

3 *Search Engine Land* (http://searchengineland.com) – This is one of the best search engine blogs for in-depth news and analysis of the search marketing industry.

4 *Search Engine Journal* (www.searchenginejournal.com) – From link building to the newest changes from Google, Search Engine Journal covers news and tactics related to the search engine marketing industry.

5 *Search Engine Roundtable* (www.seroundtable.com) – For detailed discussion and explanations of the fine details of search engine marketing, Search Engine Roundtable has you covered.

6 *SEO Book* (www.seobook.com/blog) – For reviews of the newest SEO tools to analysis of search engine changes, check out SEO Book.

7 *ReelSEO* (www.reelseo.com) – ReelSEO is a resource for marketers looking to learn more about online video's impact on search engine marketing.

8 *Yoast* (http://yoast.com) – Yoast is a how-to focused blog that covers tactics for improving SEO as well as user experience for your website.

9 *aimClear* (www.aimclearblog.com) – The aimClear blog includes articles about a wide range of search marketing topics, including SEO and PPC.

10 *Biznology* (www.mikemoran.com/biznology/blog/) – This blog discusses many SEO-related issues but has recently focused on content marketing and its connection to SEO.

11 *Blue Glass Blog* (www.blueglass.com/blog/) – The talented team over at Blue Glass discusses important industry issues as well as tools.

12 *CanuckSEO* (www.canuckseo.com/) – Jim Rudnick provides tips and tricks for improving search engine optimization as well as other search engine marketing related topics.

13 *Daily SEO Tip* (http://dailyseotip.com/) – Are you a fan of sites that provide a tip per day? Then this might be the blog for you, offering tips and tricks to help support your search engine marketing strategies.

14 *Distilled Blog* (www.distilled.co.uk/blog/) – The team at Distilled provides insights and musings about the intersection of search and social media.

15 *GeoLocalSEO* (www.geolocalseo.com/blog/) – If local and mobile search is your interest, then the GeoLocalSEO blog is a resource you should check out for tips and tricks related to the local and mobile search industry.

16 *Google Webmaster Central Blog* (http://googlewebmastercentral.blogspot.com/) – When working in the search marketing industry, you must know what the search engines are doing. Google's webmaster blog gives search marketers insights into the changes and updates to Google.

17 *Graywolf's SEO Blog* (www.wolf-howl.com/) – Michael Gray shares SEO-related commentary and advice in his blog.

18 *Industrial Search Engine Marketing* (www.industrialsearchenginemarketing.com/blog) – If you are a B2B [business-to-business] company looking for search engine marketing guidance, then this is a great resource for you.

19 *John Battelle's Search Blog* (http://battellemedia.com/) – A co-founder of *Wired* magazine and a search engine marketing pioneer, Battelle's musings cover search and much more.

20 *Junta42 Blog* (http://blog.junta42.com) – Content marketing is critical to SEO success. The team at Junta42 shares insights and tips for successful content marketing.

21 *Matt Cutts* (www.mattcutts.com/blog) – Matt is Google's most famous search engine engineer who shares his thoughts and insights on search engine optimization.

22 *Outspoken Media* (http://outspokenmedia.com/blog) – This team of bloggers discusses all aspects of search engine marketing while providing tactical information and industry commentary.

23 *SEO Copywriting* (www.seocopywriting.com/blog) – Copy is a critical part of SEO success. This blog goes into more detail than most about the best practices of SEO copywriting.

UPDATE: After some suggestions from our readers we have decided to add another blog to this list.

24 *Search Engine Watch* (http://searchenginewatch.com/) – This multi-author blog was recommended by several readers and covers a wide variety of search marketing issues.

What other blogs do you think should be added to this list?

Read more: http://blog.hubspot.com/blog/tabid/6307/bid/6482/23-Awesome-SEO-Blogs-Everyone-Should-Read.aspx#ixzz1ACtQgm3w. (*List courtesy of HubSpot, www.hubspot.com.*[21])

Learning digital media from online experts

If you're going to learn, learn from the best. One of the most recognized names in the digital industry today is Alessandra (Ale) Lariu, Senior Vice President, Digital Group Creative Director at McCann Erickson. *Fast Company* named her number 29 out of "The Top 100 Most Creative People in 2010."[22]

At a 2010 presentation in Denver at the annual AEJMC (Association for Education in Journalism and Mass Communication) Conference, Lariu made a few pointed comments about her work and the creative process at McCann Erickson. We'll discuss them here.

1 I wanted to do digital work where people said, "What? McCann?"

2 Idea is king, not the media.

3 New talent THINK this way. (You) don't want to be "siloed." You're a copywriter. We look for T structures when attracting talent (T = breadth and depth of knowledge).

4 The old process was: The client asked for a TV spot. (Then added,) "Can you do digital for my idea?"

5 We're trying to change process. Now everyone gets briefed at the same time. We talk about (the) client's problem. Then, we did TV (created TV spots) about what they said. For example: MasterCard.

6 We collaborate a lot. We mix up the group: Creatives and Technologists come at problem from a different angle.

7 You should incorporate people who are passionate about the product.[23]

Her goal (#1) when she joined McCann was to create breakthrough work and grab the digital world's attention. She didn't just accept the job. She looked to raise eyebrows. New writers should challenge themselves to develop unexpected work in the digital landscape.

The notion (#2) that "idea is king" is more relevant now because creatives may get sidetracked, distracted, or mesmerized by the allure of developing messages for digital media. Remember every word of copy must be based on a strong conceptual idea backed by a solid creative strategy.

The belief that creative talent today should have a breath of wide knowledge paired with a depth in a single expertise (#3) is commonly accepted among agencies today. Young writers should strive to be versed in many areas and experts in copywriting. Try new brands. Listen to different music. Read a variety of magazines. Watch diverse TV shows. Read books in a myriad topics. Expand your breath of knowledge wherever you can. This will make you not only an interesting person, but also a more creative writer.

Let's return to Lariu's comments. She suggested that years ago major brands were concentrating on TV first (#4, #5, and #6). Then, the other media vehicles would spin out from TV. Now, the entire team, from creative talent to media planners and digital designers, called "technologists," meets together to plan campaign solutions. Many agencies today are working this way. The greater number of insights, the better quality of ideas.

She emphasized, when hiring creative talent (#7), looking for people passionate about the product. That seems expected. But, how many people think about how enthusiastic their creative team members are about a particular account when they're interviewing? Often, the decision makers are focused on skill sets, expertise, and experience. Remember, the next time you're offered a position and then given an assignment, become an enthusiastic fan of the brand. This excitement will translate into your writing, whether it's online or out-of-home.

Also, realize that conceptual thinking today is normally a collaborative effort. As a writer, you must be able to interact with others, listen to their points, and integrate ideas from every contributor, regardless of title or department. A writer's greatest gift is the ability to be open to suggestion and be able to accept criticism.

Keep in mind all the writing tips offered throughout this chapter. You'll find digital writing is not that far removed from other media. You need to know your *audience*,

 ADVICE FROM THE PROS 11.4 **Alessandra Lariu's digital writing tips**

1 Imagine that you are writing to one person. Try and engage that one person rather than everyone.

2 Less is more. Edit, edit, edit.

3 Keep it simple. No one likes a smart ass.

4 The message is more important than the specific words. Don't agonize over one word.

5 Above all else you are trying to sell something.[24]

tone of voice, *point of view*, and *unique selling point(s)*. Make your message *relevant*, yet concise.

To continuously improve your digital writing skills, be sure you're reading websites, microsites, blogs, articles, industry publications, tweets, and other comments from industry experts. This will help you stay current with writing examples and changes that constantly take place in the industry, and strategic digital work that's both innovative and utilitarian.

Pay close attention to how people are communicating, which platforms they're using, and how these interact with one another. This infographic shows how conversations are taking place online. Notice how many digital vehicles intersect to create an open dialogue thoroughfare.

Brian Solis, author of *Engage!* and JESS3, as well as a principal at Altimeter Group, designed an ingenious infographic, "The Conversation Prism," in August of 2008. It represented the breadth and scope of "social topography" and showed how digital communication expanded beyond the typically referenced social networks like Facebook and Twitter. The infographic was based on the "Social Media Starfish" (http://scobleizer.com/2007/11/02/social-media-starfish/), which was created by Darren Barefoot and Robert Scoble in November 2007. Take a careful look at this detailed depiction of the vast impact of social media in the updated 3.0 version Solis created (Figure 11.1).

According to Solis, it was designed with three goals in mind.

Goal #1: create social map based on observation and study

I was inspired to map the social media universe by both features and capabilities and also how people were really using these tools, networks and services. Doing so would help us better understand how to survey the landscape by approachable groups rather than as a single entity.

Goal #2: search, listen, and learn

It occurred to me that each network featured a search box and as budding brand managers, both personal and professional, we could use keywords to reveal conversations and determine whether or not our presence was required. In the networks where activity was flourishing, I was able to listen, document, and learn how to engage in each community with a mission, purpose, and value-added perspective.

Goal #3: set the foundation for sCRM and introduce new social technologies + methodologies

The Conversation Prism visualized Social CRM (sCRM, or Social Customer Relationship Management) to help businesses recognize the opportunity to listen, learn and adapt. The hub was now a rotating visualization of conversational workflow to inspire the socialization of business and to introduce conversational touchpoints across the organization.[25]

In looking at this visual depiction of how we create multimedia conversations and how those dialogues converge and influence one another, it almost seems as if sCRM could stand

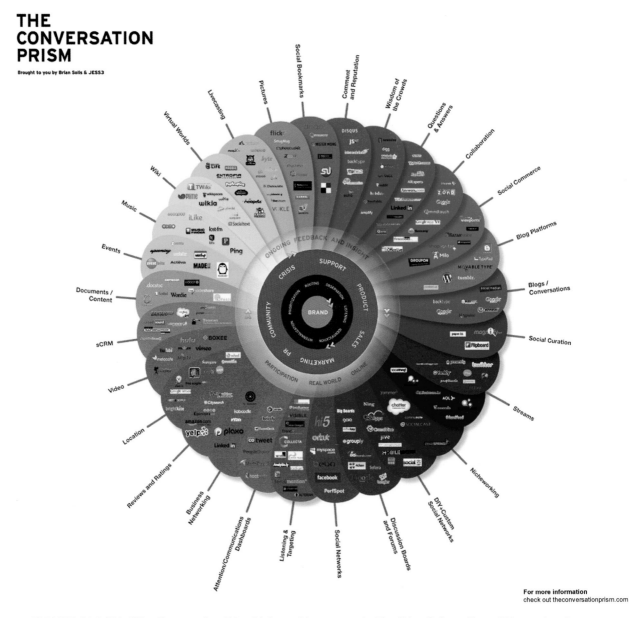

FIGURE 11.1 This "The Conversation Prism" infographic was created by Brian Solis, author of *Engage!* and JESS3. Image courtesy of Brian Solis.

for Social *Conversation* Relationship Management. Take your time to analyze and absorb the channels of interactivity. Then, think about how each of your advertising messages can influence these conversations.

Be sure you're familiar with the newest terminology. Read articles, follow bloggers, and look for new information. This is a partial list of some key, Internet-related words you'll need to know. As technology changes, new Internet-related words are created. You must promise yourself to become a forever student just to keep up. Now, let's review some of these words in an ever-growing list of terms so you can become more fluent with "Webanese."

USEFUL INFO 11.5 Common Internet terms

Adsense®	This is a program where Google places ads on websites and pays owners for placement.
Adwords®	These are key words used as ads. In the US, advertiser pays Google who then shares the proceeds with the website owners. In the UK, advertiser pays to place ads in relevant search results driven by keywords in the content.
Affiliate	This is a website, company, or marketing program that enables fee-paid links to other websites in order to drive traffic to their sites in exchange for commission.
Aggregator	This software or website gathers ("aggregates") information from various sites and sources, like news, videos, polls, reviews (for books, movies, etc.), search (can organize search results, etc.) into a consolidated view.
Analytics	This is a free analytical service by Google for all website owners so they can track visitors in various ways: by volume, geography, dates, etc.
Apps	(A nickname for "applications") These mobile web applications are software programs that facilitate searches by topic. They were designed for handheld Web-enabled digital devices like Kindle and iPad, as well as smartphones like the iPhone, BlackBerry, Android, etc.
Blog	This is the accessible online journal of a person, corporation, or association, normally encouraging interaction with its readers through a forum for comments.
Bookmark	This is a method of highlighting and saving links to websites so users can revisit them later.
Browser	This software application allows web pages to be displayed and then found by users conducting Internet searches or "browsing the Web." Some browsers are Firefox, Google Chrome, Internet Explorer, Netscape, Opera, among others.
Chat and text acronyms	This is a list of commonly used shorthand for text messaging and online chatting, such as "121" for "one-to-one," "AITR" for "adult in the room," or "CSN" for "chuckle, snicker, grin." See handy list at http://www.netlingo.com/acronyms.php.
Click-through	This is when a web user clicks on hyperlink to another site.
Comment	This is what followers do when they post (place) their opinion on websites, blogs, microblogs, etc.
Content	This is the topic expressed in website copy.
Crowdsourcing	Unlike social bookmarking, these are sites that share news stories and other types of information, not just the links to those sites. These include Reddit, Mixx, Gabbr, etc.
Domain name	This is a site's name created by website owner.
Download	This is how users copy files, images, music, etc. to their digital devices, such as computers, mp3s, etc. (See "upload.")

Facebook fan page	This Facebook page lets website owners increase traffic by establishing a loyal fan base of people who show their support by clicking the "Like" button. Search engines notice fan pages and that helps improve a website's ranking.
Flog	This fake blog is sponsored, but is written as if it were a personal, unbiased blog. (See example in chapter 10.)
Google	This is a search portal site or search engine that enables users to surf the Web.
Hashtag	This sign, a pound sign, is what Twitter users add before a word to categorize their tweets (140-character comments). Today people use hashtags to show a sense of humor, irony, coolness or to billboard a word, like "#Pound award!" It's crept into everyday speech with people saying, "Hashtag sorry I'm late." The hashtag was created by Anthony D. Weisner in August 2007.[26]
HTML	(Hyper Text Markup Language) This is the language, "code" or "source code" website programmers and designers use to indicate how the website and its pages should appear (italics, bold, indented, etc.).
Hyperlink	These are website links that are included ("embedded") appear as buttons or underlined text and allow users to click-through to other sites.
IM	This is the abbreviation for "Instant Messaging" and represents real-time digital (online and mobile) communication.
Landing page	This is a web page that acts like an ad and invites people to take action, like placing an order or subscribing to a blog, newsletter, e-store, etc.
Keyword	These main words in copy are used to help search engines track site content and traffic. Also known as "Key Term" or "Tag."
Media newsroom	This kind of web page targets members of the press and provides information to facilitate coverage.
Menu bar	This allows users to select where they'd like to go next from a "menu" of options listed.
Navigation	This is how users move around websites. The simpler the navigation, the better the online experience.
Opt-In	This is how consumers request information from a company or individual. They could subscribe to receive the information for free or for a fee.
Pay-Per-Click (PPC)	This advertising service allows sponsors to generate income each time a user clicks on a hyperlink.
Permalink	Also known as a permanent link, this is a URL that links to a specific news story or posting. Permalinks are commonly used for blog entries, so followers can get right to that specific post and not have to scroll through the entire site.
Ping	This is a test to see if the Internet is working. The Ping site (http://ping.fm) provides connectivity so consumers can post on one social networking site, and the others are updated automatically.

Platforms	Several meanings. (See figure 11.1.)
	1 Executional platform – This describes the Internet as a technologically driven environment allowing the execution of programs and ideas via websites.[27]
	2 Developmental platform – This shows users have used the Internet as building blocks to create new connections and interactions.[28]
	3 Personal or brand platform – This identifies what you, your firm, or your client are famous for, such as your main message, hook, big idea, or slogan. One example would be the political platform of candidates that exemplifies their beliefs.
	4 Media platforms – This includes all communication vehicles, digital, print, broadcast, interactive, etc.
	5 Social media platforms – These social networking sites and aggregators let you
	a network (Facebook, LinkedIn, Meet The Boss)
	b share (Digg, Delicious, Flickr, Tumblr, StumbleUpon, foursquare) (*see Social Networking*)
	c promote (YouTube, vidcasts, podcasts, blogs).[29]
Platform neutral	This demonstrates the ability to be understood or used regardless of the media vehicle. Here are a few examples:
	1 A PDF (portable document format) file can be read by any computer, whether it has a PC- or Mac-based operating system.
	2 Advertising ideas that can work equally well in all media.
	3 Programs, like Flash, that run on all computer systems.
Plog	This kind of blog has a few meanings:
	1 A political blog.
	2 A photo blog.
	3 A personal, not corporate, blog.
Podcasts	These user-created digital audio recordings allow consumers to present their own speeches, programs, workshops, musical performances, etc. for people to download to their computers or other digital devices and play at their convenience.
RSS feeds	(Really Simple Syndication or Rich Site Summary) This digital format allows users to publish and broadcast (syndicate) frequently updated information like blog posts, news reports, financial news, etc. as web feeds.
Search engine	These are applications that search for information using keywords that allow users to find web pages.
Search portal site	This search engine site allows users to search the Internet using Google, Yahoo!, etc.

SEO	(Search engine optimization) These are various techniques used to improve website rankings. Read more here:
	• Google Webmaster Guidelines (http://www.google.com/support/webmasters/bin/answer.py?answer=35769)
	• Google 101: how Google crawls, indexes, and serves the Web (http://www.google.com/support/webmasters/bin/answer.py?answer=70897)
Search engine results pages	(SERPs) These web pages display the statistics gathered from searches that show keywords and where they appeared (on which sites).
Server	Master computer that houses and organizes website pages, so other computers can access them.
Share	This is how users send others links to and examples of their favorite finds, from photos, music, information, websites, blogs, etc.
Social bookmarking	This allows users to save their favorite sites on a site other than their own. Many social bookmarking sites become popular sources of shared information like Digg, Delicious, and Shelfari. StumbleUpon recommends popular sites others have "stumbled upon."[30]
Social networking	These sites enable users to interact with each other for many reasons, like to stay in touch, network, promote themselves, and share information, such as Facebook, Twitter, LinkedIn, foursquare, MySpace, FriendFeed, Flickr, Tumblr, StumbleUpon, Digg, Delicious, Shelfari, Friendster, Naymz, among many others.
Spamming	These unsolicited e-mail messages are usually sent as an online promotional or advertising message.
Streaming	*On the Internet*, it means broadcasting something as it is happening or "in real time," like streaming video. *In media*, it's the difference between media that are being updated, like radio and TV, versus non-streaming, non-changing media, like books, CDs, DVDs, etc.
Surf	This is how users look for information or browse and navigate the Web.
Swicki	This is a social search portal like Google that anyone can create from their website, so users can learn more about a specific topic and search right from the same site.[31]
Syndicate	This describes the act of distributing and making available sections of websites on other sites or to opted-in subscribers.
Tags	These are words that put blog posts, websites, etc. into categories for easy search engine recognition.
Twitter	This popular micro blog site and real-time short messaging service limits each post or "tweet" to 140 characters.

Upload	This is how users transfer files, images, music, etc. from their digital devices to the Internet. (*See "download."*)
URL	This is each website's actual name and Internet address that describes the location and access method of a site.
Vidcasting (or webcasting)	This is the abridged word for "video casting."
Virtual worlds	These alternate universes "live" in cyberspace, like www.secondlife.com.
Vlog	Like a blog, this is the video version of an online journal.
Vodcasts	These online videos can be user-created or produced by corporations to showcase a talent, highlight a product, or show news, among other video "stories."
Webcasts	These are audio or video presentations or programs that are broadcast over the Internet, such as consumer-created content, radio, and TV shows.
Web host	This is a business site that houses and connects websites to the Internet.
Web master ("Meister")	This is the person responsible for designing and maintaining a website.
Webinars	These online seminars let people participate in a program in real time. They often download the PowerPoint presentation and follow along as the presenter delivers the workshop.
Widget (Badge or Gadget)	Tiny pieces of HTML code that appear as icons and: 1 Allow portions of website information to be syndicated (distributed and available on other computers) 2 enable interactivity.
Wiki	These websites allow users to post, update, and edit, like Wikipedia or Webopedia, and can be used by open or restricted collaborators who want to share research on specific topics, work on corporate projects, etc.
World wide web	This is another term for the Internet, commonly known as "the Web." The letters "www" are the abbreviation for World Wide Web.
Wordpress	An easy-to-use Web content management program that has syndication and widget capability already built in. Users can update data without using HTML code and can readily expand their digital footprint through the use of social media.

There are many other extensive glossaries online, including some on analytics like http://www.webtrends.com/Education/Glossary. Some lists include more technical terms, like the "Glossary of Internet Terms," created by system and software designer, J Matisse Enzer, found at http://www.matisse.net/files/glossary.html.

CHECKLIST 11.6 Online writing checklist

Notice how these points are the same as writing for other media.

1 Consider the reader. They're in a rush. (Time's up! See?)

2 Understand the objective (what you're trying to accomplish in this medium).

3 Get to the point. Be succinct.

4 Show the brand's or blogger's personality.

5 Create a message that ties into other media.

6 Determine the appropriate *tone of voice*.

7 Chose a *point of view*:

   a The brand (self-serving).

   b The consumer (testimonial).

   c The conscience (emotional blackmail).

   d The brand's personality (brand stand).

8 Don't overstuff the copy with irrelevant keywords.

9 Make your digital communication effortless to navigate and/or digest.

10 Engage the reader though interactivity: Q&A, links, comments, case studies, votes, purchases, invitations to follow via myriad social media.

Creative online writing exercises

Exercise 1

Part 1 Find two websites for (a) similar brands, (b) same-industry businesses, or (c) competing advertising agencies, digital agencies, or design firms.

   1 Compare the copy on both sites. Are they alike or distinctive?

   2 Do they use a similar *tone of voice* and *point of view*?

   3 Determine if they are targeting the same audience.

   4 Could you tell one brand, business or agency apart from the other?

   5 How would you rewrite the copy to make it more effective?

   6 How could you make the site more interactive and engaging? What links would you add? What participatory activities would you include? Perhaps a drawing tool to customize a product.

Part 2 Choose one of the two competing brands, businesses, or agencies. Think about how you would create a distinctive *tone of voice* with a clear, identifiable personality.

Part 3 Write copy for one page. You could choose the home page, or about the company, or case study, or whatever page you want. Be sure to include headlines and subheads for each page.

Exercise 2: take the same brand, business, or agency and reduce the copy to better fit a microsite

Think small screen and small space. Less is more. You might have to not only cut copy, but also use fewer subheads per page. Perhaps you would include more links and less copy. Focus on what are the most important points to cover. Edit out everything unnecessary.

Exercise 3

Part 1 Select a client, or advertise your advertising services, or your new company's website. Some students and creative talents are developing websites, writing copy, shooting videos, and so on. Create an ad for Google AdWords. Go to http://www.google .com/adwords/smallbusinesscenter/ for some tips on writing ads and deciding keywords (used to drive traffic to your site). Check out this page for a list of tips for beginners, intermediate AdWord users, and for seasoned pros: http://www.google.com/adwords/smallbusinesscenter/write-great-ads.html.

Part 2 Be sure to think about your audience, their values, and what would be a relevant message for them.

Part 3 Write a second AdWord ad for another audience or for another service or product.

Notes

1   Matt Ziselman, personal communication, January 30, 2009.

2   Matt Ziselman, personal communication, January 30, 2009.

3   Pat Sloan, personal communication, April 13, 2011.

4   http://www.ddb.com/who-we-are/roots.html (accessed April 10, 2011).

5   Sheena Brady, personal communication, May 8, 2009.

6   http://www.digitalsurgeons.com (accessed February 3, 2011).

7   http://www.f-i.com (accessed February 5, 2011).

8   http://www.f-i.com (accessed February 5, 2011).

9   http://www.f-i.com (accessed February 5, 2011).

10   http://www.f-i.com/work/all (accessed February 5, 2011).

11   http://www.f-i.com/fi/about-us (accessed February 5, 2011).

12   http://www.f-i.com/fi/about-us (accessed February 5, 2011).

13   http://www.f-i.com/services/technology (accessed February 5, 2011).

14   http://www.f-i.com/services/technology (accessed February 5, 2011).

15   http://www.f-i.com (accessed February 5, 2011).

16   Vinny Warren, personal communication, September 4, 2009.

17   Vinny Warren, personal communication, September 4, 2009.

18   Vinny Warren, personal communication, September 4, 2009.

19   http://thunderbaymedia.net/blog/website-copywriting-your-articles-do-not-apply (accessed August 26, 2010).

20   Drayton Bird, *Commonsense Direct & Digital Marketing*, 5th ed. (Kogan Page, 2007), 154.

21   http://blog.hubspot.com/blog/tabid/6307/bid/6482/23-Awesome-SEO-Blogs-Everyone-Should-Read.aspx (accessed January 5, 2011).

22   http://www.fastcompany.com/100/2010/29/alessandra-lariu (accessed January 19, 2011).

23   Alessandra Lariu, personal communication, October 16, 2010.

24   Alessandra Lariu, personal communication, October 16, 2010.

25   http://www.briansolis.com/2010/10/introducing-the-conversation-prism-version-3-0 (accessed June 12, 2011).

26   Ashley Parker, "Twitter's Secret Handshake," *New York Times*, June 12, 2011.

27   http://www.cutter.com/content-and-analysis/resource-centers/business-technology-trends/sample-our-research/bttu0902.html (accessed June 11, 2011).

28   http://www.cutter.com/content-and-analysis/resource-centers/business-technology-trends/sample-our-research/bttu0902.html (accessed June 11, 2011).

29   http://60secondmarketer.com/blog/2010/04/09/top-52-social-media-platforms (accessed June 7, 2011).

30   Deltina Hay, *A Survival Guide to Social Media and Web 2.0 Optimization: Strategies, Tactics, and Tools for Succeeding in the Social Web* (Austin, TX: Dalton Publishing, 2009), 177–179.

31   Hay, *Survival Guide*, 288.

12

THE BUZZ WORD

Interactive engagement, social media, viral marketing

 Technology is a tool, not a weapon.

PETER SENA II, FOUNDER AND CHIEF TECHNOLOGY OFFICER, DIGITAL SURGEONS[1]

Understanding interactivity

Asking: what's the point of interaction?

Considering sendable campaigns

Asking consumers to share their stories

Thinking about interactivity

Creating other ways to use interactivity

Discovering how to create buzz

Creating buzz with viral marketing / word of mouth

Asking why you responded

Understanding when buzz goes wrong

Looking at social networking: Facebook, Twitter, and more

Communicating online is similar to other media

Watching new media

Using new media for marketing messages

Using social media to create viral reactions

Designing games to recruit staff

Final interactive media checklist

Creative interactive exercises

Before you begin reading this chapter, ask yourself how often you participate in interactive campaigns. How frequently do you post on your social networking sites? How often do you tweet? The best way to build your toolkit is to immerse yourself in all forms of social, digital, and interactive media. The sooner you join the two-way conversation with brands, the sooner you'll be able to create them yourself.

For example, if you haven't "Elfed Yourself" (at http://www.elfyourself.com), you haven't seen how much fun consumer-created "sendables" are. These are messages that you create and send to your friends, family members, and associates.

This chapter will help you become adept at developing interactive, social networking-based, and viral campaigns. Here you'll see how consumer sharing builds a brand's impact, as in the Golden Grahams Cereal interactive campaign: "Golden Grahams Grant." You'll see how ASICS spoke directly to its audience through the ingenious "New York City Marathon" interactive campaign. You'll find out how Domino's not only revamped its entire pizza formula, but also created a fun, interactive campaign, "Pizza Holdouts," to spread the message. You'll discover why the innovative Burger King campaigns "Whooper Freakout" and "Whopper Virgins" went viral.

You'll realize how each social media platform (online communication sites) can be used to support the other. For example, when you use services like Ping.fm and HootSuite you're able to post in one place and have it appear on all your networking sites. Most importantly, you should commit to being a permanent student. Learn from what's already out there and consider how you could create a new way of using the Internet.

Understanding interactivity

As you have seen with blogs, online articles, and websites many messages today request the participation of the viewer. You can never underestimate the importance of engaging the consumer to strengthen the emotional bond to the brand. Information and entertainment are key in this new medium. The direction you choose depends, again, on your brand and audience. You could create a game with clues, they would find in a book and reward the winner with a free, autographed copy. You could create online banner ads that ask yoga aficionados to fill in a blank, identify advanced poses, and win a free, instructional video. Or you could ask the audience to participate with the brand by creating online content in an ongoing brand-related story and reward all participants with a fun experience, or one winner with a grand prize for the best story idea.

Pay attention to all interactive campaigns whether they're online or offline. Look for those that excel in establishing a unique, two-way communication. In client and internal meetings, you cannot stress enough the significance of this exciting consumer-engaging opportunity. If done well, it can strengthen the consumer's brand loyalty and emotional connection.

Soon, we'll discuss some successful, interactive campaigns. First let's look at the thinking behind interactivity.

Asking: what's the point of interaction?

Before you create any interactive promotion, you must completely understand the ultimate objective. What do you want from the audience? Why are you engaging their participation? Is it for any of these reasons?

- Get an opinion.
- Challenge the reader.
- Share information.
- Entertain the audience.
- Pose a problem.
- Share a solution.
- Create a contest.
- Support a charity.

You get the point. Think of interactivity as the old "call to action." Let the audience understand what you want them to do and show them why they should want to get involved. Below are a few fun sites that became viral (spread across the Web) because everyone enjoyed playing and sharing.

Considering sendable campaigns

Sendables are messages, videos, and fill-in-the-blank animations or characters that you can create and share with friends. If you haven't "Elfed Yourself" yet (www.elfyourself.com), you're one of the few people who hasn't joined in the OfficeMax fun. So many millions of people have that the campaign went viral. We'll talk more about viral videos later in the chapter.

Besides sendables, you can ask consumers to share their photos, ideas, stories, dieting progress, or life experiences. HP created a website (http://www.hp.com/united-states/consumer/digital_photography/share_photos_creative/tips/sharing_snapfish.html) where people can share their photos with each other via Snapfish (HP's online sharing service) after they establish an online account. Other companies have done the same, as we'll see.

Asking consumers to share their stories

Companies today realize they need not just to communicate with their audience, but also to interact with them in a variety of ways and at different touchpoints (places where they reach the consumer, as we mentioned earlier). Weight Watchers Online (www.weightwatchers.com) invites dieters to sign up so they can customize their own diet plans using the PointsPlus program, read about celebrity weight-loss successes like Jennifer Hudson, learn low-calorie recipes, find out how to exercise with their pets, and more. The clever slogan sums up the online campaign: "Weight Watchers Online. Finally, losing weight clicks." Notice the *play on words* slogan technique (#4) discussed in chapter 4.

Alessandra Lariu, senior vice president and digital group creative director, McCann Erickson, headed up the team that created the Golden Grahams Golden Grant Stimulus Package campaign, and won a Cannes Cyber Lions Award. Lariu explained the strategy behind the campaign:

> *Times are tough for young college grads who will be looking for jobs during a recession. So why not offer them a cathartic place where they can share their frustrations in a light-hearted way? The Golden Grahams Golden Grant was born.*[2]

The short campaign, which ran from February 3 through April 27 in 2010, asked job hunters to tweet their whacky interview predicaments for the chance to win 12 free boxes of Golden Grahams cereal as a "stimulus package" for the unemployed. You can already see the humor in the campaign. The most hilarious and ridiculous job search stories were recreated in animated cartoons and posted on the site (www.goldengrant.com). Some are just too funny to make up. One guy had to go to the bathroom so urgently that he urinated outside the building, unknowingly in full view of the interviewer. Yes, I know you're asking, "Who wouldn't go inside to relieve himself?" Well, apparently this guy figured no one was watching.

The website offered some interviewing Golden Graham tips like "Don't exaggerate your abilities" and then showed why. Here's one example. When asked if she spoke Dutch, one job candidate lied. Then, she was told the business partner, who was sitting in the interview, was Dutch. She faked her foreign-language fluency by making up Dutch-sounding words and was instantly caught in a fib.

When asked if she worked backwards, by developing the message to fit the medium, to develop the campaign, Lariu explained:

We didn't work backwards in this occasion but what was interesting was that we offered tools for people to create their own content.[3]

She said that the client clearly explained in the brief that it wanted Golden Grahams cereal to target beyond its traditionally young market and reach college graduates with an age range spanning 18 to 25. Just by asking for people to share stories about interviews that went awry, the campaign instantly raised the age of the targeted audience.

The question often asked is, "Yeah, great. But, did it work?" Here's the answer. The Twitter-driven campaign yielded more than 2.5 million video views and presented Golden Grahams Cereal Grants to 1,000 winners. The campaign was also

- picked up and commented on online by high-profile digital influencers: Rob Corddry (actor/comedian), Tony Hawk (pro skateboarder) and Tosh.O (comedian Daniel Tosh's website);

- mentioned on several blogs including, Smart Blog on Social Media: http://smartblogs.com/socialmedia/2010/02/09/golden-grahams-uses-social-media-to-get-the-job-done/.

You'll enjoy seeing these hilarious stories shown in the case study video at http://alelariuwork.tumblr.com/post/1039848983/golden-grahams-golden-grant-tweets-of-nightmare. It's obvious that this campaign idea was inspired by a desire to offer some levity to struggling, out-of-work college grads.

"

The most important thing you can get from your [website] visitors is permission to talk to them. **DRAYTON BIRD, WRITER, SPEAKER, MARKETER, AND AUTHOR**[4]

Thinking about interactivity

Whether you're asking your audience to participate in a contest, tweet about their lives, respond to an online offer, comment on blogger's post, and so on, the real question is whether there's a significant difference in writing interactive online messages, specifically between blogging or website copy. Vinny Warren, founder and creative director of The Escape Pod emphasized that the concept, and not necessarily the writing, triggers a response:

> *I think it's more of a case of, not necessarily writing, as it is thinking. If you want people to interact with something, that's tough. It's tougher to get someone to literally interact with something than it is to get someone to watch a video. If you truly want to get someone to interact with something, then that something has to be very attractive and appealing. So it's not necessarily how you write it. It's what's the idea? Is it something that's exciting or not? If it isn't you're just open to a battle.[5]*

Peter Sena II, founder & chief technology officer of Digital Surgeons, explained that you must realize that there are different kinds of site visitors or "users" and you need to create different online media vehicles to reach them: video, headlines, copy, coupons, and more. Sena explained:

> *One of the complaints that some people have with video blogs is that they want to just read the information. They want to get to it really quickly.*

One interactive campaign, "Jill's Secret Solution," focuses on product benefits and rewards consumers with information and cost-saving, digital coupons. (See the case study at http://www.digitalsurgeons.com/our-work/#/interactive.) Digital Surgeons, partnering with the agency of record for Church & Dwight, did all the digital development, interactive components, and the interactive build out (execution) of that site for Arm & Hammer, but didn't contribute to the writing or the content. Consumers looking for answers to stain removal and cleaning challenges logged on and would be able to see a spokesperson named "Jill" use Arm & Hammer baking soda to solve specific problems, like cleaning the outdoor grill, microwave, or oven. It's interactive because visitors could ask Jill a question. Then, watch the video, read the answer, and redeem the coupon. What was interesting was that Sena said among the various users, there were still some people who like to read:

> *Some just want a quick answer, which I think is a very large basis. Some want to dig an extra tier deeper and get access to more information. If you present information to a user and you give them a multitude of options as to how they can experience that data, you then let them experience it how they want to experience it, giving them a few different options.[6]*

What's important to retain is how the campaign considers the consumers' experience preferences, having prepared three choices: a visual (copy), auditory (video), and kinesthetic (coupon) delivery. These neuro-linguistic terms describe the primary ways the people absorb information, as discussed in chapter 3. If you always focus on the message's recipient, you'll drive your point home faster. Look how the short, problem-stating headlines were easy to understand and focused on the senses:

1 A Cleaner Coffee Maker
2 Clean & Green
3 Grungy Grills
4 Smelly Sneakers

(Did you identify the headline techniques used? The second one used rhyme and the other three used alliteration, as explained in chapter 4.) Sena described why this site was so user friendly.

> Where that site shined the most was it leveraged video with standard text that you could read on the page and it was connected to offers. So what they (the client) were seeing was a great deal of coupon redemption through the website as opposed to standard, in-store redemption.[7]

As we discussed in chapter 8, print coupons have morphed into digital, e-mail, mobile (like QR codes), and other redeemable formats. As with all new media, the challenge is to create new ways to communicate all types of messages in an innovative and interactive way.

Creating other ways to use interactivity

As you're working on different creative assignments think about how you could extend the message to different touchpoints (places where you reach your audience.) Consider how you might modify the message. Where could you engage the audience in an unexpected way?

Take a quick look back at the ASICS image in chapter 9 (Figure 9.17). We'll discuss the campaign in more detail in chapter 13. The creative team at Vitro wanted to connect to the New York City Marathon runners in a unique way. They developed the "Support Your Marathoner" website (www.supportyourmarathoner.com), where people could create a personal video and/or text message to motivate their loved ones during the grueling 26.2 miles. The New York Road Runners Club promoted the site, as did bloggers and other runners using social media like Facebook.

Instead of just being the standard sponsor, the week preceding the marathon, ASICS set up special stands where people could record their messages. Runners would read the message on huge LED screens set along the course. "Trigger chips" were set on RFID tags given to every runner to place on the top of their shoes. As the marathoners ran across sensors on the road, their trigger chips sent their personalized message to the screen, so they could see their unique note of encouragement as they were running. The response was amazing. People from 17 countries sent messages in all media, from printed words and still photos, to videos to 7,000 runners. Once again, a company used consumer-created content to develop relevant messages to a very special and targeted audience. With the name ASICS along the course, 45,000 runners were reminded of a brand that sold something they would need: running shoes. Watch a video of this campaign at: http://www.youtube.com/watch?v=SnrzClsOlyU&feature=player_embedded#at=45.

There are many other excellent interactive campaigns. Some help charitable causes in new ways. One such is the Unicef "Tap Project." Started in 2007 in New York City restaurants, where people who were used to receiving a free glass of tap water were asked to add one dollar to their bill as a donation to help bring drinkable water to areas of the world without clean water. This free, word-of-mouth campaign spread and soon vending machines selling "Dirty Water" allowed people to make

> **"**
> So it really does start at the beginning with defining the essence of what the project is about. **MATT ZISELMAN, CREATIVE DIRECTOR, SAPIENTNITRO**[8]

a $1.00 donation to the Unicef Tap Project. Celebrity spokespeople like Mario Lopez and Sarah Jessica Parker got on board. Corporations made donations and advertising and other agencies volunteered their time and talent. Visit www.tapproject.org for more information. And see the international agency's case study (Droga5) at www.droga5.com.

Other campaigns that created consumer interaction involved donating unused items like eyeglasses or slightly used winter coats and receiving a coupon for a future purchase. For example in 2010 in Florida, people dropped off their old eyeglasses at Hollywood Eyes and received a $25.00 coupon towards a new pair. In New York, during the 2010 "Coats for Clunkers" campaign donors of lightly worn coats at Penn Station, Amtrak, and the LIRR Concourse received a $100.00 coupon towards the purchase of a Weatherproof coat. (To read more visit www.weatherproofgarment.com or www.valleynewslive.com/Global/story. asp?S=13685658.)

In 2005, DDB London and Tribal DDB created a highly creative interactive campaign: "Monopoly Live" (Figure 12.1). You can read all the details at http://awards.digivault.co.uk/ hasbro/monopoly. The game celebrated the seventieth anniversary of Monopoly, using the first-ever updated version of London properties as they exist today. It was the first time cabs were fitted with GPS devices and functioned like Monopoly pieces traveling in real time around London.[9]

FIGURE 12.1 This "Monopoly Live" website image was created by Tribal for DDB Monopoly. Image courtesy of Tribal DDB.

With so many people in the target already familiar with and owners of Monopoly, the challenge was to get them to buy a new version of an all-time-favorite game. Consumers could register free at www.monopolylive.com and select how they should spend their £15 million Monopoly play money. Here is an overview of the campaign as a case study.

Background

This was the "first interactive, real-time, life-size Monopoly game using GPS-transmitter-fitted cabs, functioning like Monopoly pieces, throughout the streets of London."[10]

Campaign objectives

1   To spark sales of the new Monopoly game
2   To increase core value of the Monopoly game
3   To reignite people's passion for Monopoly and appeal to a new, younger generation of consumers[11]

Target audience

The traditional target for Monopoly is mums with kids aged 8 to 13 years, although due to the modern appeal of the updated game, we also targeted teens, and people in their 20s and 30s.[12]

Strategy

We decided the best way for people to rediscover Monopoly and experience the updated board was to actually play it! So, we turned London into a life-size, real-time Monopoly board by creating a true to life interactive version of Monopoly. Eighteen black cabs, fitted with GPS transmitters and liveried in Monopoly colours, acted as the real-life playing pieces.

Taking this approach allowed the communication to resonate much more strongly, as consumers could familiarise themselves with the changes to the new Monopoly board over a period of days, in their own time, rather than having these changes communicated to them in the seconds of a TV ad.[13]

Execution

The 18 Monopoly-branded taxis were fitted with a GPS transmitter using top-of-the range security technology, so that their location was known at all times.

As the taxis went about their normal day, picking up and dropping off passengers, players would pay out rent as their cabs passed properties they didn't own, and receive rent when other cabs passed their properties. The grand prize was winning your mortgage paid for a year, and there were also daily and weekly prizes to play for.

There was also an SMS element to the game allowing people to SMS for bonus cash, which deepened their involvement with the game.[14]

Media

The media involved ranged from online marketing to TV, radio, and public relations.

Results

- *Monopoly was the **best selling** board game of 2005*
- *At campaign launch, **sales of Monopoly were up 200%** on the same period of the previous year*
- *Demand for the game was so great that Hasbro **sold out** of the limited edition game two weeks before Christmas!*
- *Monopoly Live bolstered Hasbro's CRM database by over **100,000** names*
- *Over **1 million people** visited the site; **200,000 people** played the game and on average, played three times over the 4 weeks the campaign was live*
- ***45,000*** *text messages were sent*
- *Shortlisted for **Cannes Titanium Lion**, winner of **Gold Media Lion**, and winner of **2 IPA Effectiveness Awards**[15] (IPA, Institute of Practitioners in Advertising, is the UK's top association for advertising, media and marketing communications agencies.)*

This campaign, although not a copy-centric one, is a perfect example of how to reenergize buying interest in a beloved brand that most already owned. By adding consumer engagement via digital interactivity the updated Monopoly game generated renewed appeal.

Although there are many interactive campaigns today, a few worth your time are the following:

1   Special K Challenge www.specialk.com/challenge. Here consumers can find diet plans for specific tastes: chocolate-lovers, on-the-go, classic plan, food variety so they can fit into "skinny jeans."

2   www.agencypizzamaker.com. This is how a design firm created an interactive, digital self-promotion: "Gus & Joe's Agency Pizza Maker." Guests can make their own pizza with a list of toppings and post their own designs like a happy face on social networks like Facebook and Twitter. There's even a pizza that's spinning like an old LP record, playing authentic, Italian songs sounding like an old, scratchy recording. The arm that holds the play needle retracts when you hit the pause button and resumes the play position when you hit the play button.

3   The "Girl Effect" campaign (www.girleffect.org). This was created by Nike to save 600 million young girls from ending up impoverished, uneducated, forced into an arranged marriage, pregnant, and/or infected with a sexually transmitted disease (STD). The online video invites people to participate by donating money, so a young girl can get a uniform, go to school, give her family a cow, so they can sell the milk and change her future. Visitors can also share the video via social networks by retweeting it on Twitter, e-mailing it, posting it on Facebook, or following the Girl Effect Networks (on Facebook and Twitter).

4   The "Help Remedies" campaign. This has an interactive page (http://www.helpineedhelp.com/bored.html) where consumers can pick the "help" link they want (like "Help! [a] I'm bored, [b] I'm stuck in a snowstorm, [c] I have writer's block," etc.). Then, they can read about a clever solution and watch an entertaining cartoon demonstrating the solution. So, for example if you choose "Help, I feel like I'm being followed," visitors are suggested to paint the pattern of a brick wall on their clothes. Then, stand in front of a brick wall to become invisible and therefore,

undetectable, so they can't be followed. Another page explains that Help Remedies can help put small illnesses into perspective with a few kind words and some information. If you click on the "Sniffles" button, you are prompted to answer what you're suffering from. Some of the choices are health-related, like a cough, and others are very funny, like devouring an excess of bagels.

5   Coca-Cola interactive vending machine uVend ("Freestyle"), created by SapientNitro, won 2009 Gold Cannes Lions Awards for design/point of sale and viral marketing, as well as other Cannes Lions for ambient marketing (http://video.cnbc.com/gallery/?video=1325599149). The machine was equipped with touch-screen and Bluetooth and had an image of a Coke bottle that spun 360 degrees. It allowed users to download music, wallpaper, and ringtones for their cellphones. After you put your money in, a message would pop up and say, "Vending." Once you take your bottle, another message would come up on the screen that read, "Give it back." (See the machine in use at http://www.trendhunter.com/youtube/r9EA_dQvtQM or read more about it at www.thecocacolacompany.com/presscenter/nr_20090629_gold_lion.html.)[16]

You may want to check out the 2009 Freestyle Coke machine that allowed consumers to create their own flavors from 106 carbonated and noncarbonated drinks, dispensed in cups, not bottles. The machine would electronically send back daily reports of customer choices to Atlanta headquarters, so product designers could anticipate and then create the next great flavor.

The point is that not only are advertising campaigns creating interactive vehicles, like Monopoly Live, exciting product dispensers are also being developed to engage the consumer. Each time you come across an interactive vehicle, like the Unicef Tap Project donation vending machine, pay attention. Make a mental note. Think about what other products or companies would be able to participate in interactive campaigns. Some interactive campaigns are so much fun, they become viral and create buzz.

Discovering how to create buzz

If you're trying to understand exactly what goes viral, pay attention to what you retweet, post on your blog, link to on one of your social networking sites, locate and highlight on foursquare, became a Facebook fan, or share with friends. Most likely, you loved it and couldn't wait for someone else to see it, hear it, experience it, or chat about it. Become a better observer the next time you become an interactive participant. Be sure you start noticing examples of campaigns that created buzz. Study these and other effective viral campaigns, some of which we'll discuss below:

- Crispin Porter + Bogusky's classic sites for these and other clients:
  - Burger King:
    - www.subservientchicken.com;
    - www.whopperfreakout.com;
    - www.whoppervirgins.com.
  - Domino's Pizza:
    - www.pizzaholdouts.com.

- Nike and its strong relationship with Sneakerheads, the avid Nike sneaker collectors, (www.sneakerhead.com) and its famous Nike stores.
- Apple and its new product introductions from iMacs and iPods to iPhones and iPads through its online and retail (bricks-and-mortar) Apple stores.

Let's first take a look at a few of the viral Whopper campaigns. Rob Reilly, partner/co-executive/creative at Crispin Porter + Bogusky, offered insights into the viral phenomenon for Burger King: "Whopper Freakout." The agency wanted to say the Whopper was number one without sounding boastful. Reilly stated no one likes a "chest pounder." So, how do you show that people really preferred the Whopper and make it sound authentic?

> So that's where the essence of Whopper Freakout was born: Well, what if you had consumers saying it? But the problem with that is: Well sure, the consumers got paid. You know, you asked them a question. We started peeling away the layers of why something was going to be perceived as right or wrong, or what was going to work. So, then it was: What if we did the opposite? What if we took the thing they loved and took it away? Would people actually care?[17]

That strategy, as we discussed in chapter 2, is the *deprivation strategy*: having people miss something they once had, as in the first "Got Milk" commercials. The idea behind "Whopper Freakout" (www.whopperfreakout.com) was to record people's real reactions when they were told that the Whopper was no longer on the menu. The reactions were hilarious. Being created for an online viewer, the video didn't have the time restraints as for standard TV spots. Here the story could be told in 7.5 minutes, not in under 30 seconds.

The video, which got two million hits, quickly created consumer interest. People soon created their own versions and posted them on YouTube. Another Burger King viral campaign you should look at is www.whoppervirgins.com. An entire team of videographers and cooks searched the world to find people who had never had a hamburger. They wanted to create a "real taste test" and have these fast-food virgins compare the Burger King Whopper to a McDonald's burger. When you watch the video, you see all the preparation it took. Looking at people in native costumes attempt to eat a Whopper for the first time is very funny. Most had to be coached into using two hands and taking a big bite. Once again, consumers created their own YouTube parodies, which added viral fuel to the fire.

For the Domino's "Pizza Holdouts" campaign, the pizza chain admitted on camera that it had received negative feedback about its product line. It decided to change the entire formula, ingredient by ingredient. To convince consumers that it had really created a new recipe and to attract people who had never tried the new "inspired" Domino's Pizza, it created a no-holds-barred multimedia campaign that went viral. It selected three "holdouts" and persuaded these consumers to call Domino's by putting their names on giant billboards, trucks and signage with a call to action. Cameras were standing by to capture their surprise when they saw messages specifically and singularly targeting them. Of course each of them ordered a pizza and naturally cameras caught their positive reactions. Friends were invited to vote for their favorite holdouts on Facebook. See the entire video at: http://www.pizzaholdouts.com/index.php/video.

Each of the above-mentioned campaigns deserves your attention. Write yourself a note so you remember to visit these sites and see why they were imaginative and effective.

Nike knew it had a loyal, almost fanatical, fan base called Sneakerheads. Many of these devout loyalists would sit on the sidewalk for days on end waiting for the release of a new Nike sneaker model, especially when the new arrivals were limited editions. Some had as many as

300 pairs and were still collecting them. To recognize them, Nike created an entire site in their honor (www.sneakerhead.com) and continued to produce sneakers with the cool factor. This only strengthened the already deep emotional bond consumers had with the brand.

Apple also created one cool product after another and spoke directly to its audience through its humorous "Mac versus PC" (also called the "Get a Mac") campaign showing the benefits of Mac (strategy #1) with *product demonstration* (strategy #7), *product comparison* (#8), *humor* (#25) and *continuing characters* (#41) strategies. (Be sure to review the list of strategies in chapter 2 so you can identify the techniques being used.) See the complete campaign at http://adweek.blogs.com/adfreak/get-a-mac-the-complete-campaign.html. Pay attention to the copy when you listen to the spots. Notice the laid back, casual *tone of voice* of Mac and the stiff delivery of the PC. Observe how Mac introduced each new product with spots that showed consumers how easy it would be to use the new technology, implying a short learning curve because of Mac's intuitive design.

Realize that the campaigns' concepts in all of these examples are what created the response. Big ideas that are entertaining create reactions, not just great copy. Wonderful writing won't rescue a poor idea. Sometimes straightforward copy with consumer benefits and clear product demonstrations, as in the Apple new product introductions, are all that's needed for a response. Dissect every campaign you see. As you read industry news look for campaigns that spark ideas.

Creating buzz with viral marketing / word of mouth

Make it a point to analyze campaigns, videos, images, and so on that you receive and pass along. Think about what captured your attention. Consider how you would create messages that are engaging and interactive. In looking at how to create campaigns that go viral, consider the following list:

1 Develop an irresistible idea.
   - Can you make it interactive?
   - Does it reflect your audience's perspective?
   - Can you use humor?
   - Would being irreverent fit the brand?

2 Highlight the brand's benefit.
   - How does it help the audience?
   - What problem does it solve?
   - How user friendly is it?
   - Can you get consumers to create brand-related content (develop videos, comment on blogs, tweet, or shoot commercials about the brand)?

3 Understand why you're creating this message. Ask:
   - Can you make it relevant to the audience?
   - Does it reflect the brand's image?
   - Does it reach a new audience?
   - Does it showcase something unique or new?

As you become more familiar with viral campaigns, be sure to go The Viral Factory website (www.theviralfactory.com). This digital shop generated more than a billion views for its clients. While on the site, read the case studies and see what ideas they created that went viral. For example, when US brand Trojan wanted to break into the UK market, it created "The Trojan Games" (also called "SFW XXX," i.e. "safe for work") viral campaign using adult-content humorous viral videos: "The vault," "Weightlifting," and "Judo." The campaign went viral and resulted in 14 million views. It can be seen at www.trojangames.co.uk.

Another campaign, unique in its visual creativity, is also from The Viral Factory: "LED Sheep," aptly nicknamed "Extreme Shepherding." Created for Samsung, it generated 13 million views. Although, this is not an example of viral writing, the creativity behind the campaign drove users to immediately share it with everyone they could. The object was to show the brilliance of Samsung's LED TVs. This viral video can also be found at the agency website, www.theviralfactory.com, under "Case Studies." It's nothing short of absolutely amazing. Just to come up with the idea of creating images with sheep in LED-adorned jackets driven by herding dogs directed by expert Welsh shepherds is mindboggling. The sheep are remarkably herded by "extreme sheepherding" into amazing, moving images, most with lights on the back of the sheep to create

- a video game;
- a mosaic-light display of the Mona Lisa;
- a series of fireworks displaying as sheep bursting out in different directions.

You'll instantly see why the campaign went viral. The images aired on BBC, ABC's *Good Morning America*, Digg.com (front page), Sky News, ITV News, and other media outlets. Best of all, each video closes with a call-to-action to visit Samsung's LED TV: www.samsung.com/ledtv. So, the creators drove traffic to the client.

Check out unexpected viral videos from all over the world. Once you've passed an amazing video to a friend, who's passed it to a friend, you can easily see how a video, image, blog, tweet, or on-camera comment, and so on, can circle the world in less than 24 hours. Because of this instant global effect one campaign, like the Unicef Tap Project, can influence millions and even change lives.

Everyone recognizes the undeniable power of the Web. It has single-handedly launched musical careers of unknown artists via YouTube video postings, like the instant fame of two singers: 10-year-old phenom, Jackie Evancho, the 2010 *America's Got Talent* runner-up, and 48-year-old Susan Boyle, the 2009 *Britain's Got Talent* runner-up. These online videos were shared around the world, being "viral videos."

A 10-member a cappella musical group, Straight No Chaser, an Indiana University 10-member, received a five-album record deal from Atlantic Records after a video, *Twelve Days of Christmas*, which it posted on YouTube in 1998, went viral a dozen years later, in 2007, generating 7,000,000 views.

Ingrid Michaelson posted a song, "The Way I Am," on Myspace and got 10,000,000 views

> So I think the interactive world inherently has very different requirements in terms of messaging. It's a totally different animal than print. But at the same time, to me – and this is how I have always felt – a story is a story. **MATT ZISELMAN, CREATIVE DIRECTOR, SAPIENTNITRO**[18]

just on Myspace alone. As a result, LeAnn Rimes and Kylie Minoque both tweeted about her talent. Taylor Swift called Michaelson one of her favorites. This created instant visibility for the undiscovered talent. She ultimately became a best-selling independent artist.

After viewing some of the above-mentioned talents, you should think about creating messages that can go viral. To have a better idea of the kinds of campaigns that generate buzz, look at a few of these examples below. Go to YouTube and type in the words and/or copy the links:

1   Evian "Roller Babies" – http://www.youtube.com/watch?v=XQcVllWpwGs

2   "Japanese/Thai" tea commercial with caterpillars – http://www.youtube.com/watch?v=ysAKZfhQWDk&feature=related

3   Wario Land "Wii LOL" – http://www.youtube.com/watch?v=dxQ93-blOnQ

4   Wario Land "Shake It" – http://www.youtube.com/watch?v=yLJzo72vnzI (not clear, but you can still see the amazing footage and brilliant visual concept)

5   "Beautiful" Coca-Cola commercial – http://www.youtube.com/watch?v=zum9_pXpftc

6   Coca-Cola "It's Mine" – http://www.youtube.com/watch?v=xiMf5cCDy1I&feature=related

7   Tostitos viral campaign – "And Then There Was Salsa" http://www.youtube.com/watch?v=ucz039aF5l4

8   YouTube breakdown – http://www.youtube.com/experiencere

Besides online video clips, budding musicians' YouTube videos, great commercials, and other types of messages have also gone viral. The use of "flashmob" (also spelled as "flash mob") videos has become popular. Flashmob is a word that became popular in 2003. When a group of people spontaneously breaks into a pre-choreographed dance in a public place, it's called a flashmob. You should be familiar with the following flashmob videos that went viral. Try to understand and pick out which ones were product-related. The reason it's difficult is that some messages today are disguised as noncommercials or consumer-generated content. Notice in the T-Mobile flash mob, the brand name does not appear. Then, notice the people in the video shooting the images on their cellphones and sharing them with friends. That is a very subtle way to show the product. Also, when you search for the video, the title includes the brand name T-Mobile "Dance."

1   T-Mobile – "Dance" http://www.youtube.com/watch?v=VQ3d3KigPQM (January 16, 2009)

2   Oprah Winfrey's birthday surprise – Black Eyed Peas Flash Mob Chicago http://www.youtube.com/watch?v=zvt3chGuU8I&feature=related (September 10, 2009)

3   Sound of Music Central Station Antwerp – http://www.youtube.com/watch?v=7EYAUazLI9k&feature=related (March 23, 2009)

4   Glee II Flash Mob in Rome – http://www.youtube.com/watch?v=NhbK2bMTRbI&feature=related (December 29, 2009)

5   "Bollywood Hero" Flash Mob in Times Square, New York – http://www.youtube.com/watch?v=NXclwb_6LkE (August 4, 2009)

6   Paris – world's biggest "Freeze" Flash Mob – http://www.youtube.com/watch?v=8GfrfDmXDb0&feature=related (March 8, 2008)

There are also improvisation groups that create live "events" like the two Improv Everywhere videos below:

1   "Human Mirror" (15 pairs of twins on subway 6 Train sit or stand across from each and "mirror" each other's movements and postures) – http://www.youtube.com/watch?v=9MBBr-a2KnM&feature=related

2   "Frozen Grand Central Station" (207 people freeze in the station at Bryant Park at the same time for 5 minutes, then unfreeze and leave) – http://www.youtube.com/watch?v=jwMj3PJDxuo

Notice how people react in these videos. Some are filming, some are talking on the phone, and some are asking strangers about what's happening. Consider what kinds of brands could leverage this kind of footage and integrate it into a campaign. Have you noticed that smartphone commercials like Dell and AT&T have used Flashmob parodies in their spots?

Here are a few more YouTube video viral favorites. Type in the title and enjoy:

●   "Panda sneeze" (baby panda startles mom with loud sneeze)

●   "Skateboarding English Bulldog"

●   "Scuba cat" (real cat wearing custom-made scuba diving equipment and swimming under water)

●   HBO "Voyeur" (enables users to look into windows of skyscraper buildings and see everyday people in their daily routines)

●   "Charlie Bit My Finger" (baby bites brother's finger)

●   "Christian the Lion" (baby lion cub rescued from zoo in London is released into the wild and reunited with human "foster parents")

●   Oscar the "Grim Reaper" (cat accurately predicts death and has been written up in the *New England Journal of Medicine*)

●   "Nora the piano-playing cat" (cat gently caresses the piano keys with paws)

●   "Cat in a box" (cat dives into open box and slides across the floor)

Notice how Fresh Step, the product used in litter boxes, integrated the "Cat in a box" viral video clip (http://www.youtube.com/freshstep) into a commercial. Whenever you see an engaging video, you should ask, Could I use this to promote a product? It doesn't matter whether only one in a hundred might work. You're thinking in a creative way.

Asking why you responded

If you made your own mixed tape music or shared your story on www.fredperry.com, created an avatar on www.secondlife.com, found a colorful background for your Myspace page at www.whateverlife.com (created by teen artist sensation, Ashley Quails), played the game to help the Adachi family rescue the last glass of milk on www.gettheglass.com, or watched a cow fly into space at www.cowabduction.com because it was abducted by aliens who wanted milk, you discovered that the temptation to participate was too great to resist.

To make these messages irresistible, some of them are presented in the guise of "nonmessages." Advertisers are trying to find ways to speak to consumers without sounding like the used car salespeople of years gone by. The two interactive milk websites, created by TBWA\Chiat\Day for the California Milk Processor Board, are campaigns that engaged the audience without a traditional sales pitch.

Today many messages actually avoid sounding like advertising. The "brand" could offer blog posts, tweet, or engage in blog discussions. It could have its own online community. And it could speak to the audience in the *vernacular*. Sometimes, if consumers aren't happy with the brand, they answer back, not necessarily as a quiet complaint.

Understanding when buzz goes wrong

Consumers use the Internet to vent or create parodies. They may want to share a frustrating experience, point out brand flaws or get satisfaction instead of being dismissed. Brands must be aware of the possible repercussions of their actions. Disgruntled customers today don't just tell their friends. They tell the world. Although the following story was mentioned in chapter 1, it's worth repeating because of its relevance here. An original song about a Taylor guitar damaged by United Airlines handlers became a YouTube video hit when it was performed by the injured party: Canadian Dave Carroll and other members of the Sons of Maxwell band. The negative press damaged the airline's reputation. (See the "United Breaks Guitars" story and video at http://www.dailymail.co.uk/news/worldnews/ article-1201671/Singer-Dave-Carroll-pens-YouTube-hit-United-Airlines-breaks-guitar-shares-plunge-10.html.)

Bob Garfield, columnist for *Advertising Age* was so unhappy with Comcast that he created the website www.comcastmustdie.com, where other frustrated customers could log on, share their nightmare experiences, and vent their dissatisfaction. At www.angieslist.com, consumers can brag or criticize service they've received from any company, resulting in a rating system.

You've probably already seen consumer-created parodies of commercials and political issues on YouTube, www.jibjab.com, and www.funnyordie.com. The point is if you have an online presence, be prepared for an online response. It could range from admiration to possible assault. This is why most large firms have specialists who track consumer comments on blogs, tweets, Facebook, and other social networks.

Miami Ad School graduates created the Dockers 2010 Super Bowl spot "We Wear No Pants." President, Pippa Seichrist, shared this information from the school's blog site (http://blog.miamiadschool.com/) posted on February 17, 2010:

> SF alums James Davis and Nicolas Howell's Dockers "We Wear No Pants" spot won one post-Big Game competition, perhaps the one that matters most in these interconnected, digital times. The day after the Super Bowl the top two most searched keywords in Google.com were "Dockers Free Pants" and "dockers.com/freepants" (Google's hot searches for Feb. 7 [2010], at: http://blog.miamiadschool.com/posts/ dockers-free-pants-top-searches-on-google-the-day-after-the-super-bowl)[19]

The impact didn't stop there. The blog post continued, explaining how the spot, created interactivity by inviting users to "tag" the commercial, register to win a pair of pants and download music. Here are the blog posted details:

> The spot also featured an innovative link-up with Shazam, the interactive music discovery service. Viewers were invited to "tag" the TV spot with their smartphones. Once tagged,

the Shazam application gave users a shortcut to get in on the free pants giveaway, and invited them to download the original "I Wear No Pants" track from the Poxy Boggards [a Renaissance-sounding musical singing group].[20]

It's not just about creating broadcast commercials, print and online ads, or out-of-home messages. It's about connecting with your audience at multiple *touchpoints* and engaging them with interactivity that's rewarding.

Looking at social networking: Facebook, Twitter, and more

Interactivity is not going away. Neither is social networking and constant connectivity. This means people are creating new online communities every day and are staying connected with contacts and online content via more mobile devices like smartphones, in-vehicle mobile communication gadgets, and blended-technology apparatuses like iPads, and so on.

All the information you could want is delivered to consumers wherever they are. With more than a quarter of a million smartphone apps, there's one for just about everything. New technology and delivery systems bring an endless flow of data to anyone searching. Smart marketers are taking advantage of every new medium and top social networks from Facebook and Twitter to other popular sites like YouTube. Some companies reward foursquare enthusiasts with points each time they check in (tell others where they are) from participating venues. (Foursquare is a friend and city-site mobile locator.) Other companies post photos on www.flickr.com and agency talent post creative work, complete with links, music, text, videos and more on www.tumblr.com.

Normally cautious financial firms concerned about complying with regulatory guidelines have used social networks. For example, toward the end of 2009, Vanguard created a financial-question scavenger hunt on Facebook. Each question directed participants to its website, where the answers were revealed under gold coins spread out all over www.vanguard.com. Fidelity Investments created a consumer-created content contest on YouTube, offering $5,000 for the winning video, which it planned to use as one of its ads.[21]

For a quick idea of what can be accomplished just with Twitter, think about not just sending the message, but having the message read by your targeted audience. The first thing you want to do is let your followers know what you're tweeting about. This is very simple to do. Create a hashtag. How? Just go to http://hashtags.org. There, you'll find a list of topics. Select one, and insert a pound sign (#) before the name, like this: #advertising. Then just add that to your message. This will alert others looking to read about advertising how to find you. Remember the hashtags are included in your word count.

You should also send followers to sites of interest. Because of Twitter's short 140-word count, you want to shorten all URLs (website addresses.) There are several sites that allow you to do this, like http://bit.ly/, http://trim.li/, or www.tinyurl.com, among others. At the last site, all you have to do is just type in the long

> " What can this campaign do to get attention? Rather than what kind of ad can I do for Dominos? **CRAIG MILLER, CREATIVE DIRECTOR, CRISPIN, PORTER + BOGUSKY**[22]

URL and hit the "Make tiny URL!" button. Copy that to your tweet, and you're all set. By sharing valuable, inspiring, or creative information, you're helping your followers deepen their understanding of your message while establishing credibility. Be generous with your knowledge. It pays.

Another important suggestion to leverage your online communication and expand your digital footprint is to incorporate Ping.fm at http://ping.fm. This service allows you to update all your social network communications at the same time. So one of your posts will be broadcasted to all of your sites, like Facebook, Twitter, LinkedIn, MySpace, FriendFeed, Tumblr, Mashable, and other familiar social networks.

Next you can connect your ping account to "hootsuite.com." at http://hootsuite.com. This will give you insight into the effectiveness of your tweet links. Because with HootSuite, self-nicknamed the "Social Media Dashboard," you can see how many people clicked on the links you posted. How? Click on the "Shrink It" button and the statistics appear. You can also write a series of tweets and send them later by selecting the "Send Later" button. Because HootSuite is connected to Ping.fm, you only need to send your messages through one site and it's broadcasted to all the social networks you preselected.

Another way to write tweets and post them later is through http://tweetlater.com. This site charges to connect you to Ping.fm, but it offers a service Ping.fm doesn't. It sends an automatic welcome message to each of your new followers. The reason this is important is that it gives small business owners and marketers a chance to see who's following them and to welcome them aboard. In short, it personalizes Twitter. It quickly allows you to follow your followers and to disconnect from those that have chosen to "unfollow" you.

Twollo, at http://twollo.com, enables you to discover people on Twitter who share a common interest with you or your client. This service instantly identifies your target audience. You just need to log on to your Twitter account and list your interests. To hone in on local tweets, you can use TwitterLocal at http://twitterlocal.net. You just type in the city and the mile radius around that location (like 5 miles, 10 miles, etc.) and you may find there's a potential client right near by.

There's also TweetDeck at http://tweetdeck.com. It's free as a download from Adobe. It gives you the ability to organize your followers, so you don't miss key people tweeting. It helps you connect to them very quickly. In addition, it highlights in red tweets that are too lengthy, so you can immediately edit them. If you click "TweetShrinkThisUpdate," it will edit the tweet down by using text message shortcut language, by changing "you" to "U" or "want" to "wnt." You can also send pictures, create groups, or create a 12-second video from your web cam and post it via the "12second" button, automatically (1) retweet (by hitting "Share"), (2) create a direct message, or (3) reply to incoming messages, and more.[23]

Organizations that use Twitter also have "Tweet Ups" where their followers meet face to face at an organized event. People running late to a conference can follow what's happening by reading audience tweets. The same goes for people trying to follow a news story or a particular agency's latest creations. Twitter has fast become the go-to source for staying abreast in a quickly changing digital landscape.

Smart marketers are following those who are tweeting about them for many reasons, including, two key ones:

1   To know what fans rave about.

2   To know what consumers complain about.

The more you know about what consumers are saying about you, your firm, or your clients, the better prepared you are to respond or react. Most important is to tap into those groups with which you have a natural bond: those interested in your interests.

With so many interest groups online, writers should have an understanding of different top social marketing sites, like those that offer image sharing, bookmarking, gaming, general searches, info exchange, niche markets (social media), news, and special interests (books, entertainment, magazines, movies, music).

Communicating online is similar to other media

The main difference between online communication and interactive messages is media leveraging based on consumer-engaging mechanisms. Just as every medium requires strategic thinking, online dialogues force writers to consider how consumers could respond. Could they poke fun at or continue the message through video parodies? Show their loyalty through tweets or blogs? Demonstrate their support as Facebook fans? Be sure you consider the following:

1 Know the creative goal.

   a Decide the ultimate take-away message.

   b Know the expected audience reaction or response.

   c State what you want the audience to do.

2 Be sure your messages stayed on course; being creative isn't enough.

   a Check that they are relevant and effective.

   b Verify that they are on-strategy for the advertiser.

   c Leverage them in each medium for maximum effect.

3 Create interactivity in each medium.

4 Target your audience. Take a closer look at how they engage in social media.

   a Find your niche. Search for that specific online community.

   b Look for the influencers. For example, those with many Twitter followers.

   c Think about how each medium can engage the audience differently.

   d Recognize their loyalty with unexpected and cool rewards in different media. Remember, the cooler the better.

It's always useful to discover where people are responding to brand messages. More people follow brands on Facebook than on Twitter. However, the Twitter followers are 18% more likely to buy that brand and its related products than its Facebook followers.[24]

Notice how even theatrical productions are using social media. For instance, the Broadway show "Allegiance" generated 46,000 Facebook fans in 2011. These loyal "Allegianites" are waiting patiently for the show to be staged in another year. Word-of-mouth can boost, or bury, a show. According to the show's producer, Lorenzo Thione, there's no greater way to create buzz then through social media.[25]

Peter Sena II, founder and chief technology officer of Digital Surgeons, explained how his agency created www.addicted2coffee.com, a website to celebrate coffee lovers everywhere. The online video posted there was created just for fun. That playful little "exercise" attracted 10,000

ADVICE FROM THE PROS 12.1 Three digital writing tips from Peter Sena II

1 Online writing is a digital storybook. Where brands should focus on telling stories and creating experiences that fit their audiences.

2 Writing successful copy online is all about filtering out the noise and tuning into the channel.

3 Digital content has to focus on developing a meaningful connection with the consumer. Without engagement you could just as easily use *lorum ipsum* ("Greek" or fake language) as your content.[26]

views in the first week. Although the site shows cups of coffee with the Starbucks logo, this was not created for that company. However, Starbucks found out about it. As Sena explained:

The person in charge of their social media actually tweeted it. They were aware of it.[27]

The video even included a musical track from a popular artist. Although the website was never part of an official Starbucks campaign, the Seattle-based company still benefited from social media exposure. Plus, coffee addicts everywhere could enjoy a site created just for them.

Watching new media

Regardless of which medium you're writing for, you need to be intimately familiar with it. If you haven't been on any social networking site, especially Facebook, you don't understand its full impact. Now, what started out in second place to Myspace, Facebook has dominated the market and become a chosen advertising outlet. Between its launch in 2004 and the beginning of 2011, Facebook went from a college student-based site to a global networking megastar with more than 600 million members worldwide.

People connect with each other and share their favorite links for a variety of reasons. It's not always just for entertainment. Some social media sites are designed for business networking. For example, professionals use LinkedIn (www.linkedin.com) to reconnect with colleagues, gain and post job recommendations, and network in their respective industries.

Facebook, in 2010, has finally become an advertising budget contender in part because of its new automated buying platform to streamline online ad placement. It has gone from just a social networking site to a business-building site with its Facebook Connect (to share information on third-party websites and other applications), the ever-present "like" button, (to voice your vote of approval) and its popularity-boosting "Fan" pages (to generate loyal followers).

According to 2011 digital marketing predictions from the January 10 *Ad Age*, three digital powerhouse areas will continue to grow: (1) social media, (2) gaming, and (3) mobile marketing. In addition to the universal appeal of Twitter, Facebook, YouTube, and now the above-mentioned foursquare, Quora, an open-source Q&A – similar in content to www. ask.com and in compilation to Wikipedia – is expected to gain popularity.

This means that writers need to be comfortable writing for all platforms and audiences. Gamers used to be primarily young males, but now they're appealing to a more mainstream market who are playing on computers, on mobile phones, on home consoles and more. Many iPhone apps like Angry Birds have fueled the widespread use of games and increased the gaming market. Also, for the first time, more Americans with cellphones will be carrying Internet-connected smartphones than ones not enabled for the Web.

What these means to advertisers is that they – like Clorox, Axe Body Spray, and Dove – can sponsor items inside the games and reach their target audiences while engaged in "play mode."[28]

New writers may be asked to help promote or develop games, apps, and other upcoming technology. They must be staying current with new devices and media. How can you persuade anyone to buy anything you yourself don't understand? If you're afraid of technology, immerse yourself. Soon, you'll become more comfortable.

Using new media for marketing messages

As you post your photos on Flickr, share your short thoughts on Twitter, highlight your location on foursquare, announce your next event on Facebook, and write a recommendation for a colleague on LinkedIn, notice any advertising you see on these sites. Consider what kind of future (or possibly, present) clients would work well in these venues. Would a humorous, animated banner ad (narrow, horizontal "strip ad") work? Could you write a short, catchy headline? Or develop a clever animated story?

Even if you're creating an everyday e-mail or a promotional or informational e-zine (online magazine) message, think about breaking up the copy with bold subheads that move the reader along. Charlie Hopper, creative director and copywriter at Young & Laramore explained, "You can't think of the writing without thinking of how and where and when people will encounter it. The Web has made it very relevant, but it's all in context."[29] He continued:

> You have to think about what order people are reading it, where they're entering it, where they're exiting, what little stations you give them to get in and out, and that's why the design is very relevant. Because like it or not, your writing is part of a great deluge of words and thoughts and images, not even just in an advertising context, in any context these days. Even if you send an e-mail, don't send a long e-mail. Break it up. Put a little bit up at the top and introduce it with something relevant and deliver your message and get it out.[30]

Messages read differently in different venues. What sounds natural in one medium may sound awkward in another. Consider where your audience is encountering the message. If you plan on reaching the same audience in a different medium, think about how the message "translates."

One more thing to consider is how you want to use a particular social media platform (online communication sites). You may be using them for networking, like Facebook or LinkedIn. You may be using them for self-promotion, as in YouTube, blogging, or tweeting (through Twitter). Or you may be using them for exchanging or sharing of ideas like Digg or Delicious.[32] Think about what you're trying to accomplish in your posts and

> " Tweet. Learning to be relevant and humorous and interesting (and retweetable!) in 140 characters is a great exercise. Besides, it's a fun way to meet strangers without having to make eye contact or think about how you're dressed. **CHARLIE HOPPER ,CREATIVE DIRECTOR AND COPYWRITER, YOUNG & LARAMORE**[31]

interactive exchanges and you'll be better armed to select the medium or media that will help you succeed.

Using social media to create viral reactions

In the fall of 2009, to promote its new store in Malmö, Sweden, Ikea used Facebook's popular function "the Tag" to create a viral campaign via social media. The "Ikea Facebook Tag" campaign developed a Facebook page for store manager Gordon Gustavsson, and displayed 12 rooms decorated with Ikea furnishings in his photo album. The first person to "tag" an item won it for free. People all over the world begged for new pictures to be uploaded so they could try again if they missed out the first time. People showed off what they won on their profile pages. The word spread via newsfeeds and links people sent to their friends and followers. The word about free Ikea products spread quickly. Read the entire article at http://viralingoutofcontrol.wordpress.com/page/2/.

Designing games to recruit staff

Recruiting games aren't exactly new. In the early 2000s, the US Army created a highly successful and affordable game as a recruiting tool. Today, companies are using interactive recruiting more frequently and in novel ways. For example, in the hospitality industry, Marriott International developed an online game as a recruiting tool. Based on different aspects of hotel service, the game allows prospective employees to see how specific areas work. So, they could "work" in the kitchen and find out that there aren't enough croutons for the Caesar salad, or that the budget is too tight to replace a nonworking oven. The virtual challenges allow recruits to see how they would measure up as they solve various problems. They also learn how a particular department operates to see if they're interested in pursuing a career there.

In the pharmaceutical field, the Siemens AG unit bought the game *Plantville* because it could allow players to act as managers for different companies, including a bottling plant, a vitamin manufacturer, or a train-building facility.

Other games focus on time-management assignments and would be particularly suitable as a recruiting tool for hair, nail, or tanning salons; event planning businesses; fitness or yoga centers; design studios, and other service-focused entities.[33] As you start developing interactive campaigns, don't limit yourself to what has been done. Think about how you can continue, as well as innovate new kinds of consumer engagement.

Final interactive media checklist

To become familiar with interactivity, there are several steps that will increase your digital concepting and writing skills. Review this list:

1   Immerse yourself in interactive campaigns.
    a   Learn by doing. Become a participant.
    b   Deconstruct what enticed you to participate.
    c   Analyze the relationship between the interactivity and the brand.

2   Become an investigative reporter.

   a   Speak to the innovators. Ask digital creative talent about their work.

   b   Collect resources and digital examples. Look for applicable solutions.

   c   Dig for innovative answers. Be tireless in your pursuit of digital knowledge.

Enough cannot be said about stretching your creative and strategic skills. Look beyond everyday use of each medium and think about how you could apply it in a novel way. Also consider how you could connect one medium to another, engage the audience, and create interactivity. Every campaign and each piece of copy has to solve a marketing challenge and follow a predetermined, brief-guided creative direction. Creative talent must also look at the most mundane assignments and strive to find breakthrough ideas that deliver targeted messages in a unique way. That's the beauty of technology. There are fewer executional limitations. That allows you to free your mind and think like a child. Let your work be unpredictable. Unanticipated. Unexpected. Go on. Be bold. Be outrageous. Even be irreverent. Don't say, "Oh, that can't be done." Instead say, "Here's a great idea. Let's figure out how to do."

Creative interactive exercises

Exercise 1: find three great examples of interactive campaigns not mentioned in this chapter

Choose one to work on.

Exercise 2: consider how you could create a new, interactive dialogue

How could you include more consumer engagement, like consumer-created content? Look to surprise and reward your audience to build loyalty.

- What could you do to invite them to respond?
- What offers or rewards could you create to persuade people to become a Facebook fan or share their location on foursquare for points? What interactive contests or fun activities could you invent to get people tweeting?

Exercise 3: now, identify the strategic direction you used

(Refer to the list in chapter 2.) Did you use more than one strategy? Could you find another strategy that would support the one(s) you used?

Notes

1   Peter Sena II, personal communication, February 1, 2011.

2   Alessandra Lariu, personal communication, October 16, 2010.

3   Alessandra Lariu, personal communication, October 16, 2010.

4   Drayton Bird, *Commonsense Direct & Digital Marketing*, 5th ed. (London: Kogan Page, 2007), 159.

5   Vinny Warren, personal communication, September 4, 2009.

6   Peter Sena II, personal communication, February 1, 2011.

7   Peter Sena II, personal communication, February 1, 2011.

8   Matt Ziselman, personal communication, January 30, 2009.

9   Grace Wright, personal communication, February 12, 2009.

10 Grace Wright, personal communication, February 12, 2009.

11 Grace Wright, personal communication, February 12, 2009.

12 Grace Wright, personal communication, February 12, 2009.

13 Grace Wright, personal communication, February 12, 2009.

14 Grace Wright, personal communication, February 12, 2009.

15 Grace Wright, personal communication, February 12, 2009.

16 http://www.thecocacolacompany.com/presscenter/nr_20090629_gold_lion.html (accessed January 15, 2011).

17 Rob Reilly, personal communication, December 15, 2008.

18 Matt Ziselman, personal communication, January 30, 2009.

19 http://blog.miamiadschool.com/posts/archived/02-2010 (accessed February 1, 2011).

20 http://blog.miamiadschool.com/posts/archived/02-2010 (accessed February 1, 2011).

21 Emily Glazer, "Fund Firms Cautiously Tweet Their Way Into a New World," *Wall Street Journal*, February 7, 2011: R1.

22 "Creativity and the Digital Age," AEJMC (Association for Education in Journalism and Mass Communication) Conference presentation, Denver, Colorado August 4, 2010.

23 http://www.youtube.com/watch?v=UvVg8PtaGWs&feature=fvwk (accessed June 7, 2011).

24 http://thenextweb.com/socialmedia/2010/12/20/facebook-vs-twitter-by-the-numbers-infographic (accessed January 5, 2011).

25 Irina Slutsky, "Great White Way Getting Big Boost From Chatter on World Wide Web," http://adage.com/results?endeca=1&return=endeca&search_offset=0&search_order_by=score&search_phrase=01/10/201, January 22, 2011 (accessed January 11, 2011).

26 Peter Sena II, personal communication, February 1, 2011.

27 Peter Sena II, personal communication, February 1, 2011.

28 http://adage.com/digital/article?article_id=148091 (accessed January 11, 2011).

29 Charlie Hopper, personal communication, March 4, 2009.

30 Charlie Hopper, personal communication, March 4, 2009.

31 Charlie Hopper, personal communication, February 15, 2011.

32 http://60secondmarketer.com/blog/2010/04/09/top-52-social-media-platforms (accessed June 7, 2011).

33 Alexandra Berzon, "Enough With 'Call of Duty,' Answer the Call in Room 417," *Wall Street Journal*, June 6, 2011, B1, B7.

THE MULTIMEDIA WORD

Integrated campaigns

" Saturate yourself with great advertising from around the world. The best work is coming from all over "

TOM AMICO, CREATIVE DIRECTOR/COPYWRITER, KAPLAN THALER GROUP [1]

Developing ideas that spin out

Thinking about how small-space writing differs from other media

Creating messages that move from one medium into another

Thinking about multimedia from the beginning

Checking that you're writing for the eye, ear, and imagination

Reminding consumers of the benefits in all media

Including target-specific ambient and interactive advertising

Being irreverent can create unforgettable messages

Creating a new approach to a normally stuffy category

Learning Charlie Hopper's media-focused writing tips

Gaining some insights into how Crispin Porter + Bogusky think

Looking at more multimedia campaigns

Single medium campaigns

Multimedia messaging exercises

It's important to analyze as many references in myriad media and different languages. Compile examples that will help you become mentally flexible and consider various ways of executing multimedia campaigns. By doing this, you'll see how strategic thinking and considering the media and idea execution first will guide the creative process.

Most of all, you'll discover that creating communication that addresses people's needs and desires (as discussed in chapter one), while solving problems will always be relevant. And how interacting with consumers in an exciting way will create dialogues, build relationships, and strengthen brand loyalty. By paying attention to campaigns that spark your attention, engage your imagination, and stimulate your response, you'll see what kinds of ideas work and use them as reference points. Powerful campaigns, not only work in many different media; they also stick around for a while. This is because their messages are unique, unexpected, and engaging. We'll begin our exploration of multimedia advertising by looking at a campaign with big ideas.

Developing ideas that spin out

A "*big idea*," as you've probably heard many times before is one that has legs, a long "shelf life," and can work in all media. With so many new communication vehicles emerging, writers must be thinking about conceptual flexibility. They must strive to develop ideas that can be chameleons and blend easily into diverse media environments. If you're creating a magazine ad, you may want to think about where else the message could be used. Take Ugly Mug Coffee for example. Young & Laramore created print ads that ran in *Memphis Magazine* and a free, local newspaper. They were also used for PR blogger relations and intended for use as shelf talkers in a POP (point-of-purchase) program. This campaign was extended into a website. In totality, the campaign included digital, print, on-site (in-store), and PR components.

As you can see in the examples below (Figure 13.1, Figure 13.2, Figure 13.3, Figure 13.4), regardless of medium, this is a campaign with a consistent message. One that easily *spins out*. The message here addresses a *universal truth*: Mornings are better with coffee. Just look at the copy. It speaks to anyone who has trouble waking up in the morning. Notice in Figure 13.2, the humorous *tone of voice* and the unexpected reference to alien abductions. The headline asks:

Who is this person I wake up next to every morning?

The all-too-honest copy answers:

Completely unrecognizable. Certainly not the same sweet, caring wife I went to bed with. No. That woman is gone. And for the passingest of passing moments, I'm open to the concept of alien abduction.

Go and read the message in Figure 13.3. The headline addresses "Morning People," the often-despised individuals who can fly out of bed wide awake. The copy talks to them directly and shares an easy-to-apply plan for revenge:

They begin with a seemingly boundless supply of energy and pluck. Luckily for the rest of us they usually slow down around eleven o'clock. At which point they're pretty easy to pick off, swat down, and crush the hope out of.

FIGURE 13.1 This website homepage, "Oh, what a beautiful morning," was created by Young & Laramore for Ugly Mug Coffee. Image courtesy of Young & Laramore.

FIGURE 13.2 This unexpected package display message was created by Young & Laramore for Ugly Mug coffee. Image courtesy of Young & Laramore.

FIGURE 13.3 This unexpected package display message was created by Young & Laramore for Ugly Mug coffee. Image courtesy of Young & Laramore.

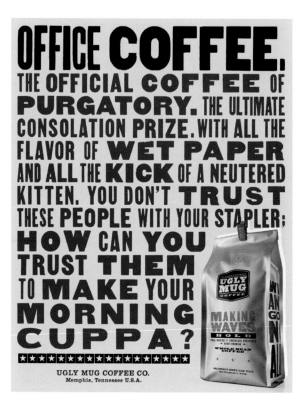

FIGURE 13.4 This unexpected package display message was created by Young & Laramore for Ugly Mug coffee. Image courtesy of Young & Laramore.

Writers must consider which media will be used and look for a way to create a message that will be equally effective in each, as well as have a definitive plan to weave them together. Realizing that what works in TV may not be relevant or applicable in radio may force writers to reexamine their initial creative direction and refocus their message.

Creative teams are always looking for a *big idea*. One that transcends media and cultural barriers. Ideas that "*spin out*" and have legs. Ideas that are flexible and nimble. Like catchy slogans (Nike's "Just Do It"), long-running characters or icons (Planter's "Mr. Peanut"), and seemingly endless campaigns (Absolut's "The Bottle"). See *Ad Age*'s list of "Top 10 Advertising Icons of the Century" at http://adage.com/century/ad_icons. The top five are The Marlboro Man, Ronald McDonald, The Green Giant, Betty Crocker, and The Energizer Bunny. The bottom five are The Pillsbury Doughboy, Aunt Jemima, The Michelin Man, **Kellogg's® Tony the Tiger®**, and Elsie (the cow).[2]

Thinking about how small-space writing differs from other media

Each medium has its challenges. And, as we've seen in writing for direct mail and small-space messages like coupons and packaging (chapter 8), the trick is to say something memorable in as few words as possible. Charlie Hopper, creative director/copywriter at Young & Laramore, adds this bit of insight:

> Well, I think it's an example of always being sure you understand who is going to see your work, where they're going to see it, and how. It's definitely different than a temporal medium, like radio or TV, which has to tease you into staying interested from moment to moment – and in this case, it's different than a billboard or Web banner or coupon tucked into a "ValPak" with a bunch of other coupons, that has to grab you quickly with a focused message and then assume you've moved past.
>
> Here, you know the person is going to hold the door hanger – or, if it's stitched into a magazine, the ad – in their hand. So if you're clever enough into charming them into spending a moment satisfying their curiosity (if you've managed to arouse their curiosity), you have the chance to say a little more than in some other media.[3]

Regardless of the medium, it's always crucial to understand where the consumer will encounter it. This helps writers comprehend the readers' mindset. Are they surfing online? Texting on their phones? Reading a magazine? Driving past a billboard on the highway? Watching TV? Listening to the radio? Following or answering a blogger? Chatting on a social network? Participating in a contest? Creating consumer content? And so on. Where they are mentally can help writers talk to them in a more personal way.

For instance, if you catch people in the middle of their everyday activities, like walking across a park, riding a mall escalator, or hailing a cab, you're using ambient or transit messages to reach them. You've already interrupted their day and, if the ad is strong enough, caught their attention. Just to see how one message can convert to another medium, let's take a glance at other ambient ads that started out as something else.

> " If you think of the production and media opportunities out there, that's where you've got to make your innovation **ROB REILLY, PARTNER/CO-EXECUTIVE/CREATIVE DIRECTOR, CRISPIN PORTER + BOGUSKY**[4]

Creating messages that move from one medium into another

Not all ads remain ads. The following magazine inserts are not just seen inside publications. They were designed with an ongoing afterlife. Young & Laramore also developed the Peerless Faucet door hanger magazine inserts. Read the copy first. Then look at the visuals.

Figure 13.5 Peerless Faucet door hanger magazine insert (cf pp312)

Headline: Right now, I'm feeling (image of an angry face):
   Subhead: If you really want to help me, you can give me:

- 10 Minutes of "Quiet Time"
- A couple of aspirin
- A little moral support

Copy: Installation hit a rough patch? We can give you the tools to cope. Between you and us, we're going to get this faucet in. And no matter where you are with your project, faucetcoach.com is prepared to help.

Figure 13.6 Peerless Faucet door hanger magazine insert (cf pp312)

Headline: Right now, I'm feeling (image of a happy face):
   Subhead: When you have a moment, I sure could go for:

- A cool glass of lemonade
- A snack
- Some applause

Copy: When weekend projects are going well, we're there to applaud your success. We've been cheering on do-it-yourselfers since 1971. And wherever you are with your project, faucetcoach.com can help.

Figure 13.7 Peerless Faucet two-sided magazine insert ad (side one) (cf pp312)

Headline: Dominate water cooler conversation
   Subhead: Instructions:
   Copy:

1 Cut out frame.
2 Photograph faucet you just installed.
3 Place picture in frame.
4 Display frame on desk, in full view of co-workers.
5 Accept accolades.

Copy: Installation hit a rough patch? We can give you the tools to cope. Between you and us, we're going to get this faucet in. And no matter where you are with your project, faucetcoach.com is prepared to help.

Figure 13.8 Peerless Faucet two-sided magazine insert ad (side two) (cf pp312)

Headline: Kick-Start Your Bragging With These Conversation Openers:

   Copy: Co-Worker, to You: *Did you catch that ball game last weekend?*

   You (seizing the moment): *Nope, didn't have time. I was under the sink – installing my new faucet.*

   You (to new hire): *Hi there, my name's (state your name). But everybody here just calls me, "That guy who installed his own faucet last weekend."*

   You (to co-worker): *Let's knock off for the day. We can make a clean start of things tomorrow. Hey, speaking of clean – have I mentioned that* I installed my own faucet last weekend?

   (Block exit and proceed with story.)

FIGURE 13.5 This door hanger magazine insert created by Young & Laramore for Peerless Faucet. Image courtesy of Young & Laramore.

FIGURE 13.6 This door hanger magazine insert was created by Young & Laramore for Peerless Faucet. Image courtesy of Young & Laramore.

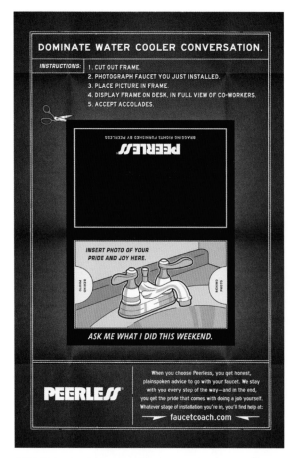

FIGURE 13.7 This two-sided magazine insert ad (side one) was created by Young & Laramore for Peerless Faucet. Image courtesy of Young & Laramore.

FIGURE 13.8 This two-sided magazine insert ad (side two) was created by Young & Laramore for Peerless Faucet. Image courtesy of Young & Laramore.

Carolyn Hadlock, the executive creative director who handled this account explained the strategic thinking behind the campaign. Observational research at people's homes told the creative team that the biggest headache of replacing a faucet was removing the old one. It turned out that people really struggled to get the old one out. By the time they were ready to install the new faucet, they were in a state of frustration. The creative team used this insight and offered consumers help with the installation process. Here's what Hadlock said:

> We decided people needed a coach. A voice who said, "You can do this. I'll help you through it." Each piece of the campaign is a trigger point or part of the process of installing a new faucet. The door hanger is for the "during". The next piece was 2-sided ad insert in a magazine celebrating the post. On the front, you could punch out the frame and insert your own photo of the finished job. The back was ways to steer the conversation towards your installation story. The door hanger was also inserted into the magazine. We had a modest media budget so we knew we needed to do something to break the book [magazine].[5]

The message showed compassion for the home-installers. It told them they weren't alone and that they could count Peerless Faucets to give them support. After they were guided through their installations, the promotional materials gave consumers a sense of accomplishment and pride, which they could share with co-workers.

In this case, the agency came up with the "tools" to help the consumers. Besides door hangers, the multimedia campaign included:

- Online banner ads.
- Video and animated images.
- A faucet coach website.
- Ad inserts in home improvement magazines.
- Messages on package brochures that explained the de-installation process.

The campaign used the "*product as hero*" strategy (#13, as mentioned in chapter two) and came to the consumer's rescue equally well in all media. That's the key to a strong multimedia campaign: present a message that's flexible enough to perform well wherever it runs.

Thinking about multimedia from the beginning

Don't just think about a concept. Think about a fleet of delivery vehicles. Right from the beginning, allow yourself to consider other idea modes of transportation. Stretch your strategic thinking. Challenge yourself. As if any of these message delivery systems would work:

- Ambient.
- Transit.
- Out-of-home messages.
- Print.
- Broadcast.
- Digital.
- Online.
- Interactive.
- Packaging.
- Indoor signage.
- Social media.
- Coupons.
- Emerging media.

Checking that you're writing for the eye, ear, and imagination

Consider what else you can do to specifically target a particular target. After you've considered various media, now ponder how you can use that specific medium to leverage its communication capabilities. For example, look at this short list. Could you add to it?

- Use *eyebrows* in print.
- Create *opt-in* messages.
- Develop an online reward point system for repeat customers.
- Offer e-coupons, *shelf talker* coupons (automated coupon distributers on store shelves), mobile coupons, and *QR codes*.
- Establish a Facebook Fan page.
- Create an interactive vehicle: online product size matching (like Levi's jean "Curve ID" shape quiz at http://.us.levi.com), e-catalogue, mall kiosks (booth or free-standing terminal), in-store imaging (like showing clothes on you without trying them on.
- Invite *consumer-created* or *user-generated content* (like TV commercials or logos).

Remember, with interactive campaigns, you can ask their opinion. Engage their curiosity. Create intrigue. You want to connect consumers' creativity to the brand in a new and compelling way.

Also think about how you could reach a broader audience. What could you integrate into your campaign to broaden your market? Consider future media. What new media could you create? Here are some examples that were breakthrough ideas when they were first introduced:

- Manhole covers in New York City – The realistic image of a cup of Folger's coffee looked as if it were steaming by the air being released under the manhole.
- Bus tires – The tire looked like the lens of a Canon camera.
- Subway platform pillars – The pillars were painted to look like brown markers to remind commuters of the UPS "Whiteboard" campaign.

Reminding consumers of the benefits in all media

Always examine how a campaign modulates from one medium to another. Earlier (in chapters 1, 2, 4, 7, and 8), we looked at the "It's All About the Roosevelts," which was part of the "Why Pay More" campaign. Teddy Brown, senior vice president, executive creative director of the Orange County office at Draftfcb, explained how the agency developed an entire multimedia campaign around the "Roosevelts" video, which was followed by 30- and 15-second TV spots, iPhone apps, and iTunes music:

> *Our Web components basically end up being at Taco Bell.com. We have our takeover pages. We did a "Why Pay More" app for the iPhone that allows you to enter your change or how much money you have. You shake up the app and it tells you how many items off the "Why Pay More" menu you can get. We made the song available on iTunes and we made the song available for download. You can watch the video online. We did a two-minute version of the video that actually ran. Taco Bell bought the two-minute spot on the All-Star game and then they bought six 60s [sixty-second spots] for the cinema [movie theaters].*[6]

This was significant because most of the advertisers in this category, including Taco Bell, usually chose TV as the preferred medium and ran 30- or 15-second commercials. Brown went on to explain how the "Why Pay More" concept was implemented online and what the challenges were.

> The online thing is, I think, one of those things in particular for this category that people are still starting to figure out. How people, particularly young people, are accessing the brand. The television gives us the most eyeballs. Our biggest challenge with online is turning our online into a transaction driver. So it doesn't just become an experience online with the brand. Something that's fun for people to do that they may or may not do. They're participating, but it's in a way that actually can translate into sales.[7]

Notice how the word "fun" wraps up his comments. If people are engaged and entertained in a dialogue that addresses their needs, they're more likely to support the brand. Focusing on the savings with the catchy "Why Pay More" slogan, the benefit is reinforced at all touchpoints.

Now we'll look back at the ASICS campaign discussed in chapters 5, 9, and 12.

Including target-specific ambient and interactive advertising

When asked about the strategic thinking behind the ASICS "New York City Marathon" campaign, KT Thayer, creative director at Vitro, explained that the objective was to build awareness. The creative team realized this was a "challenger brand" and was competing head-to-head with the category megastars, including Nike and Adidas. The idea was to showcase the unique qualities of ASICS and to offer consumers another option.

Thayer went on to explain how "Sound Mind, Sound Body" was more than just the ASICS slogan. He said:

> It is the founding philosophy and the root of the name. Anima Sana In Corpore Sano is a Latin phrase that translates to, "a sound mind, in a sound body." This position drives every decision, innovation, and communication that comes from ASICS.

Fitness is one way of creating a "Sound Mind" resting in a "Sound Body." Consumers could choose any activity. Running would be one solution. The campaign wanted to present another reason to run besides the physical benefits. It also emphasized the mental and emotional benefits. This distinguished ASICS from its competitors and enabled it to create and continue to grow its own identifiable message in the market. In just a few years (2009–11), it steadily moved into second place, behind Nike, and overtook Adidas and New Balance.[8] During the same time, it informed and reminded consumers of the benefits of every sport, specifically running.

> The 2009 campaign was internally called, "Running Truths" as the message had to come from a genuine, honest place that any level of runner could understand and believe.[9]

One interesting question with this campaign was whether the language or images came first. Thayer explained that although some of the headlines may have been created first, the graphics impacted the message. Once the art director designed the layout, chose the font, set the type, and added bright colors, the copy was rewritten to be "shorter, bolder, and punchier."[10] In case you can't recall the campaign, take a moment to review it in chapters 5 and 12. For a quick reference and to refresh your memory, look at Figure 5.5, Figure 5.6, and Figure 5.7 and Figure 9.14 and Figure 9.15. Can you see how the typography gave the ads a three-dimensional perspective and a sense of movement?

When asked to give new copywriters a few helpful tips, Thayer offered the following advice.

> *Try to learn discipline. Don't be satisfied too quickly. It's tough when you write something you like but it doesn't fit for one reason or another (it's too long, sounds like another brand, it's not on strategy, etc.), but more times than not if you keep at it, you get to a better place than where you started.*

As other writers have suggested, be tough on yourself. Don't settle with your first idea. Think about it. Ask if that's the best you can do? Remember to challenge yourself. Always stretch yourself creatively. Try to demand more from yourself. You may not only surprise, but even amaze, yourself!

Take a look again at the Legal Sea Foods campaign also found in chapter 9 and read the irreverent headlines (Figures 9.16–9.22).

Being irreverent can create unforgettable messages

If you're wondering how the creative team came up with the sassy, high-impact "Fresh Fish" campaign for Legal Sea Foods, Paul McCormick, director of new business at DeVito/Verdi answered the question. He explained that Legal Sea Foods prides itself in being able to prove ultimate freshness by its "ability to track every meal from pier to plate."[11] The Boston-based company conducts on-dock testing of all fish and buys only top-of-catch and freshly caught fish and shellfish from day boats.

The question was how to relay that freshest-fish-anywhere message in a penetrable message. The result was a remarkably cheeky, yet undeniably clever, "play on words" (as described in chapter 4) slogan "If it isn't fresh, it isn't Legal." The entire campaign drives home the benefit to the consumer in an intrusive, yet fun, manner in just three strong, simple words: "Really Fresh Fish."

The agency created a cost-effective, multimedia campaign with various *touchpoints* and a consistently whimsical *tone of voice*. The carefully integrated use of media included:

- 15- and 30-second TV spots.
- Local radio.
- Viral videos.
- Out-of-home messages.
- Cinema advertising.
- Guerilla street signs (like *floor talkers*, giant sticky notes, and creative street signs).
- Newspaper.
- *Wild postings* (repeated, often edgy posters placed in nontraditional locations like construction sites, building sides, alleys, windows, bus shelter sides).
- On-going public relations.

This campaign ran exclusively in Boston and was tailored for the cabs and MTBA ("T") Green Line trolleys. To make the campaign particularly relevant to the medium, the creatives knew where the ads would run.[12] This is why the marriage between the messages and the media are so perfectly matched. You can quickly see that from the examples below:

- "This movie sucks."
- "This cab gets around more than your sister." (Later adapted for the "T.")
- "This cab driver has a face like a halibut." (Later also adopted as "conductor" on the "T.")

With campaigns like Legal Sea Foods, it's no surprise that DeVito/Verdi has been voted "The Best Ad Agency in the US" six times by the American Association of Advertising Agencies.

Agencies of all sizes can generate national attention. And campaigns that start out as a spark of an idea can go global. Just think back to the Wendy's "Where's the Beef" and Budweiser "Whassup!" campaigns.

Creating a new approach to a normally stuffy category

One campaign that shattered the standard "stuffy" *tone of voice* was the Charles Schwab "Talk to Chuck" campaign, as mentioned in chapters 5, 7, and 9. (See Figure 5.3 and Figure 5.4, Figure 7.1 and Figure 7.2, and Figure 9.12 and Figure 9.13.) Speaking in a sincere and truthful *tone of voice* using a "*play on words*" technique in the headlines and an "*honesty strategy*" (#26, as discussed in chapter 2).

Drummond Berman, the copywriter/creative director on the account at Euro RSCG, explained that he and his creative partner, Simon Nickson, art director/creative director, look to create concepts that project "absolute realism."[13] He explained how they come up with and then develop their ideas:

> Our planners go out and they, as we said, they do these ethnographies. They go to people's houses. They talk to them. They find common patterns between the things people believe and what they don't believe and all of that. Then they share that with us. We use that to create the advertising. Then we sit with our client and we pick the best stuff, and then we put it straight out in market. We don't show it to anyone. We don't ask anyone's permission. We just run it. It's very much an instinctively built campaign.[14]

He shared how they work with the research to create an authentic voice that sounds genuine. He continued to talk about the creative process:

> We try to just capture the way people truly feel. Very often, somebody will say something in one of the ethnographies that is put in their way rather than just the kind of stereotypical way, and we'll use that word-for-word. Or we'll always try to write something so that it sounds like a real person talking the way they really speak by using those kind of idiosyncratic words that only they use. So if you look at all the spots, there's always something in there that makes it not just a person speaking, but that person speaking.

Nickson explained that the TV scripts tended to be "incredibly real,"[15] which is slightly different than print and out-of-home messages, which interpret people's feelings in a witty way, rather than "just writing exactly the way people speak."[16] Whereas with TV, Nickson said:

We write scripts that are based on one person and not one person that's talking for 100,000 people, but **one person** *who is talking* **for himself** *about* **his situation** *and how he feels about it in* **his language** *that then obviously resonates with other people.*[17]

He likened the scripts to natural conversations you might have a dinner party with someone who's expressing how you feel, but in his or her own manner of speech, using different expressions, clichés, or choice of language. But yet, you're being drawn into the conversation because it resonates with you and you agree with what they're saying.

The communication feels more like a dialogue rather than an advertising message. Although it's contemporary, Nickson said, "there's also something slightly retro about it as well, slightly comforting. Like you feel like you've seen it before, or you've been around it before."[18]

To create one cohesive message, Drummond said a team of people work on the account, who handle reports, design exhibitions and create direct mail pieces and create elements, that keep this well integrated campaign "really unified and consistent."[19]

When you look at the campaign, it's the TV campaign that adds depth to the copy, while the print and out-of-home deliver smartly written headlines that articulate commonly shared opinions. People do feel "Nickeled and Dimed" to death with hidden fees.

Drummond added another tip on writing for print, explaining that there are multiple elements to consider and writers need to think about the "hierarchy of messaging."[20] In other words, writers need to decide what part of the message should be emphasized as a headline. What should be a subhead. And what needs to be stated in the body copy. He explained:

Very often you have copy with a subhead that sort of summarizes what this ad is about in a very simple, non-creative, more informational way. So you **don't** *have to have everything in the headline. You* **do** *have to have everything in the ad. So you constantly need to be thinking about what that hierarchy of the ads going to be and what you're going to say to pay that off in order for it to quickly make total sense to people.*[21]

According to Drummond, the campaign exceeded the agency's expectations. The "Talk to Chuck Bubble" made the brand name as recognizable as Nike's "Just Do It."

Learning Charlie Hopper's media-focused writing tips

As mentioned in chapter 2, Hopper stated that creative teams begin thinking about where people will see the work. Creatives look to catch consumers off guard, interrupt their lives, and create a personal communication. Each message is perfectly tailored to that specific medium. Hopper explained the creative process this way.

Today there are more imaginative vehicles to reach the consumer, as we've discussed throughout this work. In addition to the innovative outdoor signs of years ago, now there are websites, blogs, cellphones, ambient, transit, and other unexpected places. Hopper explained that the most important strategy is to keep the consumer interested long enough for them to see there's a reason to stay engaged. He compared it to dating, and said:

You're doing the same thing with the ads. You're trying to keep them from moving on before they get what's good about you.[22]

ADVICE FROM THE PROS 13.1 Hopper's top writing tips

1 *Just stay away from the puns.* What the pun will do is distract you. The pun wins. But the pun is always off topic. The pun is never making any new ideas. The pun is never really convincing anybody about anything new. Even feeling as I do, I can't get rid of them entirely, like cockroaches or crabgrass.

2 *Write less.* You can always write less. You can always shock yourself at how concise you can get. You can take out all kinds of unnecessary clauses and qualifying words that don't get you anywhere. You can almost 100% of the time cut off the first paragraph, no matter what you're writing. Just cut off the first paragraph. That always works.

3 *Don't let grammar freak you out.* Concentrate on expressing an original thought. A lot of great thinkers would not be able to summon an example of a subordinate clause or tell you what the subjunctive mood is.

4 *Learn grammar.* It frees you. Picasso could draw an accurate, controlled and identifiable picture of a woman, that's why it was okay for him not to. If you can develop a certain comfort with grammar, it gives you confidence to mess around with it a little.

5 *Don't let bad grammar get you expelled before you make your point.* People are unaware of good grammar and really aware of bad grammar. It's like manners. And if you have good manners, you have a chance of making your point. If you do the English grammar equivalent of scratching your armpits while you talk, you may be rejected without a fair hearing.

6 *Pretend your reader has an excited dog on a leash, or impatient child repeatedly saying her name.* That way, you'll make sure you're concise, and you won't make people figure stuff out and guess what you're trying to say. And you won't be as interested in making them say, "Gosh, that person was quite clever."

7 *Don't ask a question that is easily answered "no."* Like "Are you tired of never having enough ice cubes?" or "Isn't it time you considered making a will?" It's for two reasons: people are impatient and if you ask them hypothetical questions as a way of supposedly trapping them into following you, it's just annoying and they think they have you sized up and think to themselves "forget it." And about three-quarters of the time when you do ask a question like that, it's a trite, tired question-device that automatically signals, "No need to read this. It's full of old ideas you've seen before."

8 *Be the first to say something.* Don't just mush around things other people have said. It's ambitious to think you'll be first. But it's the difference between being a writer and being a supplier of verbiage.

9 *Provide variety.* Switch it up. Be almost mechanically aware of varying the lengths of your sentences. Don't write the same length of sentence over and over and over. It's just a simple, mechanical thing to try.[23]

Gaining some insights into how Crispin Porter + Bogusky think

You can a great deal by being an attentive observer. You can also increase your knowledge by reading what agencies doing groundbreaking work are saying. Here's a little insight into how Crispin Porter + Bogusky (CP+B) looks at creating multimedia messages. Rob Reilly, the agency's partner/co-executive / creative director, had to say:

> *Normally, we think almost everything we do, work wise, whether it's TV or print, should be interactive. That's always been the philosophy of an interactive agency. Then, we do things in the digital world. We do things in the TV world. We do things in broadcast. We do a lot of things. Everything we've approached that way. That's why I think we've been successful over the years. The agency philosophy has always been: How do we play with consumers? What game can we play with consumers? I think probably the biggest example for us was Subservient Chicken.*[24]

Looking at more multimedia campaigns

Before we move on to multilingual and international campaigns, let's examine a few more multimedia campaigns. The campaign for Mount Sinai Medical Center, created by DeVito/Verdi (Figure 13.9, Figure 13.10, Figure 13.11, and Figure 13.12), shows how writers can create a series of unexpected, thought-provoking headlines. Again, the benefits of going to Mount Sinai are summarized in the *combination* (#16) slogan "Another day. Another breakthrough." (This line combines these three types of slogans: [1] #5 *parallel construction*, [2] #6 *statement of use or purpose*, and [3] #14 *reason why*, as discussed in chapter 3.) Notice also how it closes the copy in every ad, rather than sitting in its normal position: close to the logo.

Let's look at the ads one at a time. Then, we'll read the radio script. Each ad has a *call to action*, the *mandatory* information or the signature lines ("*sig*"), including the phone number and website. Pay special attention to how the copy jumps into the story, without an introduction. This way the reader is drawn in and not turned off before absorbing the information.

"Two-year-old" (figure 13.9)

Headline: We Turned a Child Who Couldn't Hear into a Typical 2-Year-Old Child Who Doesn't Listen.

Copy: Two-year-old Patricia Puia sat on her mother's lap, unable to hear the gentle voice that tried to comfort her. Deaf from birth, her life in Romania was lived in silence. But a month after undergoing cochlear implant surgery at Mount Sinai, the silence was filled with sounds of a world Patricia never knew existed. "I feel like I've just given birth to this child for the second time," her mother said tearfully. "But this time she hears." 1-800-MD SINAI. www.mountsinai.org.

Look at how the headline catches the reader off-guard. It talks about a deaf toddler who, through surgery at Mount Sinai, eventually, turns a deaf ear. Just like all little kids her age.

At first, you feel sympathy. Then, you feel joy. What a wonderful way to tell the story, in just a few words.

"Catherine" (figure 13.10)

Headline: Catherine Reynolds Had a Baby When She Was 77 Years Old.
   Subhead: Her Husband.
   Copy: He can't feed himself. He can't dress himself. He can't bathe without assistance. A victim of Alzheimer's disease, he is totally dependent on his wife of 54 years. But hope exists for those who suffer from Alzheimer's, and for family members who live with its consequences. Drugs pioneered at Mount Sinai can improve the symptoms, allowing patients to maintain a measure of dignity and independence. It's a testament to our longstanding commitment to geriatric care, and to our desire to see married couples live as husband and wife. Instead of parent and child. 1-800-MD SINAI. www .mountsinai.org.
   Here the headline makes you stop and ask, "How is that possible?" Then, the subhead explains the answer. You go from confusion to comprehension in just two words: "Her husband." Again, the woman's life experience is summed up in a headline and subhead.

"Ruby" (figure 13.11)

Headline: Ruby Gaynor's Parents Cried When She Suffered Brain Damage.
   Subhead: They Cried Even More When She Graduated Columbia.
   Copy: A car accident left Ruby Gaynor with a serious brain injury. And a severely impaired future. But doctors at Mount Sinai Rehabilitation Center weren't impaired by the constraints of ordinary care. Through intensive therapy, she relearned the basic skills she once took for granted, and fine-tuned the advanced skills that could take her through college. Which turned a tragedy into a triumph. And tears into, well, more tears. 1-800-MD SINAI. For a list of our doctors log onto www.mountsinai.org.
   This headline connects to everyone. Who wouldn't feel terrible about anyone's daughter with brain damage? Then, the subhead rewards the reader with instant relief. How wonderful that Ruby recovered. It doesn't matter whether you know her or not. You're happy for her parents. Why? Because this headline immediately conjures up empathy and compassion.

"Baseball" (figure 13.12)

Headline: Minimally Invasive Sports Surgery.
   Copy: None. (There was no need to explain it because the headline and visual said it all.)
   When the headline and the visual deliver the entire message as a unit, copy is sometimes not needed. That's the case in this "Baseball" ad. The image cleverly shows a short surgical incision as if the baseball were repaired.
   Now, let's look at how the Mount Sinai radio script paralleled the print ad copy. You'll see it recounts the two-year-old Patricia Puia's story of how her hearing was restored through surgery at the hospital. See how the script uses *parallel construction* with the second announcer repeating and then modifying the first announcer's lines.

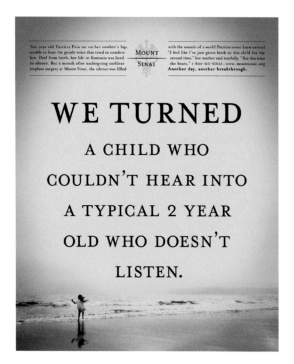

FIGURE 13.9 This "Two-Year-Old" print ad was created by DeVito/Verdi for Mount Sinai. Image courtesy of DeVito/Verdi.

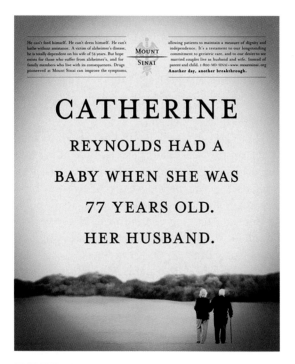

FIGURE 13.10 This "Catherine" print ad was created by DeVito/Verdi for Mount Sinai. Image courtesy of DeVito/Verdi.

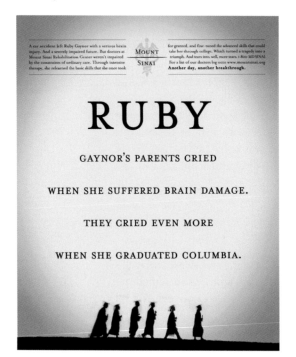

FIGURE 13.11 This "Ruby" print ad was created by DeVito/Verdi for Mount Sinai. Image courtesy of DeVito/Verdi.

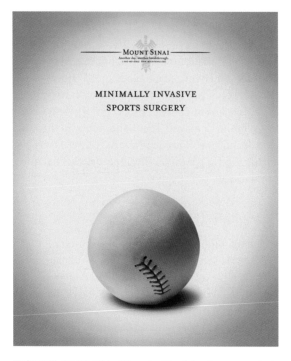

FIGURE 13.12 This "Baseball" print ad was created by DeVito/Verdi for Mount Sinai. Image courtesy of DeVito/Verdi.

SCRIPTS AND EXAMPLES 13.2 Mount Sinai, :60 radio, "Two-Year-Old"

MAN 1:	Two-year-old Patricia Puia was born deaf in Rumania.
MAN 2:	Two-year-old Patricia Puia was born deaf in Rumania.
MAN 1:	Her life was lived in silence.
MAN 2:	Her life was lived in silence.
MAN 1:	She had never heard a lullaby or the voice of another human being.
MAN 2:	She had never heard a lullaby or the voice of another human being.
MAN 1:	Her parents were told nothing could be done.
MAN 2:	Her parents were told that Mount Sinai in New York could restore Patricia's hearing.
MAN 1:	Patricia's parents were filled with despair.
MAN 2:	Patricia underwent cochlear implant surgery.
MAN 1:	Patricia withdrew into a shell.
MAN 2:	Patricia was able to hear for the very first time.
MAN 1:	Life has been difficult for Patricia and her parents.
MAN 2:	Life for Patricia is that of a typical two-year-old. She can hear, but she doesn't listen.
WOMAN:	Which hospital you choose can make all the difference in the world. Mount Sinai. Another day. Another breakthrough. For more information call 1-800-MD-SINAI.

(This "Two-Year-Old" :60 radio spot was created by DeVito/Verdi for Mount Sinai. Script courtesy of DeVito/Verdi.)

Next we'll discuss mono-medium campaigns. Those are the ones that run only in one medium.

Single medium campaigns

Some messages are so powerful, they only need to appear in one medium. The Apple "1984" TV spot, created by TBWA\Chiat\Day, that ran in the Super Bowl of that year made such an impact, it was replayed and discussed in the news. Today, it would have been shared online and viewed by thousands, if not millions of people practically overnight.

Another message, created in 1999 by DeVito/Verdi for the American Civil Liberties Union (ACLU),[25] ran only as a print ad. It drove home the problem of racial profiling with the image of Dr. Martin Luther King on the left and murderer Charles Manson on the right. Just look at how the headline clearly made the point:

Figure 13.13

Headline: The Man on the Left is 75 Times More Likely to Be Stopped by the Police While Driving Than the Man on the Right.

Copy: It happens every day on America's highways. Police stop drivers based on their skin color rather than for the way they are driving. For example, in Florida 80% of those stopped and searched were black and Hispanic, while they constituted only 5% of all drivers. These humiliating and illegal searches are violations of the Constitution and must be fought. Help us defend your rights. Support the ACLU. To learn more and to send your Members of Congress a free fax go to www.aclu.org/racialprofiling.

The copy explained that black and Hispanic drivers where pulled over by the police even thought they represented on 5% of all drivers (at that time). People profiled sarcastically

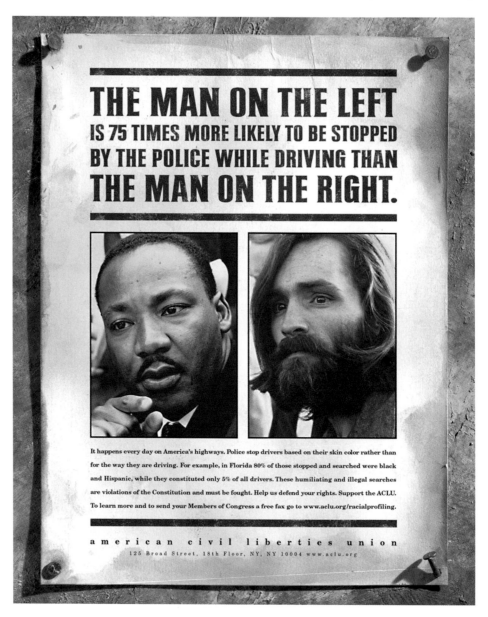

FIGURE 13.13 This "Dr. King" print ad was created by DeVito/Verdi for American Civil Liberties Union. Image courtesy of DeVito/Verdi.

coined the phrase "DWB" (driving while black) as a humorous reference or parody to the then-used phrase "DWI" (driving while intoxicated), now commonly called "DUI" (driving under the influence). The ad was designed to create pressure for those "persuaders" in political power to create change.

Another controversial campaign, also created by DeVito/Verdi, shortly after opening its agency in 1991, was for Daffy's (Figure 13.14, Figure 13.15). The first headline (below) implied that you had to be crazy to spend $100 on a fancy shirt. Unfortunately, showing a straightjacket in the ad ruffled feathers for mental-health advocacy groups, who found the image offensive.

The first headline (Figure 13.14) reads: "Shirt. Bullshirt." It shows a shirt with a $20 price tag on the left and one with a $100 price tag on the right.

The copy simply states:

Men's women's and children's fashion & designer clothes 40–75% off, every day.

It finishes with a list of addresses in Manhasset and New Jersey. Plus, the logo. That's it. The headline says it all. Under the logo is an easy-to-recall slogan that uses several techniques: *rhyming, play-on-words, statement of promise* (as discussed in chapter 4). It cleverly restates the point:

FIGURE 13.14 This "Bullshirt" print ad was created by DeVito/Verdi for Daffy's. Image courtesy of DeVito/Verdi.

FIGURE 13.15 This "Jacket" print ad was created by DeVito/Verdi for Daffy's. Image courtesy of DeVito/Verdi.

Clothes that will make you, not break you.

The second headline (Figure 13.15) boldly asks: "If you're paying over $100 for a dress shirt may we suggest a jacket to go with it?"

Again the copy just says:

With men's, women's and children's fashion & designer clothes 40–75% off, every day, you'd be crazy to shop anywhere else Elizabeth, East Hanover, Paramus, Wayne and New York.

Even though the ad uses a humorous *tone of voice*, it was still considered offensive to one group sensitive to mental health issues. However, by saying you'd have to be crazy to overpay for something is a common expression that resonates with everyday shoppers, especially in a challenging economic climate.

Humor, of course, is subjective. However, clever copy that can work in multiple media, amuse the audience, and feature benefits can be very persuasive. The humorous tone makes the audience feel comfortable, as if they know the brand and the brand knows them. They're sharing a little joke between them and the consumer feels as if the brand "gets" or understands them. The *benefits* remind shoppers their needs are recognized. The multiple *touchpoints* show consumers can be reached in their everyday activities because their lifestyles are considered. In short, reaching the consumer in a disarmingly simple, yet creative, way bears fruit.

Remember this: Sticking to the status quo is like using a compass and the North Star to fly to the moon. It's just not going to cut it.

You've got to hate big words where small words will do. The ones that come to mind immediately are "utilize" instead of "use." "Verbiage" instead of "words" or "copy." But, there are millions of other examples. You've got to hate clichés **CHARLIE HOPPER, CREATIVE DIRECTOR AND COPYWRITER, YOUNG & LARAMORE**[26]

✓ CHECKLIST 13.3 Multimedia writing tips checklist

1   Think simple. Look for a message that's instantly understood.

2   Focus on flexibility. Ask how the message would lend itself to other media.

3   Include interactivity. Make a point to engage the audience. Remember what ASICS did to target New York Marathoners and their families, as we mentioned earlier.

4   Consider specific interest groups. If you're addressing hockey or ice-skating fans, forget age and think about what unifies them. Then, speak to those common interests.

5   Remember to include *universal truths*.

6   Be irreverent when appropriate. Review the Legal Sea Foods campaign in chapter nine.

7   Decide if humor would work like it does in the Ugly Mug Coffee campaign.

8   Be sensitive to different audiences so your message will be embraced, not rejected.

9   Promote the brand through traditional, emerging, digital, social, and mobile media.

10 Create an open dialogue. Just realize, today's audience can answer back.

Multimedia messaging exercises

Exercise 1: thinking about writing for diverse audiences

Part 1 Go online and find a campaign that targets a specific ethnic or lifestyle group. For instance, cruise lines that allow specific groups to customize a cruise just for them, like art aficionados, music devotees, fitness buffs, gardening enthusiasts, wine connoisseurs, gourmands, environmentalists, fundraisers for charitable organizations, industry associates, wedding parties, same-sex couples, singles, retirees, seniors, and so on.

Part 2 Create a new campaign for the same audience. Develop a slogan and two headlines that could work in any media.

Part 3 Choose your media. Consider using:

- Interactive components, like
  - contests (for example: best new cruise activities or excursions);
  - blogs with people sharing their stories;
  - social networking site where consumers can exchange ideas.
- Mobile announcements.
- Online coupons.
- TV or radio.
- Print ads, flyers, brochures.
- eZines (online magazines) or eBrochures (online brochures).
- Ambient signs.
- Direct mail.
- Transit messages.

Exercise 2: creating another campaign for a different group

Part 1 How would you target this group? You could consider:

- *Eyebrows* (lines that appear before the headline to speak to a specific group, like: "Attention Pet lovers!" as discussed in chapter 4).
- Language *relevant* to a specific group, like "Expert Yoga instructors."
- *Benefits* that speak to an interested group, like "Strengthen your core muscles," for Pilates students.

Part 2 What other types of media would you use? Before deciding, ask yourself why you would choose those particular vehicles? Are there any other ones you should consider?

Exercise 3: thinking past age groups

Part 1 If you know which audiences you're targeting, you may be able to see if there are any common values or interests. Think about events or activities that unify people across the world like soccer, fitness, literature, art, music, and so on.

Consider how you could create a campaign that would be equally effective in both languages and speak directly to each market.

Part 2 Create a single, simple message that could easily be transcreated, if not translated. Start with a *universal* or *global truth* that could work as the slogan for both audiences.

Part 3 Modify the message to act as a series of headlines in the campaign.

Part 4 Start by creating a strictly transit-oriented campaign. Consider using:

- Taxi cabs:
  - outside (top or side of cabs);
  - inside.
- Bus:
  - sides;
  - benches;
  - shelters.
- Subways:
  - interiors;
  - exteriors;
  - platforms.
- Trolleys
- Trains:
  - cars;
  - stations.
- Airplanes:
  - in-flight magazines;
  - tray tables;
  - outside of plane (body and tail wings).

Notes

1 Tom Amico, personal communication, June 30, 2009.

2 http://adage.com/century/ad_icons.html.

3 Charlie Hopper, personal communication, November 26, 2008.

4 Rob Reilly, personal communication December 15, 2008.

5 Carolyn Hadlock, personal communication, February 15, 2011.

6 Teddy Brown, personal communication, October 26, 2009.

7 Teddy Brown, personal communication, October 26, 2009.

8 KT Thayer, personal communication, September 9, 2010.

9 KT Thayer, personal communication, September 9, 2010.

10 KT Thayer, personal communication, September 9, 2010.

11 Paul McCormick, personal communication, April 18, 2011.

12 Paul McCormick, personal communication, April 18, 2011.

13 Drummond Berman, personal communication, April 8, 2009.

14 Drummond Berman, personal communication, April 8, 2009.

15 Simon Nickson, personal communication, April 8, 2009.

16 Simon Nickson, personal communication, April 8, 2009.

17 Simon Nickson, personal communication, April 8, 2009.

18 Simon Nickson, personal communication, April 8, 2009.

19 Drummond Berman, personal communication, April 8, 2009.

20 Drummond Berman, personal communication, April 8, 2009.

21 Drummond Berman, personal communication, April 8, 2009.

22 Charlie Hopper, personal communication, November 26, 2008.

23 Charlie Hopper, personal communication, November 26, 2008.

24 Rob Reilly, personal communication December 15, 2008.

25 http://marketing-case-studies.blogspot.com/2008/02/racial-profiling-campaign.html (accessed April 27, 2011).

26 Charlie Hopper, personal communication, November 26, 2010.

14

THE GLOBAL WORD
Multicultural and International Campaigns

> *I think the first and most important thing in advertising is to be original and fresh.*

WILLIAM BERNBACH, ONE OF THE FOUNDERS OF DOYLE DANE BERNBACH (DDB)[1]

Revisiting universal truths as a core message

Writing for hispanic markets

Using global truths for today's diverse market

Creating international campaigns

Seeing how concepts move into other markets

Taking a tagline into other countries

Changing consumer behavior with fun

Reaching out with on-the-go solutions

Using the digital world to go global

Observing international campaigns

Multilingual and international messaging exercises

As you look over this chapter and examine multilingual and international campaigns, you'll recognize how to apply everything you've learned up until now. You'll see how writers on multicultural and international accounts are thinking early about how the concept will work in a range of media vehicles, for a mix of cultures, and within a combination of diverse markets across the world. You'll notice that they look at the *touchpoints* and consider how to develop a relevant, interruptive message that resonates with each audience in a unique way.

You'll also realize how writing for different markets often starts with a *global truth* that unifies a message, regardless of the audience. You'll see how a strong *slogan* (VW "Das Auto") can be used without translation in different countries in different campaigns.

Most importantly, you'll find that when you create an on-strategy, on-target message, it sounds authentic, acknowledges the audience's values, and embraces their *point of view*. The advertising sounds as if it's communicating in an intimate way, like a conversation with a close friend. One way is using *universal truths* that everyone can nod "yes" to.

Revisiting universal truths as a core message

As mentioned in the TV section (chapter 7) and in chapter 13 Sheena Brady, creative director/copywriter at Wieden+Kennedy, emphasized the important of finding a universal truth that transcended cultural barriers; yet explained that campaigns would be modified to fit the consumers' frame of reference. For instance, football is more popular in America then soccer, and these sports preferences are just the reverse in Europe and other parts of the world, like South America for example. She also said:

> If you have a voice that is in everything from your label to your messaging in the Internet, or the piece that you send out, and it's all consistent, it really gives people a sense of who you are, It's very singularly focused. It's very integrated and people get a sense of what you stand for as a brand.[2]

She continued:

> You have to take the kind of brand attributes, the kind of things that make a soda a soda, or a running shoe, a running shoe, and you have to tailor that. But, the idea of a one-on-one communication with someone, that doesn't change.[3]

Reaching audiences through multiple *touchpoints* is equally applicable to multicultural and multilingual campaigns. Those messages also need to make consumers feel as if they're having a private, one-on-one conversation with the brand. Whether you create the dialogue in one language or more, the key is to know when and where to use which language. Some agencies write differently for different markets. Others look to create a universal message that's applicable to all audiences. Let's first look at

> " Inside every fat ad there's a thinner and better one trying to get out. In short, the less said the better. **TONY COX, CREATIVE DIRECTOR (80S–90S), DDB**[4]

> " So, when we're doing national marketing messages that need to go everywhere, we use neutral Spanish. It's dialect-free and it's what we would call Tom Brokaw Spanish. **KELLY MCDONALD, PRESIDENT OF MCDONALD MARKETING**[5]

how McDonald Marketing, an agency specializing in targeting Hispanic audiences, creates messages for specific consumer groups.

Writing for hispanic markets

Kelly McDonald, the president of McDonald Marketing, shared how her agency specifically addresses one of four particular Hispanic mindsets "to identify our client's high-potential target or targets."[6] She developed an "Acculturation Stratification Model" to define each group. She explained the difference between assimilation and acculturation because many people confuse the two words and use them interchangeably. McDonald clarified them this way:

1   *Assimilation means that I forfeit my culture and I adopt yours.*

2   *Acculturation means, "I forfeit nothing." There are certain things that I really like about your culture and I want those. But, there are certain things that I really like about my primary culture and I want to keep those, too.*

   So, an overly simplistic way to look at it is, assimilation is about "either or." It's about I'm either in my culture or I'm in yours and adapted to yours. And acculturation is not about "either or" it's about "and."[7]

She gave this example of acculturation by talking about an eight-year old American little girl of Mexican descent. On Christmas, she's eating tamales *and* waiting for Santa. Then, a week later, she's celebrating Three Kings Day. She differs from the recently arrived Spanish-dominant Latinos, who are going to be immersed in their primary culture. They tend to live among other Spanish-speaking people, work among other Spanish-speaking people, live in Little Mexico, their Little Mexico part of town.[8]

McDonald then breaks the Hispanic market into four subgroups or levels of acculturation:

1   *Cultural loyalist* – They could have just arrived or could have lived in America for 20 years, yet still think they're going back "home." They still see themselves as visitors, not residents. They're the least acculturated.

2   *Cultural embracer* – Like the cultural loyalists, they were born outside the country, but have adopted the United States as their permanent home.

3   *Cross culture* – They're Latinos who are first-generation Americans. They were born here, but their parents weren't. So, they've been raised biculturally. They have a different mindset.

4   *Cultural integrator* – They're US- born Latinos who are second, third, fourth (and so on) generation. They prefer to speak English, but are proud of their Hispanic heritage. They might ask their parents to call them Joey, not Jose so they'll fit in. Today, the same kids are saying, "No, it's okay to call me José." Because now being Latino creates a professional advantage.[9]

She explained how this helps when you're marketing to each group. For example, if your client is a bank, the way you would approach a newly arrived *cultural loyalist* would be different from a *cultural integrator* or *cross culture*. You might target a *cultural loyalist* with information about a checking or savings account and money wiring. However, you wouldn't mention money wiring to any other of the Hispanic subgroups because they wouldn't be sending money home to anyone. Most of their family members are in the states. Likewise, you wouldn't try to sell a mortgage to recent arrivals because they wouldn't have the credit history needed.

For bilingual targeting, McDonald said it's not right for every market. For instance, if the same bank were targeting cultural embracers, it might use Spanish. The reason is this. Although *cultural embracers* are quickly becoming bilingual, they might still prefer to receive information in Spanish, because it's their first language and therefore easier to comprehend.

McDonald also mentioned if the client, such as a telecommunications company, were targeting youth, its natural primary audience, it would use Spanglish (a mix of English and Spanish), rather than with a bilingual campaign. And, when they create bilingual campaigns they don't "translate" the message, they "*transcreate*" it. That means they develop a similar, culturally relevant message, that isn't necessarily a word-for-word translation.

Finally, when targeting the *cultural integrator*, she would use English, the group's dominant language, peppered with cultural relevant references in the message. She explained, like African-American marketing, it's not a linguistic, but a cultural difference, which would be addressed with African-American humor, situations, family scenes, and so on.

Research delivers insights into each demographic group. For instance, if a charitable organization wanted people to donate their vehicles, that kind of message wouldn't be something Hispanics would necessarily respond to. They would tend to give their cars to family members. She became enthusiastic when she discussed the importance of research in the strategic development process:

> We love research. We believe nothing speaks like the consumer. So, wherever possible, we actually augment our own experience and insights with concrete research.[10]

She shared some interesting research results after her agency conducted 200 man-on-the-street interviews in six different cities. When they questioned people, they asked:

1 Do you have insurance?
2 Do you have a license and do you have insurance?

What they found out was surprising. Although many people didn't have a license, every one of them had insurance. When they asked consumers why they would have insurance without having a license, people answered, "Because it's the law."[11]

Another interesting insight she learned was to separate men and women in Hispanic focus groups because men will be more forthright without women in the room. On the other hand, women will be more vocal without men around them. How did she use this information? When her agency wanted to talk to the do-it-yourself painter for Sherwin-Williams, one of her clients, they spoke to the men and women separately. No macho man will admit he doesn't know how to paint something in front of a woman.

When they asked men, "Do you feel like you need to go to the paint store to get expert advice, and the proper guidance you need for the tools and the prep work?" they gathered more honest answers when there were no women in the room. Hearing from each group separately helped guide the advertising. McDonald said:

> It absolutely drives the messaging because what it does is identifies barriers to entry that we can then overcome with messaging, or identifies what their desires are that we didn't know.

One final question was telling. It was free-form: "If you had the president of Sherwin-Williams here in front of you today, what would you tell him or her?" They were able to say anything at all, like, "Oh, I like your products." Or "I wish there was a store near my house." But, here's what was said over and over: "It would be really nice if you had coupons."[12]

Just learning that this audience wanted coupons, drove the creative teams to develop them because they knew they would be appreciated and redeemed. In a direct-mail piece, Sherwin-Williams offered a coupon with $10 off a $50 purchase.

Perhaps assuming that everyone enjoys a discount and applying that as a *universal truth* would have worked. However, once the research confirmed that this audience wanted to save money, it became the core message that was definitely on target.

Using global truths for today's diverse market

We talked about universal truths earlier (chapters 1, 2, 5, 7, and 8) and explained how writers and art directors create messages that transcend cultures and geographic borders. George L. San Jose, president and COO of The San Jose Group, explained the creative process the same way:

> We call it global truth. The name of our creative model is "The 4th Dimension," or "4D," which basically is the foundation of all the creative that we generate at the agency.[13]

He discussed the change in the demographic landscape in the largest US cities and how in these areas of dominant influence (referred to as ADIs) a multicultural population has, for the most part, eclipsed the general populace. So, finding common "idea" denominators is key to the agency's creative process. The creative teams are looking for global truths relevant to all ethnic groups, including Hispanics, non-Hispanics, African-Americans, and Asians, regardless of their degree of acculturation into the American fabric San Jose stated it clearly:

> We try to find those specific golden truths, those golden nuggets, that are relevant to each of those different subgroups regardless of language preference, acculturation or socioeconomic levels, and we try to build our campaigns on that.[14]

Although the development process is the same, sometimes the agency develops only a multicultural message. Other times, it builds a multilingual message. It creates a brief based on consumer research and insights. After the team develops a "thematic concept" or "*big idea*," it is tested in multicultural and general markets. For two years (2008–10), the agency created campaigns with *global truths* that worked equally well for both markets. One campaign for American Family Insurance (AFI) won the Service Industry Advertising Awards plus two gold awards from the Aurora Awards because of its relevant, on-target message. Notice how the American Family Insurance campaign easily migrated from one medium to another, with a common theme that focused on family. For print, including bus shelters (Figure 14.1, Figure 14.2), it talked about protecting your family and referred to them as "your treasures." The headline *Protege Tus Tesoros* ("Protect Your Treasures") was a command. (It used the *imperative* technique #11, discussed in chapter 4.)

FIGURE 14.1 This "Protege Tus Tesoros" ("Protect Your Treasures") print ad was created by The San Jose Group for American Family Insurance. Image courtesy of The San Jose Group.

In another ad, both the English and Spanish versions (Figure 14.3, Figure 14.4) had long headlines. The key words were set in much larger type. The rest of the headline, although meant to be read first, was set in smaller size type, which deemphasized the line. The headlines, which essentially had the same meaning, read:

"Tu esposa sabe sobre la importancia del amor. Tu hija sabe sobre la importancia de la confianza" ("Your wife knows about the importance of love. Your daughter knows about the importance of trust.")

FIGURE 14.2 This "Protege Tus Tesoros" ("Protect Your Treasures") bus shelter was created by The San Jose Group for American Family Insurance. Image courtesy of The San Jose Group.

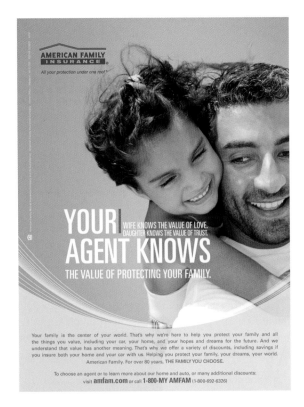

FIGURE 14.3 This "Your Agent Knows" corporate ad in English was created by The San Jose Group for American Family Insurance. Image courtesy of The San Jose Group.

FIGURE 14.4 This "Tu Agente Sabe" ("Your Agent Knows") corporate ad in Spanish was created by The San Jose Group for American Family Insurance. Image courtesy of The San Jose Group.

The larger type read: *"Tu Agente Sabe Lo Importante Que Es Protegerlas"* ("Your agent knows the importance of protecting them all.")

The English version said something similar: "Your Agent Knows The Value of Protecting Your Family." As in the Spanish version, the same three words were emphasized in larger type: "Your Agent Knows."The copy supported the headline and showed that the agent understood how important your family was to you.*Copy (in English, Figure 14.3):* Your family is the center of your world. That's why we're here to help you protect your family and all the things you value, including your car, your home, and your hopes and dreams for the future. And we understand that value has another meaning. That's why we offer a variety of discounts, including savings if you insure both your home and your car with us. Helping you protect your family, your dreams, your world. American Family. For over 80 years, THE FAMILY YOU CHOOSE. To choose an agent or to learn more about our home and auto, or many additional discounts, visit amfam.com or call 1-800-MYAMFAM (1-800-692-6326).

Copy (in Spanish) (Figure 14.4): En la vida, la familia es el centro de tu mundo. Por eso, estamos aquí para ayudarte a proteger todo por lo que has trabajado tanto, tu auto, tu hogar, tu familia. Por más de 80 años hemos protegido todo lo que quieres y aprecias. Y lo seguimos haciendo, ofreciendote un descuento al obtener seguros de casa y auto con nosotros. Ayudándote a proteger a tu familia, tus sueños, tu mundo. Escoge un agente: llama al 1-800-692-6326. www.amfamlatino.com

The copy was very much the same in both languages. Notice how the *call to action* was different. In the English version, there was a line preceding the phone number. It reinforced the company name and its 80-year tradition of taking care of families. Then, it restated the special discounts before sending readers to the website or phone number, which was presented in an easy-to-remember way, with letters. In the Spanish version, the *call to action* just said: to find an agent, call the 800 number.

For the 2009 radio campaign, which only ran in Spanish, the translated English "back copy" is provided in the scripts (Figure 14.5, Figure 14.6). Both spots were two 30-second spots, which ran back-to-back, filling a 60-second time slot. Both "José and Guadalupe" and "Carmelita and Guadalupe" talked about their children so listeners could identify with the parents in the scripts. Consumers felt connected to them because they were sharing some of the same challenges they were facing with their kids. In the first half of "José and Guadalupe" (Figure 14.5) the dad talked about being overly protective of his daughter, admitting he made her wear a face mask and extra protective padding when she learned to ride a bike. He mentioned she looked like a baseball catcher. It touched on a *global* or *universal truth*: dads are devoted to protecting their little girls. In the second half, the dad spoke about teaching his son to play baseball. The ball hit the satellite dish, cascaded down the roof and dented the car. Again, the spot featured a *global truth*: dads like to teach their sons sports. The second half closed by commending the insurance agent, Guadalupe, who "catches" everything. The one word, "catch," tied both spots together, because baseball was mentioned in each. What a clever way to unify two spots so they sound great next to each other on the air.

In the beginning of the second, combined 60-second spot, "Carmelita and Guadalupe" (Figure 14.6) the daughter, who was a young woman, was saying her parents are very traditional, so she finally moved out. But, she carried those traditions with her. It was a nice transition from "traditional" to "traditions." Although the words were similar, the meanings were different. The spot tied back to the insurance agent by her stating she called her parents' agent when she got into a fender bender. She casually stated that Carmelita was now her agent, too. The same "Guadalupe" spot mentioned above was used to fill out

CLIENT	American Family Insurance
PRODUCT	Auto/Home
TITLE	José/Guadalupe - Hispano
LENGTH	:50-10 OR
SCRIPT NO.	**ISCI 003590**
DATE	5/8/09 (as produced)

RADIO CONTINUITY

JOSE

Música:	Música Emocional / Inspiracional.
Hombre:	Siempre la sobreprotegí, de hecho cuando empezó a andar en bici hasta catcher de béisbol parecía...con careta, protección en todo el cuerpo.
	Ahora ella es lo suficientemente grande para manejar el auto de la familia.
	Pero cuando ella tuvo un accidente llamé a José, nuestro agente de American Family Insurance.
Anncr:	Visita www.amfamlatino.com
Jingle:	American Family Insurance.
Anncr:	La póliza que compres y los servicios corporativos están disponibles solamente en inglés.

GUADALUPE

Música:	Música Emocional / Inspiracional.
Padre:	Estoy enseñando a mi hijo a jugar béisbol.
Padre:	Le pegó a la antena.
Padre:	La cual se desprendió del techo, rompió la ventana y aterrizó en el auto.
Padre:	Lo bueno es que desde hace muchos años tenemos nuestra póliza con American Family Insurance y a Guadalupe, nuestra agente. Ella se asegura que nuestra póliza de seguro de casa cubra todo lo que necesitamos.
Anncr:	Visita www.amfamlatino.com
Jingle:	American Family Insurance
Anncr:	La póliza que compres y los servicios corporativos están disponibles solamente en inglés.

---

233 North Michigan Avenue, 24th Floor, Chicago, Illinois 60601-5519 TEL (312) 565-7000 FAX (312) 565-7500 E-mail sanjose@sjadv.com
An Agency of The San Jose Network, Ltd.

FIGURE 14.5 This "José and Guadalupe" :60 (combined :50 + :10) radio script was created by The San Jose Group for American Family Insurance. Script courtesy of The San Jose Group.

CLIENT	American Family Insurance
PRODUCT	Auto/Home
TITLE	Jose/Gradalupe - Hispano
LENGTH	: 50-10 OR ISCI Code: 003590
SCRIPT NO.	Back Translation
DATE	05/08/09 (As produced)

RADIO CONTINUITY

JOSE

Music:	Emotional/Inspirational music
Man:	I've always been overly protective, as a matter of fact, when she learned to ride a bike; she looked like a baseball catcher...decked out with a face mask and protective body gear.
	Now she's old enough to drive the family car.
	But when she got into an accident I called Jose, our American Family Insurance agent.
Anncr:	Visit www.amfamlatino.com
Jingle:	American Family Insurance.
Anncr:	The policy you purchase and corporate services are available only in English.

GUADALUPE

Music:	Emotional/Inspirational music up and under.
Dad:	I'm helping my son learn baseball.
Dad:	He hit the satellite.
Dad:	Which then slid off the roof, broke the window and landed on the car.
Dad:	Good thing we have our insurance policy for many years with American Family Insurance and our agent, Guadalupe. She catches everything, making sure our home policy covers everything we need.
Anncr:	Visit www.amfamlatino.com
Jingle:	American Family Insurance
Anncr:	The policy you purchase and corporate services are available only in English.

233 North Michigan Avenue, 24th Floor, Chicago, Illinois 60601-5519 TEL (312) 565-7000 FAX (312) 565-7500 E-mail sanjose@sjadv.com
An Agency of The San Jose Network, Ltd.

FIGURE 14.5 continued

RADIO CONTINUITY

CLIENT	American Family Insurance
PRODUCT	Auto/Home
TITLE	Carmelita/Guadalupe - Bicultural
LENGTH	:50-10 OR
SCRIPT NO.	ISCI Code: 003591
DATE	05/08/09 (As produced)

CARMELITA

Música:	Música Emocional / Inspiracional.
Mujer joven:	Mis padres son muy tradicionalistas finalmente he decidido mudarme de casa.
Mujer joven:	Pero me llevo sus tradiciones conmigo.
Mujer joven:	Cuando tuve un pequeño accidente conté con Carmelita, la agente de American Family Insurance de mis padres, que ahora también es mi agente.
Anncr:	Visita www.amfamlatino.com
Jingle:	American Family Insurance.
Anncr:	La póliza que compres y los servicios corporativos están disponibles solamente en inglés.

GUADALUPE

Música:	Música Emocional / Inspiracional.
Padre:	Estoy enseñando a mi hijo a jugar béisbol.
Padre:	Le pegó a la antena.
Padre:	La cual se desprendió del techo, rompió la ventana y aterrizó en el auto.
Padre:	Lo bueno es que desde hace muchos años tenemos nuestra póliza con American Family Insurance y a Guadalupe, nuestra agente. Ella se asegura que nuestra póliza de seguro de casa cubra todo lo que necesitamos.
Anncr:	Visita www.amfamlatino.com
Jingle:	American Family Insurance
Anncr:	La póliza que compres y los servicios corporativos están disponibles solamente en inglés.

233 North Michigan Avenue, 24th Floor, Chicago, Illinois 60601-5519 TEL (312) 565-7000 FAX (312) 565-7500 E-mail sanjose@sjadv.com
An Agency of The San Jose Network, Ltd.

FIGURE 14.6 This "Carmelita and Guadalupe" :60 (combined :50 + :10) radio script was created by The San Jose Group for American Family Insurance. Script courtesy of The San Jose Group.

CLIENT	American Family Insurance
PRODUCT	Auto/Home
TITLE	Carmelita/Guadalupe - Bicultural
LENGTH	:50-10 OR
SCRIPT NO.	**ISCI 003591 (Back Translation)**
DATE	5/8/09 (as produced)

RADIO CONTINUITY

CARMELITA

Music:	Emotional/Inspirational.
Young Woman:	My parents are very traditional finally decided to move out.
Young Woman:	But I will take their traditions with me.
Young Woman:	So when I got into a small accident, I had Carmelita, my parents' American Family Insurance agent, who is now my agent too.
Anncr:	Visit www.amfamlatino.com
Jingle:	American Family Insurance.
Anncr:	The policy you purchase and corporate services are available only in English.

GUADALUPE

Music:	Emotional/Inspirational music up and under.
Dad:	I'm helping my son learn baseball.
Dad:	He hit the satellite.
Dad:	Which then slid off the roof, broke the window and landed on the car.
Dad:	Good thing we have our insurance policy for many years with American Family Insurance and our agent, Guadalupe. She catches everything, making sure our home policy covers everything we need.
Anncr:	Visit www.amfamlatino.com
Jingle:	American Family Insurance
Anncr:	The policy you purchase and corporate services are available only in English.

233 North Michigan Avenue, 24th Floor, Chicago, Illinois 60601-5519 TEL (312) 565-7000 FAX (312) 565-7500 E-mail sanjose@sjadv.com
An Agency of The San Jose Network, Ltd.

FIGURE 14.6 continued

the radio time slot. Here, the agent was also a woman, "Guadalupe," which also served to connect the two spots.

Also in 2009, an AFI TV commercial called "Baseball" in English targeted the general market in 19 states. It also spoke to the Hispanic market with minor revisions ("El Batazo" or "The Hit," Figure 14.7, Figure 14.8). This multilingual, multimedia campaign ran in print, TV, digital, and radio. The one medium that ran only in Spanish was radio. Although the Spanish version used most of the same visuals from the general market campaign, the copy featured a different product, the ending (closing line) changed to address a Hispanic audience, and some of the titles of the TV spots were different. For example, it was "Baseball" in the English campaign and "El Batazo" in the Spanish one. The spot married the "José and Guadalupe" radio commercial by bringing back the baseball theme. Again, it focused on a *global truth*: kids break windows and other things when they play baseball. It's just expected. The visual showed the dad pitching to his son. Something many dads have done, making the scene easily relatable. The announcer talked about how hard parents work to protect their children by building a "world around them." The spot continued with "when your world needs a little extra protection," you can count on American Family Insurance to help. The last line reinforced the AFI promise: "Protecting your dreams, your family, your world." It closed by referring back to everything parents treasure.

Client: American Family Insurance
Product: Home Insurance
Title: El Batazo
Length: 30 sec
ISCI code: 003545/ 003546
Script No: AFI1279 / AFI3249
Date: 3/25/09

El Batazo

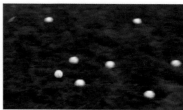

VO: En American Family Insurance sabemos lo mucho que te esfuerzas por tu familia.

VO: At American Family Insurance we know how hard you work for your family.

FIGURE 14.7 This "El Batazo" ("The Hit") :30 TV storyboard was created by The San Jose Group for American Family Insurance. Storyboard courtesy of The San Jose Group.

VO: Entendemos los sacrificios que has hecho para construir un mundo seguro para ellos.

VO: We understand the sacrifices you have made to build a safe world around them.

VO: Y cuando tu mundo necesita un poco mas de protección,

VO: And when your world needs a little extra protection,

FIGURE 14.7 continued

VO: American Family Insurance está ahí para ayudar.

VO: American Family Insurance is there to help.

VO: Protegiendo tus sueños, tu familia, tu mundo.

VO: Protecting your dreams, your family, your world.

233 North Michigan Avenue, 24th Floor, Chicago Illinois, 60601-5519 TEL (312) 565-7000 FAX (312)565-7500 E-mail sanjose@sjadv.com
An Agency of The San Jose Network, Ltd.

FIGURE 14.7 continued

FIGURE 14.8 This "El Batazo" ("The Hit") :30 TV screenshot was created by The San Jose Group for American Family Insurance. Screenshot courtesy of The San Jose Group.

In the TV spots, like "3 Kids" (Figure 14.9), the mom talked about feeling as if she lives in her car. She was always taking her kids to different activities. Like ballet, skating, swimming. What mom doesn't? This comment expressed a common feeling of a mom being the family chauffeur, and again, stating another *global truth*. The mom explained how AFI customizes its plans to fit her family's needs and budget, making her life less chaotic. Then, she saw that her son brought along his pet snake in the car. And suddenly she realized the chaos began again. Notice that there were alternate scenes that the agency created, so they could easily modify the spot.

In the English version of the "3 Kids" spot (Figure 14.9), the mom spoke about how easy it was to switch policies. The spot closed the same way again, saying that with AFI her life was tranquil. Then, she saw her son's snake and said, "Almost." You can see how similar the two versions were. The second one focused a little more on the ease of changing policies.

When you're the one creating commercials try to apply creative recycling. That way you can stretch the client's budget. When the concept is based on a *universal truth*, you may not have to change very much from language to language, as is the case here. Now, take a look at the screenshot in (Figure 14.10), so you can see how the illustrated storyboard came to life with real actors.

In the next TV spot, "Nadie Como Tu" (Figure 14.11), the copy focused on how unique everyone is. There may be six billion people in the world, but there's only one you. This is an important point because people like to be recognized as individuals and not lumped together into one group. By stating another *global truth*, "There's no one exactly like you," the copy makes viewers feel special. It closes explaining that your insurance policy needs to be as unique as you are. Notice how the word "but" is "billboarded" (emphasized, as discussed in chapter 6) because it's repeated three times before the copy continues "there's no one just like you."

The "Nadie Como Tu" radio spot (Figure 14.12) continues or spins out the "unique" concept in the TV commercial. The TV copy is slightly modified to work in radio, where there are no visual references. As discussed in chapter 6, radio is "theater of the mind," so you must create images and scenes in the listeners' imagination. Everything presented must be exceptionally clear to the audience. Remember to read the copy aloud so you can hear it as the listener would.

Although this spot was never produced in English, you can see how the English back-translation of "Nadie Como Tu" (Figure 14.13) matches the Spanish script very closely. If you speak Spanish, take a close look and compare the two. Notice the jingle lyrics that run up and under (throughout the spot, as discussed in chapter 6). Did you remember that the part of the copy that is spoken inside the jingle is called the doughnut (also in chapter 6)?

Now let's look at another multimedia campaign for SPAM, created by The San Jose Group: "Imagínalo. Prepáralo." This was the first time the product specifically targeted the Hispanic market. In the first year alone, usage by this audience increased 3%.[15] According to George L. San Jose, the product had around 87% awareness in the general market. The idea was to extend product consumption into a new market. Much like the AFI campaigns, mentioned above, SPAM was based on *global truths*. San Jose explained:

All of the creative development happened from that messaging platform. It was about owning the moment when you're hungry. If you've seen the spots you've seen people running around with these thought bubbles over their heads as they thought of what they wanted to eat.

CLIENT: <u>AMERICAN FAMILY INSURANCE</u>	
PRODUCT: <u>AUTO</u>	
TITLE: <u>3 KIDS VERSION A</u>	
LENGTH: <u>:30 TV</u>	
AD CODE: <u>004443</u>	
REV. DATE: <u>07/2010</u>	

TV Continuity

VIDEO		AUDIO
Two boys, 13 and 8, and a little girl, 6, run into a minivan where mom waits with a smile. The oldest dressed like a skater, the middle boy for karate and the cute girl for ballet. SUPER: Mi póliza llamada "Que vida la mía". **SUPER: My policy called "What a life the one I lead."**		MOM: Cuando tienes tres hijos vives en el coche. ***When you have three kids, you live in your car.***
In fast motion we see the minivan dropping the kids off at school, then picking them up. The footage is accelerated to illustrate the hectic mood.		MOM: De la casa al parque de patinetas, del parque a nadar, de nadar al ballet. ***From home to the skate park, from the skate park to swimming, from swimming to ballet.***
The woman is at the skate park watching her son skate with her friends. We hear a female voice that recommends American Family Insurance.		MOM: Y a la hora de cambiar mi póliza de seguro, decidí por irme con American Family Insurance. Mis amigas me los recomendaron porque cuentan con pólizas de auto, casa, vida y más. ***And when I had to switch auto insurance, I decided to go with American Family Insurance. My friends recommended them because they have auto, home, life and more.***
We see the whole family, even dad, inside an American Family Insurance office looking over some policy brochures.		MOM: Y crearon para mí una póliza diseñada para mis nuevas necesidades y presupuesto… ***And they created for me a policy designed to fit my new needs and budget…***

FIGURE 14.9 This "3 Kids" (Version A) :30 storyboard was created by The San Jose Group for American Family Insurance. Storyboard courtesy of The San Jose Group.

VIDEO		AUDIO

Through a series of fast paced intercuts, we now see through the minivan's rearview mirror the kids with a puppy and a hamster. On another scene the preteen kid sits on the driver's seat, mom gives him a look to scoot over.

We now see the middle child playing with a garden snake in the back seat of the minivan.

MOM: Gracias a American Family Insurance, mi vida es tranquila. ***Thanks to American Family Insurance, my life is a tranquil one.***

We see mom running out of the minivan, scared because of the snake.

MOM: Casi. ***Almost.***

Close with American Family Insurance Camera Card, 800 number and URL.

MUSIC: Jingle over and out.

FIGURE 14.9 continued

Alternate scenes

VIDEO		AUDIO

Now we see mom in the dining room on her computer looking at the Amfamlatino.com website.

MOM: Y crearon para mí una póliza diseñada para mis nuevas necesidades y presupuesto...
And they created for me a policy designed to fit my new needs and budget...

Inside the living room in the house, we see the American Family Insurance agent going over some custom policies.

MOM: Y crearon para mí una póliza diseñada para mis nuevas necesidades y presupuesto...
And they created for me a policy designed to fit my new needs and budget...

233 North Michigan Avenue, 24th Floor, Chicago, Illinois 60601-5519   TEL (312) 565-7000 FAX (312) 565-7500 E-mail sanjose@sjadv.com
An Agency of The an Jose Network, Ltd.

FIGURE 14.9 continued

TV Continuity

CLIENT:	AMERICAN FAMILY INSURANCE
PRODUCT:	AUTO
TITLE:	NADIE COMO TÚ
LENGTH:	:30 TV
AD CODE:	004442
REV. DATE:	07/2010

VIDEO		AUDIO
SUPER: La póliza llamada: "NADIE COMO TÚ" Open with millions of images of different people driving around. A man screams into a megaphone and the sound gets blasted through speakers.		LYRICS: En el mundo hay un microfono y altos parlantes. Hay 6 mil millones de habitantes. pero, pero, pero... No hay nadie como tú...
The speakers morph into car stereo speakers where we see a family singing along with the song.		... Hay mentalidades horizontales, verticales y diagonales.
We see a team bus that carries a soccer team, all the players are celebrating hanging outside the window. A car with a 30 year old man passes the bus and cheers them on.		LYRICS: ...medallas, trofeos y copas mundiales...
A business man is about to get into an expensive convertible while a college girl passes him in a classic VW Bug.		Hay Don Quijotes y Dulcineas.

233 North Michigan Avenue, 24th Floor, Chicago, Illinois 60601-5519 TEL (312) 565-7000 FAX (312) 565-7500 E-mail sanjose@sjadv.com
An Agency of The San Jose Network, Ltd.

FIGURE 14.10 This "Nadie Como Tú" :30 storyboard was created by The San Jose Group for American Family Insurance. Storyboard courtesy of The San Jose Group.

VIDEO		AUDIO
Inside another car we focus on a newborn that is just waking up, and his mom looks at him from the front seat of a car, as dad is driving. We focus on the dad and as we zoom out…		En este mundo hay mucha gente…
…we see millions of squares of different Latin people all driving different cars and doing different things. We finally focus on a couple in a car who park in front of an American Family Insurance office and walk in holding hands.	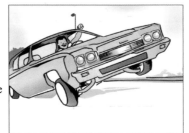	pero, pero, pero… No hay nadie como tú…
Behind them we see a couple in a truck passing with a sign that reads, "Just married" We then see an American Family Insurance Agent waving them goodbye.		AVO: En American Family Insurance tenemos pólizas de auto, casa y mucho más tan úncicas como cada uno de ustedes.
Close with American Family Insurance Camera Card, 800 number and URL.		AVO: ¿Tú póliza de seguro es tan única cómo tu familia? MUSIC: Jingle over and out.

233 North Michigan Avenue, 24th Floor, Chicago, Illinois 60601-5519 TEL (312) 565-7000 FAX (312) 565-7500 E-mail sanjose@sjadv.com
An Agency of The San Jose Network, Ltd.

FIGURE 14.10 continued

CLIENT: AMERICAN FAMILY INSURANCE

PRODUCT: AUTO

TITLE: NADIE COMO TÚ BACK TRANSLATION

LENGTH: :30 TV

AD CODE: 004442

REV. DATE: 07/2010

TV Continuity

VIDEO		AUDIO

SUPER: La póliza llamada: "NADIE COMO TÚ"
Open with millions of images of different people driving around.
A man screams into a megaphone and the sound gets blasted through speakers.

LYRICS: In this world there are microphone and speakers. There are 6 billion people, but, but, but, there's no one just like you...

The speakers morph into car stereo speakers where we see a family singing along with the song.

There are horizontal, vertical and diagonal mentalities.

We see a team bus that carries a soccer team, all the players are celebrating hanging outside the window. A car with a 30 year old man passes the bus and cheers them on.

LYRICS: ...there's medals, trophies and World Cups...

A business man is about to get into an expensive convertible while a college girl passes him in a classic VW Bug.

There are Don Quixotes and Dulcineas.

FIGURE 14.10 continued

VIDEO		AUDIO
Inside another car we focus on a newborn that is just waking up, and his mom looks at him from the front seat of a car, as dad is driving. We focus on the dad and as we zoom out…		There are a lot of people in this world.
…we see millions of squares of different Latin people all driving different cars and doing different things. We finally focus on a couple in a car who park in front of an American Family Insurance office and walk in holding hands.		But, but but, there's no one, like you.
Behind them we see a couple in a truck passing with a sign that reads, "Just married" We then see an American Family Insurance Agent waving them goodbye.		AVO: At American Family Insurance we have individual policies for home, auto and more as unique as each one of you.
Close with American Family Insurance Camera Card, 800 number and URL.		AVO: Is your policy as unique as your family? MUSIC: Jingle over and out.

AMERICAN FAMILY
INSURANCE ®
Toda tu protección bajo un solo techo"

1–800–692–6326
www.protegefamilias.com

233 North Michigan Avenue, 24th Floor, Chicago, Illinois 60601-5519 TEL (312) 565-7000 FAX (312) 565-7500 E-mail sanjose@sjadv.com
An Agency of The San Jose Network, Ltd.

FIGURE 14.10 continued

FIGURE 14.11 This "3 Kids" (Version A) :30 TV screenshot was created by The San Jose Group for American Family Insurance. Screenshot courtesy of The San Jose Group.

The thought bubbles were the *repeat graphic element* that visually connected all of the campaign elements, from TV (Figure 14.14), product integration (Figure 14.15), and out-of-home messages in billboards (Figure 14.16), bus shelters (Figure 14.17), and bus sides (Figure 14.18) to print ads (Figure 14.19, Figure 14.20). The slogan, which drove the overall message was direct and clear: "Imagínalo. Prepáralo." ("Imagine it. Prepare it."). It works equally well in all media. The TV spots used the *play on word* technique (#4, as discussed in chapter 4) in Spanish. One print ad (not shown) and a TV spot (Figure 14.14) used an image of "Huevos SPAMcheros," a reference to "Huevos Rancheros," a popular breakfast dish. In the two-minute *product integration*, "SPAMTADAS," the product was integrated (placed as part of the story) into a TV show. The coined word "SPAMTADAS" is a play off "empanadas," a favorite pastry stuffed with meat, cheese, chicken or spinach.

Look at how the slogan "Imagínalo. Prepáralo." easily lent itself to a billboard application (Figure 14.16). The message was also modified for a print ad: "Imagínalo. Saboréalo." ("Imagine it. Taste it."). The ad showed the bus side visual (Figure 14.19) and a coupon. Look at how little copy was needed to get the message across. The only area with copy was the coupon. A second coupon ad, with the headline "Tortas SPAM" ("SPAM sandwiches," Figure 14.20), visually married to the campaign, but broke away from the verbal message. Besides the coupon, however, it featured a recipe and clear cooking directions, showing how to use the product.One of the billboards used language-neutral adjectives to describe the product. "Versátil. Práctico. Delicioso." (Figure 14.21). The Spanish was so close to the English, no translation was needed. It could target multiple audiences with just three words, while presenting the benefits. Who doesn't want food that's versatile, practical, and delicious? You can see the entire campaign at http://www .thesanjosegroup.com/work/spam/.

Radio Copy

| CLIENT American Family Insurance |
| PRODUCT INSTITUTIONAL |
| TITLE NADIE VERSION 2 SPAN |
| LENGTH 60 sec. |
| SCRIPT NO. (Ad Code: 004436) |
| DATE 7/10 (Rev. Date) |

NADIE COMO TÚ LYRICS UNDER THROUGHOUT

En el mundo hay mentalidades horizontales,
verticales y diagonales.
Hay micrófonos,
y altoparlantes,
hay seis mil millones de habitantes,
hay gente ordinaria y gente elegante,
pero pero pero...
No hay nadie como tú.

ANNOUNCER:
En American Family Insurance sabemos que nuestros clientes son únicos, nuestros agentes
también y nuestras pólizas son tan únicas como la gente que protegemos. Nosotros trabajamos
contigo y tu familia para que puedan escoger entre más de 300 productos y servicios para crear
pólizas echas a la medida y proteger todo éso por lo cual han trabajado tanto. Entre nuestros
productos contamos con descuentos para gente que acaba de comprar casa nueva y grandes
descuentos para gente que combina sus pólizas.

Sabemos que eres diferente.

¿Tu póliza de seguro es tan única como tú?

Llámanos al 1-800-692-6326 o visítanos en protegefamilas.com

LYRICS CONTINUE AND LEAD TO STINGER AND TAG LINE OUT.

LYRICS:

Pero pero pero...
No hay nadie como tú.

233 North Michigan Avenue, 24th Floor, Chicago, Illinois 60601-5519 TEL (312) 565-7000 FAX (312) 565-7500 E-mail sanjose@sjadv.com
An Agency of The San Jose Network, Ltd.

FIGURE 14.12 This "Nadie Como Tú" (Version 2 – Spanish) :60 radio script was created by The San Jose Group for American Family Insurance. Script courtesy of The San Jose Group.

Radio Copy

CLIENT	American Family Insurance
PRODUCT	INSTITUTIONAL
TITLE	NADIE VERSION 2 ENG
LENGTH	60 sec.
SCRIPT NO.	(Ad Code: 004436)
DATE	7/10 (Rev. Date)

NADIE COMO TÚ LYRICS UNDER THROUGHOUT

- *In the world there are horizontal mentalities,*
- *[as well as] vertical and diagonal [ones]*
- *There are microphones,*
- *and loudspeakers,*
- *there are six billion inhabitants,*
- *there are ordinary people and elegant people,*
- *But but but...*
- *There is no one like you.*

ANNOUNCER:

At American Family Insurance we know our clients are unique, our agents one of a kind and our policies are as unique as the people we protect. We work with you and your family so you can choose from over 300 products and services to create your own custom policies to protect all the things you've worked so hard for. Among our products we have discounts for people that just bought a new home and great discounts for people that combine their policies.

We know you are different.

Is your policy as unique as you are?

Call us at 1-800-692-6326 or visit us at protegefamilias.com

LYRICS CONTINUE AND LEAD TO STINGER AND TAG LINE OUT.

LYRICS:

- *But but but...*
- *There is no one like you.*

233 North Michigan Avenue, 24th Floor, Chicago, Illinois 60601-5519 TEL (312) 565-7000 FAX (312) 565-7500 E-mail sanjose@sjadv.com
An Agency of The San Jose Network, Ltd.

FIGURE 14.13 This "Nadie Como Tú" (Version 2 – English) :60 radio script was created by The San Jose Group for American Family Insurance. Script courtesy of The San Jose Group.

TV SCRIPT

CLIENT	SPAM
PRODUCT	SPAM
TITLE	HUEVOSPAMCHEROS
LENGTH	:30 SECS
SCRIPT NO.	1177
DATE	2007

MAN: ¡Oye!

LADY: Hola mi cielo.

            [Imagínalo, Prepáralo.]

MAN: *Hey!*

LADY: *Hello darling.*

            [Imagine, Prepare it.]

233 North Michigan Avenue, 24th Floor, Chicago, Illinois 60601-5519   TEL (312) 565-7000   FAX (312) 565-7500   E-mail sanjose@sjadv.com
An Agency of The San Jose Network, Ltd.

FIGURE 14.14 This "Huevos SPAMcheros" (play on words for "Huevos Rancheros," a popular, Mexican specialty, breakfast egg dish) :30 TV spot was created by The San Jose Group for SPAM. Script courtesy of The San Jose Group.

TV SCRIPT

<table>
<tr><td>CLIENT SPAM</td></tr>
<tr><td>PRODUCT **SPAM**</td></tr>
<tr><td>TITLE SPAMTADAS® PRODUCT INTEGRATION</td></tr>
<tr><td>LENGTH 2 MINUTES</td></tr>
<tr><td>SCRIPT NO. 1177</td></tr>
<tr><td>DATE 2007</td></tr>
</table>

LADY: Gracias chulada! Cuando termino con mi trabajo me dan unas ganas de comer increíbles, y ahorita se me antoja un SPAM guisado con arroz. ¡Mmm... Delicioso!
Lo bueno es que siempre tengo SPAM cerca, es perfecto! Por que con una lata puedo complacer cualquier antojo.
Ahora mismo vamos a preparar unas riquísimas SPAMtadas ósea, unas tostadas de SPAM, lo primero que necesitamos es nuestra lata de SPAM. Es bueno tener varias latas ahí en casa para que se ahorre bastante tiempo.

Las vamos a cortar en rebanadas, así como lo tenemos por aquí, también necesitamos seis tortillas, ya las tenemos por acá, ¼ de taza de aceite vegetal, una lata de frijoles pintos fritos, aquí ya los tenemos calientitos, también tenemos nuestras rebanadas de aguacate, tenemos 2 tazas de crema por aquí, salsa fresca, dos tazas de lechuga ya cortadita y también tenemos nuestro queso fresco, ya listo.

En un sartén vamos a poner el aceite y vamos a dorar las rebanadas de SPAM ahí adentro, las vamos a colocar afuera, después de eso en otro sartén vamos a poner las tortillas y dorarla a que este bien doradita para que así este fuerte. Allí cuando la vamos a sacar la tortilla vamos a embarrarle los frijoles, le vamos a colocar las rebanadas de SPAM y le vamos a agregar nuestro aguacate, nuestro quesito, lechuga y nuestra salsa fresca y eso hace seis SPAMtadas. Ya listos para probarlo? Vámonos ¿haber como salio? ¡Mmm... Riquísimo! La verdad muy bien.

Vieron que rápido fue para prepáralo, es solo cuestión que usted se lo imagine, prepare y los saboree. Riquísimo!

Por que con SPAM es tan rápido preparar estos platillos, que hasta yo, que no tengo mucho tiempo para cocinar lo hago. Puedo preparar unos platillos deliciosos en cuestión de minutos!

Hey ven pa acá! Hay discúlpenme, discúlpenme, perdón! Hasta luego y que disfrute de sus platillos con SPAM.

233 North Michigan Avenue, 24th Floor, Chicago, Illinois 60601-5519   TEL (312) 565-7000   FAX (312) 565-7500   E-mail sanjose@sjadv.com
An Agency of The San Jose Network, Ltd.

FIGURE 14.15 This "SPAMTADAS" (play on words for "empanadas," a delicious pastry stuffed with savory meat or fruit) 2:00 (2-minute) TV product integration was created by The San Jose Group for SPAM. Script courtesy of The San Jose Group.

TV SCRIPT

CLIENT	SPAM
PRODUCT	SPAM
TITLE	SPAMTADAS® PRODUCT INTEGRATION
LENGTH	2 MINUTES
SCRIPT NO.	1177
DATE	2007

LADY: Thanks Darling. When I'm done with work, I feel like eating, and right now I am craving a SPAM® stew with Rice.
mmm… delicious!

The good thing is that I am always stocked with SPAM, it is perfect. Because with one can I can satisfy any craving.
And right now we are going to prepare some delicious SPAMTADAS®, what I mean is, SPAM tostadas, the first thing we need is a can of SPAM. It is good to have a lot of cans at home, so you can save time.

We will cut them in slices, just like we have here. We will also need 6 tortillas, we have them over here, ¼ cup of vegetable oil, as well as a can of fried pinto beans, here we have them all nice and hot. We also have our avocado slices, we have 2 cups of sour cream over here, fresh salsa, 2 cups of chopped lettuce, we also have cheese, and done. Are you ready?

We will put the oil in the pan and we will fry the SPAM slices inside, we will place them outside, after that, in a different pan we will put the tortillas to fry, until they are hard and crispy. When we are about to take the tortilla out, we will spread the beans, we will place the SPAM slices and we will add the avocado, our cheese, lettuce and our fresh salsa and that makes 6 SPAMTADAS®. Are you ready to taste them? Let's see, how did they come out? Mmm…delicious. Honestly very good.

Did you see how long it took to prepare? It is only a matter of imagining, preparing and tasting. Delicious!

With SPAM these dishes can be prepared fast, even I who doesn't have much time to cook, I do it. I can prepare delicious meals in a matter of minutes.

Hey, come over here! Oh I'm sorry, so sorry. See you later and enjoy your meals with SPAM.

English Copy Disclaimer:
Please note the English back-translation in this document may have some discrepancies due to language barriers, lost in translation and/or nuances of the Spanish language. We do our best to capture the essence of the Spanish language back to English. However, at times the English version may read different when it is being translated back from the Spanish language document. Be assured the Spanish is accurate and conveys the nuances of the language, traditions, cultural representation and of your objectives/strategies.

233 North Michigan Avenue, 24th Floor, Chicago, Illinois 60601-5519 TEL (312) 565-7000 FAX (312) 565-7500 E-mail sanjose@sjadv.com
An Agency of The San Jose Network, Ltd.

FIGURE 14.15 continued

FIGURE 14.16 This "Imagínalo. Prepáralo." ("Imagine it. Taste it.") billboard was created by The San Jose Group for SPAM. Image courtesy of The San Jose Group.

FIGURE 14.17 This "Imagínalo. Prepáralo." ("Imagine it. Prepare it.") bus shelter was created by The San Jose Group for SPAM. Image courtesy of The San Jose Group.

FIGURE 14.18 This "Imagínalo. Prepáralo." ("Imagine it. Prepare it.") bus side was created by The San Jose Group for SPAM. Image courtesy of The San Jose Group.

FIGURE 14.19 This "Imagínalo. Saboréalo." ("Imagine it. Taste it.") coupon-featured print ad was created by The San Jose Group for SPAM. Image courtesy of The San Jose Group.

Tortas SPAM™

Ingredientes

1	lata de **SPAM**® Classic (12 onzas)
4	bolillos
1	taza de frijoles pintos calientes (opcional)
1	taza de queso fresco en polvo
2	tazas de lechuga picada
1	tomate grande rebanado
1	aguacate rebanado (opcional)
*	rebanadas de chiles jalapeños en vinagre
*	sal al gusto
*	salsa casera (opcional)

Preparación

Corte **SPAM**® en rebanadas delgadas y fríalas hasta que se doren de ambos lados. Corte el pan a la mitad y tuéstelo o dórelo a la parrilla con mantequilla si lo desea. Unte la base del pan con los frijoles refritos. Cubra cada uno con 4 rebanadas de **SPAM**® caliente y espolvoree un poco de queso. Reparta la lechuga, el tomate y el aguacate en porciones iguales sobre las tortas. Adorne cada una con 2 o 3 rebanadas de jalapeño. Sazone con sal al gusto. Coloque la cubierta del pan en la torta y presione. Corte las tortas a la mitad usando un cuchillo afilado. Sírvalas en platos individuales con jalapeños adicionales y salsa casera. Para 4 tortas.

FIGURE 14.20 This "Tortas SPAM." ("SPAM sandwiches.") coupon-featured print ad was created by The San Jose Group for SPAM. Image courtesy of The San Jose Group.

FIGURE 14.21 This "Versátil. Práctico. Delicioso." ("Versatile. Practical. Delicious.") billboard was created by The San Jose Group for SPAM. Image courtesy of The San Jose Group.

San Jose identified a common copywriting error is writing too much or too little copy. Here's what happens as a result:

> You lose half of the audience in the sea of minutia, or they do not provide enough and they expect consumers to connect the dots by themselves. Again, you didn't kick on the theater of the mind your creative message is wasted. So, how do I give you enough to get your movie to play? When you're visualizing your movie and you're producing your movie, my product is in it. Apart from that, whether I use TV, radio, print, out-of-home or digital, I've accomplished the mission. Make it relevant and write to the medium.[16]

The same principles apply whether you're creating a campaign in two languages or more. Encouraging the audience to see how the product or service fits into and improves

ADVICE FROM THE PROS 14.1 Five writing tips from George L. San Jose

1   Each consumer message was based on a strategic, creative foundation.

2   The strategies for each medium are going to be quite different in terms of how to write for radio, versus how to write for TV, versus how to write for print.

3   Avoid the executional *faux pas*. Those are messages based on a good creative strategy, but are not in sync with the attributes of the medium.

4   The language has to be in the right cultural context. That's the key denominator.

5   Give the prospective customer enough information to kick their theater of the mind on. That's the best copywriting that you can write.[17]

their lives is key to any "hit-them-in-the-core" communication. Solve problems. Promise benefits. Create an interactive dialogue. Show them the brand "gets" them. And you'll create a loyal consumer.

Creating international campaigns

Looking back at chapter 7, where we also discussed the power of universal truths, it's clear to see how a globally understood message can go beyond cultural and geographic borders. The key is to create an idea that can transcend parameters, shed restrictions, and be relevant to people everywhere. You need to be thinking of writing in the international language of *benefits, needs,* and *desires,* expressed as specific *strategies,* as mentioned in chapters 1 and 2.

Keep in mind that studying differences in cultures, as you would examine differences and similarities in audiences, will help you create appropriate messages for specific markets. Strategists must look to create a message that will lend itself to *transcreation* in various languages. Important attention must be paid to develop a concept than can *spin out* in multiple media as well as multiple cultures. Noticing what is effective in the US may or may not be transferable to France, Argentina, or China. Copywriters are challenged to look for broad messages that hit a universal truth in people around the world for a greater chance at success.

Seeing how concepts move into other markets

One recognizable brand is Aflac, created by the copywriter and art director team of Tom Amico and Eric David from the Kaplan Thaler Group (as mentioned in chapter 7). What might not be commonly known is that 80% of its business is in Japan. However, after the Aflac Duck campaign was so successful in the US – with tripling in just four years – it was adopted and executed by the insurance company's ad agency in Japan. *Advertising Age* named the icon, which has 94% brand awareness (up from 8% to 10%), the second most popular brand in history. Sales have reached over a billion dollars with "a persnickety Duck who just wanted to be heard."[18] The fact that the client was so eager to have people know the company name, the CEO's creative directive was: "I want people to remember the name of my company even if you have to have a naked man on a roof shouting it."[19] Well, how about a naked, yes naked, Duck that's as endearing as it is unforgettable?

Taking a tagline into other countries

When writers create a simple, instantly understandable, and easily adoptable slogan, it can stay in its original language and transcend borders. One tagline, "Das Auto," created by Volkswagen, was first introduced in Germany at the 2007 International Automobile Association conference in Frankfurt, and then included in campaigns developed by DDB for Mexico, India, Singapore, and elsewhere.

> My main piece of advice is to always do something different. **BEN WALKER, CREATIVE DIRECTOR, WIEDEN+KENNEDY, LONDON**[20]

The campaigns differed for each market, and the copy for each would be positioned from a distinctly different strategy and positioning. For example, one campaign might focus on new technology features. Another might focus on the launch of a brand new model. Nevertheless, the tagline accompanied all messages and stayed in its original German. It was so strong it didn't need translation. Everyone grasped "Das Auto" meant "The Car." It had a secondary meaning if you emphasized the first word "Das" or "The," implying it's "the car" to own. The subtle play on words strengthened the message and drove home the point that consumers who purchased a Volkswagen were getting the best car out there.

Most advertising messages across the world just used "Das Auto." However, in some markets, like India and Singapore, the brand name, Volkswagen, was included before "Das Auto" to strengthen brand awareness and recognition.[21]

Not only did "Das Auto" run in different countries, but it also appeared in multiple media, from print to TV and online worldwide. It's important to understand that each vehicle had its own specific positioning platform. Look at the visuals below (Figure 14.22, Figure 14.23, Figure 14.24, Figure 14.25) and see how this slogan was the foundation for all the following advertising vehicles.

Let's look at the copy in a few ads in two languages. We'll start with the ads that ran in Germany (in German and English). Then, we'll look at the ones that ran in India (in English). Finally, we'll examine one that ran in Mexico (in Spanish). You can see how the overall creative direction showcases features that are specific benefits to consumers: keyless entry, iPad connectivity, automatic battery recharging, and other technological advances. In these ads, consumers can instantly see why they should buy a new VW and enjoy the latest make-your-life- easier devices.

"Time out modern ice" (German, Figure 14.22)

Headline: Technische Geräte Haben Einen Ruhezustand. Menschen Jetzt Auch.

Subhead: Der neue Eos. Das Auszeitauto.

Copy: Manchmal muss man Dinge starten, um abzuschalten. Den neuen Eos zum Beispiel. Bereits das Einsteigen ist Entspannungssache und dank optionalem Keyless Access auch ohne Schlüssel möglich. Dafür ist danach fast alles möglich, um den Kopf wieder frei zu bekommen. Und während Sie auf Ihrer Fahrt wieder Energie tanken, sorgen die effizienten TSI-Motoren für noch weniger Tankstopps. Zusätzliche Informationen bietet Ihnen der neue Eos-Katalog für das iPad. Ab sofort kostenfrei im App Store erhältlich.

Call to Action: Vor der Auszeit noch einmal schnell ins Netz und die Auszeit-App herunterladen: www.eos-auszeit.de.

"Time out modern ice" (English, Figure 14.23)

Headline: Technical Devices Have a Standby Mode. People Now, Too.

Subhead: The New Eos. The Time-Off Car.

Copy: Sometimes you need to start things – to switch off. The new Eos, for example. Getting in is already pure relaxation and thanks to keyless access also possible without a key. After that, almost everything is possible to clear your head again. And while you're recharging your battery, the efficient TSI® engines ensure less refueling stops. Additional information can be found in the new Eos catalogue for the iPad. Now available for free on App Store.

Der neue Eos. Das Auszeitauto.

Manchmal muss man Dinge starten, um abzuschalten. Den neuen Eos zum Beispiel. Bereits das Einsteigen ist Entspannungssache und dank optionalem Keyless Access auch ohne Schlüssel möglich. Dafür ist durch das alles möglich, um den Kopf wieder frei zu bekommen. Und während Sie auf Ihrer Fahrt wieder Energie tanken, sorgen die effizienten TSI-Motoren für noch weniger Tankstopps. Zusätzliche Informationen bietet Ihnen der neue Eos-Katalog für das iPad. Ab sofort kostenfrei im App Store erhältlich.

Vor der Auszeit noch einmal schnell ins Netz und die Auszeit-App herunterladen: www.eos-auszeit.de

FIGURE 14.22 This "Eos Time Out Modern Ice" (in German) print ad was created by DDB Berlin for Volkswagen. Image courtesy of DDB Berlin. All rights reserved.

The new Eos. The time-off car.

Sometimes you need to start things – to switch off. The new Eos, for example. Getting in is already pure relaxation and thanks to keyless access also possible without a key. After that, almost everything is possible to clear your head again. And while you're recharging your battery, the efficient TSI® engines ensure less refuelling stops. Additional information can be found in the new Eos catalogue for the iPad. Now available for free on App Store.

So before taking your time off, quickly check the web and download the time-off app: www.eos-auszeit.de

FIGURE 14.23 This "Eos Time Out Modern Ice" (in English) print ad was created by DDB Berlin for Volkswagen. Image courtesy of DDB Berlin. All rights reserved.

Der neue Eos. Das Auszeitauto.

Insgeheim wissen wir es alle: So schön die virtuelle Welt auch ist, die echte Welt ist schöner – und im neuen Eos auch entspannender. Statt vieler offener Fenster im Browser genügt in ihm ein offenes Dach. Auch die optionalen Ledensitze bieten nicht nur eine besonders bequeme Sitzposition, sondern vor allem Halt. Und den könnten Sie brauchen. Dafür sorgen die dynamischen TSI-Motoren serienmäßig. Zusätzliche Informationen bietet Ihnen der neue Eos-Katalog für das iPad. Ab sofort kostenfrei im App Store erhältlich.

Vor der Auszeit noch einmal schnell ins Netz und die Auszeit-App herunterladen: www.eos-auszeit.de

Das Auto.

FIGURE 14.24 This "Eos Time Out Modern Coast" (in German) print ad was created by DDB Berlin for Volkswagen. Image courtesy of DDB Berlin. All rights reserved.

The new Eos. The time-off car.

Secretly we all know it: As beautiful as virtual reality may be, reality is way more stunning – and in the new Eos way more relaxing too. Instead of countless open windows in your browser, one open roof suffices there. In addition, the optional leather seats not only provide a particularly comfortable seating position but most of all secure hold. Which you will need. The standard dynamic TSI® engines will ensure this. Additional information can be found in the new Eos catalogue for the iPad. Now available for free on App Store.

So before taking your time off, quickly check the web and download the time-off app: www.eos-auszeit.de

Das Auto.

FIGURE 14.25 This "Eos Time Out Modern Coast" (in English) print ad was created by DDB Berlin for Volkswagen. Image courtesy of DDB Berlin. All rights reserved.

Call to action: So before taking your time off, quickly check the Web and download the time-off app: www.eos-auszeit.de

Pay attention to how the copy just begins. It jumps in without an introduction or preface. As mentioned in chapter 3, and in the radio and TV chapters (6 and 7), start in act two. "Sometimes you need to start things, to switch off." You don't know what the line means until you keep reading. Then, it's an "ah-ha!" moment. You think to yourself, "Oh, I get it. I need to start my car to shut off the chaos around me and the noise in my head." Immediately, you're hit with all the ways you can relax and clear your mind as soon as you start your engine. It makes driving sound pleasurable and practically effortless.

"Time out modern coast" (German, Figure 14.24):

Headline: Die Datenautobahn Hat Millionen Spuren. Und Eine Ausfahrt.

Subhead: Der neue Eos. Das Auszeitauto.

Copy: Insgeheim wissen wir es alle: So schön die virtuelle Welt auch ist, die echte Welt ist schöner – und im neuen Eos auch entspannender. Statt vieler offener Fenster im Browser genügt in ihm ein offenes Dach. Auch die optinalen Ledersitze bieten nicht nur eine besonders bequeme Sitzposition, sondern vor allem Halt. Und den könnten Sie brauchen. Dafür sorgen die dynamischen TSI-Motoren serienmäßig. Zusätzliche Informationen bietet Ihnen der neue Eos-Katalog für das iPad. Ab sofort kostenfrei im App Store erhältlich.

Call to action: Vor der Auszeit noch einmal schnell ins Netz und die Auszeit-App herunterladen: www.eos-auszeit.de

Below is the English *transcreation*. (To remind you, that means the copy was recreated into English, not translated word-for-word.)

"Time out modern coast" (English, Figure 14.25)

Headline: The Information Highway Has Millions of Lanes. And One Exit.

Subhead: The New Eos. The Time-Off Car.

Copy: Secretly we all know it: As beautiful as virtual reality may be reality is way more stunning – and in the new Eos way more relaxing too. Instead of countless open windows in your browser, one open roof suffices there. In addition, the optional leather seats not only provide a particularly comfortable seating position but most of all secure hold. Which you will need. The standard dynamic TSI® engines will ensure this. Additional information can be found in the new Eos catalogue for the iPad. Now available for free on App Store.

Call to action: So before taking your time off, quickly check the Web and download the time-off app: www.eos-auszeit.de

Again, the copy just begins with something we all intuitively sense. An unspoken, *global truth*: Nothing beats reality. There's nothing like getting in a car and driving off. No video game can duplicate the wind in your hair when you let the windows down. Or the feeling of freedom when you're behind the wheel. Here the copy reminds consumers of the pure joy of driving, especially in a well-designed, luxurious leather seat.

These ads (Figure 14.26, Figure 14.27, Figure 14.28, Figure 14.29) ran in India, also using the "Das Auto" slogan. Notice how the visuals represent images indicative of areas around the world: cattle in the roads in India, ostriches and rhinos in South Africa, and jungles in South America and other parts of the world.

The copy and slogan remains the same in each ad, while the stacked headlines (as discussed in chapter 4) and images change. Let's look at the four headlines first, then the

The Polo Road Handling Test

1. Gather buffaloes on both sides of the road.
2. Get a friend to whack them on their rear.
3. Drive as fast as you can through the herd.
4. Slip under the Polo as the herd thunders past you.

Or take our word for it.

The New Volkswagen Polo.

Renowned the world over for its superior quality and technology, Volkswagen brings the best of German engineering with the new Polo. Its 1.2L, 75 PS common rail diesel engine delivers exceptional performance. This together with its perfectly designed suspension system makes it one of the most agile cars around. It also has a 22.07 km/l* of fuel-efficiency, higher ground clearance, dual airbags and an Anti-lock Braking System. Of course, if you still have your doubts, take the ultimate test drive. And watch the new Polo live up to the test. **German engineering. Made in India.**

Terms and conditions apply. Accessories shown and features listed may not be part of standard equipment. Please visit your nearest dealer for further details. *Test results of rule 115 CMVR.

• 1.2L, 75 PS Petrol and Diesel engine • Tilt and telescopic steering wheel • Height-adjustable driver's seat • 60/40 folding rear seat • Remote opening and closing window • Boot opener in Volkswagen emblem • World Car of the Year 2010
Authorised Dealers: West Bengal: Kolkata: Volkswagen Kolkata: (033) 24014470-1, 9051498024, 9836107882; Orissa: Bhubaneshwar: Volkswagen Bhubaneshwar: (0674) 3251587, 9337013752.
Volkswagen India Assistance: 24x7. Anytime. Anywhere. Toll-free: 18001020909, 18002090909.

FIGURE 14.26 This "Polo Cattle" print ad was created by DDB India for Volkswagen. Image courtesy of DDB. All rights reserved.

The Polo Ground Clearance Test

1. Find a big ostrich egg and place it in front of the new Volkswagen Polo.
2. Drive over it.
3. Get out to find it intact.
4. Run for your life as Momma ostrich chases you.

Or take our word for it.

The New Volkswagen Polo.

Renowned the world over for its superior quality and technology, Volkswagen brings the best of German engineering with the new Polo. Its 15" alloy wheels and higher ground clearance can clear all the bumps and hurdles it encounters. It also has 22.07 km/l* of fuel-efficiency, dual airbags, and an Anti-lock Braking System. Of course, if you still have your doubts, take the ultimate test drive. And watch the new Polo live up to the test. **German engineering. Made in India.**

Terms and conditions apply. Accessories shown and features listed may not be part of standard equipment. Please visit your nearest dealer for further details. *Test results of rule 115 CMVR.

• 1.2L, 75 PS Petrol and Diesel engine • Tilt and telescopic steering wheel • Height-adjustable driver's seat • 60/40 folding rear seat • Remote opening and closing window • Boot opener in Volkswagen emblem • World Car of the Year 2010
Authorised Dealers: Delhi NCR: Volkswagen Delhi South: (011) 42077777, 9560492919; Volkswagen Delhi West: (011) 45340000, 9873421646; Gurgaon: Volkswagen Gurgaon: (0124) 4788888, 9540019801; Noida: Kashyap Vehicle Works: (0120) 2462601-5, 9910298881/3.
Volkswagen India Assistance: 24x7. Anytime. Anywhere. Toll-free: 18001020909, 18002090909.

FIGURE 14.27 This "Polo Ostrich" print ad was created by DDB India for Volkswagen. Image courtesy of DDB. All rights reserved.

The Polo Safety and Toughness Test

1. Drive your Volkswagen Polo to a wildlife sanctuary.
2. Search for the meanest looking rhino.
3. Inch the Polo towards the above-mentioned rhino.
4. Take a deep breath and blast the horn as hard as you can.

Or take our word for it.

The New Volkswagen Polo.

Renowned the world over for its superior quality and technology. Volkswagen brings the best of German engineering with the new Polo. It is built tough with a high-strength steel body, and its dual airbags along with an Anti-lock Braking System makes it one of the safest cars around. It also has 22.07 km/l* of fuel-efficiency, along with higher ground clearance and a perfectly designed suspension system. Of course, if you still have your doubts, take the ultimate test drive. And watch the new Polo live up to the test. German engineering. Made in India.

Terms and conditions apply. Accessories shown and features listed may not be part of standard equipment. Please visit your nearest dealer for further details. *Test results of rule 115 CMVR.

• 1.2L, 75 PS Petrol and Diesel engine • Tilt and telescopic steering wheel • Height-adjustable driver's seat • 60/40 folding rear seat • Remote opening and closing window • Boot opener in Volkswagen emblem • World Car of the Year 2010
Authorised Dealers: Chennai: Volkswagen Chennai: (044) 39175000, 24334115, 9600099960, 9500099882; Annanagar Showroom: (044) 30544000, 9600099940/37; **Coimbatore:** Volkswagen Coimbatore: (0422) 3223666/999; 9500944494, 9500944474.
Volkswagen India Assistance: 24x7. Anytime. Anywhere. Toll-free: 18001020909, 18002090909.

FIGURE 14.28 This "Polo Rhino" print ad was created by DDB India for Volkswagen. Image courtesy of DDB.

The Polo Mileage Test

1. Clean and dry out a 1.0 litre bottle of mineral water.
2. Fill it with petrol.
3. Transfer the petrol into the empty tank of your new Volkswagen Polo.
4. Cross your fingers and drive through a 17 km stretch of dangerous jungle.

Or take our word for it.

The New Volkswagen Polo.

Renowned the world over for its superior quality and technology. Volkswagen brings the best of German engineering with the new Polo. Its 1.2L petrol engine delivers best in-class fuel-efficiency of 17.24 km/l and 75 PS of power, making it one of the most economical cars around. It also has dual airbags, an Anti-lock Braking System and higher ground clearance. Of course, if you still have your doubts, take the ultimate test drive. And watch the new Polo live up to the test. German engineering. Made in India.

Terms and conditions apply. Accessories shown and features listed may not be part of standard equipment. Please visit your nearest dealer for further details. *Test results of rule 115 CMVR.

• 1.2L, 75 PS Petrol and Diesel engine • Tilt and telescopic steering wheel • Height-adjustable driver's seat • 60/40 folding rear seat • Remote opening and closing window • Boot opener in Volkswagen emblem • World Car of the Year 2010
Authorised Dealers: Ahmedabad: Volkswagen Ahmedabad: (079) 66120000, 9099044399, 9879591229; **Rajkot:** Volkswagen Rajkot: (0281) 6693333, 9825034882; **Surat:** Volkswagen Surat: (0261) 2211011, 9374395999, 9374396999; **Vadodara:** Volkswagen Vadodara: (0265) 6191900, 9687671637.
Volkswagen India Assistance: 24x7. Anytime. Anywhere. Toll-free: 18001020909, 18002090909.

FIGURE 14.29 This "Polo Tribal" print ad was created by DDB India for Volkswagen. Image courtesy of DDB.

body copy. See how each ad is related to the next, using the same reference to a different type of road test, followed by four steps, set one under the next, in a humorous *tone of voice*, closing with a repeated, clever closing line (set in italics below), or "*button*" mentioned in chapter 3). Usually the buttons appear at the end of the copy. Below is how they appear at the end of the stacked headlines.

"Polo Cattle" Ad (Figure 14.26)

Headline: The Polo Road Handling Test

1   Gather buffaloes on both sides of the road.
2   Get a friend to whack them on their rear.
3   Drive as fast as you can through the herd.
4   Slip under the Polo as the herd thunders past you.

Or take our word for it.

"Polo Ostrich" Ad (Figure 14.27)

Headline: The Polo Ground Clearance Test

1   Find a big ostrich egg and place it in front of the new Volkswagen Polo.
2   Drive over it.
3   Get out to find it intact.
4   Run for your life as Momma ostrich chases you.

Or take our word for it.

"Polo Rhino" Ad (Figure 14.28)

Headline: The Polo Safety and Toughness Test

1   Drive your Volkswagen Polo to a wildlife sanctuary.
2   Search for the meanest looking rhino.
3   Inch the Polo towards the above-mentioned rhino.
4   Take a deep breath and blast the horn as hard as you can.

Or take our word for it.

"Polo Tribal" Ad (Figure 14.29)

Headline: The Polo Mileage Test

1   Clean and dry out a 1.0 litre bottle of mineral water.
2   Fill it with petrol.
3   Transfer the petrol into the empty tank of your new Volkswagen Polo.
4   Cross your fingers and drive through a 17 km stretch of dangerous jungle.

Or take our word for it.

Copy: Renowned the world over for its superior quality and technology, Volkswagen brings the best of German engineering with the new Polo. Its 1.2L, 75 PS common rail diesel engine delivers exceptional performance. This together with its perfectly designed suspension system makes it one of the most agile cars around. It also has a 22.07 km/l of fuel-efficiency, higher ground clearance, dual airbags and an Anti-lock Braking System. *Of course, if you still have your doubts, take the ultimate test drive.* **And watch the new Polo live up to the test**. German engineering. Made in India.

Additional features are listed just under the disclaimer section, below a thin line. See how discretely the important line "World Car of the Year 2010" is included just next to the added features. Quietly stated, in a virtual whisper, for those who happen to catch it. The "*sig*" or signature lines (discussed in chapter 5), packed with *mandatory* text (phone numbers, websites, local authorized dealers, etc.), appear last after all the other copy.

Notice how the *call to action* (in italics above) is not set apart as in the German ads. It's built into the copy. It's answered with a promise that the Polo will live up to your expectations. That line (set in bold type) also uses ABA construction (as explained in chapter 3), where the closing line reinforces the headline to bring closure to the copy. In this case, the last two lines act as a punctuation mark. They remind readers that the Polo was developed through German engineering, yet made in the country where the ads run: India, to increase national pride. When you see the ad for Jetta, which ran in Mexico, notice the last two lines state German engineering and boast that the cars were made in Mexico for the whole world.

The "Jetta" ad (Figure 14.30) talks about a *universal truth*: how everyone likes being a step ahead. How people like to be leaders rather than followers. And how they like being "up with" (informed about) the latest trends. The English *transcreation* is provided below for easy reference. The copy is almost the same in both languages and is easy to understand with a basic comprehension of Spanish.

Headline: Nuevo Jetta. El siguiente paso. (In English: New Jetta. The next step.)

Copy: Siempre es mejor estar un paso adelante, construir caminos, marcar tendencias, siempre es mejor ser seguido, que ir siguiendo; no hay duda, siempre es mejor ser los primeros en dar el siguiente paso. Por eso, estamos seguros de que te va a gustar el nuevo Jetta con su motor de 170 HP, un diseño innovador de carácter deportivo, equipado de serie con Bluetooth® y MDI (conexión multimedia para iPod®), entre muchas otras cosas que te harán entender por qué el nuevo Jetta está un paso adelante. Con orgullo, de México para todo el mundo.

Call to action: Ve a tu concesionaria más cercana y descubre cómo dar el siguiente paso. (In English: Go to your nearest dealer and discover how to take the next step.)

Copy in English: It's always better to be one step ahead, to blaze new trails, to set trends. It's always better to be followed, than to be following. Without a doubt, it's better to be first, to be one step ahead. For that reason, we are sure you will love the new Jetta with its 170 horsepower, innovative, sporty design, equipped with Bluetooth® and MDI (multimedia iPod connection), among many other features that will make you see why the new Jetta is a step ahead. With pride, from Mexico for the entire world.

The slogan is the glue that unifies all of these campaigns that ran across the world in print, on TV, and online. One slogan. One voice. One big message: the benefits of owning a Volkswagen.

> "
> Most original thinking isn't even verbal. It requires a groping experimentation with ideas, governed by intuitive hunches and inspired by the unconscious. **DAVID OGILVY, FOUNDER OF OGILVY & MATHER (ORIGINALLY HEWITT, OGILVY, BENSON & MATHER)**[22]

elsiguientepaso.mx

Nuevo Jetta. El siguiente paso.

Siempre es mejor estar un paso adelante, construir caminos, marcar tendencias, siempre es mejor ser seguido, que ir siguiendo; no hay duda, siempre es mejor ser los primeros en dar el siguiente paso. Por eso, estamos seguros de que te va a gustar el nuevo Jetta con su motor de 170 HP, un diseño innovador de carácter deportivo, equipado de serie con Bluetooth® y MDI (conexión multimedia para iPod®), entre muchas otras cosas que te harán entender por qué el nuevo Jetta está un paso adelante. Con orgullo, de México para todo el mundo.

Ve a tu concesionaria más cercana y descubre cómo dar el siguiente paso.

Climatic

Rines de aluminio de 17"

Nuevo diseño de faros y parrilla longitudinal

Mayor confort y espacio interior

Das Auto.

FIGURE 14.30 This "Jetta One Step Ahead" (in Spanish) print ad was created by DDB Mexico for Volkswagen. Image courtesy of DDB.

Changing consumer behavior with fun

One of the hardest things to do is to change how people behave. Many people want to help save the planet, but making them more environmentally conscious is easier in theory than in practice. That is until the VW "The Fun Theory" campaign emerged in mid October of 2009. By creating "The Fun Theory Award," this global contest allowed anyone to upload ideas at www.rolighetsteorin.se and awarded 2,500 Euros as its grand prize. The deadline was extended to January 15, 2011, because of heightened interest. Ultimately, there were 1,000 total entries, with 400 coming in over the last two days. Almost 700 entries were posted on "The Fun Theory" website (www.thefuntheory.com).[23]

VW rewarded people for developing suggestions that would change consumers' behavior to benefit themselves, each other, and ultimately the planet. For example, instead of lecturing to people about the benefits of recycling, it made the actual act of recycling fun. To encourage people to recycle glass bottles, not just cans and plastic, it introduced the interactive recycling bin, "The Bottle Arcade." It lit up like video arcade room games and gave people points just for depositing their glass bottles in this interactive bin. The bins rewarded recyclers with fun and excitement. In one night alone, the Bottle Bank Arcade Machine was used by hundreds of people, while the nearby, standard recycling bin was used only two times. The flashing lights drew people's attention. Their curiosity drove them to come back and drop off their bottles. Here's the link on YouTube: http://www.youtube.com/watch?v=zSiHjMU-MUo.

By making everyday tasks more fun, people were intrigued when VW asked consumers to come up with their fun-filled, problem-solving, "green" ideas. And they did. In fact, there have been almost six million views on YouTube of VW "The Fun Theory" ideas. Take a look at the ingenious solutions.[24] Be sure you check out the videos listed below on YouTube. Also, look at "The Fun Theory" winners and images at http://www.flickr.com/photos/43503544@N03/5145518464/#/, so you can see exactly how the apparatuses worked.

1   *Speed Camera Lottery* – How to get people to observe the speed limit? Create a Speed Camera Lottery. Everyone who drives at or below the speed limit is captured on camera. Their registration numbers are entered into a lottery. The winner was notified by SMS and received a cash award. So, they might get paid just to drive more safely. Likewise, those who broke the law and drove too fast were also photographed, but they were issued traffic citations.

This particular idea was created by American, Kevin Richardson and was chosen as the best "The Fun Theory" concept. The Swedish National Society for Road Safety in Stockholm, Sweden, implemented the idea. See it at http://www.youtube.com/watch?v=iynzHWwJXaA.

2   *Give Parents Some Peace* – How do parents get kids to clean up their rooms? Build a magnetic wall by installing a sheet of metal where kids can "hang up" their clothes with magnets. Everything gets picked up off the floor and the kids enjoy watching their clothes dangle from a wall. See it at http://www.youtube.com/watch?v=vWG6 IWgX0Q8&feature=related.

3   *Scratch Mat* – How do you get shoppers to wipe their feet when they enter a store?

Felix Möller and Daniel Westhof developed a scratch mat that simulates a DJ's scratching, moving a vinyl record back and forth to create a sound often used in Hip Hop, Pop and Nu Metal. Instead of ignoring an ordinary floor mat, people enjoyed wiping their feet and creating a scratch track. See it at: http://www.youtube.com/watch?v=lZ9uT23ixLc&feature=related.

4   *Mind Your Engines* – How do you get drivers to shut off their engines at red lights? Ask them to and reward them with a fun video. Paris drivers were asked via a billboard sign to turn off their engines at a red light to reduce CO_2 emissions, which are created by idling vehicle engines and are considered a contributing factor to global warming. They were shown a short funny video of a groomsman fainting during a wedding, while they waited for the light to change. Sensors measured how many drivers shut off their cars. When the light turned green, a billboard reminded them to turn on their engines and their headlights.
   See it at http://www.youtube.com/watch?v=0eLah9B-Ma0&feature=related.

5   *Piano Staircase* – How do you get people to choose the stairs and not the escalator or elevator? Let them play the piano stairs with their feet. Piano keys, which played the notes when stepped on, were painted on the stairs. People were running up and down the steps like kids just to hear the sounds they could make. Almost two-thirds more people chose the stairs. Impressive, right?
   See it at http://www.youtube.com/watch?v=2lXh2n0aPyw&feature=related.

6   *The World's Deepest Bin* – How do you make people throw their trash in a dumpster, not on the ground? Establish the world's deepest trashcan by inserting a sound track that resembles something falling into a deep ravine. The sound is so surprising that people and children pick up more trash just to hear it again. See it at http://www.youtube.com/watch?v=cbEKAwCoCKw&feature=related.

Earlier in the book (in chapters 1, 7 and 12), you read about *consumer-created content* (CCC). Here you're looking at consumer-created solutions. People who interact with the brand become more emotionally connected to it. This is why interactivity is integrated into campaigns today. However, the real question is: Does all of this environmental consciousness impact sales? According to Stefan Dahlin, Product Manager at Volkswagen in Sweden and jury panelist on "The Fun Theory Award," it has.[25] By emphasizing Volkswagen's ongoing improvements to lower fuel emissions and increase driving pleasure, it has embraced change and become an automotive role model.

The blend of entertainment, interactivity, and connectivity creates or strengthens an existing consumer relationship with the brand. Brands that show they understand what's important to their audience will move towards dominance and generate loyalty. Especially when it offers tangible results, like diet programs.

Reaching out with on-the-go solutions

Think about the number of people trying to lose weight. Examine the campaigns that address the dieters' challenges. Go online and see Weight Watchers (www .weightwatchers.com). It offers dieting tools, recipes, and mobile help with its "Food Tracker" to keep dieters on course. The slogan uses both the *vernacular* and *play on word* techniques (#4 and #13, as mentioned in chapter 4): "Finally, losing weight clicks." What a sticky slogan!

Also be sure you look at how Special K addressed the audience in its UK "My Special K" campaign at http://myspecialk.co.uk/, where consumers could find Special K snacks, professional advice, a free, personal weight loss plan, food suggestions; download an iPhone app; ask questions; see testimonials; and so on. Read more about the UK Special K online campaign, at http://www.brandrepublic.com/News/870505/Kelloggs-Special-K-creates-new-website-slimming-challenge/.

Now go to the US site at www.specialk.com. Check out the "Special K Challenge." See how it invites dieters to discover tips, plans, mobile applications, information about the challenge, and more. There's another site with specific instructions on how to participate in the "Special K Challenge" at http://www.specialk.com/challenge/instructions.

Smart marketers integrate all media and use new technology to connect to their audiences wherever they are.

Using the digital world to go global

In 2010, when GUESS? Watches™ (from Timex subsidiary, Sequel International) wanted to go digital and introduce its fall line into more than 50 countries, it turned to Digital Surgeons According to Peter Sena II, the agency's founder and chief technology officer. "The initiative needed to be handled in an innovative, sexy, yet careful way." He added, "It also helped that the brief said that they were ready to go digital, which is sort of our forte."

Since its introduction in 1981, GUESS? Watches(tm) has epitomized fashion and coolness. In the past, new lines were presented through distributer or dealer conferences, fashion expos, and traditional media including print catalogs and POP (point-of-purchase) displays. In 2010, the agency incorporated online advertising, an interactive e-catalog, QR codes, plus social media sites like Facebook and Twitter, as well as digital and print POP (point of purchase) displays with strong call-to-action language to launch the campaign. The interactive catalog (viewable at http://vimeo.com/15463104) enabled interested dealers to see all the watch features, join in the social networking fun, and connect with local dealers. Ultimately, the campaign spoke to three markets: distributors, retailers, and consumers.

Sena explained the challenges like this:

> Communicating to both the distributors and retailers required before, during, and after presentations of the plan. This required particular attention; we needed to excite while balancing the use of technology and social media that varied from country to country.
>
> We added a Facebook application with the new catalogs to the Facebook page so users could experience and share the new lines. We planned and placed an entire media campaign using advanced and dynamic online ad-targeting techniques so we could get the most bang for our client's buck. We crossed a small amount of high-profile-publishers impressions (mostly to satisfy the brand gods) with some social ads then sprinkled in some targeted/retargeted impressions through one of the ad exchanges.[26]

Sena shared the campaign results:

- *Organic brand searches spiked 20% for six straight months.*
- *Distribution of the media plan was well spread throughout the 50 target countries.*
- *The Facebook insights and Google Analytics numbers represented that fact well.*
- *Overall the Facebook audience grew by 15,000%.*

- *The brand received a combination of 300+MM paid and earned impressions globally. Netting them well north of 200,000 catalog views over three months.*

- *Each visitor we touched through the integrated digital campaigned spent 65% more time on the site than the average GUESS Watches visitor.*

- *When compared to prior years, online sales were up 20% in the first four weeks.*

- *Internationally distributors and retailers were thrilled and it showed through showcase upgrades and increases in co-op advertising dollars.*[27]

Wander around online and look for results of other campaigns. For instance, look at the Kosiuko campaign. You could start by viewing a video about the entire campaign: http://ny.beam.tv/archive/play/zDXNrnSXTR and go to its Facebook page: http://www.facebook.com/pages/Kosiuko/18726049342?sk=info. It was the first Argentine jeans that launched worldwide and showed celebrities on MTV and TV wearing jeans like Shakira did, and like those Britney Spears wore in her video and on her CD cover, as did stars of *The Sopranos* TV series. This resulted in Kosiuko Jeans stores across the world: US, Latin America, Eastern Europe, and Asia.

It received the Best Female Jeans of the World Award in 2002. In 2004, it was the first jeans brand to launch a radio station using a brand name: the 90-MHz KSK-FM Radio (101.9). Part one used TV and billboards that showcased the rebellious nature of its target audience. Part two positioned mannequins dressed in Kosiuko Jeans and headsets, tuned to KSK-FM, that were placed in the streets of Buenos Aires for an ambient message. Part three showed interesting billboards with a symbol and station's call numbers 101.9.

The symbol was made up of 6,000 CDs, placed side by side. It followed the radio station with a new record label: KSK Records. The first CD of the artist Capri had the visual of a jeans pocket. It was recognized by Latin America MTV Music Awards, winning the 2004 Best Latin America Independent Artist Award. Then, it opened the ultra-cool KSK Bar where people could be seen.[28]

The campaign made the jeans a world brand through traditional media, ambient messaging, innovative entrepreneurship (launching an unknown artist via a new record label), and enthusiastic celebrity acceptance. It shows how ingenuity can be the catalyst for a new product introduction.

Observing international campaigns

Spend time reviewing awards books, surfing websites for global agencies, participating in interactive online campaigns, following mobile marketing efforts, noticing all kinds of advertising from ambient messages to global communications. Become an ardent observer, a vigorous analyzer, and an eager participant. Immerse yourself in all kinds of enriching experiences so you can be a more interesting person. The fact is boring people don't create exciting advertising. To come up with a fresh idea, you need to refresh your mind, boost your imagination, and stimulate your creativity.

Pay attention to campaigns that successfully translate an unforgettable message and reach out and touch the audience, the ones that generate press, and those that show how they can resolve everyday challenges. They can work on multiple platforms in different languages because they start from a big idea that has legs.

"

Don't be boring. **DAVID ABBOTT, CO-FOUNDER**

ABBOTT MEAD VICKERS BBDO[29]

Look at how easily "Das Auto" moved from country to country without translation. Study messages that transcend borders and boundaries.

Whenever you see a multicultural or international campaign, examine it. Don't be an indifferent bystander. Jump in. Challenge yourself intellectually. Stretch your creative muscles. Dig down and ask yourself what you would do to enhance the campaign. Reenergize your imagination. Become your own creative catalyst. Then, each idea will spark another. Soon your campaigns will attract attention and inspire others.

 ADVICE FROM THE PROS 14.2 Three tips for writing to biculturals from Carlos Menendez

Define Your Target

When writing to a bicultural audience it is extremely important to know exactly who you are trying to communicate with. More so than when writing either to a strictly English-speaking or strictly Spanish-speaking consumer, it is very important to have your subject clearly defined. This tip applies to writing in any type of advertising, or medium, but when you are specifically writing to biculturals, there can be a very big difference between a 20-year-old's perspective and a 30-year-old's perspective. For this reason, I really try to pin down my target to a very specific description. For example, if I'm working with a brief that tells me that our target is bilingual women, ages 24 thru 45, with a median household income of $50K- I would try to pin down someone that I know who fits that description or even make that person up. This way I am really clear on what I have to say to them, and how I am going to say it. If you try talking to everyone, you will end up talking to no one. Again, when writing to less dynamic targets, you can probably get away with writing to the masses, but when reaching biculturals it helps to be very defined because there tends to be a large gap in acculturation and behavior with only slight differences in age, income, and even gender.

> When writing to biculturals, define that person down to the very last detail and then simply talk to them. If you can't picture them, everything about them, you can't effectively reach them. **CARLOS MENENDEZ, SENIOR COPYWRITER, ZUBI ADVERTISING**[30]

 CHECKLIST 14.3 Multilingual and multicultural writing tips checklist

1 Write for clarity. No one has time to "translate" a message, regardless of the language.
2 Work on creating a message that can *spin out* into different media platforms, from print and broadcast to ambient and digital.
3 Include interactivity. Make a point to engage the audience. Consider what Weight Watchers and Special K are doing online, as we mentioned earlier.

4   Remember to include *universal* or *global truths*. This helps the message reach a broader market.

5   Create ideas that cross geographic borders and transcend cultural divides.

6   Think about words that are understood by people everywhere, like "happy" as in Coke's "Open Happiness" campaign. Or the SPAM campaign, "Imagínalo. Prepáralo." It's easily understood by English- and Spanish-speaking audiences.

7   Present the cool factor when it is aligned with the product and audience.

8   Strive to create slogans that need no translation, like VW "Das Auto."

9   Incorporate fun when appropriate, like VW "The Fun Theory" campaign.

10   Integrate other *touchpoints*, like celebrities to wear clothing or new record labels to promote the brand like Kosiuko did.

11   Consider cultural differences for every medium.

12   Pay attention to the values of specific ethnic groups. If you're addressing a Hispanic market, use Kelly McDonald's "Acculturation Stratification Model" mentioned earlier (McDonald Marketing).

13   Use themes that are easily relatable, like family values as in the American Family Insurance campaigns.

14   Don't translate. *Transcreate*.

15   Expand your audience by tweeting, blogging, engaging, and interacting in myriad media. Look for new or create new media *touchpoints*.

16   Remember the Internet has no international borders. You can reach any audience at any time.

One important point is to realize that everything is in a state of flux. New markets and exciting media emerge. Technology evolves. Attitudes changes. To be current and relevant, you must keep up with new trends. Be the scout of the universe, always searching to have your pulse on new developments. Read. Surf. Watch. Listen. Most of all, observe and absorb. Find out new information. Did you know that there's even an iPhone app where you can discover how David Ogilvy would evaluate your client pitch? Well, there is. Check it out at *Ad Age*: http://adage.com/article/adages/iphone-app-lets-pitch-david-ogilvy/228572/.

Realize this: If you keep doing what's been done, you'll be predictable. And predictability is the enemy of creativity.

Multilingual and international messaging exercises

Exercise 1: analyzing two websites of the same product

Part 1 Compare the UK and US Special K sites http://myspecialk.co.uk and http://www.specialk.com.

Part 2 Examine the look, tone, and approach. Notice how vibrant the US site is compared to the more subdued UK one.

Part 3 Analyze the similarities and pay attention to the choice of:

- Language
- Images

- Colors
- Interactive activities

Exercise 2: taking national campaign global

Part 1 Choose a campaign you think is terrific. Ask yourself why you like it so much? Does it speak to you in a personal way? Does it solve a problem? Does it make you feel cool?

Part 2 Think about another audience outside the United States that would like this product. You can pick the same age group or another target in a different country.

Part 3 Consider how you could adapt the campaign or create a new one that would be effective.

Part 4 Write one unifying slogan that could work here and abroad.

Part 5 Decide what media to use: transit, ambient, digital, mobile, and so on.

Part 6 Create one main thematic message ("*big idea*") that would "*spin out*" to all media. Think about including a universal or global truth.

Exercise 3: developing a message for two languages

Part 1 If you know which audiences you're targeting, you may be able to see if there are any common values or interests. Think about events or activities that unify people across the world, like soccer, fitness, literature, art, music, and so on.

Consider how you could create a campaign that would be equally effective in both languages and speak directly to each market.

Part 2 Create a single, simple message that could easily be *transcreated*, if not translated. Start with a *universal* or *global truth* that could work as the slogan for both audiences.

Part 3 Modify the message to act as a series of headlines in the campaign.

Part 4 Start by creating a strictly transit-oriented campaign. Consider using:

- Taxi cabs:
  - outside top of cabs;
  - inside.
- Bus:
  - sides;
  - benches;
  - shelters.
- Subways:
  - interiors;
  - exteriors;
  - platforms.
- Trolleys.
- Trains:
  - cars;
  - stations.

- Airplanes:
  - in-flight magazines;
  - tray tables;
  - outside of plane (body and tail wings).

Notes

1   Dennis Higgins, *The Art of Writing Advertising: Conversations with Masters of the Craft* (Chicago: NTC Business Books, 1965), 12.

2   Sheena Brady, personal communication, May 8, 2009.

3   Sheena Brady, personal communication, May 8, 2009.

4   Tony Cox, quoted in *The Copywriter's Bible*, by The Designers and Art Directors Association of the United Kingdom (Switzerland: Roto Vision SA, 2000), 31.

5   Kelly McDonald, personal communication, May 12, 2009.

6   Kelly McDonald, personal communication, May 12, 2009.

7   Kelly McDonald, personal communication, May 12, 2009.

8   Kelly McDonald, personal communication, May 12, 2009.

9   Kelly McDonald, personal communication, May 12, 2009.

10 Kelly McDonald, personal communication, May 12, 2009.

11 Kelly McDonald, personal communication, May 12, 2009.

12 Kelly McDonald, personal communication, May 12, 2009.

13 George L. San Jose, personal communication, March 21, 2011.

14 George L. San Jose, personal communication, March 21, 2011.

15 http://thesanjosegroup.com/work/spam/ (accessed May 19, 2011).

16 George L. San Jose, personal communication, March 21, 2011.

17 George L. San Jose, personal communication, March 21, 2011.

18 Tom Amico, personal communication, June 30, 2009.

19 Tom Amico, personal communication, June 30, 2009.

20 Ben Walker, personal communication, January 19, 2009.

21 Sylvia Phipps, personal communication, May 3, 2011.

22 David Ogilvy, *Confessions of an Advertising Man* (New York: Atheneum, 1981), 20.

23 Michael Bugaj, personal communication, May 7, 2011.

24 http://www.thefuntheory.com (accessed April 28, 2011).

25 http://www.thefuntheory.com (accessed April 28, 2011).

26 Peter Sena II, personal communication, February 1, 2011.

27 Peter Sena II, personal communication, February 1, 2011.

28 Fabiana Antacli (at DDB), Victoria Cossentino and Rodrigo Figueroa (FiRe Advertaiment), personal communication, March 31, 2009.

29 David Abbott, quoted in *The Copywriter's Bible*, by The Designers and Art Directors Association of the United Kingdom (Switzerland: Roto Vision SA, 2000), 11.

30 Carlos Menendez, personal communication, September 3, 2010.

SUGGESTED READING

Bendinger, Bruce. 2009. *The Copy Workshop Workbook.* Chicago, IL: The Copy Workshop.

Berger, Arthur Asa. 2000. *Ads, Fads and Consumer Culture: Advertising's Impact on American Character and Society.* Lanham, MD: Rowman & Littlefield.

Berman, Margo. 2010. *Street-Smart Advertising: How to Win the Battle of the Buzz.* Lanham, MD: Rowman & Littlefield.

Berman, Margo and Blakeman, Robyn. 2009. *The Brains Behind Great Ad Campaigns: Creative Collaboration Between Copywriters and Art Directors.* Lanham, MD: Rowman & Littlefield.

Bird, Drayton. 2004. *How to Write Sales Letters That Sell: Learn the Secrets of Successful Direct Mail.* London: Kogan Page.

Blakeman, Robyn. 2011. *Strategic Uses of Alternative Media: Just the Essentials.* Armonk, NY: M.E. Sharpe.

Bly, Robert W. 2005. *The Copywriter's Handbook: A Step-by-Step Guide to Writing Copy That Sells.* New York, NY: Henry Holt.

Bogusky, Alex and Winsor, John. 2009. *Baked In: Creating Products and Businesses That Market Themselves.* Chicago, IL: Agate.

Caples, John. 1998. *Tested Advertising Methods.* Upper Saddle River, NJ: Prentice Hall.

Czerniawski, Richard D. and Maloney, Michael W. 1999. *Creating Brand Loyalty: The Management of Power Positioning and Really Great Advertising.* New York, NY: Amacom.

De Bono, Edward. 1999. *Six Thinking Hats.* New York, NY: Little, Brown.

Drewiany Bonnie L., and Jewler, Jerome A. 2008. *Creative Strategy in Advertising.* Boston, MA: Thomson Wadsworth.

Dushinski, Kim. 2009. *The Mobile Marketing Handbook: A Step-by-Step Guide to Creating Dynamic Mobile Marketing Campaigns.* Medford, NJ: CyberAge Books.

Fortini-Campbell, Lisa. 2001. *Hitting the Sweet Spot: How Consumer Insights Can Inspire Better Marketing and Advertising.* Chicago, IL: The Copy Workshop.

Gladwell, Malcolm. 2002. *The Tipping Point: How Little Things Can Make a Big Difference.* Boston, MA: Back Bay Publishing.

Gladwell, Malcolm. 2007. *Blink: The Power of Thinking Without Thinking.* New York, NY: Little, Brown.

Griffin, Glenn W. and Morrison, Deborah. 2010. *The Creative Process Illustrated: How Advertising's Big Ideas Are Born.* Cincinnati, OH: HOW Books.

Hall, Doug. 2007. *Jump Start Your Brain.* Cincinnati, OH: Clerisy Press.

Hay, Deltina. 2009. *A Survival Guide to Social Media and Web 2.0 Optimization: Strategies, Tactics, and Tools for Succeeding in the Social Web.* Austin, TX: Dalton Publishing.

Heath, Chip and Heath, Dan. 2008. *Made to Stick: Why Some Ideas Survive and Others Die.* New York, NY: Random House.

Holzner, Steven. 2009. *Facebook Marketing: Leverage Social Media to Grow Your Business.* Indianapolis, IN: Que.

Iezzi, Teressa. 2010. *The Idea Writers: Copywriting in a New Media and Marketing Era.* New York, NY: Palgrave MacMillan.

Johnson, Spencer and Blanchard, Kenneth. 2002. *Who Moved My Cheese? An Amazing Way to Deal With Change in Your Work and in Your Life.* New York, NY: G.P. Putnam.

Kizorek, Jessica. 2008. *Show Me: Marketing With Video on the Internet.* Wheaton, IL: PSI Publications.

Kleinman, Sharon. 2011. *The Media and Communication Dictionary: A Guide for Students, Educators, and Professionals.* New York: Peter Lang.

Krum, Cindy. 2010. *Mobile Marketing: Finding Your Customers No Matter Where They Are.* Indianapolis, IN: Que.

Lewis, Richard W. 1996. *Absolut Book: The Absolut Vodka Advertising Story.* Boston, MA: Journey Editions.

Lewis, Richard W. 2005. *Absolut Sequel: The Absolut Vodka Advertising Story Continues.* North Clarendon, VT: Periplus Editions.

Lindstrom, Martin. 2010. *Buyology: Truth and Lies About Why We Buy.* New York, NY: Broadway Books.

McDonald, Kelly. 2011. *How to Market to People Not Like You: "Know It or Blow It" Rules for Reaching Diverse Customers.* Hoboken, NJ: John Wiley & Sons.

Maciuba-Koppel, Darlene. 2002. *The Web Writer's Guide: Tips & Tools.* Woburn, MA: Focal Press.

Micek, Deborah and Whitlock, Warren. 2008. *Twitter Revolution: How Social Media and Mobile Marketing Is Changing the Way We Do Business and Market Online.* Las Vegas, NV: Xeno Press.

Michalko, Michael. 2006. *Thinkertoys: A Handbook of Creative-Thinking Techniques.* Berkeley, CA: Ten Speed Press.

Newman, Michael. 2003. *Creative Leaps: 10 Lessons in Effective Advertising Inspired at Saatchi & Saatchi.* Singapore: John Wiley & Sons.

Newman, Michael. 2004. *The 22 Irrefutable Laws of Advertising (and When to Violate Them).* Singapore: John Wiley & Sons.

Ogilvy, David. 1981. *Confessions of an Advertising Man.* New York, NY: Atheneum.

Ogilvy, David. 1985. *Ogilvy on Advertising.* New York, NY: Random House.

Ogilvy, David. 2004. *Confessions of an Advertising Man.* London: Southbank Publishing.

Popcorn, Faith. 1992. *The Popcorn Report: Faith Popcorn on the Future of Your Company, Your World, Your Life.* New York, NY: Doubleday.

Postman, Joel. 2009. *SocialCorp: Social Media Goes Corporate.* Berkeley, CA: New Riders.

Ries, Al and Trout, Jack. 1990. *The 22 Immutable Laws of Marketing: Violate Them at Your Own Risk!* New York, NY: HarperBusiness.

Ries, Al and Trout, Jack. 2000. *Positioning: The Battle for Your Mind.* New York, NY: McGraw-Hill.

Ries, Al and Trout, Jack. 2005. *Marketing Warfare: 20th Anniversary Edition.* New York, NY: McGraw-Hill.

Roberts, Kevin. 2005. *Lovemarks: The Future beyond Brands.* New York, NY: Powerhouse Books.

Roman, Kenneth and Maas, Jane. 2003. *How to Advertise*, 3rd edn. New York, NY: Thomas Duane Books.

Rowse, Darren and Garrett, Chris. 2010. *ProBlogger: Secrets for Blogging Your Way to a Six-Figure Income*, 2nd edn. Indianapolis, IN: Wiley Publishing.

Schulberg, Jay. 1998. *The Milk Mustache Book: A Behind-the-Scenes Look at America's Favorite Advertising Campaign.* New York, NY: The Ballantine Publishing Group.

Sullivan, Luke. 2008. *Hey Whipple, Squeeze This: A Guide to Creating Great Ads.* New York, NY: John Wiley & Sons.

Thaler, Linda Kaplan and Koval, Robin, with Marshall, Delia. 2003. *Bang! Getting Your Message Heard in a Noisy World.* New York, NY: Doubleday.

Underhill, Paco. 2009. *Why We Buy: The Science of Shopping.* New York, NY: Simon & Schuster.

INDEX